Greece:
The Peloponnese
with Athens, Delphi and Kythira

the Bradt Travel Guide

Andrew Bostock
with Philip Briggs

edition
4

www.bradtguides.com

Bradt Travel Guides Ltd, UK
The Globe Pequot Press Inc, USA

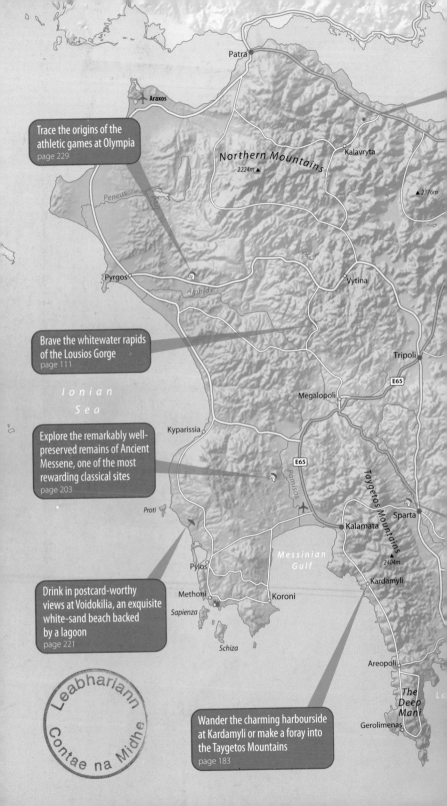

Trace the origins of the athletic games at Olympia
page 229

Brave the whitewater rapids of the Lousios Gorge
page 111

Explore the remarkably well-preserved remains of Ancient Messene, one of the most rewarding classical sites
page 203

Drink in postcard-worthy views at Voidokilia, an exquisite white-sand beach backed by a lagoon
page 221

Wander the charming harbourside at Kardamyli or make a foray into the Taygetos Mountains
page 183

Patra

Araxos

Kalavryta

Northern Mountains

2224m ▲

▲ 2376m

Peneus

Pyrgos

Alphios

Vytina

Tripoli

E65

Ionian Sea

Megalopoli

Kyparissia

E65

Pamisos

Taygetos Mountains

Sparta

Proti

2404m ▲

Kalamata

Pylos

Messinian Gulf

Methoni

Koroni

Kardamyli

Sapienza

Schiza

Areopoli

The Deep Mani

Gerolimenas

AUTHOR

Andrew Bostock first travelled to the Peloponnese as a 15-year-old backpacker and spent his first night sleeping under a bush in the carpark, having watched a performance of *Oedipus at Colunus* at the great theatre of Epidavros. He kept coming back with various companions before moving there with his pregnant partner in 2005 – their daughter was born in Kalamata. Andrew spent the next five years  guiding tours around the area, exploring its lesser-known bits, and writing about it for magazines and newspapers. The first edition of his Bradt guide was published in 2010. The family return to Greece most years, and dream about the olive groves, mountains and the sea when they are not there.

CONTRIBUTOR AND UPDATER

Philip Briggs (e *philip.briggs@bradtguides.com*) has been an inveterate traveller since he first backpacked between Nairobi and Cape Town in 1986. His association with Bradt dates to 1991, when he wrote the first internationally published guidebook to South Africa following the release of Nelson Mandela. Philip has since written Bradt guides to Tanzania, Uganda, Ethiopia, Malawi, Mozambique, Ghana, Rwanda, The Gambia, Somaliland, Suriname and Sri Lanka, all of which are still regularly updated for several subsequent editions.

PUBLISHER'S FOREWORD *Adrian Phillips, Managing Director*

Bradt and its authors come together in a variety of ways – sometimes, indeed, they do so almost by accident. Andrew entered the Bradt–*Independent on Sunday* travel-writing competition, got chatting to Hilary Bradt, and ended up moving his family to Greece to write the first edition of this guide to the Peloponnese! It was a chain of events that culminated in a wonderful guidebook. Philip Briggs, one of the world's most experienced guidebook writers, has taken up the mantle for this fourth edition, and done his usual excellent job. It's a special region: there are few places in the world where you can relax on the beach before stepping back in time to visit sites that feature in some of the greatest epic literature ever written!

Fourth edition published March 2019
First published 2010

Bradt Travel Guides Ltd, IDC House, The Vale, Chalfont St Peter, Bucks SL9 9RZ, England
www.bradtguides.com
Print edition published in the USA by The Globe Pequot Press Inc, PO Box 480, Guilford, Connecticut 06437-0480

Text copyright © 2019 Andrew Bostock
Maps copyright © 2019 Bradt Travel Guides Ltd; includes map data © OpenStreetMap contributors
Photographs copyright © 2019 individual photographers (see below)
Project manager: Claire Strange
Cover research: Marta Bescos

British Library Cataloguing in Publication Data
A catalogue record for this book is available from the British Library

ISBN: 978 1 78477 633 6 (print)

Photographs Alamy: Peter Eastland (PE/A); Andrew Bostock (AB); Ariadne Van Zandbergen (AVZ); AWL: Hemis (H/AWL); Dreamstime: Barbar1 (B1/DT), Dbdella (D/DT), Dinosmichail (DM/DT), Panagiotis Karapanagiotis (PK/DT), Joop Kleuskens (JK/DT), Oliver Meerson (OM/DT), Nikos Pavlakis (NP/DT), Georgios Tsichlis (GT/DT); Shutterstock.com: Takis Bks (TB/S), elgreko (e/S), EQRoy (EQR/S), f8grapher (F8/S), Milan Gonda (MG/S), Andronos Haris (AH/S), Inu (I/S), Panos Karas (PK/S), Nick Pavlakis (NP/S), PNIK (PNIK/S), Anatoly Vartanov (AV/S), Lydia Vero (LV/S), siete vidas (sv/S), Voyagerix (V/S), WitR (W/S); SuperStock (SS)
Front cover Theatre at Epidavros (GT/DT)
Back cover Spartan helmet (AV/S); Monemvasia (V/S)
Title page Bougainvillea (AH/S); Taverna sign (EQR/S); Gythio harbour (I/S)

Maps David McCutcheon FBCart.S (based on source material from Road Editions; www.road.gr); colour map relief base by Nick Rowland FRGS

Typeset by Lee55–Lee Riches; www.dataworks.in; Ian Spick, Bradt Travel Guides
Production managed by Jellyfish Print Solutions; printed in India
Digital conversion by www.dataworks.co.in

Acknowledgements

Thanks are due first to Hilary Bradt, who had the confidence to back this project in its infancy, and help sell it to the rest of her team. This time around it has been helped along by Rachel, Anna and Claire at Bradt. I'd also like to make special mention of Philip, the updater of this edition. This is the first time 'other hands' have touched 'my' book, and I couldn't have asked for better. His fresh eyes have improved things greatly.

Thanks are also due to many in Greece and elsewhere who provided help and encouragement. The list has now become too long to go through, and includes old and new friends, as well as all those who read and commented on the first three editions.

We have seen sadly too little of Greece in the last few years, but my family has still had to been open to travelling, as we relocated first to Egypt then China. As always they have coped with everything gamely. The book still belongs to Jemima, who was born in the Peloponnese.

FEEDBACK REQUEST AND UPDATES WEBSITE

At Bradt Travel Guides we're aware that guidebooks start to go out of date on the day they're published – and that you, our readers, are out there in the field doing research of your own. You'll find out before us when a fine new family-run hotel opens or a favourite restaurant changes hands and goes downhill. So why not write and tell us about your experiences? Contact us on ☎ 01753 893444 or e info@bradtguides.com. We will forward emails to the author, who may post updates on the Bradt website at w bradtupdates. com/peloponnese. Alternatively, you can add a review of the book to w bradtguides.com.

AUTHOR'S STORY

When researching the first edition of this book in 2008 I often found myself having to justify why I thought Greece needed another guide. Pausanias had started the whole industry back in the 2nd century, and since then Greece has remained one of the most written about, and travelled, countries on Earth. On top of this the perceived wisdom was that Greece had had its day as a destination. It was a staid country where nothing much would now change apart from steadily rising prices. Things have changed since then, of course, and Greece has shown that it is a country with plenty more to offer than just history.

The economic and political crises of the last few years, however, have not changed the reasons I gave for writing this guidebook in the first place. In 25 years of travelling around the Peloponnese I never found the guidebook of my dreams; the book that would lead me from secret coves to unexplored ruins via vibrant festivals in mountaintop villages. I still haven't found that book, but I hope I have written something that comes close.

I first visited the area, in particular the Mani, as a 15-year-old backpacker, inspired equally by my mum and the author Sir Patrick (Paddy) Leigh Fermor, and slept under the stars on beaches, in ruined tower houses and olive groves. My love for the place has continued, and is fortunately shared by my partner. Jemima, our daughter, was born in Kalamata in 2006; not strictly the Mani, but close enough, at least according to Paddy himself.

My small family lived in the Mani while the first edition of this book was researched and written, a sometimes problematic decision, but ultimately rewarding. I drove over from the UK with a carload consisting of Greek history books stuffed down footwells, a doll's house, a cot, and a Fisher Price garage. A full-sized garage would have been more appropriate; in the course of two years exploring, my car went through a passenger door, a full set of tyres, brake pads, an exhaust, and a clutch.

Recent years have brought new adventures. Now a Physics teacher, of all things, we lived in Suffolk for 8 years before relocating first to the old Greek city of Alexandria in Egypt, and then the very un-Greek Suzhou in China. I regretfully gave up the updating of this edition to Philip Briggs, but couldn't be happier with the result. Hopefully we will be back in Greece soon.

Contents

Any encounter with a foreign script leads to problems, and this is especially true of Greek, where there is a weight of tradition to be grappled with. Most of us would be dubious over the merits of visiting Olimbia, but when you realise that this is the same as Olympia it becomes more attractive.

For place names, this guidebook has used the most well-known spelling where appropriate (Corinth for Korinthos, Athens for Athina, etc), and the transliteration used by the latest Peloponnese map from Road Editions otherwise, with a few exceptions on aesthetic grounds. For other names and words, a spelling that best conveys their pronunciation has been the aim. If this is all a bit confusing, I can only apologise.

It is perfectly possible to travel in Greece without learning the alphabet. Most road signs are transliterated, and menus at restaurants are either unnecessary or translated (sometimes hilariously) into English. Despite this the Greek script for most place names has been included at their first introduction. This can help with their pronunciation, and is a good way to start learning the alphabet for those who are interested.

AUTHOR'S FAVOURITES Finding genuinely characterful accommodation or that unmissable off-the-beaten-track café can be difficult, so the author has chosen a few of his favourite places throughout the country to point you in the right direction. These 'author's favourites' are marked with a ✳.

MAPS
Keys and symbols Maps include alphabetical keys covering the locations of those places to stay, eat or drink that are featured in the book. Note that regional maps may not show all hotels and restaurants in the area: other establishments may be located in towns shown on the map.

Grids and grid references Several maps use gridlines to allow easy location of sites. Map grid references are listed in square brackets after the name of the place or site of interest in the text, with page number followed by grid number, eg: [191 C3].

HISTORIC SITES Prices and opening hours are included where they apply, although government-run archaeological sites and museums largely use standard opening times and entrance fees. See page 52. Otherwise, assume the site is free and always open.

RECOMMENDED WALKS Each of the main chapters includes a recommended walk. These are an ideal way to experience the stunning natural landscape of the region. Be aware, however, that this environment is always changing, and that walks should be undertaken with care. See page 42 for more details.

Introduction

Forget the islands. This statement will come as a shock to most travellers to Greece, and rightly so. The Greek islands contain some of the most stunning destinations on Earth, and consistently feature in bucket lists and polls of where to visit 'before you die'. Their fame, however, means that mainland Greece is often ignored, and this is unjust. In fact, parts of the mainland could make a claim to beat the islands in scenery, history, wildlife and culture. The Peloponnese, a distinct area the size of Wales, is the best place to experience this.

If you want the white-sand beaches lined with azure water, or the sleepy, whitewashed villages that the islands are famous for, then the Peloponnese has them too, but it also has so much else: towering mountains in which you can hike, and even ski; some of the most famous Classical remains, from Olympia to the theatre at Epidavros, as well as countless 'minor' sites, where you might find yourself alone in the ruins; olive groves that produce the finest fruit and oil in the world; medieval castles and churches from several different civilisations; hills covered in wild flowers; villages that vary from modern, farming communities to stone-built, mountain retreats; inland gorges with white-water rivers running down them... the list could go on and on.

The Peloponnese also offers something of a time machine. Twenty years ago in Greece you could still see old men going to their fields on donkey back, old women clad in black preparing vegetables on their doorsteps, main roads blocked by herds of goats, olives being picked with no more aid than a triangular wooden ladder and a big stick, tractors made from converted lawnmowers, and village shops seemingly unchanged since the 1940s. This Greece has disappeared in most of the more visited islands, but in the Peloponnese it endures.

This is not to say that nothing has changed. In fact the Peloponnese has been at the forefront of an important shift in the emphasis of Greek tourism. As people realise that 'beach holidays' are available more cheaply elsewhere, Greece has had to concentrate on its other strengths, and also realise that its old standards of cheap and cheerful accommodation, and food, can no longer apply. Fundamentally this is a rethinking of what the country has to offer, a concentration on 'culture and nature' rather than 'sun and sand'. Greece, and particularly the Peloponnese, has always had these aspects, but they have been limited to the more adventurous traveller. Now it is slowly being opened up to all, with due care that it is not spoilt in the process.

This re-evaluation has only grown more acute with the economic crisis. Businesses in the tourism sector are now finding that they must offer something different or better than the competition. Times are undeniably tough for many, but most Greeks have responded in their usual manner when faced with adversity – with a mixture of hard work and ingenuity.

In the introduction to the first edition I wrote that it was an exciting time to be writing a guidebook. It has only become more so.

Part One

GENERAL INFORMATION

THE PELOPONNESE AT A GLANCE

Location The southern peninsula of the Greek mainland, jutting out into the Mediterranean and almost entirely surrounded by sea

Size Approximately 21,439km^2 (*Encyclopaedia Britannica*), just larger than Wales, and slightly smaller than the state of New Jersey, USA

Climate Mediterranean

Status Parliamentary republic and member of the European Union (EU)

Head of state President Prokopis Pavlopoulos

Head of government Prime Minister Alexis Tsipras

Capital and large towns The national capital is Athens (population 3.8 million). The only towns in the Peloponnese with more than 50,000 inhabitants are Patras (215,000), Kalamata (85,000) and Corinth (58,000).

Population 1,100,000 (2011 census), almost 10% of the national population of 10.75 million

Life expectancy Male 77 years, female 83 years

Economy Agriculture and tourism

GDP per capita US$19,500 (Peloponnese), slightly below the national figure of US$22,300

Language Greek

Religion Greek Orthodox Christian

Currency Euro (pronounced evro) and divided into 100 cents (*lepta*)

Exchange rate US$1 = €0.88; £1 = €1.12 (December 2018)

International telephone code +30

Time GMT +2 (+3 in summer)

Electrical voltage 230V, 50Hz; standard European plug

Flag Blue and white horizontal stripes with a white cross on a blue background in the top left

1

Background Information

GEOGRAPHY AND CLIMATE

The Peloponnese is the last southern thrust of mainland Greece, and thus of the entire Balkans, into the waters of the Mediterranean. It looks, somewhat, like the palm of a hand with three fingers pointing down and a thumb poked out to the east. Its one connection with the rest of Europe is a thin isthmus to the northeast, in fact the original 'Isthmus', joining it to the continent above. Or at least it would be, had not the late 19th-century Corinth Canal separated it.

It can be useful to think of the Peloponnese as Greece's biggest island: it has a long coastline and you are never that far from the sea, but you must also remember that two-thirds of its landmass comprises mountains. The majority of these form a central spine heading south down to the Mani, the central 'finger'. The highest point in the region is Profitis Ilias (2,404m), which caps the Taygetos range to the south in the southern administrative region of Laconia. There are also two peaks of comparable altitude in the north, namely Helmos (2,338m) and Killini (2,374m). Snow seldom falls on the plains, but it can cover the high mountains from November to early June. The majority of the rainfall is in the winter and, owing to this, the majority of streams and rivers are seasonal. The average monthly temperatures in degrees Celsius are 10.6°C in February, 19.7°C in May, 26°C in August, and 14.8°C in November. Note that these averages hide the fact that in the summer temperatures can soar to 40°C and beyond.

NATURAL HISTORY

The Peloponnese provides many diverse habitats, from the sea that surrounds it, through its Mediterranean shores, to its alpine slopes. It even has several wetland areas, beloved by migratory birds. The outlines below are just the barest introduction to the natural beauty on offer. Just remember that one of the chief delights of all those old temples and churches is the magnificence of the countryside they are in.

WILD FLOWERS The best time to come to see the extraordinary displays of wild flowers that the Peloponnese puts on is in the spring. They start blooming as early as January and then continue in waves. April is, perhaps, the most stunning month. This is not to say that there is nothing to see at other times of year. While the summer months can seem arid, with bare and dusty hillsides, there are still gems to be found, while the rains of autumn bring on a mini revival of vegetation. There is no way a guide such as this can do justice to the extraordinary variety of flora, and fauna, of this region. An excellent starter guide is *Complete Mediterranean Wildlife* by Paul Sterry (page 273), and a good website for plant

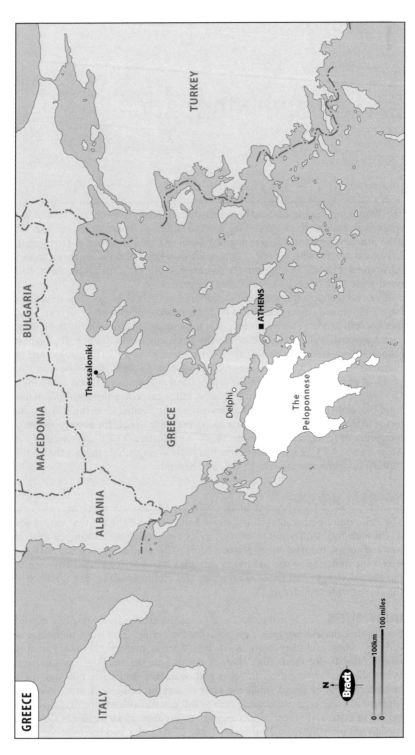

lovers is **w** mediterraneangardensociety.org. They have a Greek branch if you want to meet fellow enthusiasts and tour local gardens. See also, box, page 6.

ORCHIDS Orchids grow from two underground bulbs or tubers, and get their name from the Greek for testicle (which is why you need to be a bit wary in the Peloponnese when asking someone to show you their orchids). In Greece they fall into three main groups – *Ophrys* (bee orchids), *Serapias* (with veined sheaths) and *Orchis* (helmet-shaped on a juicy stem). They flower through the spring and summer. There are over 80 species of orchids in Greece, and all are rare and protected by law. Below are a few to look out for. If you are lucky enough to see one be sure to take no more than a photograph.

Ophrys scolopax The various bee orchids are generally regarded as highly variable in colouring and markings, but do have an overall flower shape in common, often with purple petals and a rounded lower lip that is meant to look like a bee. This attracts male bees to 'mate' with the flower, which then pollinates it. The brown bottom lip of the woodcock orchid, and its two hairy sideburns, mark this flower out from the others. The markings can be lime green, and have a leopard-skin look about them. They are unscented as their looks alone are good enough to attract pollination by bees.

Ophrys tenthredinifera The sawfly orchid has a lime-green and brown-marked lower lip, which some compare to the stubborn jaw line of a bearded terrier. It grows up to 40cm, on rocky or grassy ground throughout the region, and flowers through to May.

Serapias cordigera Also flowering through to May, and reaching 40cm in height, these striking and colourful orchids have a pronounced heart-shaped tongue of burgundy and upright lilac leaves that have the dark veins characteristic of this genus. It has a robust look and appears in damp grassland, hillsides, and many other situations.

Serapias lingua Coastal olive groves provide the optimum habitat for these spiky, architectural-looking tongue orchids. They hide in patches of tall grass and are shade lovers. Each bud bursts into a long, horizontal tongue of deep magenta. It is reminiscent of an iris, and has similar lance-shaped leaves of mid green.

Orchis simia The monkey orchid gets its name because the lower part of each flower is the outline of a pink monkey, as if hanging from a tree, which stands out against the white, speckled, appearance of the rest of the flower. These are grouped on a stem to form a loose helmet shape, which is a characteristic of the genus.

Orchis coriophora Flowering through to June, this orchid's stem holds up to 40 flowers with delicate green, upward-facing spurs, and deep pink to purple tongues. It is a very variable species so can be many colours and heights.

Barlia robertiana The giant orchid stands head and shoulders above its surrounding scrub or grass. The flower is a complex mass of florets shaped in a spire on a juicy green stem. The florets have a light pink-coloured, hanging tongue, and a darker, almost brown, hood. Their amazing scent, in the sunshine, will pull you towards them from several metres away. It can grow up to 80cm, although the usual height is about 40cm.

This intentionally basic month-by-month list describes 12 flowers to look out for at different times of year, to give you a small feel for what is out there.

January
Iris reticulata This purple flower, standing 15–20cm on a bare stem, grows out of rocky hillsides, and provides welcome colour in this sometimes grey month.

February
Muscari neglectum The grape hyacinth is so named because the dark-blue flowers look like bunches of grapes. It is often found in rocky olive groves.

March
Lupinus angustifolia The narrow-leaved lupin has a long central stem topped by a hairy bud that bursts into pale-blue flowers, surrounded by thin leaflets on branching stems.

April
Salvia officinalis The wrinkled, silver leaves of the common sage are strongly scented, often used in Greek cooking, and said to be good for liver problems. Its spires of flowers, which can poke up almost 1m, appear two-toned: the flowers themselves being white to purple and the sepals below green to maroon.

May
Foeniculum vulgare Fennel tends to grow in patches and its tall stems (2m) are topped with yellow 'plates' of tiny flowers. Crushing these produces a strong aniseed scent. It carries on flowering into September. An even larger version grows to 3m, but smells more of celery.

June
Acanthus spinosus The leaves of this imposing flower stalk are the inspiration for the Corinthian order of capital carving on columns. The huge flower spike protrudes to 80cm with many purple spiny leaves under each white petal, which is covered by a burgundy hood. The flowers crowd the stem like a foxglove.

July
Urginea maritima Sea squill grows from a large, half-buried, bulb in rocky ground, often near the coast. It produces large, succulent leaves in the spring and then a bare flower stem reaching up to 1.5m high, topped by hundreds of white, star-shaped flowers. Each petal has a purple stripe.

TREES The **olive** is now ubiquitous in the Peloponnese, and its spread, from ancient times onward, was due to its economic worth (see box, page 184). Its common companion in the countryside is the **cypress tree** – standing alone, or in groves, it acts like an exclamation mark in the landscape. Some of them are now sadly bare of leaves, victims of a disease called cypress canker.

Almost every village square you enter is covered by the welcome shade of a spreading **plane tree**, some of which grow to an enormous size. In fact its Greek name is the derivation for what these squares, great or small, are called – *platea*. For

August
Euphorbia paralias The euphorbia is a beautiful sight throughout the spring and summer in Greece. Topped with lime-green flowers, this amazingly varied species hugs the mountainsides, grows near the sea and looks like anything from a prickly pin cushion to a beady-eyed mound. Euphorbias can have feathery foliage or structured, architectural stems. This particular variety, sea spurge, is blue-green with red stems at the base and grows on sandy beaches between grasses on dunes.

September
Datura stramonium The elegant white, trumpet-shaped flowers of the thorn apple start erect and then hang down. They can be 15–20cm long and look like they belong in a carefully cared-for garden rather than wild on field margins and roadsides. The spiky, almost conker-like, seed capsules are 10–15cm long and round. The plant is poisonous.

October
Plantago coronopus The buck's-horn plantain is one to look out for on the beach. A low rosette of leaves grows out of sandy soil, with green flower spikes pointing upwards in a candelabra shape some 20cm tall.

November
Bougainvillea glabra Now hugely characteristic of the region, the bougainvillea originally comes from Brazil. It flowers almost all year in the Peloponnese, and is often still in bloom in November. It comes in various colours – the most popular is cerise pink, but purple and white varieties are also plentiful. The 'flowers' are in fact bracts, brightly coloured leaves, and the real flowers contained within are creamy white and almost insignificant. The bracts attract butterflies, bees and birds as pollinators.

Bougainvillea can be a huge climber and will cover house walls and sprawl over trees up to, and beyond, 10m high.

December
Clematis cirrhosa Known as virgin's bower, this evergreen clematis is coveted by many an English garden owner, as it flowers through the winter months and will give out an amazing honey scent on a cold winter's day. It sports a nodding, elegant white or cream, bell-shaped flower with a speckled inside. The leaves are shiny and dark green and usually have three fingers. This climber clings and covers trees and shrubs in wild fields and on cliffsides.

similar reasons, shade and ornamentation, the foreign **eucalyptus** is often planted along avenues, and the hardy tamarisk by beaches, although it has the annoying habit of turning the sand to earth. The **Judas tree** is a bushy, deciduous, small tree with heart-shaped leaves coloured from brown to green to red through the seasons. The pink pea-shaped flowers come first in March before the leaves, and you will see them as splashes of dramatic colour on mountain slopes.

Fruit trees are also a common sight, with huge groves of lemon and orange. The pretty, red flowers of the pomegranate are transformed by the sun into a hard-skinned fruit, whose interior of plentiful seeds means that it is a symbol of fecundity and good luck. Figs, particularly around Kalamata, are enjoyed both fresh, and more famously, dried. Nowadays the mulberry, with its tall, fast-growing branches, is enjoyed for its purple or white fruit, and the leaves used for goat fodder, but it was once important for feeding silk worms. The Peloponnese was famed for silk production, so much so that its medieval name, *Morea*, means mulberry tree.

One last tree worth mentioning is the **carob**. The hard seeds, contained in long, hanging pods, were once ground down to flour and baked into a kind of bread for the poor. This rustic loaf has had a recent resurgence among wholefood shops and trendy restaurants, as has the oil the carob also produces.

ANIMAL LIFE For a good guide to the fauna of the Peloponnese, see page 273.

Birds Of 440 bird species recorded in Greece, around 275 occur in the Peloponnese as residents or seasonal migrants from outside Europe. The wetlands of the Peloponnese are an important habitat for migratory birds such as herons, egrets and the magnificent greater flamingo. The best place to view these is the lagoon at Gialova (page 220). Other good sites for aquatic birds include the Limenas Geraka, Europe's most southerly fjord (page 156), and the Stymfalian Lake (page 257). Up in the mountains you will often spot large birds of prey. Most conspicuous is the common buzzard, but eagles, vultures and kites are also about. Small owls can often be spotted perching on rooftops and in ruins, and their distinctive call can be heard at night. Other conspicuous birds include common hoopoe, Alpine swift, Eurasian jay, Eurasian magpie and common starling. A full checklist for the Peloponnese can be found at w avibase.bsc-eoc.org, while an excellent overview of the region's key birdwatching sites is posted at w ecotourism-greece.com.

Mammals Hare and wild boar still exist in the mountains, and are favourite animals to hunt. In the lowlands there are foxes, badgers and stone marten, a ferret-like creature who is the scourge of gardens everywhere. Sadly, the only state in which you are likely to see any of these secretive wild creatures is as roadkills.

Reptiles Lizards are common, mostly smallish and brown in colour. A few species of gecko might be seen scarpering up and down walls in hotels and resorts during summer; be nice to them, as they are harmless to people but devour plenty of mosquitoes. One of the most visible and striking species is the Balkan green lizard (*Lacerta trilineata*), which is bright green in colour, can be more than 50cm long from the nose to the end of its tail, and is most often seen sprinting smartly across the road in front of your vehicle. Two species are endemic to the peninsula: the Peloponnese wall lizard (*Podarcis peloponnesiacus*), a rather stout inhabitant of rocks and walls close to the coast, and the more strikingly marked Greek rock lizard (*Lacerta graeca*), which occupies a similar niche but generally at higher altitudes.

Snakes and tortoises may also be spotted on the road. The former generally leave you alone if you leave them alone, and only one species is somewhat venomous (page 35). The Greeks are bizarrely terrified of them and will swerve their cars to run them down – a practice infinitely more likely to kill them than a snake bite. Tortoises also get run over, by accident, but seem to survive pretty well as a species. They are undeniably cute, but can give a sharp bite with far from clean teeth, so you should keep your distance.

Insects For a visitor used to urban life in northern climes the Peloponnese seems to teem with insects, some of them alarmingly large. The vast majority are harmless, if sometimes irritating (page 34). The most vocal are cicadas, whose shrill mating call can be a constant background in the summer months. The prettiest are butterflies, around from spring to autumn.

Marine life Dolphins are a not uncommon sight in the surrounding waters. Much rarer are the endangered loggerhead turtles, who use the long beaches of the western Peloponnese as a breeding ground.

CONSERVATION The conservation movement came late to Greece, and in some cases missed the boat rather, but it is gaining momentum. Fly tipping over the sides of mountain roads is becoming much less of a problem than it once was, and large blue recycling bins usually stand by the normal ones.

As far as wildlife goes, the most visible effort in the Peloponnese is that to conserve the nesting grounds of the loggerhead turtle (page 228). Various areas have also been declared protected under the NATURA 2000 programme, under the auspices of the EU. These include all of the Mani, much of the northern mountains, and the area around Mount Parnonas.

MYTHOLOGY

One of the problems with Greece is that before tackling the history, you first have to deal with the myth. The first thing to learn is that this is a far more complicated subject than it is sometimes portrayed. The Greek belief system was fluid and adaptable, rather than a rigidly defined structure. It also had the nifty trick, common to many religions, of being able to accommodate several contradictory ideas at once. Added to this is a large amount of regionalism; the Apollo worshipped in Delphi probably had a very different character from the Apollo worshipped in Arcadia.

That said, it would be useful for any traveller in Greece to have some basic knowledge of the beings to whom all these temples are dedicated, as well as of some of the stories that formed the backbone of Classical Greek thought. So, here we go:

THE OLYMPIANS It comes as a surprise to many that the main Greek gods did not create the world, but were merely by-products of the process (which apparently took the form of mother earth coming forth out of chaos). They weren't even the first generation of beings to appear, but a later dynasty who usurped their forebears' power. It was a sign of things to come. You must not imagine these deities as otherworldly creatures, divorced from reality. On the contrary, in their actions and emotions they were all too human; they often fell victim to anger and lust, and weren't above a bit of treachery and deceit. In fact the only thing that really separated them from normal mortals was their immense power.

The main pantheon were said to live on Mount Olympus, still the tallest mountain in Greece (it is located in northern Greece, and should not be confused with Olympia in the Peloponnese). Tradition says that there were 12 major gods and goddesses, although there is often dispute over exactly who made up this elite, and there were countless lesser deities. For most of us an acquaintance with just the main players is more than sufficient.

Zeus The king of the gods, Zeus sometimes comes across as a bit of a stereotype nowadays, with his big, white beard and penchant for flinging thunderbolts at those who angered him. He was also known for sleeping with almost any woman available, usually by force. This started with his own sister, who then became his wife.

Hera Wife (and sister!) to Zeus, she was known as a protector of women and family values, which was somewhat ironic given her own situation. She spent much of her time plotting revenge for her husband's many indiscretions. She particularly went after his illegitimate offspring, the living reminders of his infidelity.

Apollo Apollo was one of these children, the progeny of Zeus and the nymph Leto, but he seems to have bypassed Hera's wrath and become one of the most important Greek deities. He was known as the god of light, and of music and the arts. In contrast to his father he was normally portrayed as an unbearded youth, the Classical ideal of beauty.

Artemis Apollo's twin sister is primarily known as the goddess of the hunt, which was one of the reasons that she was popular in the Peloponnese, an area still famous for the quality of its game.

Athena The goddess of wisdom, Athena sprang fully formed, and in armour, from Zeus's forehead. She was always most associated with the city of Athens, which she won in a competition with Poseidon, Zeus's brother and god of the sea and earthquakes. He gave the city a spring, but Athena trumped him by presenting them with the olive tree, thus showing that the ancient Greeks valued the olive over water (and they still do, given how much you see the latter wasted).

Other gods Other gods pop up here and there over the Peloponnese. **Pan**, who had the legs of a goat, was associated with the wilderness and shepherds, and can often still be glimpsed on the mountainsides of Arcadia. **Aphrodite** was goddess of love and beauty, and Greek girls are still named after her, sometimes rather optimistically. **Ares** was the god of war, the Greek equivalent to Roman Mars, and was especially beloved by the Spartans who sometimes offered him human sacrifices. Their modern descendants in the Deep Mani renamed their capital in his honour (page 169). **Hermes** was the messenger of the gods and something of a trickster, although he was also the patron of travellers – something to keep in mind.

HERACLES One of the most important mythological figures of the Peloponnese was only part divine. He is more commonly known by his Romanised name, Hercules, but nowadays this brings to mind daytime TV serials and Disney movies rather than heroic deeds. He was a demigod: part human and part god. His mother was the mortal Alcmene, and his father, unsurprisingly, was Zeus.

His name, meaning 'the glory of Hera', may have been an attempt to allay Zeus's bride's wrath, but if so it failed. Hera sent snakes to kill the young baby, but she hadn't realised yet who she was dealing with, and the infant easily strangled the serpents. The goddess then grew more cunning, and inflicted on the now adult Heracles a bout of madness, during which he killed his wife and children. As punishment for this crime the Oracle at Delphi put Heracles under the command of his enemy Eurystheus, King of Mycenae, who made him perform his famous Twelve Labours. The first six of these, and the final one, took place on the Peloponnese, and they are worth listing in full, although note that their order and nature is disputed among ancient sources.

The Nemean Lion Heracles' First Labour is one of the more believable ones, as in ancient times lions were still native to southern Europe. This particular one was laying waste to the people and animals of Nemea (page 65), again not unusual behaviour for a rogue animal. Its skin was probably not really impregnable, however, but this didn't stop the hero skinning it and using the hide as a cloak from this time on.

The Lernian Hydra The Hydra was a many-headed monster who lurked in the swamps near Lerna (page 96). Some speculate that it represented a river delta, and that 'slaying' it involved taming the waters for irrigation. Many of the Labours do seem to represent some sort of taming of wild nature by civilisation. In the myth the monster's heads kept growing back until Heracles cauterised each stump with a burning brand.

The Arcadian Stag This golden-horned animal was a favourite of the goddess Artemis. Heracles, with her tacit approval, captured the beast, but later released it.

The Erymanthian Boar Another fearsome beastie, this one was the terror of the slopes of Mount Erimanthos (page 253). Heracles quickly dispatched him and delivered the body to King Eurystheus.

The Augean Stables Seeing that killing or capturing animals and monsters was second nature to Heracles, King Eurystheus changed tack, and for his next Labour tried to gross the hero out. The stables of King Augeas can be safely described as one big pile of horseshit, which Heracles was given the task of clearing in just one day. Ever cunning, he diverted a nearby river through the building, simultaneously inventing the flush toilet.

The Stymfalian Birds Stymfalian Lake (page 257) was the home to horrendous, man-eating birds, who shot their feathers out like arrows. They were, perhaps, metaphors for the area's endemic malaria. The indefatigable Heracles drove them away.

The Capture of Cerberus Cerberus, the subject of the last Labour, was the terrifying three-headed dog who guarded the entrance to Hades, the underworld, reputedly located at Cape Tenaro at the foot of the Mani Peninsula (page 175). Heracles tamed the beast by the simple expedient of being nice to it. He then put a leash on him and dragged him up to the world of light.

THE WAR AGAINST TROY Our main source for the battle between the Greeks and the Trojans are the two epic poems of Homer, the *Iliad* and the *Odyssey* (page 126), and they formed one of the main pillars of Greek thought and education. For a long period they were also required reading for any educated European, but this is no longer the case. This is unfortunate, not because the 'classics' should still be the centre of a modern education, but because they are great stories. The summary below is intentionally sketchy, and a look at the poems themselves, which have many excellent translations, is highly recommended. Many legends surround the tale, and Homer only tells part of the story.

It all starts with Helen, the wife of King Menelaus of Sparta, running off with Paris, a handsome young prince from Troy, a city on the coast of what is now Turkey. Menelaus enlists the help of his brother, King Agamemnon of Mycenae, who is the overlord of all the 'Greeks' (a word never actually used by Homer). Agamemnon rallies the various Greek kingdoms, who amass a fleet and sail on Troy.

The Peloponnese may be named after him, but not many people nowadays are aware of who he is. His father, Tantalus, is a little more famous, if only for a rather gruesome cause. For some reason he took it into his head to cut up his young son and serve him in a stew to the Olympian gods. Apparently he was curious to see if any of them would notice. One of them, Demeter, had recently lost her daughter Persephone, and distracted by grief she took a mouthful.

The rest of the gods were up to the challenge; they refused to eat and brought Pelops back to life. Unfortunately he was missing a shoulder as Demeter had eaten it, but Hephaestus, god of the forge, soon fashioned him a new one.

Tantalus himself had to undergo eternal punishment in the underworld. Afflicted by great thirst and hunger he stood in a pool that receded from him when he tried to drink it, while above him fruit-laden branches blew away in the wind when he tried to grasp them. What could be more 'tantalising'?

Pelops went on to feature in one of the early myths of Olympia. It was said he sought the hand of Hippodamia, whose father King Oenomaus had been told that his son-in-law would kill him. Not keen on the idea, he had decreed that his daughter's suitors must beat him in a chariot race or die. Several had already failed. Pelops, cleverly, managed to replace the lynchpins of the king's chariot with ones made of wax. These broke during the race and Oenomaus was dragged to his death by his horses.

Killing your father-in-law is perhaps not the best start to a marriage, but it didn't seem to do any harm and Pelops was admired as one of the founding fathers of the area that still bears his name.

The siege of the city, which eventually lasts ten years, is prolonged by disputes among the Greek leaders. Most importantly Achilles, their greatest warrior, falls out with Agamemnon over a captured slave girl, and goes off to sulk in his tent. The Greek forces suffer without him, and to raise their morale, Achilles' best friend, and probable lover, Patroclus, dresses in his armour and joins the fight. He is killed by Hector, another prince of Troy.

A furious Achilles challenges Hector, killing him and then ignominiously dragging his body behind his chariot around the walls of Troy. Paris, in return, slays Achilles; shooting him with an arrow in his only weak spot (his heel, as you might be unsurprised to learn). The siege only comes to an end when another of the Greeks, Odysseus, comes up with one of history's first 'cunning plans', building a wooden horse and filling it with troops. The Trojans, clearly unaware of the dangers of Greeks bearing gifts, drag the thing inside the city walls where the Greeks overcome them. Foolishly they let a Trojan named Aeneas escape, who goes on to found Rome, the eventual ruler of Greece.

One of the few people to come out well from the whole affair was Menelaus. Helen returned to him and, by all accounts, they lived happily ever after. Agamemnon, the great king, was murdered by his wife Clytemnestra and her lover. Most famously Odysseus got profoundly lost on his way home. His son Telemachus criss-crossed the Peloponnese searching for news of him. After another ten years Odysseus, in disguise, made it home to find his wife, Penelope, besieged by suitors, whom he quickly killed. Unfortunately Odysseus was fated to continue his wanderings, but the saddest part of the whole story concerns his neglected dog, Argos. Lying on a rubbish tip, he is the first to recognise his old master on his return after a 20-year absence. With a last wag of his tail, the dog promptly dies.

HISTORY

The history of the Peloponnese, and that of Greece in general, is long, complex and extremely well covered by an innumerable number of books and, nowadays, websites and podcasts. A generation or two ago it could be assumed that the average, educated, person, knew at least the bare bones of the story from the Persian invasions right up to the Roman conquest. This is no longer the case.

Enthusiasts of the subject will not need yet another history of Greece, but for those less acquainted with its Classical past, and for those whose knowledge ends somewhere in the murk of Byzantine times, an unapologetically 'potted' history of the Peloponnese might prove useful, at least in placing the various ruins that dot the landscape in some sort of a context.

THE MYCENAEANS (1600–1100BC) Traces of human settlement in the Peloponnese go back 30,000 years or so, but we can safely ignore much of this 'prehistory', which left little in the way of remains, and skip straight to the first great civilisation of the area, the Mycenaeans. They were more a loose federation of states, based around individual palace complexes, than a homogenous people, but they clearly shared aspects of culture, much of which was assimilated from that of the Minoans of Crete, including their written language, Linear B (see box, page 226). Their main centres included Mycenae itself, Pylos, Tiryns and Sparta, among others.

The main written source for this culture is Homer, and was set down a few hundred years later, but it is reasonably well backed up by modern archaeology. Each Mycenaean palace was the centre of a mini kingdom, whose ruler dispensed security and justice to his people, and hospitality to visitors. Whether these various kingdoms did band together to make an assault on a city in Asia Minor round about the 12th century BC (the attack on Troy related in the *Iliad*) is disputed, but not particularly unlikely. The reasons probably had more to do with trade disputes than runaway wives, however.

The Mycenaean civilisation went into a rapid decline shortly after the supposed dates of the Trojan War, for reasons that are unclear. Some modern speculation, always trying to link the past and the present, blames climatic changes that brought a long period of drought. Whatever the real cause, Greece now entered a 'dark age', brightly illuminated by one shining light.

THE AGE OF HOMER (1100–800BC) These dark ages saw a wave of migrations into the Peloponnese, most importantly that of the Dorians. Where these people came from, what they spoke, and their relationship to 'proper' Greeks is, for our purposes, of little import. The chief achievement of this age was the emergence of a national myth, delineated in two epic poems.

Endless speculations can be made over whether there was in fact a man named Homer, a blind poet who wrote the two great epics of the *Iliad* and the *Odyssey*. If he existed at all he was probably a compiler of the oral histories, in poetical form, which originated in these years between the Mycenaean age and the rise of Classical Greece. The poems look back to a preceding time, when men were heroes and gods walked the Earth, but they also look forward. The culture and philosophy of Homer's characters not only deeply influenced Greek and Roman culture, but continue to play a part in the intellectual life of Europe, America and the rest of the world.

THE RISE OF SPARTA (800–490BC) Over the centuries that marked the transition between these dark ages and the Classical period, one city emerged as the force to be reckoned with in the Peloponnese. Although the Spartans did not invent the tactics of the phalanx, they certainly perfected it. They began with subduing their neighbours to the west, the Messinians, before bringing much of the Peloponnese under their control, either directly, or under an alliance which they dominated.

At the same time as the steadfast, but somewhat plodding, Spartans were securing a land empire, the Athenians, more flexible and forward-thinking, were starting to do the same thing over the islands and the sea. They also managed to invent one of the first forms of democracy, albeit a limited one – women and slaves, obviously, weren't allowed a vote.

These two differing styles of governance were bound to come to blows at some point, but before they could an outside force brought them together: a not uncommon theme in Greek history.

PERSIAN INVASIONS (490–479BC) The Persian invasions hardly touched the Peloponnese, but were vitally important. For a full, and engrossing, history of these years, with plenty of diversions down interesting sidelines, go no farther than the 'Father of History', Herodotus. His account fills a few hundred pages of a modern paperback, but the basic facts are clear, and easily summed up.

In 490BC, Darius, the great king of the highly monarchical Persian Empire, invaded Greece from the north. He got as far as the plain of Marathon, not far from Athens, where a heavily outnumbered, but clearly inspired, army sent them packing. In 480BC, Xerxes, Darius' son, gave it another shot, bringing with him an army of, allegedly, some five million. This time Sparta led the defence, first at the heroic stand at Thermopylae (page 127), and then in the decisive battle at Plataea. These, along with a stunning Athenian naval victory at Salamis, put paid to Persian attempts to conquer Greece.

It is a gross simplification, but not completely unreasonable, to see this – the surprising defeat of the overwhelming forces of the Persian Empire by a small alliance of freedom-loving Greek cities – as one of the turning points of world history. For those on the lookout for such momentous events, another one was soon to follow.

THE PELOPONNESIAN WAR (431–404BC) The defeat of the Persians marks the start of what is known as the Classical Age, which includes the building of the Parthenon, the writing of the great plays of Sophocles and his fellows, and the philosophy of Socrates. Most of this is a story that involves Athens, and it marks the start of a decline in the Peloponnese's fortunes, at least in historical terms, that does not revive until medieval times. There is one last salute, however.

The Persian assault had brought a brief pause to the Spartan and Athenian rivalry, but had not stopped their inevitable conflict. This has been known, mainly thanks to its chronicler Thucydides, the second great historian of the western world, as a battle between democratic Athens and anti-democratic Sparta. Things are not nearly that simple; although it is worth noting that without Thucydides we would have little information about this war at all, despite the endless discussion and analysis that surround it.

In the end the Athenians lost, due in part to some bad luck (the city was struck by disease), but also because of some really bad decisions. Sparta was left as the dominant city of what, slowly, was becoming a more cohesive 'nation' of Greeks. They wouldn't hold the position for long.

THE DECLINE OF SPARTA (371–146BC)

After the Spartan victory over Athens history seems to move out from the Peloponnese. Their hoplites, supposedly undefeatable in pitched battle, were soundly thrashed by the Thebans under Epaminondas. All this was soon to be made irrelevant by the rise of two new powers: firstly the Macedons under Philip, and then his son, Alexander the Great, to the north; and then a little-known city that had been making waves in the western Mediterranean – Rome.

The various cities of the Peloponnese seem to have pretty much accepted Macedonian dominance, and they were not much involved in Alexander's extraordinary conquest of much of Asia, in his eyes a revenge for the Persian invasions of the previous century. After Alexander's death, at a young age, his empire was divided under a number of generals, and the Peloponnese came under the – disputed – jurisdiction of Macedon itself.

It is a fascinating question what may have happened if Alexander, indisputably one of the finest military minds of all time, had ignored his desire for revenge on the Persians, and instead turned west.

In Italy he would have met a few Greek colonies and, to the north, a small, but growing, city state. He probably would have crushed them without noticing. Instead they were free to expand, and after Alexander's death a series of wars cemented Roman control over Macedon and the rest of Greece. In 146BC, to make a point, the Romans utterly destroyed Corinth.

ROMAN RULE (146BC–AD330)

Under the *Pax Romana*, the peace brought about by being under Roman subjection, the Peloponnese became the province of Achaea, ruled from Corinth. The Romans' main occupation seems to have been building, both new structures and converting old ones to their own tastes (many stadiums were closed in so that they could show gladiatorial contests).

This placid period allowed two famous travellers to pass through the Peloponnese. The first was St Paul, who spent an extended period preaching in Corinth. A century later the writer Pausanias (see box, page 60) toured the area, noting down what remained of the old Greek civilisation.

THE BYZANTINE EMPIRE (AD330–1204)

The Roman emperor Constantine I, called 'the Great', is remembered for two things. The first is the founding, in AD330, of a new capital city, Constantinople (now Istanbul in Turkey, though many Greeks stick to the old name). The second is overseeing the start of the ascension of Christianity into a state religion. Under Theodosius I, in the late 4th century, these innovations were formalised, although the new faith spread only slowly into some of the more remote corners of the Peloponnese.

At the same time Greece was suffering from a series of invasions and population migrations from the north. First in line was Alaric and his Visigoths, who sacked Sparta, but perhaps the most lasting incursion was that of various Slavic tribes, who settled permanently. Although many Greeks would like to deny it, these Slavs formed a significant part of the demographic, as proved by the countless villages still called by their 'old', Slavic, name.

At least the Eastern, or Byzantine, Empire did better than the West. In AD476, the last emperor of Rome was executed by the 'barbarians'. It is worth noting that the surviving half of the empire still saw itself as Roman, and that even the Greeks of today will sometimes refer to themselves as such. The term Byzantine is a later invention of historians, and refers to an old name for their capital. Presumably the Constantioplean Empire was a mouthful too far.

MEDIEVAL CONFUSION (1204–1460) Allegedly aimed at the 'Holy Land', the knights of the Fourth Crusade were diverted by the lure of riches, and in 1204 shamefully sacked Constantinople, a city of fellow Christians. One of the Frankish forces, led by Geoffrey de Villehardouin, on its way to join in the plunder, embarked at the bottom of Messinia that year. Geoffrey was indeed French, but the term 'Frank' was used in Greece to describe any foreigner from northwestern Europe.

Realising that there were plenty of riches to be gained where he was, Geoffrey set about conquering the Peloponnese and founding a dynasty. His son, William, was an inveterate castle builder – point to any medieval ruin in the Peloponnese and say it was built by him, and you have a good chance of being right.

The Franks in Greece are an intriguing prospect, and they are often overlooked. This was at the height of the chivalric tradition, and the knights of the Peloponnese were acknowledged as some of its finest flowers. When you picture noble ladies giving favours to knights in shining armour, before they run at each other in the lists, sun glancing off the tips of their lances, you do not often place the image in Greece, but there it is.

The Franks never had total control, however. The Venetians also took over those parts of the Peloponnese that were useful to them, generally coastal fortresses such as Koroni and Methoni. At the same time the Byzantines did not disappear. On the contrary, they made Mystra, near Sparta, into the second city of their empire, and it enjoyed an artistic and intellectual revival.

Many places in the Peloponnese spent this period being juggled between these three rival powers. A fourth was soon to join them, and bring some measure of continuity to the area.

TURKISH OCCUPATION (1460–1821) The Ottoman tribe had emerged as the leader of the Turkic peoples in Asia Minor and had begun forming an empire that would last right into the 20th century. In this book they are referred to interchangeably as either Turkish or Ottoman, and it is also worth remembering that their troops, especially in later times, could come from anywhere in the empire, from Albania to Egypt.

They had conquered the great city of Constantinople on 29 May 1453, and its last emperor, another Constantine, crowned at Mystra a few years before, died fighting on its walls. It was a Tuesday, still deemed an unlucky day by modern Greeks. Mystra fell in turn, in 1460, and the Peloponnese came under the control of the Ottomans, although the Venetians managed to hang on to some of their ports, and were a constant thorn in the Turkish side.

The Greeks make much of their years of repression under the Turkish yoke, and a lot that is still wrong with the modern country is blamed on this period. Some of this is true, but it is also the case that if you had to choose a repressive regime to live under, then that of the Ottomans wouldn't be a bad choice. The Greeks maintained a large degree of religious freedom, and talented individuals could rise high in the civil service, no matter what their nationality.

That said, it was never going to sit well with the freedom-loving Greeks to be ruled by a foreign power, especially one based in the 'holy city' of Constantinople. It was all too easy, looking back over history, to see the Turks as another wave of the dreaded Persians – a tyrannical Eastern power subjugating the free West. At some point, they had to go.

THE WAR OF INDEPENDENCE (1821–29) The Peloponnese was the central battleground of the Greeks' struggle against their Turkish overlords. The rebellion started here, officially on 25 March 1821, when Bishop Germanos of Patra raised the flag at Kalavryta, and the most effective Greek general, Theodoros Kolokotronis, made it his heartland. Early success, marred by massacres on both sides, soon got bogged down in petty rivalries between the Greek leaders and even, in 1824, civil war.

The Ottomans took advantage, and in 1825 a large Egyptian force under the command of Ibrahim Pasha landed in southern Messinia and started ravaging the countryside. Foreign sympathy had slowly been growing for the Greeks, most manifest in the numbers of philhellenes ('lovers of Greece') who flocked to fight against the Turks. The most famous of these was the poet Byron, whose death at Missolonghi, just to the north of the Peloponnese, forever won him a place in the Greek heart (hence the number of streets named *Vironis*).

In 1827, the foreign powers finally acted (see box, page 218), when a combined British, French and Russian fleet destroyed that of Ibrahim, effectively ending the war, although skirmishes continued until 1829.

THE 'MEGALI IDEA' (1830–1923) The new Greek nation consisted only of the Peloponnese, a small part of the northern mainland including Athens, and the Cycladic islands – less than half of its present-day area. Much of the country's first hundred years was an effort to capture all the territory seen as rightfully Greek, up to and including Constantinople itself. This was the Megali Idea, the 'Great Idea'.

Its greatest proponent was Prime Minister Venizelos, after whom Athens airport is now named, who managed to regain much of what is now northern Greece in the Balkan Wars of the early 20th century.

After the Allies defeated the Ottoman Empire in World War I, Greece saw the chance to complete its project. Initially Greeks were allowed to occupy Smyrna (modern Izmir), in what had become the new nation of Turkey, as it had a substantial Greek population. Seeking to overwhelm the young country, and regain Constantinople, they then decided to march on the capital, Ankara. They underestimated the enemy, and its new leader, Ataturk, and, in 1922, the Greeks were pushed back into the sea. The 1923 Treaty of Lausanne established, for the most part, the modern borders, and saw a large population exchange, with 400,000 Muslims living in Greece moving to Turkey, and 1.3 million Christians leaving their homes in what was now Turkey to settle in Greece.

RESISTANCE AND CIVIL WAR (1935–49) Coping with this huge influx of refugees from Turkey, most of whom settled around Athens (as is still evidenced by the names of areas like Nea Smyrna, 'New Smyrna'), was not helped by the world slipping into a huge economic slump. The era saw the start of mass immigration to countries such as the US and Australia in search of a better life.

Political chaos led to the rise of a fascist dictatorship under General Metaxas in 1935. At the start of World War II the general's sympathies clearly lay with Hitler and Mussolini, and the expectation was that the country would, at the least, remain neutral. Never underestimate Greek pride, however.

On 28 October 1940, Mussolini asked his good pal Metaxas if he wouldn't mind a few thousand Italian troops moving through Greece. The bridled Metaxas is said to have answered with a resounding '*Ohi!*' ('No!'). The hurriedly gathered Greek forces rushed up to the snowy Albanian border where, in hideous conditions, they soundly thrashed the Italians. The day is still celebrated as a national holiday.

Hitler could not allow this and, in 1941, the German war machine rolled over the country. The British and Commonwealth troops who had been aiding the Greeks were evacuated from the Peloponnese, although many were captured. A few avoided the Germans by running into the mountains, where they were often protected, at great risk, by local villagers.

The Greek resistance started as a spontaneous movement, and was much inspired by the struggle against the Turkish occupation which had, after all, ended not too long before. It was, without doubt, the most effective resistance effort in Europe, most of it organised under the auspices of ELAS, a liberation army with a communist leadership.

The latter fact did not sit well with the Allied leadership, particularly Churchill, who was already mentally divvying up post-war Europe. He gave his support to the exiled King George in Cairo, and persuaded him to reject offers of a coalition government. These machinations led, soon after the defeat of the Germans, to a vicious civil war between the Left and Right which lasted until 1949 and in which more Greeks died than in World War II itself. British support for the royalist forces was soon replaced by that of America (Greece saw the first ever use of napalm), and by the end of it all the country was little more than a US client state.

The civil war can still be a contentious subject, and is only just starting to be discussed with any openness. Massacres and atrocities took place on both sides, and a coherent, and accurate, argument could be made demonising both. Most people have realised that it is time to forgive and forget, but some villages, even today, are often defined by which side they were on.

DICTATORSHIP TO DEMOCRACY (1967–2012) George Papandreou had become prime minister in 1963, but his constant arguments with the Greek king, Constantine II, led to political instability. In 1967, a military coup installed a junta that became known as the Colonels. It was a harsh and oppressive regime, with mass arrests and the suppression of any dissent, although the Colonels also tried to court popular opinion with measures such as the cancelling of bank debts of peasant farmers.

At the time Cyprus, with its large Turkish minority, was an independent nation, and various international agreements prevented its union with Greece. In 1974, the military dictatorship sent troops to overthrow the government of the island, and the Turkish army, in response, invaded from the north. The result was the still divided nation we see today.

Back in Greece the crisis had made the Colonels look incompetent, and they were forced to hand back power to a civilian government. An election brought the right-wing New Democracy (ND) to power under the leadership of Constantine Karamanlis. The king had fled the country back in 1967, a referendum decided that the Greeks did not want him back and the country became a republic.

The 1980s were dominated by PASOK (the Panhellic Socialist Movement) under Andreas Papandreou (George's son), while the next two decades saw power swap backwards and forwards between the two main parties.

RECENT POLITICS

The Greek government works on a fairly standard model, somewhere between that of France and Germany. The president is largely ceremonial and power lies with the prime minister, a large cabinet, and a parliament. For a long time after the fall of the Colonels, the prime minister came from either PASOK or the ND, and Greek politics could have put the Bush or Clinton dynasties to shame. The then prime minister and leader of ND, Costas Karamanlis (nephew of Constantine – see above) called snap elections in October 2009 and was replaced by the leader of the PASOK opposition, George Papandreou, who is the old George's grandson and Andreas' son (again, see above). Antonis Samaras of ND at least provided a new surname to the list, although it might be noted that he was a dormitory roommate of George Papandreou while at college in the US. In 2012, after some turmoil, he entered a rather uneasy coalition with PASOK, led by one Evangelos Venizelos (who claimed to be completely unrelated to Eleftherios Venizelos, the former prime minister after whom Athens airport is named – see page 31).

The big story of the 2012 elections was the rise of former fringe parties, including extremes on both sides of the political spectrum. This included the KKE (the Communist Party of Greece) who have historically always won around 10% of the Greek vote, and, more worryingly, Golden Dawn, an unashamed bunch of fascists. Most importantly it saw the rise of Syriza, the 'Coalition of the Radical Left', led by the relatively fresh-faced Alexis Tsipras.

Indicative of Greece's volatile economic and political state is the fact that two snap legislative elections were held in 2015. The January elections resulted in a victory for Syriza, and the almost complete collapse of PASOK, the old party of the left. This began an extended set of negotiations between Greece and its creditors over new bailout deals, almost leading to a Greek exit ('Grexit') from the Eurozone (page 20). Compromise, of a kind, was eventually reached. Nevertheless, Tsipras was left with little choice but to resign in August 2015, only seven months into his term, in the wake of a rebellion by members of his own party. Another snap election was held in September 2015, and Tsipras led Syriza to another victory, taking 145 out of 300 seats and forming the coalition with the right-wing Independent Greeks party, which took nine seats. The next quadrennial election is due in September 2019, but few would be surprised were a snap election to be called well before that deadline.

Greek politics have not yet fully settled down into what must be seen as a new era. Austerity, in one form or another, looks set to continue for the foreseeable future, with the national debt still on the increase according to quarter-on-quarter figures for 2017, despite the implementation of another substantial credit, loan and debt relief package by the Eurozone in June of that year. One thing the crisis has shown is that, for one reason or another, Greece still seems to matter. The stories that emerge from the historical home of democracy still have the power to resonate on the world stage.

The other big story of 2015 was the refugee crisis, largely caused by the ongoing civil war in Syria. Greece is one of the easiest EU countries to enter from the Middle East, with some of its islands mere kilometres away from the Turkish coast. Figures are hard to verify, but close to a million people entered Greece in 2015, and the country, already under stress, was barely able to cope (although it is worth noting that this has had little impact in the Peloponnese). The volume of new arrivals has subsequently abated, but it is estimated that more than 60,000 refugees were trapped in Greece in 2017, and many people worry who else might be entering among the waves of desperate refugees.

While the government has been slow to react to the issue, possibly understandably given its other problems, the people of Greece themselves have shown almost universal compassion for the refugees arriving on their shores (see box, page 21).

ADMINISTRATIVE REGIONS

The Peloponnese is divided up into seven primary administrative regions, whose borders are based on ancient divisions. Following their coastlines in a clockwise direction from the northeast (where the peninsula links to the rest of mainland Greece at the Corinth Canal), these are Corinthia (whose capital is Corinth), Argolis (Nafplio), Arcadia (Tripoli), Laconia (Sparta), Messinia (Kalamata), Elis (Pyrgos) and Achaea (Patras).

This guidebook is divided into six chapters, each of which more-or-less covers one or two of the traditional administrative regions. Corinthia and Argolis are combined into one chapter, as are Elis and Achaea, though the latter also incorporates the mountainous far west of Corinthia. A full chapter is dedicated to each of Arcadia, Laconia and Messinia, though the culturally cohesive region known as the Mani, which is divided between Laconia and Messinia, has been accorded its own chapter. If these minor liberties annoy or offend any locals, I extend my humble apologies. I have done it for the benefit of travellers to the region.

ECONOMY *with thanks to Nicholas Walton*

Anybody with even the vaguest awareness of what's in the newspapers will know that Greece has been having a rough time of it in recent years. Some aspects of Greece's current economic and political problems are a potential issue for travellers, but some aren't. Either way, it's worth taking a few moments to take stock of the situation before you go.

Greece's problems started – or at least were widely noticed – when George Papandreou's PASOK party won elections in 2009 and announced to the world that Greek debt figures were wildly inaccurate. To cut a long story short, this then called into question the country's solvency and its membership of the European single currency, the euro. Concerns about Greece's position within the euro then spread to other members of the euro, prompting enormous questions about the viability of the single currency and the current structure of the EU itself.

The Greek government was only able to pay its way thanks to billions of euros of emergency funds provided by the EU and International Monetary Fund (IMF), with strict conditions attached that required Greece to cut its budget and enact structural reforms. Although it is undeniable that Greece already had deep structural problems in its economy, there is also no doubt that these reforms caused the country to enter a deep recession, which in turn threatened or outright destroyed many people's livelihoods. While some restructuring of the economy was undeniably necessary, the negative results of the austerity measures seemed to fall unfairly on the poor and the young – unemployment rose to an extraordinary 75% among those in their 20s. Understandably, this led to political turmoil, with some riots and public unrest on the streets of Greek cities, and the emergence of parties on the extreme ends of the political spectrum.

The victory of far-left Syriza in 2015 was largely a reaction to these harsh austerity measures. Prime Minister Tsipras put a team in place to negotiate with what had come to be known as the troika; the European Commission, the European Central Bank, and the IMF. The poster boy for these was the new Greek Finance Minister, Yanis Varoufakis, a motorbike-riding former academic and unashamed Marxist. Talks were often tense and Greece came close to leaving the euro. The high point of these came in the summer of 2015 when the Greek stock market and banks were closed down, and a limit was put on cash withdrawals from ATMs. At the same time, Greece announced that the latest bailout deal would be put to a national referendum on 5 July, which Tsipras and Syriza urged the population to reject, even though they themselves had negotiated it. They received the support they wanted with 63.1% voting 'No', but not everyone was pleased with the outcome – Varoufakis, who had become a divisive figure, then resigned.

Despite the referendum result, Greece was offered few concessions to the deal, and was forced to capitulate to its terms (further austerity and a loss of fiscal sovereignty). On 20 July, banks reopened and the immediate crisis was averted.

The snap election in September 2015 showed that Tsipras still had popular support, even though many think he bent too far under the pressure from the troika. In 2018 Greece finally exited its bailout programme. The economy, although it shows some glimmers of recovery, still dips in and out of recession, and the years ahead will remain tough for the long-suffering Greek people.

So what does this mean for the visitor? First of all, it does not mean that Greece is suddenly an unsafe place to visit. With care and common sense, the traveller in the Peloponnese will still find the country beautiful and the people welcoming. Some public services may be at breaking point, so it's reasonable to expect minor problems, for instance in rubbish collection or medical services, so have a close read of your insurance policy. Pharmacies have also been a target of reforms thanks to the unpicking of cosy deals they had with governments, and this means that you ought to take along an adequate supply of any prescription or emergency medicines you might require. Also be aware that transport services such as buses may be cut back.

The situation also calls for sensitivity. It's always best not to overtly bring up the subject of politics (although the Greeks are normally happy to raise it themselves – just be led by your hosts). You should also be aware that, despite the troubled times, the already strong sense of Greek patriotism is likely to be running high. Recognise that a lot of people and communities are undergoing extremely hard times, and a little extra thought or a tip will go a long way.

Most importantly, check news websites before you travel for updates on the situation and possible flashpoints in the near future, and make sure you have adequate and suitable cover from your insurance company and the businesses providing services like flights, car rental and accommodation. Trouble is most likely to occur in Athens and other centres, but be wary of political rallies in any city. In late 2015, farmers in Sparta, Kalamata and Tripoli staged peaceful protests in objection to increased taxes, while more recently, in May 2017, police fired teargas during a violent anti-austerity demonstration in Athens, while an associated strike led to more than 150 flights bring grounded for 4 hours and the closure of ferry services to the islands for several days.

If Greece did ever fall out of the euro – which looks far less likely than it did at the height of the crisis – it would probably happen very suddenly, causing a good deal of unrest and loss of services. Just in case of further economic turmoil, it makes sense to take precautions, such as having an extra source of cash, and keep important phone numbers – embassy, insurance company, airline – at hand. It is worth noting that even at the height of the crisis in summer 2015, ATM

ON THE SHORES OF LESVOS

In October 2015, a photo depicting three old Greek ladies went viral on the internet. What was interesting was not their black clothes and long socks – these are still typical of old Greek ladies everywhere. What had caught attention was the lady on the right who was cuddling and bottle-feeding a refugee baby who had recently arrived on the beach of her island of Lesvos. This was 83-year-old Emilia Kavisi, who has been one of the many locals to have volunteered to help with the influx of desperate people who have arrived on the shores of Greece. Like other Greeks she was motivated not just by compassion but by history. Her father, like many others on the island, was also a refugee from Turkey, arriving with the population exchanges of 1922 with nothing more than a pair of shoes and a sewing machine.

withdrawal limits did not apply to tourists and few problems were reported by the multitude of visitors who continued to flock to the country.

In the longer term, a return to the drachma should lead to a dramatic drop in comparative prices for those travelling from countries such as the UK, meaning that Greece may once again become a Mecca for backpackers and other budget-conscious travellers. Interesting times, indeed.

PEOPLE

At first glance the population of Greece is, ethnically, pretty homogenous, especially outside of Athens. Even before the recent refugee crisis (page 19), it had the highest proportion of immigrants of any EU country. Estimates put one in ten of the population as having been born outside of Greece, the vast majority of these being Albanian, and these still provide a vital base-level workforce in agriculture and construction. Even in out-of-the-way areas in the Peloponnese, you will see groups of immigrant workers gathering in the early morning, waiting to be picked up for a day's labour. Recent years in the Peloponnese have also seen an increasing number of agricultural labourers coming from Asia, as well as a scattering of knick-knack salesmen from North and West Africa. While there is some inevitable tension, most Greeks treat the immigrants well. Looked at historically, this is hardly surprising as the Greeks have much experience with immigration, both to and from their country. Most families have also grown up with stories of living in harsh conditions in the aftermath of the various upheavals of the 20th century, giving them a greater empathy with immigrants.

ORTHODOXY AND GREEK EASTER

Greece is one of the few countries where religion is still a major part of the national identity. The vast majority of the population, whatever their church-going habits, would describe themselves as Orthodox. There is also a still tight link between Church and State, one example of which is that only foreigners can be cremated, a practice forbidden under Orthodox laws. In most Greek minds you cannot be Greek unless you are Orthodox. This is true of everyone from the most pious to those who hardly ever set foot in a church and find the practice somewhat old-fashioned.

The Orthodox Church was one of the anchor stones of Greek identity during Turkish occupation. In modern times this has led to a unique attitude to religion in all spheres of life. In political life the mentioning of 'God' is almost a taboo in Britain, carrying an embarrassing taint with it. In the USA, however, it is practically obligatory and a president can happily mention that God talks to him and helps him make geopolitical decisions. To the Greek mind both these attitudes would seem strange. The Orthodox faith here is simply a given, informing and providing an undercurrent to everything else. To reject it is unfathomable and would involve turning your back on an essential part of what being Greek is; akin to an Englishman not supporting the national football team, or an American decrying the constitution (although this might be slowly changing – see below).

The Orthodox year is littered with observance and celebration. Each saint, down to the most parochial and minor, has their own festival; commemorated at churches dedicated to them, in villages they are patron of, and by people who share their name. Even a fairly short journey through Greece is not unlikely to throw the traveller into the midst of one of these. One of these *paneyiri*, or 'celebrations', will always involve a church service, but they are more noticeable for

LANGUAGE

Greek is not the easiest of languages, not helped by the fact that the alphabet is different. The reasons for not learning it are compounded by the number of Greeks who speak excellent English, especially the younger generation (it is compulsory in school), and the fact that almost all road signs are now transliterated.

It's worth trying to learn the basics, however. A simple greeting can promote you from the level of a 'tourist' to that of a *xenos*, a word that means 'stranger', but also, tellingly, 'guest'. A knowledge of the alphabet will also help if you want to explore more isolated areas, both with signs and menus.

Something worth remembering is that Greek is a stress-based language. While words are pronounced as written, if you put the stress in the wrong place then Greeks will find it hard to understand you. It's often worth trying again if this happens. The stress is indicated by the accent on individual letters.

RELIGION

Almost the entire population identify themselves as Greek Orthodox Christian (95–98%). Priests are a fairly common sight, and you can't miss them in their dark, flowing cassocks, wearing cylindrical hats and often sporting flowing beards (they are forbidden from cutting their hair). A priest (or *papas*) is allowed to marry, although this excludes him from promotion up the Church hierarchy. Most village priests have a wife. For more on the part religion plays in Greek life

their partying,with eating and drinking continuing in the village square until the early hours.This combination of religious festival with secular bacchanalia – wine, food, good company and dancing – also applies to the more universal celebrations of the Christian year. The most important of these, from the Orthodox perspective, is Easter; still far overshadowing the observance of Christmas, despite a recent influx of Western traditions. This makes a lot of sense, when looked at objectively.

The earliest sign that Easter is on the way is a slowly increasing chorus of loud explosions in the weeks before. These come from firecrackers of a sort long banned in most countries, and walking past teenagers, and even younger children, at this time of year becomes a hazardous occupation. It is a harbinger of the celebrations to come.

To prepare for these the Greeks tend to fast in the weeks preceding. This can vary from 'giving chocolate up for Lent' to not eating any meat, fish or oil. On Good Friday processions of icons of Christ, rested on funeral biers, are solemnly paraded around villages and towns.

The main event is the next night, when an evening service culminates in the extinguishing of all lights in the church. At the stroke of midnight a single candle is lit in the inner sanctuary, symbolising Christ's rebirth. This is passed from candle to candle until every family has a light. To ensure good luck for the year they must return home with it still lit, and draw a sooty cross above their front doors.

The fast is broken that night with a soup of lamb's guts and lemon, but the main feast is the next day when the whole lamb is roasted on a spit. Greek Easter eggs are hard-boiled and dyed red, and a game, similar to conkers without the strings, is played with them. The eating and drinking will generally continue for much of the day.

1

see box, page 22. The supremacy of the Greek Church has been somewhat rocked in recent years, as they have been involved in several scandals including dodgy property deals, and many have begun to question its favourable tax deals in the light of austerity measures for everyone else. An indication of this disquiet was evident when Tsipras chose not to undergo the normal religious swearing in of the prime minister, and surprisingly little fuss was made. The fact that the young Greek leader is unmarried, but has a family, and is an unashamed atheist, would have been almost unthinkable a few short years ago.

EDUCATION

State education is free at all levels and is compulsory from ages 6 to 15. Before this children can also join kindergarten from the age of 4. From 6 to 12 they attend a primary school, and then junior school up to 15. Senior school, 15 to 18, is optional, but the final exams are necessary for entry into university, as well as government-controlled professions.

School generally only takes place in the mornings, and children often attend supplementary private schools in the early evening. Holidays are two weeks at Christmas, two weeks at Easter, and a whopping 12 weeks in the summer.

Schools in Greece were already in dire need of reform before the debt crisis, and they have not escaped the universal cuts since then. This has led to what many see as a two-tier system. State schools are free, but not up to the job, and only the well-off can now afford the extra private schooling that a student needs in order to succeed in exams.

CULTURE

The modern culture of Greece is, in many ways, not much different from that of the rest of Europe and America, with the young absorbing much of their view of the world from the same movies, music and websites as the young everywhere else.

This has to be weighed against the importance the Greeks put on their history, and the customs and culture that have arisen from it. This includes not just the glories of the Classical Age, but also the flowering of Christianity under Byzantium, the 400 years of 'oppression' under the Turks, and the events of the 20th century – in which, it would be fair to say, Greece suffered more than any other country that is normally included in 'Western' Europe.

This contradiction can be often seen in the Peloponnese, where the people are surrounded by tangible reminders of this past, and the region is known as a conservative one. Everyone, even iPod-wearing teenagers, would agree on the importance of preserving Greek heritage and tradition.

The most obvious signs of this, at least for a visitor to the Peloponnese, are likely to come in the form of music and dance. **Music** is generally based around the *bouzouki* – an instrument a bit like a mandolin which used to have six paired strings, but now generally has eight strings. Nowadays its players form the backbone of both traditional folk music and of *rembetika*, the 'Greek blues', which started in the hashish dens of Piraeus (the port of Athens), mainly sung by the Greek refugees from Asia Minor in the 1920s. Another characteristic instrument for folk music is the clarinet, whose wailing tones often give it a distinctly Eastern flavour.

Traditional Greek **dancing** is familiar, at least in its basic form, to many of us, but the surface similarities between the various dances actually hide a wide diversity of styles. The *kalamatianos*, said to have originated in Kalamata, is a classic, with the dancers standing in a row with their hands on each other's shoulders. Performances of music and dance often take place in touristy areas, but are sometimes of dubious quality. You are better off hunting down a village *paneyiri*, or 'celebration', where live music will be accompanied by spontaneous dancing. You might also keep an eye on the Greek men late at night in a taverna, as occasionally one of them will be possessed by the spirit of the evening and will perform a *zeibekiko*. This intense, solo dance also originated in the hash dens where *rembetika* was played.

Finally, as we are discussing music and dance, a word on **plate smashing**, which outsiders often regard as an essential part of a Greek evening. It used to be a rare expression of celebration, but is now actually illegal because of the injuries it sometimes caused. Nowadays, Greeks confine themselves to throwing flower petals over the heads of the dancers and musicians.

Background Information CULTURE

1

2

Practical Information

WHEN TO VISIT

Spring is one of the best times to come to the Peloponnese. The climate can be very pleasant and, although the Greeks will think you mad, you can swim from April onwards. Greek Easter is the biggest festival of the year and it's usually possible to get involved (see box, page 22). Above all, the mountainsides, bare and forbidding for the rest of the year, are covered with swathes of wild flowers in every colour imaginable.

Summer is for the sun worshippers. Temperatures in July and August can soar above 40°C, making anything more energetic than walking into the sea a daunting prospect. It is also the busiest time of year, and not only with foreigners. In August the entirety of Athens decamps to the beaches and accommodation can be hard to come by.

Things start to calm down again in **autumn** from September onwards. The sea stays warm and swimming remains pleasant into October, which marks the end of the usual 'holiday season' that began in April. Don't discount coming in the **winter** months, however. There are often sunny and enjoyable days, even in December, and there's also the opportunity to ski in the mountains.

HIGHLIGHTS AND SUGGESTED ITINERARIES

The shape of the Peloponnese lends itself to a **circular tour**, with one or more excursions inland, but, as distances are not that great, it is also easy enough to base yourself somewhere and make excursions around. **One week** will give you a taster for the area, but is not enough for a proper tour. You are probably best to stick to one of the regions, perhaps the Argolid to see the famous ancient sites, or the Mani for its walking and nature. **Two weeks** does allow enough time to explore, especially with your own transport, but try and allow enough time to chill out as well. If you can come for more than two weeks, then do – there is plenty to keep you occupied for a month or more.

TEN MUST-SEES These are not places that *must* be included in any Peloponnese trip, but rather the pick of its various attractions. You don't need to visit all of them, but, if you're near one, you should probably stop in. As is inevitable in Greece, the list is heavy on the ancient sites. Don't be put off by these: even if you have no interest in history these places are often a good excuse to get into the countryside, and they are almost always in beautiful settings. Note that Athens and Delphi are highlights all of their own, and are not included in this list – see page 259.

Ancient Corinth   The streets where St Paul preached can still be walked on, and the bulk of Acrocorinth above delivers on the majestic views it seems to promise (page 62).

Nafplio Easily the prettiest town on the Peloponnese, and an excellent base for exploring, it also provides a bit of culture and sophistication among the rural backwaters (page 79).

Epidavros The Classical theatre of the ancient Greeks is something most people have an image of in their head. Epidavros is where this image steps, spectacularly, into reality. Try and catch a play here (page 88).

The rack-and-pinion railway This scenic short ride between Kalavryta and Diakopto is definitely not just for the railway buffs and, if you are not a walker, it's your best chance to see a mountain gorge up close (page 251).

Mycenae A monumental structure of stone perched on a ridge between two mountains, Mycenae was already old at the time of the ancient Greeks (page 68).

Diros Caves For something completely different allow yourself to be punted around these extraordinary sea caves (page 171).

Mystra Many visitors are surprised by the exquisite beauty of Byzantine churches. This ghost town, in the foothills of the mountains, is full of them (page 134).

Olympia Set in a peaceful river valley, it is hard to ignore the atmosphere of Olympia, which saw the athletic games take place for more than 1,000 years (page 229).

Voidokilia There are plenty of fantastic beaches around, but this one, backed by a lagoon, is among the best. The postcard printers certainly seem to think so (page 221).

Monemvasia The little village that is hidden away on this 'Greek Gibraltar' has never seen a car. It is almost impossibly romantic (page 146).

TEN HIDDEN GEMS Some of these places are better known than others, but all of them have a sense of discovery about them. At some you might find yourself the only visitor, even in midsummer. Like the list above they are in no particular order.

Ancient Messene The site of this ancient city is bigger than Olympia, and it really belongs in the list above, but because it's a little hard to get to almost no-one visits (page 203).

Kastania This little village could represent the Mani. There is an imposing tower house and several Byzantine churches, plus a basic, but excellent, taverna. Despite being in the mountains just above the 'resort' of Stoupa, few people seem to make it up here (page 193).

Orchomenos There are countless small ruins in the Peloponnese, many of them little more than a jumble of rocks. This is a bit more impressive, and you will be on your own with the magnificent views (page 103).

Kyparissia Getting here is half the fun, as the village is at the dead end of a long and stunning cliffside road. Once there it looks like a sleepy corner of one of the islands, and the beaches are superb (page 228).

Prodromou The most dramatic of the monasteries of the Lousios Gorge, which is itself the most beautiful corner of the evocative region of Arcadia (page 116).

Mylopotamos The island of Kythira could count as a hidden gem all on its own. This village, with its chilled tavernas, waterfall pools, and cliffside caves, sums it up well (page 160).

Geraki If you liked Mystra, this is a smaller version of the same thing, with beautiful churches, stupendous views, and newly upgraded onsite interpretive material. Anywhere else this would be a premier site. Check out the nearby village as well (page 144).

Polilimnio In an area where most rivers are dry for much of the year this place makes a welcome change, with a beautiful series of pools and waterfalls that offer a different swimming experience from the sea (page 226).

Pheneos This flat plain, surrounded by mountains, is striking and intriguing. In the forests above is a picture-perfect lake, and the monastery of Agios Giorgios, whose two friendly monks always welcome visitors (page 256).

Gerolimenas Little Greek fishing villages always have charm, but this has more than most, along with several good tavernas that will cook the catch, and some startlingly nice places to stay (page 173).

TOUR OPERATORS

Many tours can be booked without a flight, so could be done from any country.

ABROAD
UK
Andante Travels ☎01722 713800; e tours@andantetravels.co.uk; w andantetravels.co.uk. 12-day tours of the major archaeological sites accompanied by an expert & gentle walking tours of the Argolid.
Explore ☎01252 884709; e sales@explore.co.uk; w explore.co.uk. 2-week tours of the major sites as well as the Mani.
Inntravel ☎01653 617001; e inntravel@inntravel.co.uk; w inntravel.co.uk. Fly/drive tours that include self-guided walking in the southern Peloponnese.
Martin Randall Travel ☎020 8742 3355 or +1 800 988 6168 (toll-free) in the US; e info@martinrandall.co.uk; w martinrandall.co.uk. 10-day tours of the Classical sites with an expert.
Naturetrek ☎01962 733051; e info@naturetrek.co.uk; w naturetrek.co.uk. Flower- & butterfly-related tours.
Responsible Travel ☎01273 823700; e rosy@responsibletravel.com; w responsibletravel.com. Small group tours of the Peloponnese that include

biking, rafting, sailing & horseriding.
Sunvil ☎020 8758 4499; w sunvil.co.uk. International operator offering tailor-made trips, fly-drives, island hopping & beach holidays.

USA
Classic Adventures ☎+1 800 777 8090; e benton@classicadventures.com; w classicadventures.com. 11-day cycling tour which includes the Peloponnese.
Hellenic Adventures ☎+1 800 851 6349; e info@hellenicadventures.com; w hellenicadventures.com. Expert-led tours that include Olympia & Nafplio.
Homeric Tours ☎+1 800 223 5570; e info@homerictours.com; w homerictours.com. Various coach tours & cruises.

Australia
Grecian Tours ☎+61 3 9663 3711; e greciantours@bigpond.com; w greciantours.com.au. Various tours & other services.

IN GREECE There are countless tours and excursions that can be booked on the ground in Greece, usually coach tours to the sites. Contact the travel agents listed in the guide. There are also several companies that specialise in unusual tours of specific areas; these are highlighted in specific chapters. The two companies below offer something a bit different.

Cycle Greece \+30 21092 18160; e info@ cyclegreece.com; w cyclegreece.com; see ad, page 54. As the name suggests, cycling tours, which can also be combined with sailing.

Trekking Hellas \+30 21033 10323; e info@ trekking.gr; w trekking.gr. All sorts of outdoor activities from hiking to rafting offered as well as traditional cooking workshops. Highly recommended. They have a branch in Arcadia.

RED TAPE

UK visitors must have a passport. Schengen area visitors face no entry restrictions, but should have a valid passport (this, or a photo driving licence, are supposed to be carried at all times, but you will rarely be called out on this).

Most non-EU visitors (including those from the US, Canada, Australia and New Zealand) can stay a maximum of 90 days in Greece and other Schengen-zone countries (most of the EU, but not the UK). Your passport may not be checked if arriving from another EU country, but you need to have it stamped to avoid problems leaving the country. After the UK leaves the European Union, documentation requirements for UK citizens may change. Check before travelling. If you want to stay longer you are best to contact a Greek embassy before you make your trip.

EMBASSIES

For a list of Greek embassies abroad, see w embassy.goabroad.com/embassies-of/ greece. Otherwise, the following can be found in Athens:

Australia Level 6, Thon Bldg, Cnr Kifisias & Alexandras Av, Ambelokipi, 11523 Athens; \21087 04000; w greece.embassy.gov.au/athn/home. html

Canada 48 Ethnikis Antistaseos St, Chalandri, 15231 Athens; \21072 73400; w canadainternational.gc.ca/greece-grece

Ireland 7 Leo Vas Konstantinou Av, 11526 Athens; \21072 32771; w dfa.ie/irish-embassy/ greece

New Zealand (consulate) 76 Kifissias Av, 15226 Athens; \21069 24136; w mfat.govt. nz/en/countries-and-regions/europe/italy/ new-zealand-embassy/new-zealand-consulate-general-athens-greece/

UK 1 Ploutarhou St, 10675 Athens; \21072 72600; w gov.uk/world/organisations/british-embassy-athens

USA 91 Vassilisis Sofias Av, 10160 Athens; \21072 12951; w gr.usembassy.gov

GETTING THERE AND AWAY

BY AIR The Peloponnese has only two 'main' airports at the present time, Kalamata and Araxos (near Patra), which used to cater mainly to charter flights, and these are still available in the high season. These two airports have minimal facilities and you would be wise to organise your onward transport in advance.

Flights to the Greek capital, Athens, are a good alternative. It is only an hour by road from the Peloponnese and there are reasonable bus and train connections (see below). Kalamata also has internal flights daily to and from Thessaloniki (in northern Greece – see w olympicair.com).

Direct flights   Most direct flights to the Peloponnese from the UK (*3½–4hrs*) and the rest of Europe are for the benefit of package holiday companies and only run from May to October. The schedules and departure airports are never static. There are also weekend flights from Manchester, Birmingham and Gatwick to Kalamata, as well as several other European countries to both airports.

Things are now improving for the independent traveller. EasyJet (w *easyjet.com*) flies to Kalamata between May and November, and British Airways does the same from Heathrow (w *britishairways.com*).

At least from the UK, w skyscanner.net is a good website to check on and compare flights. Another good option is to find out who is offering package holidays in the area and check their websites for flight-only deals. Prices can fluctuate wildly, and often it can be cheaper to book a package itself than just the flight – remember you don't actually have to stay in their accommodation.

Flights to Athens   Direct flights to Athens leave from London, and less frequently Manchester (*3½–4hrs*). EasyJet (w *easyjet.com*) is often cheapest, but you have to book well in advance to take advantage of this. Other airlines that currently serve these routes are British Airways (w *britishairways.com*), Aegean (w *en.aegeanair.com*) and Olympic (w *olympicair.com*) – w skyscanner.net can compare them all over a wide range of dates.

Athens is also accessible by air from most of the rest of the world. A good place to start is one of the various 'cheapflights' websites: try w cheapflights.com (USA), w cheapflights.ca (Canada) or w cheapflights.com.au (Australia and New Zealand).

To and from Athens airport   Athens airport, officially named Eleftherios Venizelos (☏ *21035 30000*; w *aia.gr*), opened in 2001 to the southeast of the city, and was a massive improvement on its predecessor. It is now a reasonable international airport with all the facilities you would expect.

Among these are the usual range of car-hire company desks that keep long hours; however, you are best to pre-book a car over the internet. If you are picking up a **car** here then getting to the Peloponnese is simple, with two toll roads taking you first round Athens (there's no need to cope with the notorious city traffic), and then along the coast to cross the Corinth Canal. Follow the signs for Athens, ('ΑΘΗΝΑ', 'ΑΘΗΝΑ' or 'Αθήνα'), out of the airport, and then the signs to Elefsina ('ΕΛΕΥΣΙΝΑ' or 'Ελευσίνα'), and then Corinth ('ΚΟΡΙΝΘΟΣ' or 'Κόρινθος'). The two toll charges are currently around €3 each (it's a good idea to have change, but the toll booth operators can normally split most notes). The drive to the canal, the start of the Peloponnese, takes an hour on a good day. Bad traffic can occasionally double this, and is usually encountered on big holiday weekends.

Getting to the Peloponnese by **bus** is a slightly more complicated procedure, but could be your best option if you are heading directly to the southern part of the area. If you aren't overnighting in Athens, number X93 bus (w athensairportbus.com/en/timetable/x93airporttokifisos.html) runs directly from the airport to the main bus terminal in Athens (known as Kifissou 100), or you catch a taxi (*expect to pay around €40 05.00–midnight, €55 at other times*). The bus stop is outside the airport building to the right. Buy a ticket from the booth here (€6) and remember to validate it in the machine on board the bus. The buses leave pretty frequently and run through the night (although you will be better off waiting at the airport rather than the bus terminal for the first buses to the Peloponnese to start in the morning). The journey to the bus terminal takes about an hour, but this can be doubled in heavy traffic. The bus also passes the other major bus terminal of Athens, so be sure to check you have the right stop (it's the last one and pretty obvious). At the Kifissou 100 bus terminal things are a bit more hectic than the airport. There are plentiful buses to all the main towns of the Peloponnese, and lots of the smaller ones as well. These are all run under the auspices of KTEL, the national bus company, but are in fact managed by a number of different companies depending on the area. The main ticket hall has several different ticket desks which are organised by destination. Once you have your ticket be sure to ask for the number of the bay from which your bus will depart. If you find the bus station chaotic and frustrating then you're not alone, but it's actually got a lot better in the last few years. If you get here after 07.00 you will probably be on your way to any of the major towns in the Peloponnese within an hour or so.

The easiest way to get to Corinth is by **train** using the Proastiakos suburban rail network. This will one day be extended to run as far as Patra, but for the time being it only runs as far as Kiato (just past Corinth), from where a bus service connects onward. There are hourly trains to Corinth from 05.44 to 22.44, although this schedule changes regularly. The journey takes just over 1½ hours and costs €12.

Finally, don't totally discount a **taxi**. If shared between four people fares are not that bad (currently around €170 to Corinth and €280 to Kalamata), but you are much better to organise these in advance.

BY TRAIN The most practical train route joins up with the ferries from Italy to Patra. The quickest ferry option could get you from St Pancras, London, to Patra in just 48 hours. If you book in advance and go for the cheapest seats this would cost about £150–300, depending on the season and not including expenses along the way or a cabin on the ferry.

For the adventurous it is now possible to travel the whole way to Athens by train via eastern Europe (international trains into Greece were suspended from 2011 to 2014). This option takes two nights and would cost around £220 if you include the cheapest couchette options for the night trains.

The premier resource for planning either of these trips is the website **w** seat61.com.

BY CAR If you are planning to be in Greece for any length of time it is perfectly possible to bring your car over from the UK. You are allowed to keep it in the country for six months (keep hold of your ferry ticket to prove when you came in). Although this is rarely checked, if you are caught out (for instance if you have an accident or are caught speeding) your car will be immediately impounded and the fine to release it can be more than it is worth. Driving a UK car on the right-hand side of the road is not as difficult as everyone seems to think it is.

Those of us who do this trip often could debate the various routes to take for hours (and do). Undeniably the quickest route leads from Calais, through France and Switzerland, to Italy where you catch a ferry (page 33), but this entails quite heavy road tolls in France and also the Swiss road tax. If you sail from Venice then this drive can be done in 13 hours (you should have two drivers for this), meaning you could do the whole trip over a long two days (sleeping on the ferry from Italy to Patra).

My preferred route is via Brussels and Munich and then down through Austria to the Italian ferries. Venice is a fantastic place to sail out of or into (the ferry seems to go through the old city), but the ferry ride is then very long. Ancona is a good compromise, although you can also continue to Bari or Brindisi if you want to minimise your time afloat. For comfort and safety you should plan at least one overnight stop before you reach the ferry (more if you are driving solo).

A good resource for planning the overland part of this trip is **w** viamichelin. com, although you need to be aware that their timings do not include any stops. If you were driving a normal car, stopping overnight on the way to or from Italy at a campsite or budget hotel, and travelling deck class on the ferry, an estimate for total costs would be around €400–500 one way. If you are going to be in Greece for a month or more this can compare quite favourably with the cost of flying and then hiring a car once you are there. The added advantage is the amount of stuff you can bring with you.

BY FERRY Several companies run daily ferries from Italy to Patra in the northeast of the Peloponnese, usually via Corfu. They leave from Venice, Ancona, Bari and Brindisi, with the crossing times getting progressively shorter (from Venice they can be as long as 35 hours, from Brindisi as short as 14 hours). The longer ferry journeys are more expensive, but this is somewhat offset by the price of driving further down Italy. You are always best to book in advance (which you can do via **w** directferries.co.uk, **w** ferries.gr or **w** aferry.co.uk). There are various forms of accommodation aboard, and these can raise the price quite considerably. It is worth knowing that 'deck' class does not mean you are confined outside! You are allowed in the communal areas inside, and in the low season will often find a spot to stretch out and sleep. In the high season you are likely to be obliged to sleep out on the deck, although there are usually plenty of sheltered areas (a sleeping mat or even a pop-up tent is an advantage). An option for those with camper vans is the ability to stay in them overnight.

You can also get local ferries from Piraeus, the port of Athens, to various ports along the east and south coast of the Peloponnese.

HEALTH *with Dr Felicity Nicholson*

Greece is no longer the back of beyond, and the health issues you will face here are little different from those of most Western countries. There are no inoculations needed for entry, although it's always wise to be up to date on your tetanus, which these days comes combined with diphtheria and polio. EU citizens are entitled to a certain level of free medical care (apply for an EHIC card before travelling), although proper health insurance is always advisable. Also be aware that 'free' health care in Greece doesn't cover all you might expect, especially in these days of austerity. There are charges, generally small, for prescriptions, tests and, increasingly, even just check-ups. If you need hospitalisation note that nursing care tends to be minimal (Greek families provide this for hospital patients, along with food).

Prescription medicines are widely available, but you would be advised to bring along enough for your trip, along with your prescription itself. Codeine is considered a narcotic in Greece and should be covered by a prescription. However, try not to take codeine-based medicines with you unless there is no other option. Carry a letter from your doctor too. Pharmacists used to be the first port of call for the ill in Greece. They are well trained and able to prescribe an extensive amount of medication. This is still mostly the case and pharmacies are the best place to deal with most medical issues. In some touristy areas, however, they are getting more cagey, doubtless fearful of being sued, and are more likely to refer you to a doctor.

Most areas are served by a health centre, which is generally staffed around the clock and open for drop-in enquiries in the morning from 08.00. It's first come first served, so get there as early as possible. These places used to check you out for free, as did hospital casualty wards, but due to the economic situation there are, increasingly, small costs even for this. If you think you have been charged inappropriately then hang on to receipts.

SUN AND HEAT By far the biggest health problems for the majority of travellers to Greece come from unaccustomed exposure to sun and heat. Even ignoring the possibility of skin cancer, **sunburn** can spoil any holiday, and in serious cases can put you out of action for days at a time. It also makes you turn a ridiculous lobster colour and causes your skin to flake off – it's just not worth it. Wear a high-SPF suncream and a hat whenever you are out in the sun, and try to introduce yourself to the sun slowly. Also have a look at how the Greeks cope: they tend to sit in the shade when possible. Heatstroke is also a risk so make sure to drink plenty of water.

FOOD AND WATER The next most common problem for travellers in the area is **stomach upsets**. Most of these are relatively minor and the vast majority are not caused by poor hygiene. **Tap water** is said to be safe to drink throughout almost all the Peloponnese (the odd coastal village has their supply tainted with salt water), but you are less likely to get an upset stomach if you stick to bottled or spring water. Food preparation is up to the same health standards as the rest of the EU. Despite this, visitors still get stomach upsets.

The main reason for this is that they are on holiday. People eat out more, and tend to have richer and oilier food than they are used to. They also tend to drink more alcohol than usual. There is nothing wrong with the occasional excess, but be cautious of over-indulging. Of course, serious problems are always a possibility, and should be dealt with by a medical professional.

NATURE There are also various plants and animals that can cause you problems, but the seriousness of these, and their prevalence, is often exaggerated, not least by the Greeks themselves.

Mosquitoes can be a major irritant, and some people react badly to their bites, but they are usually harmless. There has been of late an increase in mosquito-acquired infections, including malaria and dengue fever. Although these are rare they are still worth avoiding, so ensure that you apply insect repellent day and night if mosquitoes are about. Mosquitoes are most prevalent at dusk and can be effectively combated by a combination of nets or window screens, and plug-in repellents (the liquid ones work best and can be easily bought in supermarkets). If you are camping you have to go with the smelly option; cheap, burnable coils work reasonably well, and a good spray-on repellent is worthwhile (look for a high DEET content – 50–55% is optimum). One of the best tips is, at the first sign of dusk, to change into loose garments, such as long-sleeved shirts and trousers that cover you up. There have been recent malarial cases in Greece, but these remain extremely rare and normally limited to the immigrant community. Current advice does not include any extra precautions above the ones listed here.

Ticks can be a nuisance to hikers. If you walk through the long grass in spring it is worth checking your legs. Ticks can be gently **removed** with tweezers grasped round their heads. In rare cases they can pass on disease, so watch out for signs of fever and if you have any go to a doctor as they can sometimes be treated with antibiotics. There is a risk of tick-borne encephalitis in some parts of the country; it is a serious and potentially fatal disease. Cases have been reported around the city of Thessaloniki. Some travellers may want to consider vaccination but should seek advice. If recommended, then two doses of vaccine are needed at least 2 weeks apart.

Ticks should ideally be removed complete, and as soon as possible, to reduce the chance of infection. You can use special tick tweezers, which can be bought in good travel shops, or failing this with your finger nails, grasping the tick as close to your body as possible, and pulling it away steadily and firmly at right angles to your skin without jerking or twisting. Irritants (eg: Olbas oil) or lit cigarettes are to be discouraged since they can cause the ticks to regurgitate and therefore increase the risk of disease. Once the tick is removed, if possible douse the wound with alcohol (any spirit will do), soap and water, or iodine. If you are travelling with small children, remember to check their heads, and particularly behind the ears, for ticks. Spreading redness around the bite and/or fever and/or aching joints after a tick bite imply that you have an infection that requires antibiotic treatment. In this case seek medical advice.

Snakes are much maligned by Greeks, but rarely do anyone harm. The one venomous snake of the Peloponnese is the horned viper (the horn is more of a little bump on top of its head, and it often has a zigzag pattern going down its back). Being bitten by one of these is painful, but not lethal, and the antivenin is readily available. If you are concerned bind the wound tightly (but don't block circulation), try to limit the limb's movement, and seek the nearest medical attention.

The best advice is to try and leave the snakes alone, and let them do likewise to you. They tend to flee at any sign of human presence. If you are out in the countryside try not to creep around, and be cautious of holes and crevices in stone walls or wood piles. **Scorpions** and large, brown **centipedes** with pincers are also known to give painful stings or bites. Again, seek treatment at the nearest medical centre or pharmacy.

Bats in Greece can carry rabies. For most travellers this would be low risk but if you are thinking about going caving then you might want to consider a course of rabies vaccine. There is no rabies reported in other wild or domestic mammals.

In the water look out for **sea urchins**, especially on shallow rocks. If a spine becomes embedded it needs to be removed. Local advice, or the nearest pharmacist, is usually effective. **Jellyfish** stings are painful, but less serious. They will subside on their own, but there are various remedies available to ameliorate the discomfort.

Various **plants** have sap or oil that can cause irritation when it comes into contact with the skin. Berries can be fairly poisonous. If you're not absolutely sure what it is, don't taste it.

TOILETS You might still encounter the odd 'Turkish' toilet in Greece, which consists of two foot stands and a hole in the ground, but they are increasingly rare. What hasn't changed is the inability of the Greek sewer system to cope with toilet paper, or anything else more substantial. These all go into the bin provided next to the toilet, unless you want the embarrassment of causing a flood.

TRAVEL CLINICS AND HEALTH INFORMATION A full list of current travel clinic websites worldwide is available on w istm.org. For other journey preparation information, consult w travelhealthpro.org.uk (UK) or w wwwnc.cdc.gov/travel/ (US). Information about various medications may be found on w netdoctor.co.uk/travel. All advice found online should be used in conjunction with expert advice received prior to or during travel.

Practical Information HEALTH

2

SAFETY

Compared with many European countries, Greece is relatively safe to travel in, and the Peloponnese, because of its rural nature, is especially so. Although you would be unwise to leave your house or car unlocked, as you could do 20 years ago, crime is still relatively rare.

As noted on page 21, political unrest is increasingly an issue, but this is generally confined to Athens. The Peloponnese has seen only minor protests. If you encounter anything of this sort your best advice is simply to remove yourself from the area.

Any crime should be reported to the **tourist police** (☏ *171 – their local numbers are listed in the guide*) who will have an English speaker on their staff. They can also be useful in disputes with the likes of hotel owners and taxi drivers.

Forest fires are, unfortunately, a normal part of the Greek summer, and you should be aware of the dangers of starting one. In the countryside dispose of cigarettes and broken glass carefully. The need to evacuate an area due to fires is fairly rare, but you should keep in mind that it is a possibility (a few villages in the Peloponnese suffered this fate in 2015, but the fires did little damage in the end).

Minor earthquakes are not uncommon, and the locals hardly bat an eyelid at them. Larger ones are rarer and all Greek buildings are built to withstand them. If you do find yourself in a big earthquake then the best thing to do is go outside into an open area, if possible, quickly and safely. If not, get under the sturdiest piece of furniture available.

Woman travellers, especially on their own, might find some male attention unwelcome, although this is much rarer than it once was. Nowadays it is generally confined to some staring, and Greek women will generally be quick to help you if you need to enlist their support.

TRAVELLERS WITH A DISABILITY

If you have mobility problems then the Peloponnese is a difficult prospect, and most of its best attractions will only be appreciated with some considerable assistance.

Things are getting better, however, thanks in part to the impetus of the Olympics, and Paralympics, in 2004. More recent hotels and restaurants, especially those that have benefited from government money, have started to provide some facilities. You are best advised to contact places directly and ask exactly what kind of access they provide.

TRAVELLING WITH CHILDREN

Greeks love kids, sometimes to an over-indulgent degree. It is still a place where old ladies and men will give sweets to children they meet in the street. This can seem odd for those of us brought up in more suspicious places, but is also a pleasant change.

Almost all restaurants and places to stay will go out of their way to accommodate the needs of your children. This can sometimes be a bit makeshift; if highchairs are not available, normal chairs might be stacked until they are the requisite height, but it is always done with goodwill.

In the long summer holidays most Greek kids stay up until it's dark, if not beyond, and it is not unusual to see them in tavernas late at night, sometimes sleeping on chairs or beneath the table. Given that they then get a siesta in the afternoon, it's not that bad an idea.

Playgrounds can be found in all Greek towns and many villages. Some of these are modern and well maintained, but many leave a bit to be desired. A good tip is that Greek kids, and their families, tend to gather in the main square, or near the church, of any community to socialise and play. The main time for this is towards dusk, especially in the hot summer months. Greek children tend to be as welcoming as their parents to foreigners, and will generally be delighted to practise their English.

GAY AND LESBIAN TRAVELLERS

Homosexuality is legal in Greece. The Peloponnese, however, is a somewhat conservative area and 'out' gay Greeks are not common as in the UK or USA. Public displays of affection will probably bring you some unwelcome attention (but this is almost as true for heterosexual couples in some of the more rural areas). Greeks mostly treat visitors with respect, however. If you are reasonably discreet you will find that the worst reaction you might get will be a certain amount of bewilderment over why you and your partner want a double bed.

WHAT TO TAKE

It is tempting to say that you only need your money and passport. Everything else is available in Greece, but a few guidelines might prove helpful.

Even in summer it is advisable to pack some clothing that covers you up, if only to dissuade the mosquitoes and to give you something to wear if you visit a church or monastery. All clothing should be loose for the heat. A good floppy hat is invaluable, along with plenty of suncream, even in April and October (it's very expensive locally). Along with your swim things you might want to have some sort of rubber shoe, both for walking on the rocks and hot sand. For those who suffer in the heat the pressurised water sprays, sold in pharmacies, are expensive but can provide instant relief on the road.

Toiletries in general are expensive in Greece, so bring enough to last. Women should be aware that you are more likely to find sanitary towels than tampons in some rural areas.

Hikers will rarely need more than good trainers, but sticks can be a help on the rocky terrain. A daypack will be useful for all – for carrying water, towels, suncream and so on.

If you are bringing any electrical equipment, such as a laptop, be sure to have a European adaptor. Also be aware that Greek sockets come in two types: an indented round hole for heavy equipment, and a simple two-hole socket for lights and such. You can plug into either, but the former is more advisable for most things.

A torch is useful for exploring caves, unlit churches and the like, and also for Greece's not infrequent power cuts.

Campers will have their own list of equipment they find necessary, but it is worth noting that it is warm enough to sleep out in a light sleeping bag without a tent from June to September, and often beyond.

Everyone, no matter what style of accommodation they are staying in, would benefit from bringing the wherewithal to have a picnic (see box, page 38). A plastic plate each (these can double as chopping boards), a plastic bowl for salads, one good knife, a fork each, plastic tumblers and a bottle opener are all it takes. For water, buy one bottle when you arrive and refill it from springs, which you often find by the roadside and in villages.

2

BROWN SIGNS AND THE PERFECT PICNIC

One of the things that makes the Peloponnese so extraordinary is its plethora of ancient sites. It's not just the large, famous names, such as Olympia and Mycenae, but countless smaller ruins covering a history of 5,000 years or more. Many of these, in any other country or area, would be major sites, with ticket offices, gift shops and explanatory boards: Mycenaean bridges, ancient cities, abandoned temples. Some, it has to be admitted, are little more than a few scattered rocks of indeterminate origin. What they all get, however, from the great to the small, is a brown sign. These ubiquitous little markers point the way to everything from the 'Ancient Theatre of Epidavros', through countless 'Mycenaean Tholos Tombs', down to the slightly mournful and unspecific 'Ancient Site'.

Your brown sign can be deeply frustrating. As intriguing as an 'Ancient Tower' might sound, you will soon find yourself being pointed down a rutted, dirt track, which after 5km ends in nothing more exciting than an olive grove and a pile of rubble which could date from last year. A 'Mycenaean Tholos Tomb' could mean anything from the magnificent constructions at Mycenae itself, or Peristeria in Messinia, to a slight depression in the ground reached after a 4-hour hike along mountain paths.

In other words brown signs are a lottery, sometimes leading to riches, sometimes to ruins, and sometimes not even that. In fact, you might be best to ignore their historical aspect entirely. The thing is that these ancient peoples, be they Mycenaean, Greek, Roman, Byzantine, Frankish, Venetian, Turkish or anything in between, all seem to have had an eye for good real estate. While travelling, if you find yourself in need of a break, look for the next brown sign – it's never too far away. Even if you never find the 'Tholos Tomb' or 'Ancient Settlement', you probably will find a pleasant olive grove, or mountainside meadow, or sea view. Stop awhile, have a rest, contemplate the passing of times and maybe crack open a bottle of local wine. Which brings us on to the perfect Greek picnic.

Picnics used to be something that the British were good at, whether fancy affairs at opera festivals or fun children's events by the sea, but we seem to be losing the art. A trip through the Peloponnese is the perfect place to rediscover it, and give it an added Mediterranean twist. It's not too hard: a bottle of wine; fresh tomatoes, cucumber and feta, dressed with the oil from a jar of olives; chunks of bread torn off a fresh-baked loaf; perhaps some local smoked ham or sausage. Spread a blanket, or even a towel, sit back and relax, and wonder whether the rock you are leaning on was an ancient city wall, a temple base, or just a rock.

MONEY AND BUDGETING

MONEY The currency of Greece remains the euro (pronounced *evro*), at least for now. Notes come in denominations of 5, 10, 20, 50, 100, 200 and 500, but the last three are the most likely to be fake, and most people won't appreciate you paying with them, so try to avoid them. The euro is split into 100 cents (*lepta*). Coins come in denominations of €1 and €2, and 1, 2, 5, 10, 20 and 50 cents. People will often round change amounts if they are under five or ten cents, either in your favour or not, depending. For the exchange rate at the time of going to print, see page 2.

Greece is still largely a cash society, but it is now possible to pay directly with a **credit or debit card** at almost all hotels and restaurants, and in shops aimed at tourists.

ATMs are becoming more and more common, and allow you to take money straight out of your own account. There won't be one in every village by any means, but every small town and above will have at least one. It's best to withdraw enough for the next few days, rather than using them little and often. Be aware that a lot of accounts charge you for doing this. Check yours, and if you travel a lot consider opening a specific account for this at a bank that doesn't. Visa and Mastercard seem to be the most widely accepted ATM cards, and having a variety can help if you find yours is rejected. In general debit cards offer better terms on foreign cash withdrawals than credit cards. Preloadable ATM cards for travellers are also an option. Bank opening hours are usually confined to weekdays from 08.30 to 14.00. They tend to close a little earlier on Fridays.

Some cash for emergencies is also a worthwhile contingency.

BUDGETING It's been going this way for years, but certainly since the introduction of the euro Greece is no longer a cheap country to travel in. Indeed certain things cost much more than in other European countries. The bonus for the traveller, particularly in the Peloponnese which is still a little out of the way, is that eating out remains cheap. On the accommodation side budget options cost much what they would elsewhere in Europe, but at the other end of the scale you can get some bargains.

You could get by on €30 a day per person, but this involves camping without a tent, travelling by bus, and mostly steering clear of tavernas (maybe once a week). As part of a couple you could stay at reasonable/budget hotels, eat one meal out a day at a reasonable taverna, stop for a drink when you wanted, and have the use of a hire car for about €80 a day per person.

One option to consider is mixing up the budgets. Travelling as a pair you could bring a tent, but still hire a car from the airport. By eating a mixture of picnics and taverna meals, and staying mostly in campsites, you could save enough money for the occasional treat, such as staying in a lovely hotel at Monemvasia.

Below is a list of rough price guidelines for some common purchases (as of 2018, but only the petrol price tends to vary much):

Water (1½-litre bottle)	€1
Coffee	€2–4
Local wine (½-litre jug)	€3–5
Greek salad	€5
Cheese pie	€1
Loaf of local bread	€1–2
Petrol (1 litre)	€1.55
Suncream (medium SPF)	€10
English newspaper	€3–5

GETTING AROUND

BY TRAIN Trains are the cheapest form of public transport in Greece, mainly because they are so bad. The exception is the good connection from Athens and its airport to Corinth (page 32).

Trains used to run on two interesting, if slow, lines via either the west coast or Nafplio and Tripoli down to Kalamata, but both are currently closed, and do not look likely to reopen. Call ✎1110 in Greece, pressing 2 for an English operator, to get the latest info. Rail buffs should not despair as the short but spectacular rack-and-pinion railway line up to Kalavryta (page 251) is one of the best rides in Europe.

BY BUS   In contrast to trains, buses are normally fast and efficient, at least on main road routes, and the buses themselves are modern, comfortable and normally air conditioned (although the toilet is seldom open). Athens to Kalamata is about the longest single bus ride you might want to take (*3½–4hrs; €23*). On intercity routes such as this, you buy a ticket in advance and seating is assigned, although old Greek ladies often don't understand this.

More rural routes are a bit more casual. You buy your ticket from a conductor or the driver on the bus, and the timetable often goes out of the window. You will rarely be alone waiting for a bus, so trust what the locals tell you. Throughout this book the frequency of buses is given rather than a timetable, as these often change. If there are only a couple of buses a day they tend to be first thing and in the early afternoon.

BY CAR AND MOTORBIKE   Unless you want to confine yourself to the major towns and sites, or have a lot of time on your hands, having your own vehicle is by far the best way to explore the Peloponnese. The easiest way to do this would be to hire a car in advance and pick it up at the airport or ferry port. In peak season you can get a small car for around €30 a day (use an internet clearing house such as w travelsupermarket.com to search for deals). You are always best to get the most comprehensive cover you can.

Like the rest of Europe you drive on the right in Greece, and hire cars will have their steering wheels on the left-hand side. If you are unused to this the best advice is not to think too much about the whole left vs right dilemma. Rather concentrate on the fact that the driver's side of the car stays near the middle of the road, and the passenger's near the edge – exactly as at home. Other laws are similar to the rest of Europe with seatbelt use compulsory. A photo licence from any EU country is valid; other nationals will need to have brought an International Driving Permit.

Watch out for local speed limits. As a rule, these are 50km/h in built-up areas, 70km/h on rural roads and 100km/h or 120km/h on highways, but there are plenty of (often inexplicable) exceptions. Speed cameras are beginning to appear, but police traps with radar guns are more common. If people driving towards you flash their lights several times they are warning that you are about to pass one of these.

The Peloponnese has a few toll roads. The main one runs from Athens to Kalamata via Corinth, Tripoli and Megalopoli. Another toll road branches west at Corinth towards Patra, and a third runs southeast to Sparta from just south of Megalopoli. Toll points are around €1.50–3 each.

Unleaded 95 is the basic fuel, and currently hovers around €1.50 per litre, but changes often, and also varies by up to 10% from one filling station to the next. Diesel is a lot cheaper. In the majority of filling stations there are pump attendants. Some might close on Sundays and/or during the night.

Driving in Greece is generally no problem, but conditions and other people's driving are not what one would expect at home, and caution is the best policy. Drive with care and consideration and, while being aware, don't be put off by others' actions. Road surfaces vary widely in quality. Tarmac has a short lifespan in Greece and even newer roads can have large pot-holes. In the mountains you often encounter rockfalls as well. Smaller, rural roads and those that go through small towns and villages are often single lane. Beep your horn at blind corners and listen out for those coming the other way. Proper roundabouts are rare, and where they exist their correct usage appears to be disputed.

In villages it is normally best to park where you can in the outskirts and continue your exploration on foot, in order to avoid narrow lanes that can often lead to a dead end. In towns and cities parking can be a problem. As none of them are that large your best bet is to find a parking place as close to the centre as possible and then explore by foot.

The actions of other drivers in Greece can be alarming. Tailgating, overtaking on corners, using the hard shoulder as a personal fast lane, weaving through traffic and other idiocies are common. Someone turning on their hazard lights tends to mean 'I am about to perform a manoeuvre that is illegal and borderline suicidal – keep clear'. As stated above the best policy is to not be fazed and continue to drive with care yourself.

In case of an accident remain calm and wait for the police to arrive; they are normally efficient, polite and fair. If you have a breakdown the Greek breakdown service ELPA can be called (📞 10400). They have reciprocal agreements with companies such as the AA and RAC in the UK, and the AAA in the US.

Finally, don't let any of this put you off. The vast majority of travellers who drive around the Peloponnese do so without any problems at all. It is also worth noting that on many roads, including the most scenic, you won't actually see many other cars.

There are a few places in the Peloponnese where you can hire scooters, motorbikes or even quad bikes (see page 103 for the best option for the latter). For any but the smallest of these you should have a specific licence, and the best advice, if you are not experienced in driving these vehicles, is to steer clear entirely. The winding roads, combined with the fact that you'll often be wearing little more than a swimming costume, make for some colourful injuries.

Occasionally, to get to a nice beach or a small ruin, you might have to drive on dirt roads and these can also vary widely in quality. Even on good ones the best advice is to drive extremely slowly, often not much more than walking pace, to avoid throwing up stones and pebbles. If you are in a hire car be aware that you are often not covered for damage to its underside, or for driving off road (even if you have hired a 4x4).

BY TAXI Taxis are much cheaper than in most other European countries. While using them to travel around the whole area would probably be prohibitive, they can be a useful alternative to public transport. In towns they run on the meter (on tariff 1, changing to tariff 2 if they drive out of town). In rural areas there are normally set prices for various journeys. Agree on the charge before starting your journey. A very rough estimate of cost in rural areas would be €1 per kilometre.

CYCLING Despite its high mountains many people enjoy cycling around the Peloponnese, although high summer should be avoided. Many of the resorts hire out mountain bikes. Bringing your own bike by aeroplane is often possible as well, but should be discussed in advance with your airline.

HITCHING Hitchhiking is often risky and is not recommended alone. It also seems to have fallen out of favour in much of Greece, so you might not have much luck. The exception is rural areas where it is not uncommon for people to wave down cars to take them to the next village, most often the elderly. If you are driving then picking them up is at your own discretion, but it can be an excellent way to interact a bit.

WALKING Walking and hiking are the best ways to explore the natural landscape of the Peloponnese. Even a short wander into the olive groves can be a delight. Good trainers or lightweight walking boots are normally sufficient. Lightweight but sturdy long trousers are recommended in spring, when the grass and thorns are high. A small, comfortable, rucksack is a good idea. It should contain at least water and suncream. Modern telescopic walking sticks can provide good support, but you would be wise to test them first as they don't suit everybody. For longer hikes some snacks, a good map (see below) and a compass would also prove useful. A more sybaritic addition is some wine in a plastic bottle. There's nothing finer than sipping wine at the top of a Greek mountain. Insulating sleeves, available at outdoor shops, will even keep it cool for an hour or two.

Walking alone in the mountains is always a risk – make sure someone (perhaps your hotel owner) is aware of your intentions and knows roughly when to expect you back. A mobile phone can also be a good idea as coverage can be surprisingly extensive.

Each chapter of this guide includes a **suggested walk**. These vary in length and difficulty, with the shortest lasting not much more than 2 hours (although you will probably want to take longer). The descriptions given are designed to make the walk possible without a map, although if one is available it is worth taking along. **Important note:** timings in the walk descriptions are a guide only, and should be adjusted to your own pace. They are taken from my own walking times, which from feedback seem to be fairly fast. They also don't include any but the briefest of stops for water, so the whole walk will undoubtedly take longer than indicated. To get a much better, but still rough idea, of how long the walk will take see the initial information, which also grades the walk for difficulty (easy, medium or hard) and lists the facilities *en route*.

MAPS

Good map coverage of Greece was a dream only a few short years ago, but there are now several options. Three of the best maps dedicated to the Peloponnese in its entirety are published by Freytag & Berndt (best scale at 1:150,000, but double-sided, and non-tear/waterproof), Anavasi and Terrain Editions (both 1:200,000, one-sided, and tear and waterproof).

For more detailed coverage of regions within the Peloponnese, **Anavasi** (w *anavasi.gr*) produces a range of excellent and regularly updated 1:50,000 and 1:25,000 maps that are particularly useful to hikers and walkers. Some useful regional maps are also produced by **Terrain Maps** (w *terrainmaps.gr*) and **Road Editions** (w *travelbookstore.gr*). Also worth a mention is **Geopsis** (w *geopsis.com*), which publishes a good map of Messinia.

Bear in mind, however, that no map company could keep up with the rate of change in the Peloponnese, so be on the lookout for new roads (both dirt and tarmac), dirt roads that are now surfaced, and in rural areas surfaced roads that have reverted back to dirt.

Maps are also sold at many bookshops within the region. If you want to buy maps in advance, however, **Stanfords** (w *stanfords.co.uk*) in the UK stocks most of the maps listed above and can also process special orders. Stanfords has shops in London, Bristol and Manchester, as well as an excellent online store that ships maps all over the world.

The maps contained within this book are mainly intended as a guide to planning, and make no claims to be comprehensive. Plans of sites are intended to help identification of the various ruins in conjunction with the text.

ACCOMMODATION

Accommodation in the Peloponnese has changed dramatically in the last ten years, both in terms of the quality available (with small, boutique hotels upping the game and becoming more prevalent), and when it is open. It used to be that all but the larger hotels only opened from April to October. This is now changing as the Greeks realise they need to attract visitors to their country year round, but it is always worth checking ahead if you travel here in the winter months.

The other times that you might experience problems are around Greek Easter (see box, page 22) which is an important holiday, and throughout August, when half of Athens seems to descend on the Peloponnese. Booking ahead is advisable for both. Prices also vary widely by season. Prices quoted are always for a double room in August. Outside of summer you can expect to pay at least a third less, except near ski resorts when the opposite applies. For a list of the accommodation price codes used in this guide, please see the inside-front cover.

CAMPING Camping is easily the cheapest option. Legally this can only be done in campsites, which are plentiful along most of the coast, but rarer inland. They are mainly geared towards camper vans and caravans and charge on a sliding scale: so much per person, a charge for a tent depending on size, a charge for a vehicle depending on its size, a charge for hooking up to electricity, and so on. So the less you have, the cheaper it is. For two people with a small tent and a normal car the cost is around €15 a night, but does vary a fair bit. The facilities can also be variable. As a minimum, campsites have toilets (but not always toilet paper), and showers (but not always hot water). In general the standard is pretty good, however, with small shops, sometimes a taverna and sometimes a pool. The main benefit is that you are often right on the beach, something few hotels can offer (due to Greek building restrictions). For obvious reasons the majority of campsites still only open up for the April–October season.

Wild camping, outside of these campsites, is illegal, but often tolerated. Up in the mountains, in the middle of nowhere, you should have no problems at all. On the coast you need to be more discreet. If campsites are available, then you should use them. If you do wild camp you need to make sure you leave no sign of your presence, taking all rubbish with you. You also need to be very aware of the danger of starting forest fires. During summer months having an open fire is illegal and carries a heavy fine.

ROOMS 'Rooms places', as they are known (*domatia* in Greek), used to be one of the mainstays of travel in the Peloponnese. The other, sleeping out on the flat roofs of hotels, seems to have died out. The line between a rooms place and a small hotel is now quite blurred. Traditionally rooms would be in the owner's house, and toilet facilities were shared. This is now rarer, but rooms are still available, especially in small villages where nothing else is offered. They are usually basic, but they also tend to be friendlier and more personal than hotels. To find them look out for signs or, even better, ask around in the local *kafenion* (café) or taverna. Depending on where it is and the time of year a room can vary from a bargain €20 up to €60.

HOTELS Hotels used to be fairly anonymous concrete blocks, and of course these still exist, mostly in the larger towns and resorts. There are an increasing number, however, which are realising they have to do more to attract guests, both Greek and foreign. The Peloponnese now boasts some absolutely gorgeous places to stay, and prices are normally pretty reasonable, compared with their equivalents in other European countries. All hotels have to be licensed by EOT, the Greek tourist board, and should display prices on a notice inside each room's door. This is the maximum they are allowed to charge and is based solely on facilities. You will normally pay less, but take it up with the local tourist police if you think there is an issue. For a normal room with the basic facilities (air conditioned, with a separate bathroom with hot water) expect to pay €50–80 in August. A small double room rarely gets above €100–150, even in the smartest place, although a few do charge more. At cheaper places a little bit of haggling might lower the price – whether breakfast is included can be a negotiating point (if it is it will likely only be bread and cheese slices). Another innovation in recent years has been the rise of agri-tourism. Most of the Peloponnese relies on agriculture, and most families own a farm or at least some olive trees. Nowadays many hotels are emphasising this, with products coming from their own land, and even opportunities to join in on the harvest – these are highlighted in the guide.

VILLAS Plenty of companies offer self-catering villas for hire on a weekly basis in the Peloponnese, and this can also be sorted out privately, either from abroad or while here. Prices vary, but can be pretty reasonable when compared with hotel accommodation. A good option for self-catering accommodation in Laconia is the Laconian Collection (see ad, page124), which has more than 20 properties in the like of Sparta, Mystra, Gythio and elsewhere in the region.

EATING AND DRINKING

BREAKFAST Greeks aren't particularly big on breakfast, tending to skip it and then maybe having a mid-morning savoury pastry. There are several varieties of these, the most usual being *tiropita* (cheese pie) and *spanokopita* (spinach pie). These are best purchased at the local bakery, and often run out by noon. You should also buy your bread at the bakery, as supermarket bread tends to be foul. Greek bread can be excellent, and is perfect for mopping up olive oil, but it goes stale quickly.

If breakfast is provided by your hotel it is usually what is referred to as 'continental'. In many cases, this means bread, packet butter and jam, and perhaps some processed ham and cheese slices. That said, an ever increasing number of boutique and other superior hotels now provide large, filling and delicious spreads of local products. If you are self-catering then yoghurt and honey is an excellent option. Greek yoghurt is thick and slightly sour, absolutely nothing like 'Greek-style yoghurt' from English supermarkets, and is perfectly accompanied by a spoon of local honey, which is the best in the world.

LUNCH AND DINNER Lunch is traditionally the main meal of the day, and many people will still return home from work to eat it. If Greeks are eating out, and they do this a lot, then they often opt for a weekend lunch, and this is a good time to head for more isolated tavernas that can often be closed the rest of the week.

A lunch out starts at around 13.30, and sometimes even later, and can stretch into the early evening. Greeks tend not to eat in courses, or to have separate dishes each, although they are getting used to foreigners who do. The local way is more fun, with dishes coming when they are ready and placed centrally. You can then either eat straight from them, or serve out on to individual plates.

Bread comes with every meal whether you want it or not, as should a jug of water. It is normal for there to be a 'bread' or 'cover' charge on the bill, usually

€0.50–1 a head (you will still have to pay it even if you don't have the bread – regard it as a service charge).

The usual table covering, even at some quite smart places, is disposable plastic-backed paper, often with a useful map of the area printed on it. The wonderful advantage of these is that they are fresh on and last for only one meal, so you can make as much of a mess of them as you like. They make an excellent extra plate for squeezed lemons, bones, olive stones and chunks of bread, and you can plan out your route in biro on the map. If you have kids they make a great colouring book. At the end of the meal the plates are taken off, the paper scrunched into a ball with whatever's left in it, and the whole lot thrown away. It would be interesting to compare the environmental cost of these against the constant laundering of 'posher' tablecloths.

Dinner is also eaten late by the Greeks, and if you want a better atmosphere then you should try and follow suit. The earliest is around 19.30–20.00, although pushing midnight is not unknown in the summer. Evening meals are usually preceded and followed by a *volta*, a stroll about in the cool evening air. After the meal these often end up at a pastry shop for a dessert, which are not traditionally served at restaurants, although they are becoming more common.

WHAT'S ON OFFER Greek cuisine is pretty well known nowadays, although the British perception of it is somewhat coloured by the fact that most of the 'Greek' restaurants in the UK are in fact Cypriot. The cooking is pretty similar, but two of the mainstays of Cypriot eating, *hummus* (chickpea dip) and *haloumi* (grilled cheese), are rare in the Peloponnese – although the former is becoming more common, mainly because visitors are asking for it, and the latter has a cousin in the commonly found *saganaki* (fried cheese).

The Mediterranean diet is now known to be one of the healthiest in the world. There's no real secret to it: plentiful olive oil is combined with fresh, local products. Greek cooking, and most of what is on offer in Greek supermarkets, is still very

THE PERFECT GREEK SALAD

This will open me up to howls of derision and letters of complaint, but here's my version.

Halve a clove of garlic and wipe a bowl with the fresh flesh and discard. If you have a cucumber with thick skin (common in Greece) then slice much of it off, but don't be fussy. Slice in half lengthways, and then into quarters. Holding these together cut into large slices. Cut two or three large Greek tomatoes into bite-size chunks any old how. Add one large red onion diced up. I like to crumble my feta over, but will not complain if you like yours in large slabs. The feta should be chosen with care from the large selection at any Greek supermarket. Sprinkle on a couple of handfuls of Kalamata olives. And that's it for major ingredients – no peppers, and certainly no lettuce.

Now the important part: the dressing. This is very scientific. Take a bottle of this year's local olive oil and place your thumb so it covers about a third to a half of the opening. Then pour over the salad, moving the bottle in three circles; not too fast, but not too slow either. Take a bottle of red wine vinegar and close off the top a little more this time. Do just one circle. Finally sprinkle on half a handful of dry oregano from the nearest mountains. Do not toss the salad; the flavours will mix on your plate. Eat with Greek bread baked that day.

seasonal and this is vital (as we are starting to relearn in other countries). The ultimate proof of this is the so-called 'Greek salad'. Again, it's not complicated – just simple, fresh ingredients put together (see box, page 45). But compare one made with shipped supermarket ingredients in the middle of a UK winter, with one from the most basic of village tavernas in the Peloponnese. There is simply no comparison. It is no exaggeration to say that first-time visitors are known to go into a stunned ecstasy the first time they bite into a local tomato.

On the other hand, one reasonably legitimate complaint made against eating out in the Peloponnese is that the food can be monotonous. Every taverna seems to have the same menu and serve the same dishes. Part of this is due to the nature of the menus themselves. They are often speculative affairs, listing all the dishes that the taverna might one day serve, rather than what they have on offer right now.

However, it is true that the once clear distinctions between the types of Greek restaurant are being broken down. Once grill houses pretty much only served meat, fish tavernas only fish, tavernas only oven dishes, and ouzeries just served *meze*, small dishes of food to accompany the drinking of *ouzo*. Now they mostly all seem to do a little bit of everything and come under the general title of tavernas.

Every restaurant of any worth, however, will have its specialities, be it a particular dish that they are known to do well, or an oven dish that they have just cooked up for that day. The trick to getting these is to ask. As always it is worth learning from the Greeks themselves – they rarely glance at the menu, instead engaging the waiter in a long, and sometimes passionate, conversation about what is good today, what dishes go especially well together, and so on. Try doing the same: waiters normally have some English, and if not it is perfectly fine to go and explore the kitchen and point. Below are some of the more common things you will find.

Dips, salads and *meze*

These are often lumped together in menus as 'starters', mostly to cater to foreign tourists. Greeks will normally have them as an integral part of a larger meal. They can also provide a full meal on their own. A *horiatiki* (village salad), commonly known as Greek salad, along with one dip and accompanying bread is a good, light lunch for two. Other salads tend to be less substantial and fairly simple, but it is surprising just how good shredded cabbage and lemon juice can be. Greeks also do a warm dish called *horta*, sometimes translated as 'weed salad'. Despite the name this is a delicious mix of wild greens (often dandelion leaves, but with much variation), cooked in oil and lemon. You will often see old Greek ladies preparing and cleaning the horta, a time-consuming occupation.

Dips themselves are known as salads (*salata*) and come in many flavours. Most common is *tzatziki* (yoghurt and shredded cucumber); for those used to the tame, foreign supermarket versions, be aware that it can often have a hefty garlic kick. *Tirosalata* (cheese dip) can similarly surprise you with the amount of chilli in it. *Melitzanosalata* (aubergine dip) is always mild and delicious. *Taramosalata* is a dip made from fish roe. At its best it has a subtle and delicious flavour, quite different from the bright pink variety often found in shops.

Meze are just little plates of food, and include the dips above, but can be a small sampler of just about anything. Cheese is often served this way. It is worth trying something other than the ubiquitous, if delicious, feta. *Sfela*, a strong goat's cheese, is a speciality of the Peloponnese. Another local speciality is *pasto*. These chunks of smoked ham come under a variety of names depending on the region. Asking for a *pikilia* is often an excellent way to eat. This is a plate of mixed meze, sized according to how many people are eating. It can often be 'themed' to be meat-, fish- or vegetarian-based.

Oven dishes Meals cooked in the oven, often slowly throughout the day or night, used to be the central focus of a taverna, and often still are. These could just be one or two dishes in a small place, or up to six or so in a larger taverna. It is considered perfectly acceptable to go and have a look at these before ordering, often in the kitchen itself, but sometimes nowadays in hot plates under glass. These can be absolutely delicious, and put most fast food to shame – they can be at your table before you've sat down again (ask for them to be brought later, or actually order

GIROS PITA

Giros are fairly well known in certain parts of the US and Australia, particularly where there are large Greek communities, but less so in the UK, where the kebab shop business is dominated by the Turks. I could just tell you that giros are simply the finest fast food in the world, and leave it at that, but perhaps a bit of explanation is needed.

Giros, in literal terms, simply means 'round', or 'to turn'. The first letter of the word is the tricky gamma, so that it is pronounced somewhere in between yiros and giros, mostly closer to the former. It refers to the skewer of layered meat that, nowadays, turns slowly upright in front of an electric grill. This will remind UK readers of the Turkish doner kebab, but is nowhere near the processed sausages of suspect meat that these can often be in fast-food joints back home. As the meat cooks it is shaved off, and can just be served in a portion on a plate.

Most often, however, it is eaten in the sublime form of the giros pita. To understand this you must first banish any notion of pita bread being a flat oval with a handy little pocket in the middle. What we're talking about here is a thick disc of bread that is generally grilled with a goodly amount of olive oil brushed on. On to this is spread *tzatziki* (or more occasionally, and inauthentically, mayonnaise) and then a pile of the meat. Other toppings are to taste, but if undirected the giros chef will add them all. They are usually lined up in front of him in trays (and it's almost always a him), so just point and gesticulate. Tomato pieces and red onion are the norm. Chips used to be regarded as the devil's work, but these days it is an almost mandatory pita filling at most grill houses. Tabasco is rarely available, but is a noble addition.

This whole thing is then rolled into a cigar shape of about 5cm in diameter, usually just too big to fit into your mouth without embarrassing spillage, and further rolled in grease-proof paper with one end left open to munch on. One giros is normally enough to snack on, two is a fairly hearty meal, three or more is for students on marathon box set binges.

You can also get *souvlaki* pita, which is the same but with the meat coming from mini pork skewers on the grill. *Kotopolo* pita, with chicken bits grilled on the skewer, is also increasingly available. You could also order a pita with no meat at all, although be prepared for odd looks if you attempt this. Chips are advisable, in this case, to bulk it out.

Giros stands are common, often open windows connected to tavernas, in the larger towns and cities, but rare in the countryside. To find them look out for schoolkids at around 18.00 with greasy packages, and follow the paper trail. Whatever you do, do not underestimate the power of the giros: rich Greeks abroad have been known to get their favourite giros stand to bulk freeze their product and ship it to them in London or New York.

them later on if you don't want this). They also often aren't piping hot, although they will have been cooked properly. This is to Greek taste, and suits the hotter days.

Many of these are meat-based, and some are well known, such as *moussaka*. *Stifado* is a casserole of meat and small, sweet onions. Its best incarnation is made with rabbit or hare. *Yiouvetsi* and *pastitsio* are both meat and pasta dishes (the former is slow-baked lamb with orzo pasta, the latter pretty much what we would call lasagne, but made with macaroni rather than pasta sheets). *Kleftiko* is considered a Cypriot dish, but is also common in the Peloponnese, as it should be as the area was famed for its Klephts, after whom the dish is named. The word literally means thief, but was used to describe the people who took to the mountains during the Turkish occupation and constantly raided and attacked their oppressors. They developed a way of cooking meat, most often lamb, sealed up so that the smell would not give them away. The result is mouth-wateringly tender and falls off the bone.

Vegetables are also cooked in the oven, or on the hob and then kept warm, including lovely stews of green bean or okra with tomato or a mix of vegetables known as a *briam*. *Yemistes* are stuffed vegetables, most often large tomatoes, but also peppers and aubergines. Usually they have flavoured rice inside, but sometimes also mince.

From the grill Unlike oven dishes, meat from the grill is cooked to order. This is traditionally done over charcoal (if it isn't you might want to go somewhere else), often in plain view. Most of us know how much better meat tastes off a proper barbecue. Now imagine a barbecue run by someone who has been doing it every day for all his or her life and has perfected the art. That is what you get from a good grill house in the Peloponnese. Meats are generally simply prepared with a few herbs, salt, pepper and oil. *Souvlaki* is meat on the skewer, usually pork or chicken, but sometimes lamb. It can come in two sizes – small ones are normally served without any accompaniment but bread, and you order as many as you want, larger ones come with rice or chips and salad as a main dish. *Paidakia* means 'ribs' but generally refer to lamb chops, and are often excellent. It is rare to get *kokoretsi* outside of Easter time, when it is traditional. A kebab of lamb's lung, liver and spleen wrapped up in a sheep's intestine might not initially make your mouth water, but one smell is enough to get most meat lovers interested.

Seafood The Mediterranean has been sadly overfished, and this has hugely driven up the price of those fish that are left. Eating fish can now be an expensive affair, and one that the Greeks often reserve for a big occasion. At a proper fish taverna the day's catch will be displayed on ice for the customer to choose which fish he wants, and then how it is to be cooked (generally simply fried or grilled). The fish are priced by weight, and you can get your choice weighed in advance to check how much it will be. The current price for most fish is around €50–60 a kilo. There is a bewildering array of species on offer; among the more recognisable will be *barbouni* (red mullet) and *garides* (large prawns or shrimp).

There are cheaper ways to sample a bit of the Mediterranean. Small fish deep fried can be delicious with a squeeze of lemon juice. They seem to be defined by size rather than species. *Marides* are the smallest and are probably whitebait. *Gavros* are larger and are often translated as anchovies, although they seem more like sardines. You might want to head and tail the larger ones, and remove the backbone, but the smaller ones can be eaten whole. *Oktapodi* (octopus) is also affordable, either grilled, or boiled and served with oil and vinegar. Make sure it isn't frozen – tavernas must by law tell you if it is; several of the things hung out on a washing line outside to dry is a good sign. *Kalamaria* (squid) normally is frozen, even at good tavernas, but must not stay that way for long. It can taste fantastic, but is always a bit of a lottery and can be rather rubbery.

Vegetarians Not eating meat is not as difficult as it once was for travellers in Greece. Even out-of-the-way tavernas will offer salads and dips, or a vegetable dish, plus several non-meat meze. If you are very strict, or a vegan, things can be more problematic. Vegetable dishes might have meat stock in them, and dairy products are often used. The best time to visit is before Easter. The strict Orthodox fast bans all animal products and most tavernas will have a dish that abides by this rule.

DRINKING

Water This is the king among Greek drinks. Each village extols the virtue of their local spring, and people will travel long distances to fill up bottles from a particularly renowned one. The old men boast that they can taste a glass and tell you where in the Peloponnese it came from. The majority of Greek bottled water is excellent, but fresh spring water is the best: look out for it. Water is drunk with meals and normally accompanies coffee.

Coffee Not so long ago, the Peloponnese was the despair of coffee lovers, but that has changed in recent years. Old-fashioned 'Greek' coffee is in fact Turkish, but you'd be wise not to point this out. It is made by boiling the coffee grounds and sugar in the water, and is served in tiny cups with no milk. Old men can make these last for hours. Like all coffee in the Peloponnese it comes either *glyko* (very sweet), *metrio* (medium sweet), or *sketo* (no sugar). In a village coffee is drunk at the *kafenion*, a basic café that was until quite recently an all-male preserve.

The most usual cup of hot coffee you will find is instant, and is called a *nes* after Nescafé. For a 'real' coffee you will need to be in a bigger town, or at a resort, where Italian coffee machines are more common. However, people often seem a bit unsure as to how to use them, and the resulting 'cappuccino' can disappoint.

What the Greeks are good at is iced coffees. The frappé is now considered a bit old-fashioned. It is made with instant coffee and normally some sugar, which is shaken or whizzed up in a little bit of water to produce a foam. More water is added along with condensed milk if desired. It is surprisingly good on a hot day. The more modern equivalent is the *freddo*. This is basically a posh version of the frappé, made with chilled espresso coffee and fresh cream.

Apparently Greece does the most expensive coffee in Europe. Even in the Peloponnese a good coffee in a trendy café can set you back €3. Up in the mountains a Greek coffee or a frappé is more likely to be €1.

Alcohol Greeks normally only drink while eating. Up to very recently you couldn't even order a beer without getting something to eat with it (if only some nuts or cut-up cucumber). Even today the only time Greeks will generally drink without accompanying food is late at night in a bar or club. Extreme public drunkenness is still considered shameful.

Most beer in the Peloponnese is lager brewed under licence and imports can be expensive. The two big brands are Amstel and Heineken. Mythos, considered by many to be local, is also foreign-owned. Fix, an old brand that has been revitalised by the original family owners, is more authentically Greek, and also rather good. Recently a few micro-breweries have opened up in Greece, but they are yet to be widely stocked. In out-of-the-way places a 500ml bottle of beer starts at €1.50. In smarter cafés it can reach €4.

The Greeks drink a remarkable amount of whisky for some reason, but the best-known local spirit is *ouzo*, a clear, anise-flavoured spirit that turns white with the addition of water. It never seems to transfer well to other countries, but seems to go down well in Greece itself. Also look out for *tsipouro*, a fire water made from grapes after they have been pressed for wine. It is normally knocked back in shots and can be very strong.

Greek wine was long a matter of some amusement, but this has now changed (at least for those in the know); after all, Greece is one of the first places to have cultivated the vine, and the Peloponnese is at the heart of this (page 66). There are now some excellent wines to be had, and top Greek restaurants can keep fantastic cellars without recourse to any foreign wines at all. A good bottle of wine is comparatively expensive, starting at around €15 and upwards, but can be very good value for its quality.

There are several varieties native to the Peloponnese to look out for. Around Nemea the *Agiorghitiko* grape, named after the nearby monastery, produces a complex and velvety red wine. Further south, *Moschofilero* produces the AOC Mantinia, a dry white. In the northwest Patra region, another dry white is made from the *Roditis* grape, as well as two AOC dessert wines, Moschato Patron and Moschato Rio. *Mavrodaphne* from the same region goes into a fortified, sweet red wine of the same name. It is not to everyone's taste, but has a surprisingly dense flavour.

'House' wine in the Peloponnese is an entirely different question. This is generally very inexpensive and served by the kilo in jugs (a *meso kilo*, 'half kilo', is half a litre and good for two people – at least for starters). It normally comes from large boxes these days, but sometimes is more local, and barrelled. It is not *retsina*, as is often thought; that wine, flavoured with pine resin, usually only comes from a bottle in the Peloponnese, and is produced elsewhere.

These jugs of wine can vary hugely in quality. They are normally extremely dry, which some people dislike, and some village wine can have a sherry-like quality. It can be best not to think of it as wine at all. When drunk without prejudice it actually complements Greek food, cutting through the oil well. It also only costs about €3–5 per *meso kilo*, so you can't complain too much.

PUBLIC HOLIDAYS

1 January	New Year's Day or St Basil's Day. This is when Greeks traditionally give gifts, and St Basil is their Father Christmas.
6 January	Epiphany. Celebrated with the 'blessing of the waters', when swimmers chase a gold cross thrown into the sea by a priest.
February/March	Clean Monday. This is the start of Lent and fasting, and takes place at the start of the seventh week before Greek Easter. Celebrated with seafood picnics and kite flying.
25 March	Independence Day. Parades in many towns and villages, often of schoolchildren.
Around April	Greek Easter. Often on a different day from 'Western' Easter. The Friday and Monday are both holidays. Easter Sunday falls on: 28 April (2019), 19 April (2020), 2 May (2021), 24 April (2022) and 16 April (2023).

1 May	Labour Day. It is also seen as the start of spring and celebrated with trips into the country and the picking of wild flowers.
May/June	Pentecost. The Monday 50 days after Easter Sunday.
15 August	Assumption of the Virgin Mary. One of the biggest holiday days of the Greek year. Everyone seems to hit the beach.
28 October	'*Ohi*' Day. When Metaxas said 'no' to Mussolini; see page 17.
25–26 December	Christmas.

SHOPPING

Most shops and supermarkets now operate on hours similar to the rest of Europe, but some still close in the afternoons for siesta. Outside of tourist areas everything closes down on a Sunday. Supermarkets now sell almost everything you could want, especially the large ones at the edge of bigger towns, but independent butchers and greengrocers still thrive. In rural areas, vans go from village to village selling everything from vegetables, through fresh fish and live chickens, to plastic chairs. You can also still find the old-fashioned *pantapoleion* in some villages of the Peloponnese – these 'shops that sell everything' are not exaggerating, and often serve as the kafenion as well (see box, page 202).

As far as souvenirs go, there are several good options. Mountain honey and herbs, often sold on the roadside, are superb, as are olives and oil, but these need to be packed with care (not in hand luggage if you are flying). Jewellery is not cheap, but can be excellent quality, particularly in the mountains of Arcadia, where there is a tradition of it. The Peloponnese is increasingly attracting interesting young artists and craftspeople, and you can often view their studios. Particularly good areas for this are Nafplio, Monemvasia and the Mani.

ARTS AND ENTERTAINMENT

The Peloponnese is chiefly a rural area and an evening's entertainment is usually confined to a meal out, followed by some stargazing. There are **cinemas** in the larger towns, such as Kalamata, Sparta and Nafplio, and sometimes even open-air ones in the summer. These show the latest releases in their original language with Greek subtitles. Live music is also often available in tavernas and bars – look out for posters. Apart from that there are also various festivals. These range from village festivities to international arts events. The latter include three world-renowned events:

The **Kalamata Dance Festival** (w *kalamatadancefestival.gr*) is held in July in Kalamata. The city has always been famous for its Greek dancing, but the festival now includes renowned performers from across the globe. The traditional **carnival** at Patra includes parades and other festivities and is held in the weeks before Lent (w *carnivalpatras.gr*). It is one of the largest pre-Lentern carnivals in Europe.

Theatre performances at Epidavros take place in the summer as part of the **Athens and Epidavros Festival** (w *greekfestival.gr*), which also includes performances at the theatre of Herodes Atticus on the Acropolis. It includes both modern theatre and music with the Greek classics.

Practically all government-run archaeological sites and museums now operate the same rather elaborate schedule of opening times. During winter (November to April), they are open from 08.00 to 15.00, but hours are extended to 08.00–20.00 during the summer months (May–October). All sites are closed on certain public holidays, ie: New Year's Day (1 January), Independence Day (25 March), Easter Sunday (variable date), Labour Day (1 May), and Christmas/Boxing Day (25/26 December). These holidays aside, most archaeological sites and attached museums are open seven days a week, but museums not attached to an archaeological site are generally open Tuesday to Sunday only, closing Monday, as are some minor archaeological sites.

Except where otherwise stated, the entrance fee to most government-run archaeological sites and museums described in this guidebook is €6. Certain major sites charge €8 (Ancient Corinth) or €12 (Ancient Mycenae, The Theatre and Sanctuary of Asklepius at Epidavros, Old City of Mystra, Ancient Messene, Olympia Archaeological Site and Museum and The Sanctuary of Apollo and Archaeological Museum at Delphi). This almost invariably includes entrance to the site museum where one exists. A 50% discount on all these fees is given across the board in winter (November to March) and to certain qualifying individuals (eg: students from elsewhere in the EU) on production of suitable ID. Admission to most sites and museums is free on the following days: Melina Mercouri Memorial Day (6 March), International Monuments Day (18 April), International Museums Day (18 May), European Heritage Weekend (the last Saturday and Sunday of September) as well as 28 October and the first Sunday of every month from November to March.

PHOTOGRAPHY

Remember to pack a memory card or cards that will last for your trip, although in bigger towns internet cafés will often let you upload images on to the web.

The biggest obstacle to good photographs is the harshness of the light. Apart from anything else it can make seeing anything on your viewing screen very difficult.

In archaeological sites and museums flash photography is often forbidden. You will also be asked to pay a separate fee for the use of a tripod or video equipment, which can be hard to organise.

Most Greeks won't mind you snapping their picture, but it is always polite to ask. On the other hand, photos of military bases and airports can get you in serious trouble. Obey 'no photo' signs if you see them.

MEDIA AND COMMUNICATIONS

LOCAL NEWS The local, daily edition of the *International Herald Tribune* contains a translation of parts of *Kathimerini*, one of the better Greek newspapers. This can also be viewed at **w** ekathimerini.com.

TELEPHONE With the rise of the mobile phone, public telephones, operated by cards, are increasingly neglected and often out of order. If you are on a short trip, however, they can provide the cheapest method of phoning home. Buy a card such as the €5 Call Plus from a supermarket, phone shop or roadside kiosk (*periptero* – see box, page 202), and simply follow the instructions (given in English). Calling a UK landline, these cards allow you 2–3 hours of talk time.

If you bring your own mobile make sure that it is open to being used in foreign countries. If so it will generally pick up one of the Greek networks, but this can be expensive. Charges are capped in the EU, but can still add up – check with your provider exactly how much you will be charged for which services. If you are staying for a while the easiest option might be to buy a Greek pay-as-you-go SIM card, and put it in your phone (these cost around €5 and usually come with some free credit), but be aware some phone providers block you from changing SIM cards.

INTERNET Internet cafés have not been listed in this guide as they seem to come and go quickly. Internet connection, after a slow start, is now widespread around the Peloponnese. Many hotels and cafés now provide a Wi-Fi connection, normally for free if you are staying there or ordering a drink, and this has spread to some surprisingly rural locations. Speeds are often comparable to what you might expect in the UK or US. If you want 24/7 internet access, the best solution is to buy a local SIM card for your phone, and enough airtime to convert to a data bundle, all of which can be done online.

POST The postal service in Greece is surprisingly efficient and cheap. Most larger villages have post offices (at the very least on weekday mornings) and they will hold mail sent to you care of them. International post seems to vary for some reason. To and from the UK can be remarkably quick (two to three days), while the post to and from Germany, for instance, can take up to a week or more.

BUYING A PROPERTY

Buying or building a property in the Peloponnese, generally either as a holiday or retirement home, is less popular than it once was, for obvious reasons. However, for the canny investor, this might be a good time to buy, with prices generally stagnant or falling. The mechanics of buying are much simpler than they once were, but remain a little different from what you might be used to at home; it might be wise to use the services of local agents who have experience selling to foreigners.

One final plea. Some areas of the Peloponnese, mercifully few as yet, saw an absolute rash of new building in the early years of this century. Much of this was fuelled by the Greeks, but often it was down to foreign owners as well. This property boom has now well and truly popped, leaving unoccupied shells littering some landscapes. Think hard before you join in. For a start there are plenty of old properties around that are crying out for some tender loving care. If you do want a new house, try to think out of the box a little. Using traditional materials and styles is all well and good, but simply aping the past is often a mistake. For instance, Maniat tower houses (page 172) were never meant to be lived in. New towers, some with artfully 'ruined' battlements, tend to just look ludicrous.

CULTURAL ETIQUETTE

Greeks traditionally treat strangers as guests, and you will get on with them best if you act like one. Cultural mores are generally little different from the rest of Europe, but there are a few pointers to keep in mind.

The Peloponnese is still fairly conservative, and walking around wearing very little, except on or near the beach, will be disapproved of. Similarly, topless sunbathing for women, while generally accepted, might raise the odd eyebrow if done on the village beach in front of everyone sitting at the taverna having their family lunches. Nude bathing is illegal, at least on paper, and is best kept to isolated spots.

Tipping, at least on American scales, is not normal, and can sometimes cause offence. At restaurants, or with taxi drivers, it is practice not to bother about a few coins change, or to just round up the bill by a little.

Visitors to churches and monasteries are expected to dress respectfully, although many people ignore this. At the least you should cover knees and shoulders.

TRAVELLING POSITIVELY

Despite the hard times, and what you might read in the press, Greece has little need of overt public charity. If you want to help the country there is one excellent way you can do so: come here, travel around, spend money locally, try and understand the culture and people, and fall in love with the place.

There are a couple of organisations that could do with practical help. **ARCHELON** (*57 Solomou St, 10432 Athens; ☎ 21052 31342; e *info@archelon.gr*; w *archelon.gr*), the Sea Turtle Protection Society of Greece, welcomes enthusiastic volunteers throughout the year, but their main efforts are over the summer. Work varies from nest maintenance to public awareness. **GAIA** (e *gaia.d.manis@gmail.com*; 🄵 *GaiaWestMani*) is an organisation based in the Mani, but which works throughout the Peloponnese. Their mission is to protect and promote the natural environment, and they do work that ranges from clearing paths for hikers to fighting fires. They could do with extra volunteers, even short term, money and equipment.

Part Two

THE GUIDE

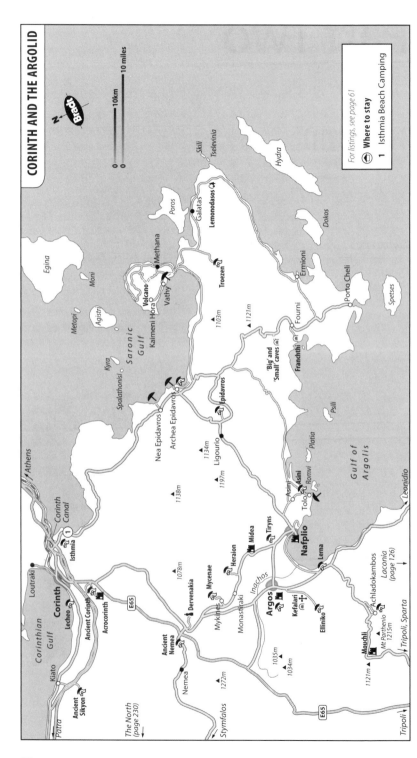

CORINTH AND THE ARGOLID

0 ___ 10km
0 ___ 10 miles

For listings, see page 61
🄰 Where to stay
1 Isthmia Beach Camping

3

Corinth and the Argolid (Κόρινθος & Αργολίδα)

Corinth is the traditional gateway into the Peloponnese, and continues to be so if you are coming from Athens. Along with the Argolid, the 'thumb' of the peninsula, it forms a historical heartland, with Classical and pre-Classical sites seeming to fall over each other.

This is as far as most tourists get into the Peloponnese, and even then they don't explore very much, often doing nothing more than a one-day whistle-stop coach tour. The main sites are most certainly worth it, but there's plenty more to be seen, and the region can surprise you. The walk from Mycenae, described in the box on page 72, is a surprising insight into the mainly rural nature of this world-famous patch of ruins.

CORINTH (ΚΌΡΙΝΘΟΣ)

Corinth seems to have suffered from an excess of history, having been variously razed to the ground and then flattened by earthquakes on several occasions. This has led to the modern city being a rather uninspiring collection of low, concrete buildings. Standing by the thin isthmus that separates the Peloponnese from the rest of the mainland, it is a rather off-putting introduction to the region. Don't be fooled – only 7km to the southwest, the small village of Ancient Corinth (Αρχαία Κόρινθος) flanks the site of the old Roman town, where you can tread the same streets as St Paul would have almost 2,000 years ago. Above it, the imposing bulk of Acrocorinth, its hilltop fortifications visible as you approach the isthmus, is a more than worthy guardian to the secret delights of the Peloponnese.

MYTHOLOGY Corinth appears in several mythological cycles. Jason and his new wife, Medea, are said to have settled here after stealing the Golden Fleece. Jason, however, soon fell for the younger Glauke, Princess of Corinth. Medea, a powerful sorceress, dispatched her rival with a poisoned cloak that burnt her to death.

An early ruler of Corinth was Sisyphus, a man so cunning he cheated death not once, but twice. When he eventually reached the underworld, Hades punished him with an unending task. He forever pushed a rock up a hill, only to have it roll to the bottom again just as he was about to reach the top; a fitting life metaphor for depressed existentialists everywhere.

Sisyphus's grandfather was Bellerophon, who was charged with killing Chimaera, a beast with the head of a lion, the body of a goat, and the tail of a serpent. To achieve this he needed the help of Pegasus, the winged horse created from Medusa's

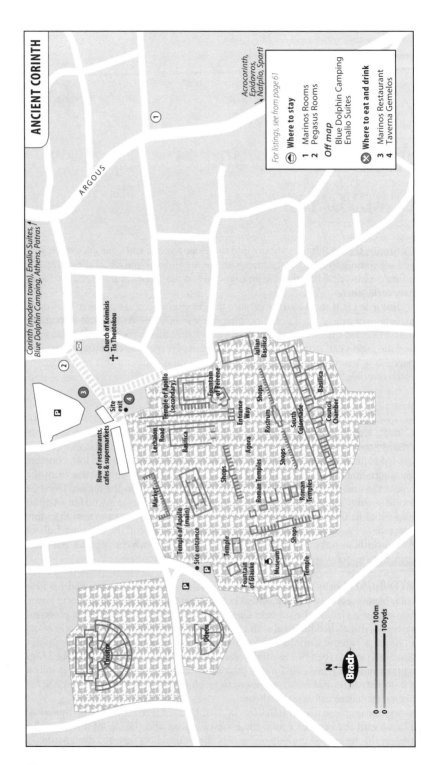

ANCIENT CORINTH

ARGOUS

Corinth (modern town), Enalio Suites, ↑
Blue Dolphin Camping, Athens, Patras

Acrocorinth,
Epidavros,
Nafplio, Sparti ↑

For listings, see from page 61

Where to stay
1 Marinos Rooms
2 Pegasus Rooms
Off map
   Blue Dolphin Camping
   Enalio Suites

Where to eat and drink
3 Marinos Restaurant
4 Taverna Gemelos

Church of Koimisis
✝ Tis Theotokou

Row of restaurants,
cafés & supermarkets

Site exit

Temple of Apollo
(secondary)

Fountain
of Peirene

Julian
Basilica

Entrance
Way

Shops

Lechaion
Road

Basilica

Rostrum

South
Colonnade

Basilica

Agora

Council
Chamber

Market

Shops

Roman Temples

Shops

Roman
Temples

Temple of Apollo
(main)

Shops

Temple

Shops

Site entrance

Fountain
of Glauke

Museum

Temple

Theatre

Odeon

N

Bradt

0   100m
0   100yds

58

blood after Perseus slew her. Pegasus used to drink from the spring on Acrocorinth, and Bellerophon captured the animal with the help of a golden bridle, a gift from Athena. Flying above Chimaera Bellerophon speared the creature with a lance tipped with lead, which melted in its fiery breath, killing it.

HISTORY The origins of Corinth, as one would expect from such a strategically important site, are prehistoric. In Homer it appears as the city of Ephyra and is home to the mythical characters above. It emerges into history in 747BC when rule passed to the oligarchy of the Bacchiads, a group of 200 aristocrats who claimed descent from Heracles. With its two harbours on either side of the isthmus, Corinth became a dominant sea power trading throughout the Mediterranean. Colonies were founded at Corfu and Syracuse and the city was the first to use triremes in battle.

In 657BC, the Bacchiads were overthrown by one of the first Greek tyrants, a man called Cypselus. Under his son, Periander (629–585BC), Corinth reached new levels of success and it is in this period that the Temple of Apollo, the Fountain of Peirene, and the Dioklos (the road for hauling ships over the isthmus) were started. Periander is often included as one of the Seven Sages of ancient Greece, despite having a noted sadistic streak (killing and *then* raping his wife being one of the more lurid stories).

During the Persian invasion of Greece Corinth's strategic location led to it being the headquarters of the allied Greek states. The city sent 40 ships to the Battle of Salamis (480BC) and then, the next year, 5,000 infantry to the decisive Battle of Plataea. After this Corinth's power waned as that of Athens, Sparta, and then Macedon, grew.

However, under Macedonian rule, the city had a bit of a renaissance, attracting playwrights such as Xenophon and, most notably, the philosopher Diogenes the Cynic. The latter based his life around his admiration for the way dogs acted – free from embarrassment and the burden of possessions, and living entirely in the moment. There are stories of him defecating and masturbating in public (he is said to have quipped that he wished hunger could be satisfied by merely rubbing the belly), and he lived in squalor in an empty tub or pot. This eccentric lifestyle earned him a certain notoriety, and Alexander the Great, when visiting Corinth, was keen to meet the philosopher. Finding him sunbathing Alexander asked if there was any favour he could grant him. 'Yes,' replied Diogenes, 'get out of my sunlight'. Five hundred years later, when he came through Corinth, Pausanias could still visit the philosopher's tomb.

Corinth was entirely destroyed by the Romans in 146BC and lay destitute until it was rebuilt by Julius Caesar in 44BC. He made it the capital of Roman Greece and the city again prospered, gaining a reputation for luxury and licentiousness. St Paul was certainly not impressed during his 18-month stay in the mid 1st century AD, admonishing the local population in his Epistles.

The later history of Corinth is a litany of disasters, with barbarian invasions interspersed with devastating earthquakes. The latter struck in AD375 and AD551, while Alaric, king of the Visigoths, sacked the city in AD395, selling much of the population into slavery. Under Byzantine rule the city gained some prosperity in the 11th and 12th centuries, but this only served to attract the unwelcome attention of Roger of Sicily, whose Norman troops plundered Corinth in 1147.

After the fall of Constantinople in the Fourth Crusade, the city was besieged by the Franks in 1205. It was defended by the Greek ruler of Nafplio, Leo Sgouros. He despaired of its fate and, in 1208, committed suicide by riding his horse off the ramparts of Acrocorinth. Perhaps he thought he was on Pegasus.

Every guidebook writer owes a debt to all the other travellers that have been before them. In the Peloponnese this goes all the way back to the man who invented the entire industry.

Pausanias probably came from Lydia, in Asia Minor, but he was a Roman through and through, and it was the peace brought about by Roman domination that allowed him to travel so widely. He is thought to have been all over the Near East, as well as seeing the pyramids in Egypt. He also travelled through northern Greece to visit Italy and the great capital of the empire.

It was in Greece that his main interest lay, however. His guide to the country doesn't cover much more than the Peloponnese, as well as the areas to the north around Athens, but it is the first comprehensive guidebook we have to anywhere. He is most at home when describing religious customs and architecture, as well as extensive histories, mainly mythological, of the places he encountered.

It seems a shame, but we have no direct evidence that any of his near contemporaries ever read the books. They survived to our age almost by chance, and for a long time were dismissed as widely fanciful and inaccurate, mostly by people who had never, themselves, travelled through the landscape he described.

The reassessment of Pausanias's work probably begins with Colonel Leake, who on an army assignment travelled through Turkish-occupied Greece in the early 19th century. His observations confirmed the accuracy of many of those of Pausanias, as does the continuing work of modern archaeology. The best modern version is the two-volume Penguin edition (page 273), which is still not a bad addition to anyone's luggage.

Corinth fell to the Ottomans in 1458, and apart from a brief Venetian interlude, remained under their control until the city was liberated in the Greek War of Independence. Up until this time the name Corinth had referred to Acrocorinth and the surrounding settlement, but this was devastated by an earthquake in 1858, and the modern town was relocated a few kilometres to the north on the coast.

GETTING THERE AND AWAY If you don't have your own transport Corinth may well end up being your first stop in the Peloponnese. This is unfortunate as it can be a confusing place to turn up in, and not very inspiring. The main thing to realise is that it is split into two, with the drab, modern city separated from its old site, now called Ancient Corinth. You are far more likely to want to head for the latter.

By car Corinth stands about 80km west of Athens, an hour's drive along the tolled multiple-lane A8 highway. If you want the modern city, take the well-signposted exit about 5km after the highway crosses the Corinth Canal. To go directly to Ancient Corinth, stick on the highway for another 5km, through an interchange where you need to take the Patra Road, until the appropriate exit is signposted. Ancient Corinth is just a few hundred metres south of the highway, and although the various slip roads blend rather confusingly, you won't go wrong if you just follow the signs to it.

By train Corinth is now connected to Athens, its airport, and the port of Piraeus by the suburban railway line, or Proastiakos, which has regular trains every hour. This service continues west to the town of Kiato (and is set to go further at some point), where there are currently connecting bus services to Patra. The station is not in the city itself, but just to the south. There are hourly buses from here to the city and Ancient Corinth, as well as a taxi rank. There is currently no service from here towards the south (page 39).

By bus Unless you want to go into the city itself you are best to get off at the large bus interchange just south of the Corinth Canal. From here you can charter a taxi or pick up one of the occasional local buses to Ancient Corinth. This is also the place to catch buses into the rest of the Peloponnese; most destinations are served several times daily – although note that most of them have come from Athens and can be full.

WHERE TO STAY *Map, page 58 unless otherwise stated*

There are several adequate small hotels in Ancient Corinth, and these form your best option if you want to get an early start on the ruins. There are also several contemporary hotels catering for all budgets in the modern city, but there's no real reason to stay there. A better option than either of the above might be to visit in passing en route from Athens to another base: the coast to the north and east has several 'resort' style hotels as well as campsites, and there are also options in mountain villages to the west, while the southerly coastal towns of Nafplio and Tolo (pages 79 and 86) are within easy striking distance.

Enalio Suites (11 rooms) 27410 87984; m 69719 69896; e info@enalio.gr; w enalio.gr. This modern but stone-built set of suites with attractive grounds & pool is on the coast at Lecheo, 5km west of modern Corinth & 4km north of Ancient Corinth. Run by a friendly family who provide a good b/fast & offer free transfers from the railway station. €€€€€

Marinos Rooms (23 rooms) 27410 31994; m 69447 41479; e marinosrooms@gmail.com; w marinos-rooms.gr. This friendly & well-signposted guesthouse has a quiet location in Ancient Corinth less than 500m east of the ruins. It is run by the hands-on Marinos family, which has been renting rooms in the village since 1968, & offers perhaps the best option in the immediate vicinity, with simple but well-priced & comfortable rooms. Rates include a good traditional b/fast. Plenty of parking space too. €€€

Pegasus Rooms (9 rooms) 27410 31366; e info@pegasurooms.gr; w pegasusrooms.gr. Situated 200m from the ruins next to a row of tavernas & bars, this agreeable small guesthouse has modern tiled rooms & serves b/fast on a rooftop terrace with a lovely view. €€€

Blue Dolphin Camping 27410 25766; e skouspos@otenet.gr; w camping-blue-dolphin. gr. About 4km from Ancient Corinth near to the ancient site of Lecheo on the old road to Patra. Small, but set on a pretty pebble beach looking north to the opposite coast. €

Isthmia Beach Camping [map, page 56] 27410 37447; e isthmia@otenet.gr; w campingisthmia.gr. This campsite is 13km to the east of Ancient Corinth, a few mins' drive from Isthmia down the road towards Epidavros. It is bigger & on a nice pebble beach. €

WHERE TO EAT AND DRINK *Map, page 58*

A row of tavernas and cafés lines the main road opposite the ruins. Most cater primarily to the tourist trade during the day, which is never a guarantee of good quality; in the evenings look out for where the locals are gathering.

Marinos Restaurant 27410 31130. Established in 1970, this family-run restaurant

on the main road in front of the ruins is widely & justifiably rated as the best place to eat in

Ancient Corinth. It's a little pricier than most of the competition, but quality is usually excellent, portions are generous & the carafe wine, sourced from the family farm, is excellent.

✗ Taverna Gemelos ✆ 27410 31361. The best feature of this long-serving family-run restaurant is the shaded rooftop terrace, which offers a fabulous close-up view over the main ruins to the more distant hilltop Acrocorinth. For those seeking a cheap lunchtime snack, it also seems to be the only place in the village that serves wallet-friendly giros pitas. Otherwise it serves a pretty standard selection of Greek stews & grills.

OTHER PRACTICALITIES The modern city has all the facilities you would expect, but it is worth planning on taking advantage of these elsewhere, so as to avoid an unnecessary trip into the centre. The village of Ancient Corinth has a couple of small but very well-stocked **supermarkets** among the tourist shops.

WHAT TO SEE AND DO
Ancient Corinth (Αρχαία Κόρινθος) (✆ 27410 31207; ⏰ *times & entrance fees, see box, page 52*) The remains of the ancient city that are still visible are mostly Roman, dating from the 1st to the 3rd century AD. This means you are looking at the same buildings, and walking the same paths, as St Paul and Pausanias. Before entering the ruins it is worth looking at the theatre and odeon; although fenced in they are visible from the opposite side of the car park. As you enter the site you first notice a prehistoric-looking mass of rock with several fissures in its sides. This is the **Fountain of Glauke**, so-named after Jason's second wife who flung herself into it to obtain relief from Medea's burning cloak. Earthquakes have destroyed the façade, leaving just the huge cube of hewn rock beneath.

Just ahead is the site's small **museum**, most of whose exhibits have labels in Greek and English. Its attractions include several good mosaics, and what might be the earliest example of a 'Keep Off The Grass' sign – the fine was 8 obols.

The present-day remains are dominated by the **Temple of Apollo**, its seven standing columns visible on a small knoll as you leave the museum. It is one of the oldest temples remaining in Greece, and certainly the oldest building on the site, dating back to c550BC. It is in an imposing position, framed either by the bulk of Acrocorinth or the blue waters of the Gulf of Corinth. Strangely Pausanias makes little mention of it.

Beyond the temple you enter the huge **Agora** (or Roman Forum). Its 210m x 90m expanse is surrounded by shops, arcaded market areas, and administrative buildings. The ruins are a little confusing, but give a real sense of the hustle and bustle of a working city. In the far corner of the agora, heading back towards the modern village, is the **Lechaion Road**, so called as it led to Lecheo, one of Corinth's twin ports. Here you can walk along the actual road itself, wondering in whose footsteps you are following.

At the beginning of the road, just to the right, the beautiful remains of the **Fountain of Peirene** come as a bit of a surprise as they are mostly sunken below ground level. The natural spring, which still supplies the modern village with water, is hidden behind a six-arched façade fronted with columns. Unfortunately you can no longer approach the fountain closely, but if you cup your ears it is just possible to hear the still-running water. This is the lower of two springs of the same name, the upper one being on Acrocorinth. The road carries on to the exit from the site.

Acrocorinth (Ακροκόρινθος) (⏰ *see box, page 52; free entrance*) Despite its spectacular position and looming presence many people give Acrocorinth a miss. This is partly because, without your own car, it is only reachable by taxi or an hour-

long uphill walk. On top of this it is an extremely large site – water, good shoes and a sun hat are a must. It is worth every effort, however, with its extensive castle ruins and astounding views. The site is reached by following the road up past the entrance to the ancient city. On your way up you will see the small castle of **Pendeskoufi** on a nearby peak. It was built by the Franks during their siege of Acrocorinth in the 13th century.

The road ends in a small car park by a modern café, below the imposing walls and gateways of the castle itself. Crossing a dry moat you come to the first of **three gateways**; a triple fortification whose history mirrors that of the various owners of the castle. The first gateway is mostly Turkish in origin, while the second is a Venetian restoration of an originally Frankish structure. The third, and perhaps most impressive, gateway is mainly Byzantine, but look closely at the large stones in the tower to the right; these probably date back to the 4th century BC.

Inside the castle most of the ruined buildings are Turkish, including a mosque with most of its dome still intact. Three paths snake away from the entrance, although they all end up in the same place. If you are in a hurry the path to the right is the quickest. Almost opposite the gateways, close to the eastern walls of the castle, the main path splits into three again. The path to the right leads to the southern walls and a **Frankish tower** that you can scramble around for views into the mountains beyond Corinth. The central path leads around to the left, skirting the walls, before it reaches the upper **Fountain of Peirene**; look out for fencing around a concrete roof that covers the underground spring. This is where the winged horse, Pegasus, liked to come to drink. Metal steps lead down to stone steps that descend into a twin-arched pool with eerily blue water (not drinkable). The spring has never been known to run dry, a fact the local flies take full advantage of. The path that continues past the spring soon peters out.

The third path goes off to the left, climbing through the centre of the castle to the higher of its two peaks (575m), close to the northern walls. This was the site of the **Temple of Aphrodite**, although all trace of this has now gone. In ancient times the goddess of love was worshipped with religious prostitution provided by 1,000 sacred courtesans. Visitors nowadays have to make do with the view. This is no hardship, as even on a hazy day it is impressive; on a clear day you can see from the Acropolis in Athens on the right, to the mouth of the Gulf of Corinth on the left.

Historical and Folklore Museum (*1 Ermou;* ✆*27410 25352;* ☉ *see box, page 52;* €2) The only reason to go into the modern city of Corinth is to visit this unusually large and well-designed folklore museum. It has a particularly good collection of traditional costumes from the early 19th to the mid 20th century, as well as other craft items. The building, which was constructed specially to house the collection, is on El Venizelou Square, on the seafront by the marina.

Lecheo and Kenchreai The strategic position of Corinth, guarding the isthmus into the Peloponnese, is obvious. The ancient city took advantage of this by having not one, but two ports; one on either side of the isthmus. Cargoes (and even ships – see page 64) could be transported overland between the two. Sadly, little remains to see of them today.

Lecheo (Λέχαιο) lies to the west among tall sand dunes. The site has yet to be excavated properly and is fenced off. The one visible building dates from a much later period, and is a huge 6th-century AD **basilica** dedicated to St Leonidas and the Virgins, who were martyred by drowning near Corinth in the 3rd century AD. Most of the remains of **Kenchreai** (Κεγχρεαί), to the east of the isthmus, are now underwater.

The Corinth Canal The Corinth Canal, nicknamed 'the ditch' in Greek, is a huge engineering achievement, and marks the start of the Peloponnese. If you are travelling on the main national road, however, it is easy to blink and miss it. To get a proper view, get on to the old road that runs parallel to it and crosses a bridge that has walkways on either side – from the direction of Athens, this is done by taking the turn-off that is marked for Loutraki and then bearing left. It is famously hard to judge the scale of the canal from above; if you are lucky a ship will pass through, scraping the sides of the cliffs far below.

One glance at a map and the advantage of a canal through the isthmus is obvious, but all attempts to build one before the 19th century failed. This, perhaps, has something to do with the Corinthians, who did not want to lose their status as a trade hub. The most famous attempt was made by the Emperor Nero, who started the digging himself using a small gold spade, so it is not surprising that he did not succeed. With the aid of modern technology the first ship travelled through the canal in 1893. The canal is just over 6km long and the cliffsides rise up to 52m above sea level. Its diminutive width (21m at its bottom) and water depth (8m) mean that it is too small for most modern cargo ships.

If you want to view the canal from the bottom up the easiest option is to take a **cruise** which can be picked up at the dock by the sinking bridge at Isthmia (about €20). The more adventurous could try a **bungy jump** from the old road bridge over the canal. This is run by Zulu Bungy who have a small office at the north end of the bridge (℡27410 49465; m 69460 89743; e info@zulubungy.com; w zulubungy.com; ⏰ Jun–Aug 10.00–17.45 Wed–Sun; May, Sep & Oct 10.00–17.45 Sat & Sun; closed Nov–Apr; €80).

At either end of the canal there are road crossings over bridges that submerge to let ships over them. Head to the western one of these to see the remains of the **Diolkos**, or 'ship haulway'. This was first built in the 7th century BC and allowed ships to be towed across the isthmus. You can see the stone trackway emerging out of the water just before the bridge on the Corinth to Loutraki road.

Isthmia (Ισθμία) (⏰ 08.30–15.00 Tue–Sun; €2) The isthmus that separates the Peloponnese from the rest of the Greek mainland is the prototype isthmus that all others in the world are named after. Games were held here of almost equal importance to those at Olympia. To reach the ruins head out on the road towards Epidavros through the small modern town of Isthmia. At the edge of the town is a badly signposted road up to the right, which leads up to the museum and ruins of Ancient Isthmia.

Isthmia is a bit of a poor relation to the other ruins nearby, and in the rest of the Peloponnese. Apparently it suffered by being so accessible, and was looted over the centuries – more remote locations have survived better. Even the archaeologists who devoted their careers to the site commented how little there was left to see. Do not be entirely put off, however; the small **Archaeological Museum of Isthmia** (*Kyra-Vrysi 20;* ℡27410 37244; ⏰ 08.30–15.00 Tue–Sun; €2) is interesting and holds some unusual glass mosaic work, and the site itself is extensive, if rather jumbled, and is surprisingly tranquil given the nearby roads. Look out for the rather peculiar sunken pits apparently used by a dining cult, and the **large mosaic floor** in the Roman baths, covered with mythological and real sea creatures.

Sikyon (Σικυώνας) (℡ 27420 28900; 08.30–15.00 Tue–Sun; €2) Situated on a plain some 5km inland of the Corinthian Gulf and 20km northwest of Corinth, the ancient city of Sikyon (Σικυώνας) was occupied more-or-less continuously from Mycenaean times into the early Christian era. According to legend, it was ruled by a succession of around 25 mythical kings prior to the Trojan War in the 12th century BC. Sikyon peaked in importance in the 4th century BC, when it was renowned as a centre of painting and sculpture. As might be expected, the ruins are impressively extensive, and include an Agora that was converted to a Basilica in early Christian times, and an unexcavated stadium. Most impressive is the large theatre, which was carved into a natural depression in the 4th century BC.

The ruins of Sikyon are somewhat difficult to find, and the site is often closed. The best approach is from the national road between Corinth and Patras. About 16km past the exit for Ancient Corinth, take the exit for the modern town of Kiato (Κιάτο), then cross the bridge over the railway and take an immediate sharp right on the other side. Make your way from here to the next bridge back over the railway, under the national road and up into the hills following the signs to the archaeological museum. The museum is right by the ruins, and despite what many guidebooks will tell you, it has been open since 2006 (after an extended closure of about 15 years). Unfortunately, due to the troubled times, it may not stay open much longer.

NEMEA (NEMEA)

In Classical times, Nemea was one of the four sanctuaries that hosted athletic festivals attended by the whole of the Greek world – the others were Olympia, Isthmia and Delphi. In the modern era, the area has become the centre for the revival of Greek wine in the Peloponnese, and now the ancient sites are surrounded by vineyards. Nearby a decisive battle in the War of Independence was fought (page 16).

MYTHOLOGY It was said that the games at Nemea were founded by the Seven Against Thebes, Argive heroes who were on their way to battle the city of Thebes, as a sign of grief at the part they played in the death of Opheltes, infant prince of Nemea. When he had been born the Delphic oracle warned that Opheltes should not touch the ground until he had learnt to walk. The Seven met Opheltes being carried by his nursemaid Hypsipyle. They asked her directions to the nearest spring, and in her eagerness to help she forgot the prophecy and laid the baby Opheltes down on a bed of wild celery. A snake, concealed in the foliage, killed the boy. Victors in the games received crowns of wild celery in commemoration of this, and the judges wore black in mourning. The Romans, however, believed that the games were held in honour of the first of Heracles' Labours: killing the Nemean Lion (page 11).

GETTING THERE AND AWAY
By car The ancient site of Nemea is located just off the main Athens–Tripoli highway (E65) and the junction is clearly signposted. It can also be approached on various back roads that come down from the mountains to the north and west and then pass through the vineyards on wine routes (page 66).

By bus Several buses a day go from Corinth to the modern town of Nemea, 5km beyond the ruins. Make it clear that you want to be dropped at Archea (ancient) Nemea, and also check return times if you don't want to be stranded here.

OTHER PRACTICALITIES Nemea is an agricultural area and is not geared up for visitors. There is no real reason to stay here anyway, and there are plenty of good options nearby (around Corinth, Mycenae and Nafplio). The modern town is fairly small, but has a few **shops** and an **ATM** if need be. By the site itself there is a friendly 'snak' bar where you can get drinks and food.

WHAT TO SEE AND DO

Temple of Nemean Zeus and the museum (☏ 27460 22739; ⏲ & *entrance fees, see box, page 52, ticket covers the museum, the main site & the stadium*) The main archaeological site at Nemea may not be as big or famous as some of its nearby companions, but it still rewards a visit, especially as it tends to be far less crowded. Set in a fertile valley of the Elissos River and surrounded by fields of vines, it is a tranquil and attractive spot.

You are best to visit the **museum** before the site itself. Not only is it full of interesting finds from Nemea and the surrounding region, but there are also two useful reconstructions of how the sanctuary used to look; both in Classical times and also in the 5th century AD when the temple had started to fall down and a large Christian basilica dominated the scene. Large windows overlook the site from the museum, allowing you to compare the models with the modern-day view. Another worthwhile exhibit is a video that explains, and re-creates, the ingenious starting mechanism used for the races in the nearby stadium.

When you venture out into the site itself you first pass over the remains of the **Christian basilica** as well as some old graves (one of these has been left *in situ*), before heading to the left where there are the remains of the **bathhouse** used by the athletes in the games. They are covered by a modern shelter, but this is the same size and shape as the ancient building would have been. Inside the basins and drainage system are interesting to look at.

The path continues past the bathhouse to the **Temple of Nemean Zeus** which was built between 340BC and 320BC. For many years only three of its slender columns remained standing, but many of the drums from the other columns still lay around and, since 2000, they are slowly being restored. The missing pieces are reconstructed with local stone, just like the originals; you can see the workshop behind the temple. Nine columns are upright currently. Below the floor level of the temple, and reached by stairs, is an *adyton*, a secret inner sanctum, from where oracular pronouncements were perhaps given.

The stadium (⏲ *same times as temple & museum & it is covered by the same ticket*) Leaving the site of the temple turn left to reach the stadium, only a short distance away. It is entered by way of a long **tunnel** that dates back to c320BC. It is a wonderfully evocative way to approach the stadium; you can almost hear the roar of the crowd as you emerge.

One interesting feature to note is the channel that runs beneath the rows of seats. This would have held running water for the spectators' refreshment. The **starting line** is also intact. The ancient athletes would have raced naked, after coating themselves in olive oil. You are probably unwise to emulate them this far, but you might want to take off your shoes and try a quick run.

The act of re-creation has been taken further by the **Society for the Revival of the Nemean Games**. Since 1996 they have been holding games in the stadium every four years. These are open to athletes of any ability and, although the victors are awarded the traditional wild celery wreath, no records are kept and the emphasis is on taking part together. Competitors come from all over the world (for the story behind this revival and the excavation of the site, see box opposite).

Wine routes and vineyards Nemea is at the heart of the revival of good Greek wine (page 65). The classic grape variety of the area is Agiorgitiko, which produces a dark, fruity red often referred to as the 'blood of Heracles'. The grapes derive their name from the monastery of Agios Giorgios, which used to own much of this land

(page 256). Other varieties are also grown, including whites, as well as grapes that are dried for currants (which take their name from nearby Corinth). Many of the back roads that snake through these charming valleys are now marked as 'wine routes' and several of the vineyards welcome visitors, including the ones below, and are signposted off the roads. These are reliably open during the summer in the mornings and afternoons, but it may be worth calling in advance. You will also see huts beside the road that sell more robust wines in plastic bottles. The region hosts a three-day wine festival in August.

Lafkiotis Winery 27460 31000; e info@lafkiotis.gr; w lafkiotis.gr; ⊕ 10.00–15.00 daily (call first). A warm welcome comes from this winery on the other side of Archea Nemea, near to the village of Ancient Kleones (Αρχαιες Κλεωνες).

Palivou Estate 27460 24190; e info@palivos.gr; w palivos.gr; ⊕ 08.30–16.30 daily. This is a more contemporary winery, founded in 1995, but it has a strong reputation & is very welcoming to visitors. The tasting room is located on the road towards the modern town of Nemea.

Papaioannou Estate 27460 23138; e info@papaioannouwines.gr; w papaioannouwines.gr. Founded in 1876, this winery really came into its own under the direction of Athanassios Papaioannou (other winemakers in Greece refer to him as 'god'). Now run by his son George, it is the biggest producer in the region. Look out for their 'Old Vines' variety. They are located near to Archea Nemea.

Dervenakia Pass (Δερβενάκια) The road from Nemea towards Mycenae, Argos and Nafplio immediately heads through the Dervenakia Pass. This was the site of a crushing victory over the Ottomans during the War of Independence. In 1822, a huge army, some 30,000 men and 6,000 cavalry, led by Dramali Pasha, invaded the Peloponnese and quickly took the citadel at Acrocorinth before pushing farther south. They were held up, however, at Argos, where a much smaller force resisted them for several days. Meanwhile the famous Greek general Kolokotronis collected together about 8,000 irregular troops and began to harry the larger, occupying force while also closing their supply lines. The Ottomans found themselves trapped on the sweltering plains of Argos, and increasingly hungry, thirsty and disease-ridden, until finally they made the decision to retreat back to Corinth. The Greeks were waiting for them in the mountain passes and on 6–8 August a massacre ensued.

Various casualty figures are given, but it is fair to say that the Ottoman losses were huge while the Greeks suffered minimal losses. One of the Greek leaders, Nikitaras, earned the epithet *Turkofagos* after the battle – the Turk Eater. Dramali himself made it back to Corinth, but died there the following December, a broken man. The battle became famous and any big setback is still referred to as a 'Dramali disaster' in Greek.

The victory is commemorated by a large statue of Kolokotronis, unusually not on horseback, which looks over the plains below. Coming from Nemea it is reached by taking the small turn to the left immediately after you cross the railway track, signposted to Dervenakia. This winds up into the mountains for a couple of kilometres before reaching the site of the statue. The views from here are well worth the detour.

MYCENAE (MYK'HNAI)

The citadel of Agamemnon, celebrated by Homer as 'rich in gold', has given its name to an entire civilisation. The ruins that it left behind were ancient even in Classical times, and already were the subject of myth and legend. Pausanias attributed the great walls of the citadel to the Cyclopes, one-eyed giants. The site is still a dramatic one, offering a stark contrast to the normal perception of 'Greek ruins'. If the white marbled temples and theatres speak of philosophy and high art, then the walls and remains of Mycenae are redolent of something darker: a blood-stained, myth-haunted past.

MYTHOLOGY When Helen eloped with Paris, a prince of Troy, her husband, King Menelaus of Sparta, called on his brother Agamemnon for help. Agamemnon, who was himself married to Helen's sister Clytemnestra, was overlord of all the Greeks and King of Mycenae. He gathered together a great fleet and prepared to set sail

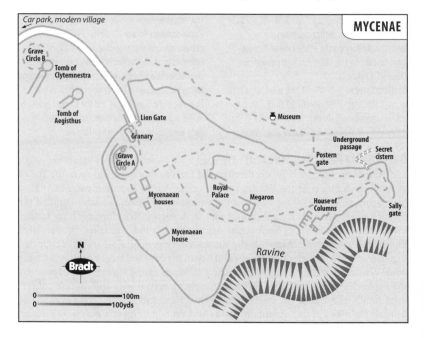

Heinrich Schliemann was born, in 1822, into a poor pastor's family in Germany. Somehow, at an early age, he fell in love with ancient Greek literature, particularly Homer, and it is said that at the age of eight he declared his intention to dig up the city of Troy.

First, however, he would need to earn his money. He became a businessman and began to travel, first to Russia and then to California at the time of the gold rush. By the end of his life he could hold a conversation in 13 languages: English, French, Dutch, Spanish, Portuguese, Swedish, Italian, Greek, Latin, Russian, Arabic and Turkish, as well as his native German.

He was either very good at business, or very lucky, and he amassed several fortunes and was able to retire by the age of 40. He could now devote himself, and his wealth, to his dreams. Most scholars of the day dismissed the epic poetry of Homer as mere mythology, with little or no basis in reality. Schliemann was convinced that his stories had their basis in fact.

There was already a tentative location for the site of a 'historical' Troy, a low hill on the west coast of Turkey named Hissarlik. In 1871, due in no small part to his money, Schliemann was able to start digging and soon discovered the remains of an extensive ancient city. In 1873, he uncovered 'Priam's Treasure', a huge cache of gold jewellery that was famously displayed by his young Greek wife Sophia. In fact we now know that Schliemann in his eagerness dug straight through the Troy of Homer's epics, and that his finds come from an even earlier period, but there's little doubt that this was Troy.

Schliemann next turned his sights on mainland Greece. At Mycenae, in 1876, he struck gold again, literally. When he uncovered a golden face mask in one of the shaft graves, it still had traces of flesh clinging to the inside. He immediately telegrammed the King of Greece saying, 'I have gazed upon the face of Agamemnon.' Once again it is now thought that his finds were earlier than he supposed.

By today's standards, Schliemann's archaeology leaves a lot to be desired, but there is no denying that his main hunches were right, and that he opened up whole new fields of study. He is also a testament to the fact that you can sometimes follow a dream.

for Troy, which was located in Asia Minor. However, he had offended the goddess Artemis, and she sent contrary winds against them. She was only placated when Agamemnon gave her a sacrifice of his own daughter, Iphigenia.

With Agamemnon away at war, Clytemnestra, understandably upset at the death of her daughter, took Aegisthus, an old enemy of Agamemnon's, as her lover. When her husband eventually returned after the long siege of Troy, Clytemnestra murdered him. According to some accounts she smothered him with a robe while he took a bath, before striking him three times with a double-headed axe – an imitation of his act of sacrifice. The cycle of revenge continued, as it always does, with Agamemnon and Clytemnestra's two remaining children, Orestes and Elektra, murdering their mother and her lover.

This tragic sequence of tales was one of the favourite subjects for Classical art. It is mentioned by Homer in both the *Odyssey* and the *Iliad*, and is used in plays by Aeschylus, Euripides and Sophocles.

HISTORY It was the German archaeologist Heinrich Schliemann who dragged the myth of Mycenae into the historical world (see box, page 69), but he himself was caught up in the romance of the place. Since his time more scientific excavation, both by the Greek Archaeological Service and the British School at Athens, has added to the understanding of the reality behind Mycenaean history and life.

The hill that Mycenae sits on was occupied from Neolithic times onward, but it only really came into its own in the Late Helladic period, when, sometime around 1500BC, six shaft graves were sunk in what is now known as Grave Circle A. Buried within them were nine women, eight men and two children, clearly members of a ruling family, as evidenced by the amount of gold and other rich artefacts that surrounded them. The fact that there is no source for such an amount of gold in the vicinity is one of the first mysteries of Mycenae – where did this sudden wealth come from? At first it was thought that Minoan Crete might have been the source, but Crete was also relatively free of gold. It is more likely to have come from Egypt, which at the time was paying for mercenaries to help fight against overseas invaders. If this is true then it might also explain the sudden elaborate burial arrangements, as veneration of the dead was a notable Egyptian custom.

The following 200 years saw the expansion of Mycenaean power into the void left by the decline of the Minoan civilisation, from which it adopted many customs, including writing in the Linear B script (see box, page 226). In about 1350BC, the first walls were built around the citadel. This period also saw the building of the magnificent tholos tombs that surround the site, misidentified by Pausanias as treasuries. This was the height of Mycenaean power, when the city held sway not only over the whole Peloponnese, but also over many of the islands and areas of northern Greece as well.

The decline and then almost total disappearance of the Mycenaean civilisation is even more mysterious than its sudden appearance. The 13th century BC had seen an increase in defensive measures at several sites, including the building of the secret cistern at Mycenae itself, a fact that speaks of either an external threat or some kind of civil war. Indeed around 1250BC all the palaces in the Peloponnese were burnt down. This might have been the result of the invasion of Dorian Greeks from the north, although this is not generally believed anymore. Other theories include a disastrous drought or some other form of climate change, seismic activity, or a plague. The real truth might remain hidden forever.

GETTING THERE AND AWAY

By car Mycenae is just off the road to Argos and Nafplio and is well signposted. To go straight to the site, drive through the modern village and on another 2km to the large car park.

By bus There are lots of buses daily to and from Argos and Nafplio (*30mins*) which will drop you at, or near to, the village of Fichti from where you can get a taxi (*5mins*) or walk (*50mins*). There are also some local buses from these two towns that serve the village and the site itself.

WHERE TO STAY AND EAT
The main road through the modern village of Mycenae (more accurately transliterated as Mykines) is lined with small guesthouses, tavernas and cafés. In the summer, it caters to the lines of tour buses that come and go each day, but once evening comes everything calms down again and it is a surprisingly pleasant place to stay a night or two.

There are two campsites in the village. **Camping Mykines** (↝*27510 76121;* €) is in the centre. It is a small site with basic facilities, but the welcome is friendly. **Camping Atreus** (↝*27510 76221, 27510 76735 in winter;* €), on the way into the village, is larger and has a small pool. They also provide food in the evening including a good grill.

La Petite Planète (29 rooms) ↝27510 76240; e info@petite-planet.gr; w petite-planet.gr. This hotel, on the left-hand side of the road on the way to the site, is where Schliemann would probably stay nowadays if he came. The rooms are simple but have everything you need; there are nice views over the plains below, & the welcome from the Dassis family is warm & friendly. Maria runs the restaurant, with its large terrace, & produces a surprisingly sophisticated take on traditional cooking. There is also a nicely situated pool in the grounds. €€€

Belle Helene (8 rooms) ↝27510 76225; e bellhel@otenet.gr. This is where Schliemann

did stay when he excavated Mycenae. In 1885, the family converted their house into a hotel, one of the earliest in Greece, to cope with the increasing number of visitors to the site. It is worth popping in here, even if you are not staying, to see the old photos & the visiting book (filled with famous, & infamous, names). The same family still runs it today. Unfortunately the front of the building has been redone, but the old rooms are still the same (& have shared bathrooms because of this). The restaurant can provide meals in the evening. It is located on the main road in the centre of the village. €€

OTHER PRACTICALITIES Mykines is primarily a tourist town, with a bit of farming thrown in on the side. You can purchase the basics here and there is an ATM opposite the Belle Helene. During the summer season the car park at the site houses a mobile post office. For all other needs you should head to the towns of Nafplio (ideally) or Argos (if you must).

WHAT TO SEE AND DO
Ancient Mycenae (↝ *27510 76585;* ⊕ *times & entrance fees, see box, page 52*)
As always it is worth exploring this archaeological site as early in the morning as possible, or later in the evening, to beat both the heat and the crowds. The stones, off the wooden walkways, can be slippery, so good shoes are advised, and there is little shade in the site. One last recommendation is a torch, which will allow you to explore the secret cistern (page 74).

Like many ancient sites in the Peloponnese, one of the best things about Mycenae is its setting. Perched on a triangular plateau slung between two mountains, the citadel is an imposing sight, even if the walls tend to blend into the rocks around them. These walls will be your first destination, but spare a glance for the few ruins to the right of the path as you approach them. First up is **Grave Circle B**, which was excavated in the early 1950s. There is not much to see today, but it produced some of the most important finds at Mycenae. It is thought to date from about 1650BC, slightly earlier than its more famous sibling within the walls. The 25 graves within the circle yielded objects of bronze, rock crystal, ivory and gold.

Nearer the walls are two tholos, or beehive, tombs with their distinctive conical roofs. They are rather fancifully named the **Tomb of Clytemnestra** and the **Tomb of Aegisthus**. The first of these is dated later in the Mycenaean period, around 1300BC, because of its sophisticated architecture. The roof was restored in the 1950s and it is possible to go inside; the entrance is on the opposite side to the main path. It is worth noting the Hellenistic theatre that has been built on top of it; one row of seats can still be made out. The next tomb is of an earlier date and its roof remains collapsed. Farther on, back along the main road towards the village, are a line of **merchants' houses** where tablets inscribed in the Mycenaean Linear B script were found (see box, page 226). The houses included one that produced perfumed oils for export.

Most of what remains at Mycenae dates from 1350–1200BC. This includes the **walls** of the citadel, which are still impressive, fully justifying the adjective 'Cyclopean'. They vary from 4m high to over 10m, and can be equally as thick. They are made of lines of gigantic, barely formed blocks of limestone. The corridor leading up to the **Lion Gate** is made of more carefully squared blocks of breccia, giving it a more formalised look. It is easy to see how exposed attackers would have been. The famous gate itself is composed of just four massive pieces of stone. The gateposts are just over 3m high and slope inwards slightly. They are topped by a huge lintel 4.5m long, 1.9m thick and 1m high. It is estimated to weigh anywhere between 12 tons and 20 tons. It in turn supports a triangular stone carved in relief. On it two headless lionesses rest their front paws on a pillar, on top of which is an abacus. To the modern eye it looks like a heraldic symbol and perhaps it was, indeed, the symbol of the city. Look out for holes on the gatepost and lintel that held the original double gate. It also used to be possible to make out the ruts of chariot wheels in the road below, but these have now been covered up. A niche to the left of the gate was perhaps a guard post. The remains of

🚶 MYCENAE TO THE HERAION

(4hrs with time to explore the ruins; easy; café at Monastiraki)
This shortish, circular walk is a lovely way to escape the hustle and bustle that tends to surround Mycenae, and also to get an insight into the rural heart of the Argolid – an aspect of the region that goes unnoticed by the majority of tourists on their coach tours. Part of it is on farm tracks, some on rural back roads, and some on paths. Your only fellow traffic is liable to be the odd tractor. See the walking guide on page 42.

0mins Begin by heading out of Mycenae in the direction of the citadel. Just before the end of the village follow a concrete road that peels off to the right and then, with your back to the building of La Petite Planète, head off straight down a dirt road.

5mins You soon come to a fork in the road. Go left, and at the fork that follows shortly after, go right.

15mins The road turns back to concrete and heads steeply down towards a village.

35mins You reach the sleepy village of Monastiraki (Μοναστηράκι), where there is a kafenion. Start heading straight through the village, but turn left after the church and head out past another church by a graveyard. Where the road forks, shortly after, head straight on, ignoring the road that curls off to the right, and begin climbing gently up.

55mins When the road reaches another church, head round to its left and continue on the dirt road.

1hr 2mins At a crossroads head straight over.

1hr 10mins You reach a junction, with a brown sign pointing straight ahead and a road off to the right. You have three options from here. If you head the building to the right past the gate was probably a two-storey guardhouse, although it has been called a **granary** as jars of wheat were found within.

From here a ramp ran up to the palace above. To the right of it is **Grave Circle A**, the royal tombs that were the site of Schliemann's famous excavations (see box, page 69). The circle consists of two rings of wall with the largest having a diameter of 27m. The gap between the walls was originally filled with rubble and capped with slabs, making one structure, whose entrance faced the Lion Gate. Within were six shaft graves, dug straight into the rock, which were filled with 19 bodies, undoubtedly from the ruling family of the citadel. The wealth and scale of the grave goods, including the famed Mask of Agamemnon, were extraordinary, one of the richest archaeological finds ever made. Much of this is on show in Athens, but the onsite museum now has excellent reproductions of some of the more famous items.

A path leads up the hill from the grave circle, partly done in wooden and metal boardwalk to protect the stones beneath. Where it forks, head right, and this will bring you up to the **royal palace** itself, with stunning views back down over the

straight ahead you will soon see a fence with a gate to the right. If this 'back door' is open you can enter the Heraion here. Otherwise you should head diagonally right through the olive trees before scrambling down into the small gorge and then immediately climbing up the other side. Make your way around the fence (which is somewhat precipitous) to the front of the Heraion. For the safest, but longest, route turn right down the road and follow the directions below.

1hr 15mins After the Heraion has come into view on the left you come to a place where a rough track goes down and crosses the gorge.

1hr 20mins The track leads you to the tarmac road up to the Heraion. Turn left up it.

1hr 25mins You reach the Heraion entrance gate. See the description on page 75.

2hrs 10mins Head back by the same route until you reach the church and graveyard just outside the village of Monastiraki. Head right up a road opposite the church.

2hrs 20mins Just after a shrine on the left-hand side of the road, turn left down a dirt road.

2hrs 25mins At a T-junction turn right and up, but then almost immediately turn left.

2hrs 30mins At another T-junction turn left and down. From here you start to see fantastic views across to the citadel of Mycenae. You quickly come to a final T-junction. Turn right and you are back on the road to the village.

2hrs 35mins You arrive back in Mykines.

fertile plains of the Argolid. The remains of the palace are somewhat sketchy, but you can make out the *megaron*, the room containing the great hearth that was the centre of palace life. The bases to four columns can be seen around it. A nearby room is said to have been a bathroom, perhaps the very place where Clytemnestra murdered Agamemnon – the tour guides will certainly tell you so.

Continuing towards the far end of the citadel you pass the **House of Columns**, perched above the dramatic ravine below. It is easy to see why this structure was so named, although only the bases now remain. It was possibly an eastern wing of the main palace, or perhaps an administrative centre. Continuing to the back wall of the citadel you come across a small gate in the wall, perhaps used as a **sally gate** from which to counterattack a besieging enemy. Tucked into a corner here is Mycenae's most surprising attraction, the **secret cistern**. This announces itself with the usual Mycenaean triangular-topped, rock-hewn doorway. From here stairs descend into the dark and you will need a torch. The entrance is often roped off, but this will not prove much of a hindrance, especially if you have arrived early and no-one is about. A total of 102 steps lead steeply down and under the wall. The engineering of this passageway is extraordinary. It used to be connected to an outside spring, providing a secure water supply, but the bottom of the cistern is dry now, despite what other guidebooks might tell you, although it often can still be slippery. If you brave the descent, the underground atmosphere is delightfully scary, helped along by the occasional scurrying rodent.

A little past the cistern, back towards the front of the citadel, is the **postern gate**, or back door, built at the same time as the Lion Gate. You can leave the citadel here and make your way over to the site **museum**, which tries its best to blend into the local landscape and ancient architecture. All the displays are usefully translated into English, but be warned, it can become very crowded. The entrance hall contains extensive information on both the mythology and the excavation of the site. A room to the right contains many finds, mostly pottery, grouped by the building they were found in. On the lower level finds are displayed in circular showcases, including reproductions of the Schliemann gold objects. There are also displays on post-Mycenaean life on the site.

The Treasury of Atreus
Situated about 500m before Ancient Mycenae, this site is included in the entrance ticket to the main ruins and lies on the west side of the approach road from the modern village.

It can be can be overrun at busy times, but it is astounding, so it is worth persevering – try to wait around for a gap between coach parties, so that you can savour the experience as much as possible.

Misidentified in ancient times by Pausanias, the 'treasury' is in fact a tholos tomb, and almost certainly has nothing to do with Atreus, the legendary father of Agamemnon. More recently, it has been (rather unsuccessfully) renamed the Tomb of Agamemnon, but this is equally speculative. It was certainly a royal tomb of some kind, however, and dates to around 1300BC.

The finest tholos tomb in existence, it is an awe-inspiring sight. The walls of the 35m-long entrance passageway rise up as they cut into the hillside before reaching the monumental gateway. The inner of the two lintel stones here weighs a staggering 120 tons, making it the largest of its kind in the world. This gateway was once richly decorated, surrounded by columns of green limestone. The characteristic 'relieving triangle' above the gateway had a façade finished in *rosso antico*, red marble, that was probably quarried down in the Mani (page 177). Walking through this entrance, look out for the bronze nails that held the ancient door frame and are still in place.

The inside of the tomb is even more spectacular. For over 1,000 years this was the largest domed structure on Earth. It is 13m high, with a diameter of 14.5m. The walls are made of snug-fitting blocks of breccia, all joined without the use of mortar. Each level, or course (there are 33 in all), moves slightly inward to form the curve of the dome – a technique known as corbelling. The overlapping edges were carved away, leaving a smooth finish to the dome. The last hole, at the top, was filled by a single slab, but unlike the keystone in an arch this is unnecessary for the structure's stability. A smaller, cubic, chamber leads off from a door to the right; an unusual feature for a tholos tomb. Outside you can scramble on to the earth-covered roof itself, and get an interesting perspective down to the entrance passage.

Archaeology buffs will want to stop at the small church of Agios Giorgios, on the right as you head back to the village. Tucked away in its cemetery is the burial place (marked by a smallish, white headstone) of **Humfry Payne**, the excavator of Perahora on the other side of the Corinth Canal, director of the British School at Athens, and the first husband of the author Dilys Powell (page 273).

The Argive Heraion (Ηραίον) (⊕ *see box, page 52; free entrance*) If you find the citadel at Mycenae too crowded then the nearby Heraion (temple of the goddess Hera) can provide welcome relief. It is a little-visited site, but that does not mean it is of no interest, and the setting is fantastic. The temple is most famous for a story about it related by Herodotus (see box below).

THE SECRET OF HAPPINESS

One day Croesus, one of the rulers of Asia Minor and reputedly the richest man in the world, received a visit from Solon, the famed Athenian law-giver. Croesus was thrilled at such a prestigious visitor and showed him all possible hospitality. After a few days he showed his guest his vast treasuries, hoping to demonstrate how rich and successful he was. When they were done Croesus turned to Solon, who was well known both for his wide travels and for his wisdom, and asked him who was the happiest man he had ever met. He was hoping, of course, to hear his own name as the answer.

Without pause Solon named an unknown Athenian called Tellus. He had had enough money to be comfortable, fine sons and grandsons, and, after living to see them, had died honourably in battle defending his city.

It was not quite the answer that Croesus had expected, but, missing the point of Solon's answer, he persisted and asked who was next on the list. Surely he would make second place? Solon decided to knock his message home and told the story of two brothers from Argos, Cleobis and Biton. There was a festival to the goddess, celebrated at the Heraion, to which their mother, a priestess, needed to be driven in her ox-cart. Unfortunately the oxen were lost in the fields. With not a moment to lose her two sons hitched themselves to the cart and pulled their mother the 10km to the shrine.

They were universally acclaimed for their act, and in recognition their mother prayed to Hera that they receive the highest 'blessing' available to mortal men. The goddess, knowing that they had reached the high point of their lives, let them die in their sleep.

Croesus still didn't get it, and asked how his own happiness might be judged. Solon, not one to mince his words, gave his terse reply, 'Not until you're dead'.

Without your own car getting to the site can be a little complicated. There are plentiful buses that travel up and down the road from Mycenae to Nafplio, but these leave you with a 2km walk up the steep, and pot-holed, road to the site entrance. As a pleasant alternative you can walk from Mycenae through the rural back roads (see box, page 72).

The remains are not particularly extensive, but the walk up is more than rewarded by the views over the Argive plain. To reach the top of the ridge head straight from the entrance and then curl to the right past a **retaining wall** built of huge blocks that has a definite Mycenaean feel to it. In fact it is believed to be contemporary with the temple that it once supported. The top of the site is a plateau, and it is here that the original **Temple of Hera** stood, built in the 7th century BC. It burnt down in 423BC, according to Pausanias because a priestess called Chryseis fell asleep on the job and her lamp lit the wreaths and garlands that decorated the temple. A **new temple** was erected soon afterwards, and its rectangular floor plan is clearly visible on the terrace below.

The view is well worth contemplating before heading down. The hills of Argos are across the plain directly ahead, while Nafplio and the Gulf of Argolis are to the left.

Just beneath the retaining wall are the remains of the **north stoa**, a kind of colonnaded walkway. It is dated to the 6th century BC, and is one of the earliest examples of this kind of structure. At the lowest level of the site is the **south stoa**, built in the middle of the 5th century BC.

Midea (Μιδέα) (⏱ *see box, page 52; free entrance*) Midea was an impressive Mycenaean citadel in its day (around the 13th century BC), although it seemed to contain several houses rather than a palace complex. Nowadays it is rather forgotten next to its more famous neighbours, but it is still worth a visit and you will likely find yourself alone among its still mighty walls (although on my last visit I stumbled upon a lone Swedish archaeologist carrying on the work begun by his fellow countrymen in the 1920s).

To find the site, look out for the signs on the road from Mycenae down to Nafplio. Carry on through the modern village and look out for the turn up to the acropolis just after it. The remains of the tholos tombs associated with the citadel are down below in the village of Dendra (they are archaeologically important and included many finds now in the Nafplio Archaeological Museum (page 78), as well as buried horses, but there is little to see now).

ARGOS (ΆΡΓΟΣ)

As far as most travellers are concerned, Argos, once the area's most important city, has been easily superseded by its more attractive neighbour, Nafplio. Even if you do end up in Argos, it's extremely easy to move on elsewhere. That said, its museum is worthwhile, there are excellent views from its castle, and the ruins of the ancient city, while not in a pretty spot for once, are impressive.

In case you're wondering, there is a link between the town and the UK's catalogue-based shopping chain: apparently its founder was on holiday here when he came up with the idea for the shop.

HISTORY Once such an important place that Homer could use the word Argive to refer to the Greeks in general, the history of the city is one of gradual decline. Nowadays it is a modest provincial town based on agriculture.

During Classical times the city's story was dominated by its rivalry with Sparta. Argos was one of the first places to adopt hoplites (heavily armed foot soldiers) and

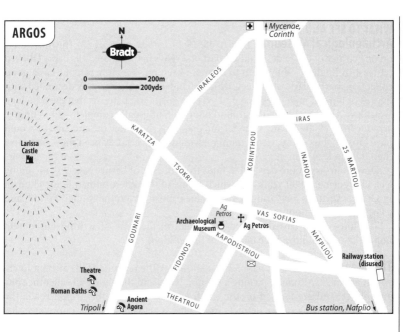

phalanxes (close-ranked infantry with interlocking shields) in its army, and it even managed to defeat mighty Sparta (in 669BC, at Hysiai; page 96), but ultimately lost out to its belligerent neighbour.

During the Persian invasions of Greece the Argives didn't contribute to its defence, a fact they were never allowed to forget. Later domination by the Romans was followed by the sacking of the city, in AD396, by Alaric the Goth. The Middle Ages saw Nafplio begin its rise to ascendancy over its neighbour, and by the 20th century it was little more than a rural village. Latter years have seen a slight return to prosperity as a central market town.

GETTING THERE AND AWAY
By car While there is no ring road, there are complicated, but clearly signed, routes through Argos from all directions. If you want to stop, be warned; parking is often a complete nightmare, both in the centre of town and out by the ancient theatre.

By bus Most buses that you might want to catch run from, or near, the bus station, which is now located to the east of the centre of town, on the main road south of the disused railway station. There are plenty of services running to and from Nafplio, a journey of 20 minutes, and they carry on until quite late, making this your best escape route if you get stuck here. Other services include Tripoli (*frequent; 1hr*), Athens (*2hrs*) and Corinth (*frequent; 50mins*), and Mycenae (*4 or 5 a day; 30mins*). There are also buses heading south down the coast to Astros (*3 a day; 40mins*).

OTHER PRACTICALITIES The centre of Argos is Agios Petros Square, based around the rather gaudy 19th-century church of the same name. It is surrounded by hotels, should you feel the urge to stay, fast-food joints and tavernas, and banks with ATMs. There are also taxi ranks here (✆*27510 67020*).

WHAT TO SEE AND DO

Archaeological Museum (↘*27510 68819; ⊕ see box, page 52; €2*) The museum is on one corner of the pedestrianised part of Argos's main square. It is badly labelled (at least in English – they seem to be more keen on French here), but has a good collection, particularly of pottery, which includes several large pots decorated with figures of horses, men wrestling and various geometric patterns that even include swastikas. Also notable on the ground floor is an unusually complete suit of bronze armour from c900–700BC. A model and diagrams show how the ancient city would have looked; the central, tiered fountain would have certainly been more attractive than the modern church.

Downstairs is a room devoted to finds from the site of Lerna (page 96), including a small figurine, 5,000 years old, which is one of the oldest human figures known in Greece. Upstairs are various larger statues, mostly from the Roman period, and a large, patterned floor mosaic.

The museum is closed for redevelopment at the time of writing but should hopefully reopen during the lifespan of this edition.

The theatre (⊕ *see box, page 52; free entrance*) The remains of the ancient town, which are mostly Roman, include a theatre, baths and the agora, among other bits and pieces, and are located on the south edge of town on the Tripoli road. The dusty, urban setting rather detracts from what is actually a hugely impressive site. The theatre, in particular, once sat 20,000 people, bigger than the one at Epidavros, and in later times the circular orchestra could be flooded in order to recreate naval battles. Those Romans certainly knew how to put on a spectacle.

Larissa Castle (Λάρισα) Visible for miles around, this hilltop castle is arguably the most worthwhile of Argos's attractions, offering some magnificent views. Whether you are on foot or in car, the best way to get there is to follow the narrow but motorable ascent road, and ignore any mention of a footpath.

The road is fairly circuitous. Follow the signs for Corinth and then turn left (brown signs) just before crossing a bridge. Passing some cement factories ignore the first brown sign to the left (to the scarcely visible remains of the

---

ROOF TILES AND ELEPHANTS

In 272BC, Argos was besieged by the famous King Pyrrhus, from northern Greece. Things were going well for him until one of the mothers of the Argive soldiers, obviously completely furious, prised up a roof tile and flung it at the king. Pyrrhus was decapitated.

One of the extraordinary aspects of this siege is that Pyrrhus deployed a battalion of war elephants, brought back from India by the troops of Alexander the Great, around the city. It is a fine image to have in your mind's eye as you stare down from the castle walls.

The king is most famous today in our use of the phrase a 'Pyrrhic victory' to describe a victory won at too great a cost. Pyrrhus had earlier taken his army over to Italy to fight an expanding Rome. He won three battles against them, but lost many troops with each victory. Rome, fighting on home turf, could replenish its legions, but Pyrrhus was eventually forced to return to Greece, his tail between his legs. 'Another such victory,' he is supposed to have commented, 'and we shall be lost'.

Temple of Athena Oxyderkes), but follow the next one, which takes you up to the castle. You will need good shoes to explore properly, and you need to watch your footing in the central keep. Look out for the large, polygonal stonework that dates back to the 6th century BC. Most of the structure is medieval. The views extend over the town towards Nafplio, across towards Mycenae, and down into the Gulf of Argolis.

NAFPLIO (ΝΑΎΠΛΙΟ)

Nafplio is easily the prettiest large town in the Peloponnese, a fact not lost on the nearby Athenians who flock to visit on weekends and holidays – times when you'd be well advised to have a reservation if you want to stay here. It is well worth the effort as Nafplio is a delight, even when thronged with people. Its faded, Neoclassical elegance has been updated over recent years with a layer of trendy chic (even the branch of the Goody's fast-food chain looks like a designer bar) and the shops, cafés and restaurants are up to Athenian standards (often with prices to match). This comes hand in hand with a beautiful setting, with the placid harbour set below two dramatic hilltop castles and lapping the shores of a third island-bound one.

MYTHOLOGY AND HISTORY Legend has it that the town was founded by Nauplios, a son of Poseidon, the sea god. Nauplios's son Palamedes fought in the Trojan War but was unjustly executed by his fellow Greeks for treachery (he had got on the wrong side of wily Odysseus). Before this ignominious end, however, he had been a busy bee and is credited with the invention of dice, navigation, lighthouses, weights and measures, several letters of the alphabet, a forerunner of chess, and, to cap it all, jokes. The higher of the town's two castles is named after him.

During the Classical period the town mostly served as the port of nearby Argos. It really came into its own in medieval times, when it was valued for its excellent harbour by Venetians, Byzantines and others. In 1210, the town was captured by the Frankish leader Geoffrey de Villehardouin, who gave its control to Otho de la Roche, the Duke of Athens. It was bought by the Venetians in 1388, although it was at the time occupied by the Byzantines. They were quickly ousted and Venice reigned supreme for over 150 years, repelling several Ottoman attacks during this period. In 1540, the Turks finally succeeded in capturing Nafplio and made it the capital of their occupation of the Peloponnese. It briefly came under the control of the famous Venetian general Morosini at the end of the 17th century.

During the War of Independence the fortresses of Nafplio were considered one of the most important strongholds of the Peloponnese. The Greeks started a long siege of the town in 1821, but it didn't fall to them until 1822, shortly after Kolokotronis's defeat of the Ottoman army under Dramali (page 67). Ioannis Kapodistrias, the first prime minister of Greece, made the town the seat of government in 1828. He was assassinated here in 1831 by the door of the church of Agios Spiridon (you can still see the bullet hole). The deed was committed by two Maniat brothers of Petrobey Mavromichalis, whom he had imprisoned here. The capital moved to Athens in 1834.

GETTING THERE AND AWAY

By car However you approach Nafplio you will likely be caught up in its one-way system, which has some confusing junctions in it. Take it slowly and keep an eye out for the signs. Your target should be the seafront/harbour where there is free parking. Don't even attempt to drive into the old town. Once you have located

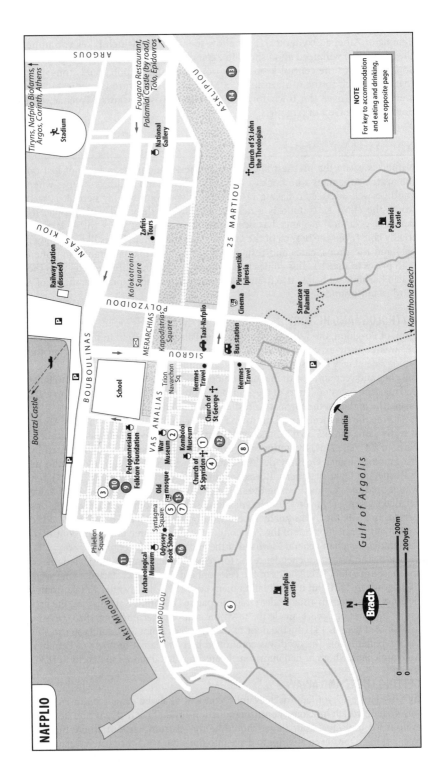

NAFPLIO

Bourtzi Castle

Tiryns, Nafplio Biofarms,
Argos, Corinth, Athens

Fougaro Restaurant,
Palamidi Castle (by road),
Tolo, Epidavros

ARGOUS

Stadium

Railway station
(disused)

NEAS KIOU

National
Gallery

BOUBOULINAS

Zafiris
Tours

25 MARTIOU

Church of St John
the Theologian

Kolokotronis
Square

School

MERARCHIAS

POLYZOIDOU

Pirosvestiki
Ipiresia

Cinema

Akti Miaouli

Philellon
Square

11

Archaeological
Museum

3

10   9

Peloponnesian
Folklore Foundation

VAS. ANALIAS

War
Museum

Komboloi
Museum

Kapodistrias
Square

Taxi-Nafplio

SIGROU

Staircase to
Palamidi

Palamidi
Castle

Syntagma
Square

Odyssey
Book Shop

16

5   7

Old
mosque

13

2

1

4

Church of
St Spyridon

Trion
Navarchon
Sq

Hermes
Travel

Church of
St George

Bus station

STAIKOPOULOU

6

Akronafplia castle

8

12

Hermes Travel

Arvanitia

Gulf of Argolis

Karathona Beach

0   200m
0   200yds

N

Bradt

13

14

ASKLIPIOU

NOTE
For key to accommodation
and eating and drinking,
see opposite page

80

NAFPLIO
For listings, see from below

Where to stay
1 Aetoma
2 Allotino Pension
  Adiandi Boutique Hotel (see 3)
3 Amymone Guesthouse
4 Byron
5 Hotel Athena
6 Nafplia Palace
7 Nafplion 1841
8 Pension Marianna

Where to eat and drink
9 3Sixty
10 Aiolos
11 Antica Gelateria di Roma
12 Kastro-Karima
13 Menta Meze Bar
14 Pidalio Mezedopoleio
15 Ta Fanaria
16 Vassilis

Off map
  Fougaro

where you are staying your hotel should be able to advise you if you can get your car any closer to them.

If you are heading south towards Sparta consider the mountain route detailed on page 119.

By bus There are plenty of buses a day to and from Corinth (*1hr*) and Athens (*2½hrs*), as well as shuttle buses to Argos and other nearby destinations. There are also services to most destinations in the Argolid as well as two a day to Tripoli, where you can connect to most of the rest of the Peloponnese. The bus station is at the end of Syngrou Street, not far from where the steps lead up to the Palamidi fortress.

TOURIST INFORMATION The **tourist office** on 25 Martiou Street is closed at the time of writing, but the municipal website **w** nafplio-tour.gr is full of useful information. **Travel agents**, who can book rental cars and provide other information, are plentiful; try the following:

Hermes Travel Syngrou 18 & Papanikolaou; **** 27520 25308; **m** 69776 06326; **e** cars@ hermestravel.gr; **w** hermestravel.gr

Zafiris Tours 11 Sideras Merarchias; **** 27520 22221; **e** info@zafiris-tours.gr; **w** zafiris-tours.gr

WHERE TO STAY *Map, opposite*
Nafplio has perhaps the largest and best choice of accommodation in the Peloponnese. Options range from basic, concrete-box hotels in the outskirts to luxury villas built within the walls of the Akronafplia, the town's lower fortress. The best places to stay are probably the various boutique hotels that have been built in restored Neoclassical buildings in the old town. Booking is highly recommended, especially for the latter, on all but out-of-season weekdays.

Nafplia Palace (84 rooms) **** 27520 70800; **e** reservations@nafplionhotels.gr; **w** nafpliapalace.gr. Set within the walls of the Akronafplia & approached by foot from a lift through the mountain at the base of the cliffs, this feels a little like staying in a 1970s Bond villain's hideout, but it's the height of luxury, with huge prices to match. Has a mixture of well-appointed rooms & standalone bungalows, all with balcony. **€€€€€**

Aetoma Hotel (8 rooms) Agios Spiridon Sq; **** 27520 27373; **e** stay@aetoma.gr; **w** aetoma.gr. This restored 18th-century Neoclassical mansion has spacious wood-floor rooms individually decorated with handmade

carpets, modern artworks & pastel-shaded walls. Several have views to Palamidi Castle. **€€€€**

Allotino Pension (7 rooms) 19 Vas Konstantinou; **** 27520 96150; **e** info@allotino-pension.gr; **w** allotino-pension.gr. Set above a café in the old town, its tall-ceilinged rooms are all based around different colour schemes & are simple but elegant. **€€€€**

Amymone Guesthouse/Adiandi Boutique Hotel (15 rooms) 31 & 39 Othonos; **** 27520 99477; **m** 69720 84554; **e** info@ amymone.gr, info@hotel-adiandi.com; **w** amymone.gr, hotel-adiandi.com. Owned by the same people & situated just down the road from each other, this chic pair of hotels shares a lovely location in the old town, just back from the seafront, & feature wooden flooring, antique furniture & quirky artwork. €€€€

🏠 **Hotel Athena** (14 rooms) Staikopoulou 11; 📞 27520 47200; e info@hotelathenanafplio.gr; w hotelathenanafplio.gr. Following extensive renovations in 2015, this medium-rise hotel is one of the best options in the old town. All the stylishly decorated rooms have private balconies overlooking Syntagma Sq. Excellent b/fast. €€€€

✳ 🏠 **Pension Marianna** (25 rooms) 9 Potamianou; 📞 27520 24256; e info@hotelmarianna.gr; w hotelmarianna.gr. Set on a slope just below the fortified wall of the Akronafplia, this guesthouse is solidly built in stone, but this is softened by sunshine colours & a warm heart. The friendly Zotos brothers, who own & manage it, also run several farms & serve their own products, many of them organic, in a hearty b/fast. Several of the rooms have great views. A superb terrace overlooks the bay &

faces directly towards Palamidi Castle, offering stunning views of its walls when they are lit up at night. €€€€

🏠 **Byron Hotel** (18 rooms) 2 Platanos; 📞 27520 22351; e byronhotel@otenet.gr; w byronhotel.gr. The Byron, a restored mansion house on several levels, led the charge in new, boutique hotels in Nafplio & it is still among the nicest (& most reasonably priced). Its position, up a steep lane, means it stays quiet. B/fast is served on a pleasant roof terrace. €€€

🏠 **Nafplion 1841** (6 rooms) 9 Ioanni Kapodistriou 9; 📞 27520 24622; e info@nafplion1841.gr; w nafplion1841.gr. Named after the year in which it was constructed, this friendly family-run traditional pension has a great location a block from Syntagma Sq & attractive restored rooms with wooden ceilings & floors. Great value in a town where accommodation tends to be on the pricey side. €€

🍴 WHERE TO EAT AND DRINK *Map, page 80*

You are not short of options in Nafplio; indeed there must be more than 100 restaurants, tavernas and other eateries dotted around town, and part of the fun is choosing where you think looks the nicest. It is one of the few places in the Peloponnese where you will be pestered by that scourge of the islands, the restaurant tout. Don't expect to quietly examine a menu without a waiter pouncing on you to extol the virtues of his kitchen. It's mostly done with a smile, however, and is all part of the bustle of the town. There are two main streets to check out in the old town: Bouboulinas, on the waterfront, is a long string of tavernas, the majority of which specialise in fish; Staikopoulou is just off the south side of the main Syntagma Square. It is allegedly pedestrianised, although the odd car still seems to make its way down, and the tables of the cheek-by-jowl tavernas spill out on to the street. Come the evening both streets are a buzz of activity. A cluster of newer and generally more affordable tavernas can be found along 25 Martiou about 200m east of the old town.

Old town centre

🍴 **3Sixty** Cnr Koletti & Papanikolaou; 📞 27520 28068; w 3sixty.life. This funky grill & wine bar, set in a Neoclassical late 19th-century building, offers the finest dining in the old town centre. Emphasis is on aged purebred steaks, but the succinct menu also includes great burgers, lobster (for 2) & other meat- & fish-based dishes. A long wine list focuses exclusively on local vineyards.

🍴 **Aiolos** 30 Vas Olgas; 📞 27520 26828. A nicely done-up, homely, taverna just back from the seafront, with some excellent food – trust the waiter's advice.

🍴 **Antica Gelateria di Roma** 3 Farmakopoulon; 📞 27520 23520. The most established & probably best of Nafplio's increasing number of gelato and frozen yoghurt shops, this stands to the northwest of Syntagma Sq, just before the sea.

🍴 **Kastro-Karima** Papanikolaou 32; 📞 27520 25279; f KastroKarima. Tucked away along a quiet alley below Pension Marianna, this small restaurant is characterised by warm décor & service, & a menu dominated by traditional Greek fare. Excellent lamb. Vegetarians are unusually well catered for.

✕ Ta Fanaria 13 Staikopoulou; ✆27520 27141; w fanaria.gr. Specialising in seafood & traditional casseroles, this old favourite among the string of tavernas on Staikopoulou spills out on to a bougainvillea-covered alleyway just behind the mosque/cinema on Syntagma Sq.

✕ Vassilis 22–24 Staikopoulou; ✆27520 25334; w tavernvasilis.gr. One of the better bets on this busy street. Have a look in the kitchen to see what's good – the lamb is reliable & the beetroot salad is tasty.

New town

✕ Fougaro 3km along the Tolo Rd; ✆27520 47347; w fougaro.gr. Named after the tall narrow brick chimney that dominates its skyline, this converted cannery doubles as a café, art gallery & market. The food – mostly light snacks – doesn't quite match the attractive ambience, but it's an ideal out-of-town lunch spot for families with children.

✕ Menta Meze Bar 25 Martiou 9; ✆27520 23603. Situated next door to the more established Pidalio, away from the hustle & bustle of the old town, this well-priced restaurant offers a varied selection of meze & mains in a subdued classic contemporary setting. The speciality is a 1kg rump steak (enough for 2 or 3 to share) at €18. Terrace seating available.

✕ Pidalio Mezedopoleio 25 Martiou 5; ✆27520 22603; w pidalio.gr. The varied selection of Greek meze & grilled seafood at this popular restaurant is supplemented by pastas, curries & a few French dishes. Terrace seating & good service.

NIGHTLIFE This goes on to the early hours and is based around the bars and cafés between Syntagma Square and the waterfront Akti Miaouli, who try to outdo each other with trendy artworks and design – it's great fun simply to walk past and people watch. If you want something more upbeat, head towards the road round the bay on the way to Nea Kios (taxi necessary) where there are a string of ever-changing nightclubs, offering either live performers doing Greek music, or 'Western' club music to dance to. Don't expect anything to get going until two in the morning, or even later/earlier.

OTHER PRACTICALITIES Taxis congregate around the squares that line Syngrou Street – if you need to book one, try Taxi-Nafplio (✆69814 02003). The post office is at the harbour end of the same street, where there is also a large supermarket. The hospital is not too far along the main road from the old town towards Epidavros (✆27523 61100). Banks and ATMs are plentiful and include a National Bank on Syntagma Square in the centre of the old town.

Odyssey Bookshop, on Syntagma Square, has a good English-language selection, including maps, newspapers, magazines, novels and guidebooks and other titles relating to Greek life and culture, and maps.

Children tend to enjoy Nafplio, with its harbour and many pedestrianised streets. There is also a good playground in the park below the steps to the Palamidi Castle, as well as at Fougaro (see above). The best place, however, is the marble flagstones of Syntagma Square itself, where great crowds of kids of all ages gather to play games in the early evening while their parents sip coffee.

WHAT TO SEE AND DO The heart of Nafplio is the harbourfront, faced by the small citadel of Bourtzi on its little island, and the old town behind it, which is centred on Syntagma Square and is mainly pedestrianised. The two main castles rise above this.

The old town and the waterfront
One of the best things to do in Nafplio is simply to wander the streets and alleys of the old town, many of them no more than narrow stairways. This is centred on the large, marble-paved **Syntagma Square**, ringed with cafés. At one end is the old town **Arsenal**, a handsome building that now houses a museum (page 84). At the other end is an old **mosque**, which now occasionally serves as a cinema. The surrounding streets are lined either with

tavernas or shops; shopping is a serious business here, with designer names mixing with local artists and crafts.

The waterfront has lovely views over to **Bourtzi Castle** (see below). The main harbour road, **Bouboulinas**, is named after Laskarina Bouboulinas, the famous female sea captain from the War of Independence, and there is a statue of her at its east end.

The castle of **Akronafplia** (⊕ *always*) looms over the old town. There have been fortifications here going back at least to Classical times. Now it is the preserve of the Nafplia Palace hotel (page 81), who try their best to discourage outsiders from disturbing their exclusive guests. Fortunately there's not much to see, anyway. If you don't feel like walking up, a free lift connects the central waterfront to the fortifications around the Nafplia Palace hotel.

Museums and galleries

Nafplio contains a surprisingly large collection of museums to explore, by far the most important of which is the **Archaeological Museum** (✆ 27520 27502; ⊕ *times & entrance fees, see box, page 52*). Located in the beautiful old Venetian Arsenal building on Syntagma Square, this museum houses one of the best collections in the Peloponnese, all attractively displayed with English signs. It contains finds from all over the surrounding area, focusing particularly on the Mycenaean period. Highlights include beautiful floor panels and fresco fragments from Tiryns, and a near-complete, 3,500-year-old suit of armour with accompanying helmet made of boar's tusks.

A showcase for the eponymous private foundation, the **Peloponnesian Folklore Foundation Museum** (*Vas Alexandrou 1;* ✆ 27520 28947; w *pli.gr;* ⊕ *09.00–14.30 Mon–Sat, 09.30–15.00 Sun; €2, €4 for a tour*) is also well worth the visit. It hosts a huge collection of costumes and household and agricultural implements from all over Greece, not all of which can be displayed, even in this large building. The accompanying shop is a good place to get high-quality local crafts.

Affiliated to its namesake in Athens, the **War Museum** (*22 Amalias;* ✆ 27520 25591; ⊕ *09.00–14.00 Tue–Fri, 10.00–14.00 Sat & Sun; free entrance*) is housed in an impressive stone four-storey building constructed as the first War Academy of Greece by Prime Minister Kapodistrias, c1830. It displays a good collection of uniforms and armoury, as well as some interesting historical photos.

Sometimes referred to as the art museum, the **National Gallery of Nafplio** (*Sidiras Merarchias 23;* ✆ 27520 21915; ⊕ *10.00–15.00 Mon & Wed–Sat, 17.00–20.00 Wed & Fri, 10.00–14.00 Sun, closed Tue; €2, free on Mon*) is housed in a handsome Neoclassical building a short walk east of the old town centre. An annex of the same institution in Athens, it houses a superb collection of art associated with the War of Independence of 1821.

Shops selling Greek worry beads, or *komboloi* (these are related to rosaries, but do not have a religious meaning in Greece), seem to be breeding like rabbits on the streets of Nafplio over the last few years. The ancestor to them all also houses the **Komboloi Museum** (*25 Staikopoulou;* ✆ 27520 21618; w *komboloi.gr;* ⊕ *09.30–20.30 Wed–Mon; €2*).

Bourtzi Castle (Μπούρτζι)

The most striking feature of Nafplio harbour front is the mini castle of Bourtzi, which occupies the entirety of a small island about 500m offshore. Formerly the site of a Byzantine church dedicated to Agios Theodoros, Bourtzi started life as a watchtower built by the Venetians in 1473, and was expanded to become a hexagonal castle under the supervision of the Italian architect Antonio Gambello. More recently, it provided sanctuary to the Greek government during a rebellion in 1826 and was used as a fort until 1865. It subsequently served as an executioner's home (it kept its unpopular inhabitant safe from vengeance) and was converted to a hotel in 1935. Recently restored following a long period of abandonment, Bourtzi is earmarked to reopen as a museum in the near future. Until that happens, cruises offering a close-up view of the castle exterior run from the harbour in summer and cost €4 per person.

Palamidi Castle (Παλαμήδι) (⏰ 08.00–19.00 daily; €8) There are two ways up to the fortress (built by the Venetians, 1711–14) that towers 200m above Nafplio. The more traditional is to take the stepped path that leads from near the reconstructed town gate at the end of Polyzoidou Street. Be warned, however, that this is quite a steep climb. The number of steps varies, depending on who you ask, from the accurate-sounding 857, through the somewhat dubious 999, to the frankly alarming 'thousands' (I have been recently contacted and told that the 'correct' count is 913 – take your pick!). Whatever the truth, it is not an ascent to be taken lightly; you're best off attempting it first thing in the morning when, for a brief period, the steps are in shade. The alternative is to take 25 Martiou Street out of town, where a circuitous, signposted route leads up to the Palamidi. A good compromise would be to take a taxi up, and then walk down the steps.

The fortress is well worth the effort and has some great views of the town and surrounding countryside. It is a large and somewhat confusing construction, which actually consists of several interconnecting, but independent, fortifications. The paths through are well laid out, and signposted with modern names for each section of the castle, and there is a welcome amount of shade, which is so often lacking in Greek castle ruins.

The ruins are worth exploring, and repay any effort you put into them, being full of surprises and hidden corners (or entire wings). If you are short of time the best idea is to follow the signs towards 'Kolokotronis's Cell', which is in the central keep of the castle. The hero of the War of Independence was imprisoned here during inter-Greek squabbling. It would have been a difficult time: the dank, windowless room, in a castle he himself had liberated only a few years before, must have strained to contain his ego. Above the cell, reached by a long ramp or a staircase, are the fortress's highest ramparts, from where you can gain an overview of the whole structure and plan which other corners you would like to visit.

Arvanitia and Karathona beaches The best place to swim in the immediate vicinity of Nafplio, pretty **Arvanitia Beach** arcs around the southeast corner of the same headland occupied by the old town. Providing welcome relief after a hot day of shopping, you can swim off the small stretch of pebbles, or use the platforms in front of the café. The easiest way to get to Arvanitia is to walk or drive south for 200m along the steepish road that runs past the base of the steps to Palamidi Castle. A more scenic walk follows a 1km-long vehicle-width track from the west end of the harbour around the uninhabited western and southern cliff base of the peninsula.

The larger, sandier and more attractive out-of-town **Karathona Beach** is known for its reliable winds, and windsurfing and parasurfing equipment can be hired there. If you don't mind a bit of a walk, the nicest way to reach it is along the dramatic 3km-long vehicle-width-track footpath that continues southeast from the car park at Arvanitia Beach. Alternatively, with your own vehicle, you could drive there along the same extension of 25 Martiou Street that leads to Palamidi, continuing past the junction for the castle itself.

The above-mentioned footpath from Nafplio harbour to Arvanitia and on to Karathona is nicknamed Dromos Discardius ('Road of the Heart'), a dual reference to its popularity with young lovers and the belief that walking along it will extend the life of anybody with heart issues. Either way, it makes for a lovely gentle stroll, roughly 4km in either direction, and is also very popular with local runners.

Nafplio Biofarms (📞 *27520 91087;* **m** *69715 04162;* **e** *nafpliobiofarms@gmail. com;* **w** *nafpliobiofarms.gr*) Operated by the same friendly brothers who own and manage Pension Marianna, this organic farm near Nea Tiryntha, 2km north of Nafplio, produces a range of typical Greek produce including oranges, lemons and olives. Guided tours of the farm provide a fascinating insight into traditional and modern farming methods, and it also arranges a wide variety of cookery lessons, culminating in a tasty lunch or dinner. Prices are in the range of €12–25 per person.

Tiryns (Τίρυνς) (🕐 & *entrance fees, see box, page 52*) Tiryns, noted by everyone from Homer onward for its amazing walls, is another **Mycenaean fortified palace**, dating from the 14th or 13th century BC. Indeed, Pausanias said that Tiryns was 'no less marvellous' than the Pyramids, which is stretching it a bit, but does give you some idea of how impressive a place it is. It probably once stood by the sea, and may well have acted as the port to Mycenae itself. Now it is in the outskirts of Nafplio, about 3km out of town. Head out on the road towards Argos and you will see the famed walls to your right (this is perhaps the best view of the citadel). Just after them turn right on the lane towards Mycenae, and immediately right again into the site's new entrance and car park.

Unfortunately large sections of the palace are currently closed owing to earthquake damage, including the vaulted passages and the secret stair, which were both highlights of the site. There is no indication as to when these might be open again, but don't be put off; the site is still well worth a visit. What you can see, on the top of the site, is rather confused, but does allow you to at least look into one of the **vaulted passages**, and it is also well worth strolling as far as you are allowed around the amazing **walls**. It is easy to see why the Greeks called them Cyclopean – only those one-eyed giants could have built such immense structures.

TOLO (ΤΟΛΌ)

Situated just 10km southeast of Nafplio, Tolo is a laid-back beach resort town whose high street is decorated with tubs of flowers donated by the British tour operator Sunvil, which has a strong presence here. Tolo lacks the dramatic setting of Nafplio and the visible sense of history that permeates its old town, but it is a pretty enough place, and better suited to those seeking a conventional beach resort. Tolo is conveniently situated for Nafplio, Mycenae, Epidavros and Nemea, while the site of Ancient Asini is just a few hundred metres to the northeast.

WHERE TO STAY

Tolo is serviced by dozens of small hotels and self-catering apartment complexes. Most of these are situated on or close to the high street, the best choices being those that offer direct beach frontage.

Hotel Tolo (64 rooms) 15 Bouboulinas; 📞27520 59248; **e** skaladis@hoteltolo.gr; **w** hoteltolo.gr. This well-run & perennially popular 4-storey beachfront hotel has bright, clean rooms with all mod cons, including a king-size bed & superb views over the harbour to the islands – it's worth forking out the slight extra for a seafront with balcony. Junior suites are in an annex set back from the inland side of the high street. **€€€** (main building) or **€€€€€** (annex)

✳ 🏠 **Nelly's Hotel Apartments** (17 rooms)
29 Bouboulinas; 🕿 27520 59212; m 69470 01302;
e info@nellys.gr; w nellys.gr. This family-run
apartment complex is difficult to flaw – great
beachfront location, good amenities, attractive
bright décor, wallet-friendly rates & the excellent
Nelly's Café situated on the ground floor. €€

🏠 **Xeni Camp & Bungalows** Asini Beach;
🕿 27520 59338; m 69340 14425; e info@xeni.gr;
w xeni.gr. Boasting an attractive & historic location on
the beach abutting Ancient Asini about 1km northeast
of town, this friendly set-up backed by olive groves
has a mini market, bar, taverna & even the remains of
some Mycenaean tombs hidden behind it. €

🍴 WHERE TO EAT AND DRINK

Several dozen tavernas and other restaurants line the high street through Tolo and
you could easily spend a week in the town without eating at the same place twice.

🍴 **Maria's Restaurant** 48 Bouboulinas;
🕿 27520 59198; w marias-restaurant.gr. This
long-serving Tolo favourite, now managed by
the daughters of its namesake founder, offers the
choice of relatively formal indoor dining on the
inland side of the high street or a semi-outdoor
setting in a plastic shielded annex overlooking
the beach. Traditional Greek fare is the speciality,
with an emphasis on seafood, but the unusually
cosmopolitan menu also embraces the likes of
curries & pasta dishes.

WHAT TO SEE AND DO

The beach and waterfront Tolo's sandy beach, which runs parallel to the high
street, and is separated from it by a row of hotels, shops, tavernas and self-catering
apartments, is long and narrow, but it widens at the northeast end. In season, the
narrower part of the beach can get crowded, but the entire bay is very well sheltered,
and the sea is particularly inviting in the early morning – a before-breakfast swim is
recommended. The setting is beautiful, with two islands in the bay providing a target
for strong swimmers and kayakers. These are tiny Koronisi Island, which houses an
old church dedicated to Petros and Paulos, and the much larger and more sloping
Romvi Island. There's also a nearby fish farm where large pods of dolphins hang out.

Ancient Asini (🕓 *see box, page 52; free entrance*) Straddling the small but steep
Paliokastro Peninsula at the northeast end of Tolo village, Ancient Asini has been
inhabited since the 3rd millennium BC. Name-checked as Asine in the ancient
writings of Homer, Ptolemy and Pausanias, the port served as a thriving Aegean trade
entrepôt for about 2,000 years prior to being destroyed by the rival army from Argos
c700BC, when its inhabitants relocated to what is now Messinia. It was revived c300BC
under Demetrius I of Macedonia, who most likely established the first fort there, and
was inhabited on-and-off for the next two millennia prior to the construction of the
present-day fortress by the Venetians during the second occupation.

The ruins today are rather modest but easily explored along a good network of
footpaths adorned with interpretative panels in Greek and English. They comprise a
Mycenaean lower town that thrived in the 12th century BC, as well as some castle walls
that date to the Venetian period. The most famous item unearthed in the lower village
is a stunning Mycenaean gold burial mask, dubbed the King of Asini in reference to
Homer's *Iliad*, and now housed in the architectural museum in Nafplio.

More contemporarily, an interesting on-site photographic display is dedicated
to the modernist poet and diplomat Giorgios Seferis, who won the Nobel Prize for
Literature in 1963, and whose melancholy Homeric poem *The King of Asine* was
written in the aftermath of a visit to Tolo in 1938. Another unusual display, set in a cave
that was dynamited into being by the Italians as a refuge during aerial bombardments
during World War II, details the history of the Argolid resistance in Tolo and Nafplio.

EPIDAVROS (ΕΠΊΔΑΥΡΟΣ)

Epidavros is most famous for its theatre, one of the best surviving buildings from the Classical period. The theatre, and its surrounding sanctuary, are actually a little bit inland from the ancient city, as are the two modern settlements that bear its name. It can be a bit confusing, so make sure you know which one you are heading for. **Nea Epidavros** (New Epidavros) is the more modern, and is split into two bits: one section on the coast and another above it in the hills. Some 8km to the south, and also on the coast, is **Archea Epidavros** (Old or Ancient Epidavros) where the ruins of the old city can be found (mostly beneath the sea). To round things off, Archea Epidavros is often referred to as **Paleo Epidavros** (which also confusingly translates as Ancient Epidavros). The **theatre and sanctuary** are separate from either of these and are 10km inland.

MYTHOLOGY AND HISTORY The sanctuary at Epidavros was dedicated to Asklepius, god of medicine and healing, and its history is bound up with the mythology that surrounds him. His father was the god Apollo, and his mother Coronis, a mortal. While she was still pregnant she had an affair and Apollo, in his rage, sent his sister, Artemis, to kill her. As she burned on the funeral pyre Apollo, or some say Hermes, saved her child and gave him to the centaur Chiron to raise.

Chiron taught Asklepius the arts of healing, and he became so proficient in them that he could even raise the dead. This angered Hades, king of the underworld, and he complained to his brother Zeus, who killed Asklepius with one of his famed thunderbolts. This, in turn, angered Apollo and he killed the Cyclopes who manufactured Zeus's thunderbolts. This was a step too far, and Apollo was sentenced to a year of hard labour. Wisely he accepted his punishment, and Zeus deified Asklepius in recognition of his good deeds.

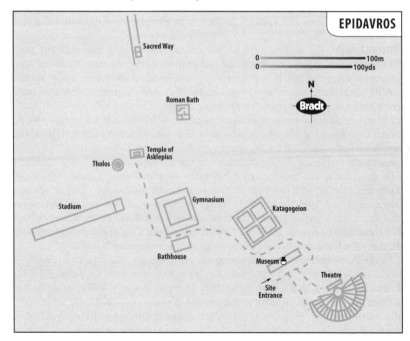

Asklepius was commonly depicted as a bearded man with a staff. A single serpent wraps itself around the staff – a symbol of doctors from Classical times to the present day. How this symbolism came about is not known for certain, but there is interesting speculation that it is related to a parasite called a guinea worm, which would have been common in historical times. These are the thickness of spaghetti, but can grow to almost a metre long, and were removed from the body by slowly wrapping them around a stick.

Asklepius was worshipped at various sanctuaries, the two most famous being Epidavros and Kos, where Hippocrates, the father of medicine, is said to have worked. People came to them to be healed, but they also developed into social centres, with athletic contests and theatres.

GETTING THERE AND AWAY

By car There are two main approaches to Epidavros. Coming from Nafplio you take the road through the centre of the Argolid past Ligourio (Λυγουριό). On the way, near the village of Arkadiko (Αρκαδικό), are the remains of a **Mycenaean bridge**, consisting of Cyclopean stones, and a **tholos tomb**. The area is now noted for the manufacture of old-fashioned smoking pipes, and there are several places where these can be purchased.

In Ligourio itself there is a small but well-presented **Natural History Museum** (✆ 27530 22587; ⏰ 10.00–16.00 Tue–Sun; €2). The collection of minerals and fossils includes 240-million-year-old ammonites found at the nearby sanctuary to Asklepius. Be warned that the museum is sometimes closed owing to lack of staff, particularly in the low season.

Coming from the north, the road skirts a stretch of coast with several small resorts on it, mainly used by weekending Athenians. The route is a scenic one, and is surrounded by pine trees in many places. A couple of kilometres before you reach Nea Epidavros look out for the **Agnoundos Monastery** on the left. Its 11th-century church is set in a beautiful courtyard and contains excellent frescoes.

By bus There are five buses a day from Nafplio to the site of the theatre and sanctuary, a couple of which carry on to Archea and Nea Epidavros (*40mins–1hr*). The latter two are also served by two buses a day that come down the coastal route from Corinth (*1hr*). During the festival (page 91) there are also special buses that run to and from the theatre before and after performances from both Nafplio and Athens.

WHERE TO STAY AND EAT
Ligourio has a few basic hotels, but unless you're desperate to be right beside the ruins it is far more pleasant to stay by the coast, particularly in the village of Archea Epidavros.

Note that on festival nights at the ancient theatre, rooms can be hard to come by. You can camp in the large car park at the site itself, as long as you don't pitch a tent until after the performance has ended. This is not allowed on other nights of the year.

🏠 **Hotel Heleni** (19 apts) ✆ 27530 41864; m 69743 96636; e helenioe@otenet.gr; w helenihotel.gr. The small road that runs south of Archea Epidavros through the orange groves is lined with holiday apartments & campsites, many of them looking on to the various sand & pebble beaches. One of the most attractive is the Heleni, with its handsome garden & warm family welcome.

Eleni, the matriarch of the house, can provide home-cooked meals in the evenings. €€€€€
🏠 **Hotel Poseidon** (11 rooms) ✆ 27530 41211; m 69466 67064; e pitsaaff@otenet.gr; w hotelposidon.com. Rubbing shoulders with Mike's on the pretty harbour front of Archea Epidavros, this homely hotel has very comfortable rooms with a balcony & sea or mountain view, &

an excellent seafood-oriented restaurant that spills out on to the cobbled harbour. €€€

🏠 **Mouria** ↘27530 41218; e info@mouria.gr; w mouria.gr. Just to the south of town & next to the thin but pleasant beach, this recently renovated complex – also known as Gikas Holidays Club – offers rooms & studios, as well as a good restaurant & a trendy café. €€€

🏠 **Hotel Mike** (15 rooms) ↘27530 41213; e hotelmaik@yahoo.gr; w mike-epidavros.com.

The more budget-friendly options are centred on the little port in the village itself, including the Mike (or 'Maik'), which has rooms with balconies overlooking the Saronic Gulf. The attached taverna offers fish from the daily catch. €€

⛺ **Camping Nicolas** ↘27530 41297; e info@mouria.gr; w mouria.gr/en/nicolas-i or mouria.gr/en/nicolas-ii. Next door to (& owned by) the Mouria are 2 sites under this name. Both are set in orange groves & lead directly on to the beach. €

OTHER PRACTICALITIES A café and drinks stands can be found at the site of the theatre. Archea Epidavros has plenty of restaurants and **shops,** as well as **banks,** **ATMs** and **taxis** (↘*27530 41723*), all based around its tiny harbour.

WHAT TO SEE AND DO
The Theatre and Sanctuary of Asklepius (↘*27530 22009*; ⊕ *& entrance fees, see box, page 52*) From the large car park at the site follow the wide path that passes by the café. After you pass the ticket office, the long, thin building to the left is the museum, but you will probably want to head straight for the **theatre**, which is up to the right.

> [W]ho can begin to rival Polykleitos for the beauty and composition of his architecture?

The theatre is as impressive today as it was in Pausanias's day when he complimented its supposed architect. It is a masterpiece of harmonious and technically clever design. Along with the Parthenon itself, it probably stands as one of the major symbols of all that is admirable in Classical Greek art and science. Most famously it has incredible acoustics. Drop a coin or rustle up a ball of paper in the middle of the circle at the centre of the theatre and the noise can be heard clearly from any of the seats, right up to the last tier (it is worth pointing out that this was not the stage in ancient times, the foundations of which are just behind it). Sit here for long enough and an obliging tour guide will demonstrate the acoustics for you, and it is also not unusual for impromptu concerts to take place: Greek schoolchildren doing the national anthem or amateur opera singers belting out a quick aria. The theatre really comes into its own, however, during the annual festival where it is used for its original purpose (page 91).

Many tour groups come and see the theatre and leave straight afterwards, ignoring the rest of the sanctuary entirely. This is a shame as it has much to offer, particularly as the careful work of restoring its monuments continues. It is easy to see why the Greeks built a sanctuary of healing here. The setting is lovely, and the ruins still exude an air of peace, especially after the crowds that normally throng the theatre have left.

The **museum** is a thin building full of various bits of statuary and some interesting medical instruments. Once rather cluttered, it now seems very well organised and the signage is quite informative.

Turning left out of the museum you ascend a staircase towards the rest of the sanctuary. The first ruin you come to, a large, square structure, is called the **Katagogeion** and served as a hotel. The main path then leads past a **bathhouse** on the left and the confusing ruins of the **gymnasium** on the right. In fact this building was more likely a banqueting hall, but it is hard to interpret as the Romans built on top of it.

Close by are the **restoration workshops** where the work of matching bright white, new marble to its old counterparts is undertaken by extremely talented workmen. If you are lucky you will be able to watch some of them on the job. Behind and below the workshops are the remains of the **stadium**.

Past the workshops are a group of buildings that have undergone major restoration. The first of these, on the left, is the **Tholos**, a peculiar round structure whose function is rather obscure. Its foundations comprised six concentric walls, the central three of which consisted of a miniature labyrinth. Above this was a floor of black-and-white marble tiles in a spiral pattern, and the whole building was surrounded by two rings of columns: 14 Corinthian ones in an inner circle, surrounded by 26 Doric. The most interesting of the various theories as to the Tholos's usage was that the labyrinth formed a snake pit, the sacred animal of Asklepius, into which patients entered for a kind of 'shock treatment'. Presumably they quickly got better lest they had to repeat the process.

To the right of the Tholos is the **Temple of Asklepius**, the centre of the god's worship. Its columns – it was originally 6 × 11 – are slowly being restored. The surrounding buildings, built in various stages, comprise the **Abaton**, where patients would sleep, hoping for a visitation by the god in their dreams. Many tablets were found here telling of miraculous cures.

Beyond these buildings, at the edge of the site, you come to the entrance gate of the **Sacred Way** that led to the city of Epidavros on the coast. Shaded by the trees, this would be the perfect spot for a picnic, although this is not strictly allowed. Notice the modern towers topped with water cannons, a protection against forest fires. Heading back into the site bear to the left. The building with tilework and a channel leading into it was a **Roman bath**. You will pass the gymnasium on its opposite side before coming back to the path towards the museum and the site entrance.

It's worth getting here soon after it opens or just before closing time. In between, the hordes of people intent on taking selfies rather spoils the atmosphere.

The Hellenic Festival (✆ *21092 82900;* w *greekfestival.gr; tickets start at under €20*) During July and August there are weekend performances at the main theatre by Greek and foreign theatre companies. The repertoire has been broadening in recent years, but the main draw is still the **Classical plays** (done in Modern Greek). Although you may not understand a word there is nothing to compare with the atmosphere of sitting in this ancient theatre, watching the sun dip behind the hills, before the lights come up and you watch the same dramas enacted that were first performed here more than 2,000 years before. It is all but mandatory to book in advance as, although the theatre is huge, parts are currently closed off for renovation, and seats are often booked up months in advance. In the cheaper seats you will be sitting on the bare stone so a cushion, if you can come by one, is a good idea. There are also performances at the small theatre in Archea Epidavros.

Archea Epidavros The modern village of 'ancient' Epidavros is extremely pleasant, with its little harbour and small beaches to the south. Evidence of the ancient city is slightly harder to come by. The **Theatre of Dionysus**, at the southern end of the village, is a small cousin to the more famous theatre inland, but to see any more remains you really need to get in the water. This is best achieved with **Epidive** (✆ *27530 41236;* m *69765 09563;* e *epidive.plongee@gmail.com;* w *epidive.net*) who can take you out **snorkelling** to see some of the ancient ruins that lie just below the surface of the water, including old walls and amphorae (*€40*). They also can take you out **scuba diving**, even if you are a complete beginner – a first-time dive costs €60. Their offices are by the village's small harbour.

South of Epidavros and east of Nafplio lies the 'thumb' of the Peloponnese, sticking out into the sea towards the various islands of the Saronic Gulf. In fact the main reason for visiting this area is often to travel to or from the islands. The coast itself, while often dramatic, can be overdeveloped.

For the adventurous, however, there is much of interest. This is especially true for lovers of geology – the area boasts volcanoes, sinkholes, prehistoric caves and a dramatic chasm full of rock pools. For the myth-hunters there are the remains of Troezen, birthplace of Theseus, the slayer of the Minotaur.

GETTING THERE AND AWAY Having your own transport is by far the most practical way to explore the southeast of the Argolid. While buses do run to the various resorts/port towns, there are usually only two or three a day. The local village buses could then take you on to most of the sights, but these mostly run first thing in the morning, making exploring a time-consuming exercise. With a car you could see much of what is on offer in a day trip.

As stated above the most common reason for visiting this area is to catch boats to the various Saronic islands. **Poros** (Πόρος) is reached by water taxi from **Galatas** (Γαλατάς), which is only a few hundred metres away. They scoot backwards and forwards several times an hour and currently cost less than €1 each way. In the summer the islands of **Egina** (Αίγινα), **Hydra** (Εδρα) and **Spetses** (Σπέτσες) are currently linked to the Peloponnesian ports of **Methana** (Μέθανα), **Ermioni** (Ερμιόνη) and **Porto Cheli** (Πορτοχέλι) by catamarans and hydrofoils run by Hellenic Seaways (w *hellenicseaways.gr*) – see website for schedules and booking. There are several sailings a day. These services also link with **Piraeus** (Πειραιώς), the port of Athens. Conventional ferries used to do these routes all year round, but do not appear to be running at present. These details are always subject to change, and no-one ever seems to know what is happening from one year to the next. As well as the above website it might be worth contacting some local agents: try **Kollias Travel** (✆ *22980 92580*) in Methana, **Fun in the Sun** (✆ *27540 31514;* w *ermionifuninthesun.com*) in Ermioni, or **Hellenic Vision Travel** (✆ *27540 51444*) in Porto Cheli. Unsurprisingly all of these have their offices by the various ports.

WHERE TO STAY AND EAT If you are just passing through to see the sights there is little reason to stay in the area. All the main towns have a range of fairly uninspiring and generally overpriced hotels.

The same rule applies to eating. The towns on the coast often feel like suburbs of Athens, and the various restaurants have prices to match. If you are doing the area as a day trip you might be best to pack a picnic; there are plenty of places inland that would make idyllic spots.

There are two possible exceptions to the above. One is the pretty little fishing village of **Vathy** (Βαθύ) on the east coast of the Methana Peninsula, where there are a couple of good fish tavernas, and a few people offering simple rooms if you ask around. It has the potential to be a great little hideaway. At the moment, it is mainly visited by yachts.

The second is the town of **Ermioni** (Ερμιόνη). At first glance it has little to offer, but it has hidden charms and is probably a more 'authentic' experience of Greece than many of the Peloponnese's more touristy destinations. A local English couple have written an excellent online introduction to the town and the surrounding area (w *ermioni.info*), where you can also find links to local accommodation.

WHAT TO SEE AND DO
Methana and its volcano (Μέθανα) The Methana Peninsula seems stuck on
to the rest of the Argolid almost as an afterthought, the thin strip attaching it to
the rest of the mainland an accident in what was intended to be an island. But it is
not just its isolation that sets Methana apart; the peninsula is part of the Aegean
volcanic arch along with Milos and Santorini, and has 32 extinct craters dotted
over its small area. They started bubbling Methana out of the sea from between
one and two million years ago, but the last activity was a submarine eruption in
1700, just off the northwest coast. The most visible reminders of volcanism come
from an eruption in c230BC near the village of Kaimeni Hora (Καημένη Χώρα).
Volcanic activity in the area is recorded by Pausanias, Ovid and Strabo.

The first evidence of all this volcanism is in the town of **Methana** itself, which
you generally smell before you see it. As you approach, the source of the old
nickname *Vromolimni* ('pongy pool') becomes immediately clear. The stench is
sulphur and it mainly emanates from a large white pool. This is the main thermal
spring of this spa town, whose healing waters have been famous since ancient
times. In modern times the baths were the source of the town's fortune, but
they have been in decline since World War II. German architects built the long,
imposing spa buildings behind the lake in the 19th century. They were bought in
2004 and renovated, and now offer many different types of therapies if you are
interested (📞22980 92079).

Unfortunately you cannot make a circuit of the peninsula. Most people will
want to head towards the western coast. This takes you past the attractive little
port of **Vathy**, with its pebble beaches. Alarmingly the deep waters off the coast
here are said to be a breeding ground for sharks, but they don't seem to be the
sort to bother swimmers. Just to the south of the village are the remains of some
Classical fortifications begun by the Athenians in the Peloponnesian War.

Heading north you slowly wind up into the mountains and there are great
views back over to the mainland. The village of **Kaimeni Hora** ('Burnt Village')
is dominated by the volcanic rocks above it. The road continues for a short while
beyond it until you reach a small parking area. Looking at the rock face, the path
up to the **volcano** starts just to the right of this parking area and once you are on
it, it is well marked. The walk to the top takes 15–20 minutes and is well worth it
for the drama of the views and the rock formations.

If you have enough time, and a vehicle, there is a worthwhile diversion into
the interior of the peninsula. On the road from Methana to Vathy you will see a
fork to the right marked with a brown sign for an **ancient tower**. The tower itself
is located in an olive grove on the left, just past a small church (the building's
original purpose, and even its date, are somewhat obscure). This road can be
followed onwards into the mountains. It is tarmac all the way, but quite narrow
with many hairpins. Ignore the next left-hand turn and at the next crossroads
take the road down to the right. You will get good views of the amazing terracing
on the hills (there are allegedly 300,000 of them in the area) and on some can be
seen grape vines growing in the fertile volcanic soil. Pausanias relates the bizarre
ritual that the inhabitants used to protect their vines against the southwest wind,
known as the 'Lips':

> The wind called Lips, striking the budding vines from the Saronic Gulf, blights their
> buds. So while the wind is still rushing on, two men cut in two a cock whose feathers
> are all white, and run round the vines in opposite directions, each carrying half of the
> cock. When they meet at their starting place, they bury the pieces there.

The road emerges just outside the village of Kypseli (Κυψέλη) on the eastern side of the peninsula.

Ancient Troezen and the Devil's Bridge

Little remains of the Classical city of **Troezen** (Τροιζήνα), located just to the south of Methana, but it has other attractions that make a visit interesting. To find it head for the modern village of Trizina, nestled in the foothills of Mount Aderes. They don't get many visitors up here so you're sure to get a warm welcome. Either ask a local for directions or follow the signs that head to the right through the village.

Shortly after leaving the village you will come to a fork in the road, presided over by a large rectangular block. This is the so-called **Theseus Stone**, under which the hero found the sword and sandals of his earthly father (he is also supposed to be the son of Poseidon), which proved that he was heir to the throne of Athens. One suspects that the identification of the story with this particular boulder is a result of some rather wishful thinking.

Both forks of the road past the stone are worth looking at. Heading right first, various signs lead you towards the few remains of the ancient city. Take a right at the next fork past a modern church and then a left. Take a further left at another modern church on to a driveable dirt road that takes you the last 250m.

The large, square ruin here, with water channels leading into it, has been identified as a **healing sanctuary** dedicated to Asklepius – a smaller version of the one at Epidavros. Beyond this is the ruin of a **Byzantine bishop's palace**, which clearly used a lot of ancient stones and pillars in its construction. This is said to be the site of the **Temple of 'Peeping' Aphrodite**, mentioned by Pausanias. The story goes that Phaedra, Theseus's wife, fell in love with her stepson Hippolytus, and used to come here to watch him exercise (which he presumably did naked). Hippolytus rebuffed her advances and she killed herself, but not before accusing him of rape. Theseus, assisted by Poseidon, then took deadly revenge on his own son; and so the soap opera of Greek mythology went on.

Heading back to the Theseus Stone the other fork (to the left if coming from the village) heads up towards an impressive chasm in the mountains, but first passes an imposing **tower** that once formed part of the city's walls. The top of this is medieval, but the unmistakable large stones of the base date back to Classical times; stairs lead up inside it.

The road continues upward from here, bearing to the right and becoming dirt. After a few hundred metres the gorge narrows and an obvious path crosses over the **Devil's Bridge**, an attractive arch spanning the narrow chasm. It is a lovely spot, enhanced by a series of tree-shaded rock pools. A path on the opposite side of the bridge traces the chasm for a distance in both directions. Depending on the time of year it should be possible to take a swim in the inviting waters.

Lemonodasos (Λεμονοδάσος)

This 'Lemon Forest' makes a nice stop just south of Galatas. Lemons grow all year, but are at their best in spring, when you will smell them from the car driving past. Various paths lead through the groves of trees, but they all seem to end up at a café that serves, obviously, fresh lemon juice.

Three 'caves'

The road that heads north from Porto Cheli on the south coast towards Epidavros is notable for a series of geological formations along its way. Only the first of these is a proper cave, but it holds the distinction of being one of the most important sites for the study of Neolithic people in Europe.

Just south of Fourni (Φούρνοι) look out for signs to the **Franchthi Cave** (Σπήλαιο Φράγχθι). The road takes you down to a pleasant beach opposite a small island that is obviously the private haunt of some reclusive millionaire. The waymarked path to the cave begins at the other end of the beach, following the rocks around a headland (it takes about 15 minutes each way). The cave itself is an impressively gaping hole in the rock side. You shouldn't need a torch as it is open at both ends, and it is easy to see the excavation pits made by the scientists who investigated the site. Here were found the oldest human burials in Greece, dating back to the Mesolithic period (roughly 8000–6000BC). One of these skeletons can be seen at the museum in Nafplio. The cave also provided the first tangible evidence of human seafaring. Obsidian tools were found, the rocks for which must have been quarried on the island of Melos, 120km away by sea. They were probably brought here on reed boats. With a bit of scrambling you can climb out of the far entrance of the cave, only to find a second, equally as large.

Back on the main road, about 5km north, you will probably notice a huge circular hole that seems to have been gouged out of the side of the mountain. To the untrained eye it looks like a meteorite crater, or perhaps the landing point of one of Zeus's thunderbolts. In fact, it is a **doline crater**, or sinkhole, and there are two of them – signposted off the road in English as 'Big Cave' and 'Small Cave'. The smaller one is actually more interesting close up. You enter it through a whitewashed tunnel through the ground that brings you out on a ledge inside the crater itself. Two small churches have been built in its interior, presumably to appease whatever powers caused this great scar in the earth. The larger crater can be viewed by following the path on from the entrance to the small one.

THE SOUTHWEST

Now that the new national road scoots people backwards and forth just to the north, few people visit this corner of the Argolid, which used to be the main route southwards. This is a shame, as not only does the old road pass through some spectacular scenery on its way to Tripoli, but there are also some interesting things to see on the way; they may not be major sites, but it's still well worthwhile making a detour on to the 'scenic route' rather than rushing south on the 'motorway'. The coastal route south is also well worthwhile – this is strictly part of Arcadia, but is described in the Laconia chapter of this book (page 125).

WHAT TO SEE AND DO
Kefalari Cave and church (Κεφαλάρι) About 1.5km south of Argos look out for the right-hand turn to the village of Kefalari. Here a **spring** gives rise to the river of the same name, issuing from below **two caves** in the hillside. In ancient times this spring was called Erasinos, and the water was believed to come underground from the Stymfalian Lake (page 257). The caves were dedicated to Pan and Dionysus and appropriately, given these gods' reputations, they were honoured in an annual festival of *tyrbe* (a kind of bacchanalia).

Times have changed and now the smaller of the two caves contains a church. The larger, which goes back around 60m into the hillside, hosts a series of icons. The surrounding park is shaded and pleasant, and houses several tavernas that cater for the modern pilgrims to this site.

The Pyramid of Kenkreai Carry on through Kefalari towards the village of Elliniko (Ελληνικό) where, on the left, you will see this mysterious **pyramid**

structure. Don't get overexcited; this is not a building on the Egyptian scale – the base is perhaps 10m square and the top is missing. It is quite impressive, however, made with large, polygonal blocks. It has an arched entrance on one side, which leads into an interior room.

No-one is quite sure what function this pyramid served. Pausanias thought it was a burial monument for the Argive warriors who fell defeating the Spartans at Hysiai (see below) in 669BC, but the archaeological evidence does not back up this claim. The main theory is that it served as the base of a lookout tower from the 4th century BC, but then why bother with the pyramid shape? It is the best preserved of a few similar structures found in this region, and nowhere else in Greece.

The House of Tiles at Lerna
(⏰ 08.30–15.00 daily; €2) On the southern edge of the village of Myli (Μύλοι) look out for the inconspicuous little lane to the left, just before an orange grove, which leads to the **House of Tiles**, the remains of a building from the Early Helladic period (3000–2000BC). This small but significant site was probably a palace, or at least an administrative centre. It is contemporary with one of the early layers of Troy, in what is now Turkey, and pottery finds show that it traded with the fabled city. What remains are the ruins of a rectangular building (25m x 12m) with mud-brick walls that were originally two storeys high. The roof was covered in tiles, giving the site its name, and many of them can still be seen lying in piles. The house was destroyed by fire, which helped preserve the mud and clay. The onsite maps of the floor plan show that in many ways this building was a precursor of the palaces at Mycenae and elsewhere. The fact that two Mycenaean shaft graves that cut across the site are more modern than the house itself only serves to emphasise its great antiquity.

The surrounding area is classical **Lerna** (Λέρνα), which has much mythology associated with it. Nearby was one of the many entrances to Hades, the kingdom of the underworld. This is the one through which Dionysus descended to bring back his mother Semele. This is also where Heracles fought, and slew, the many-headed Hydra, as one of his Labours (page 239).

Up into the mountains
After Myli and the House of Tiles the old road to Tripoli now turns west and starts to dramatically switchback up into the mountains. After about 14km it passes a turn to the village of **Achladokambos** (Αχλαδόκαμπο⊠). The name translates as 'Plain of the Wild Pear', but sadly few of these remain. Take the turn if you want to see the remains of the ancient town of **Hysiai** (Υσιαί). Here the Argives defeated the Spartans in 669BC, and the Spartans in turn destroyed the town in 417BC. All that remains is a wall of polygonal stones. The views down to the plain below are stunning, and you can trace the route of the old railway far below.

After Achladokambos, the road passes round the slopes of **Mount Parthenio** (Παρθένιο, 1,215m). It was on this mountain that the runner Phidippides saw the goat-legged god **Pan**. The Athenians, outnumbered by the invading Persians at the plain of Marathon in 490BC, had sent him to ask the Spartans for aid. The Spartans prevaricated, but Pan promised his help, duly appearing before the Persian soldiers and sending them into an eponymous panic. According to Herodotus, Phidippides arrived in Sparta the day after he left Athens, around 250km away. This was long thought to be a fanciful story, especially given the extremely mountainous nature of much of the route. However, in 1982 five RAF officers, led by Colonel John Foden, set out to test whether it was possible. Herodotus was vindicated when they completed the route in 40 hours.

If you fancy trying Phidippides's run then you can join a group of international athletes that re-create the feat each year in September. Be warned: the distance is 246km and the current record is an astonishing 20 hours 29 minutes (and four seconds), set back in 1984 by, appropriately, a Greek, Yannis Kouros (see w spartathlon.gr for details). Of course Phidippides, once he'd run the 246km to Sparta, turned around and ran all the way back.

On the slopes of the mountain, to the left, you might spot a brown sign to the Byzantine fortress of **Mouchli** (Μούχλι). It was destroyed by the Franks in 1460, apparently rather thoroughly as you'd be hard pressed to spot any actual ruins. Still, it's a dramatic spot and there is a thoughtfully provided picnic bench.

The road from the coast to Tripoli is only 41km, but will take longer than you think, even if you don't stop, owing to the mountainous nature of the terrain.

UPDATES WEBSITE

You can post your comments and recommendations, and read feedback and updates from other readers online at w bradtupdates.com/peloponnese.

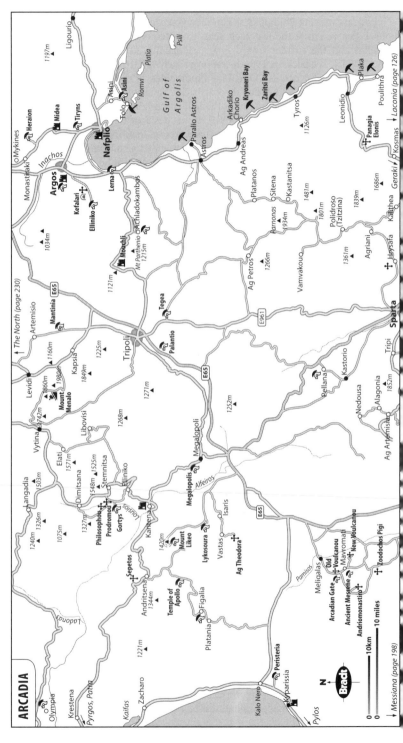

ARCADIA

4

Arcadia (Αρκαδία)

Arcadia is a name to conjure with, bringing up images of rural bliss. The reality is actually much more interesting, and Arcadia turns out instead to be a land of mountains and monasteries, stone villages and isolated ruins.

Look carefully, however, and the bucolic idyll is still to be found, by lush riverbanks and white-columned temples shaded by olive trees. As a region it is, perhaps, the best single example of what it is that the Peloponnese has to offer, and what sets it apart from the rest of Greece.

TRIPOLI (ΤΡΊΠΟΛΗ)

The capital of Arcadia, in contrast to the rest of the region, is a workaday place, not really aimed at travellers, and there's no very compelling reason to stop over here. It is not devoid of interest, however: if you are waiting for a bus then the museum is worth a look, and the surrounding countryside is filled with the remains of ancient cities.

HISTORY Tripoli is a modern settlement, especially in Greek terms. It first started to grow in the 14th century and only achieved any prominence when the Turks made it their capital in the Peloponnese because of its central position. It was they who gave it its modern name 'Three Cities', in commemoration of the ruined Classical cities of Tegea, Mantinia, and Palantio that surround it.

During the War of Independence it was a prime target for the Greeks. On 23 September 1821, an army under Kolokotronis captured the town and exacted bloody retribution on its inhabitants. Perhaps 8,000 Turks were massacred for the loss of 300 Greeks, but this went beyond a simple slaughter into the realm of sadism. Eyewitnesses described pregnant women being cut open, decapitated and then left with the heads of dogs stuck between their legs. Kolokotronis grew rich from the plunder gained in this atrocity. The Ottomans took their revenge a few months later when they killed 25,000 on the island of Chios, and in 1825 when Ibrahim Pasha retook Tripoli. It fell to the Greeks again in 1828, but Ibrahim, as he retreated, burnt it to the ground. If the modern city seems rather drab, you can't really blame it.

GETTING THERE AND AWAY One of the main reasons for coming to Tripoli is that it is a transport hub, especially for buses, owing to its central location.

By car Now that the national road bypasses the town there is no need to brave the intricacies of its road layout, unless you are desperate to visit the museum, or you use the attractive secondary road up to Vytina via Alonistena (Αλωνίσταινα)

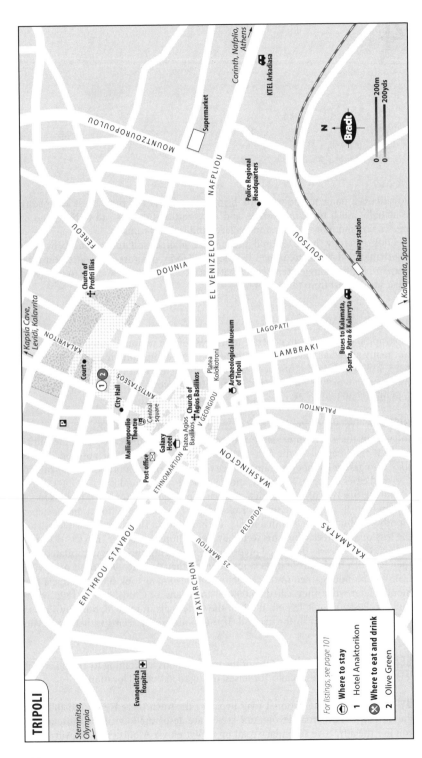

TRIPOLI

Stemmitsa,
Olympia

For listings, see page 101

Where to stay
1 Hotel Anaktorikon

Where to eat and drink
2 Olive Green

KTEL Arkadiasa

Corinth, Nafplio,
Athens

MOUNTZOUROPOULOU

Supermarket

NAFPLIOU

Police Regional
Headquarters

FEREOU

Church of
Profiti Ilias

DOUNIA

EL VENIZELOU

SOUTSOU

Railway station

Kalamata, Sparta

Kapsia Cave,
Levidi, Kalavrita

KALAVRITON

LAGOPATI

LAMBRAKI

Buses to Kalamata,
Sparta, Patra & Kalavryta

Court

City Hall

ANTISTASEOS

Central
square

Platea
Kolokotroni

Archaeological Museum
of Tripoli

PALANTIOU

Malliaropoulio
Theatre

Galaxy
Hotel

Post office

ETHNOMARTION

V GEORGIOU

Platea Agios
Basilikos

Church of
Agios Basilikos

WASHINGTON

ERITHROU STAVROU

25 MARTIOU

PELOPIDA

KALAMATAS

TAXIARCHON

Evangelistria
Hospital

N

Bradt

200m
200yds

0
0

100

– although the main route, reached via the Olympia junction on the national road north of town, is almost as nice.

If you do drive in, then good luck. Signposts are hard to spot and the one-way system always seems to lead you into narrow back alleys. You should, at some point, pass through one of the central squares, all of them set out to work as roundabouts. Try to park as near to them as possible.

By train The train station is out on the southeastern edge of town, but no trains are running here, and haven't done for years. There is a replacement bus service, but you are better off on the regular bus.

By bus The building of the new bus station on the outskirts of town seems to have brought some confusion with it, not least to the employees of the various bus companies. The current situation is as follows.

The main bus station, **KTEL Arkadia** (*50 Nafpliou;* ✆ *27102 23614*) is reached by following El Venizelou Street east from Platea Kolokotroni. It becomes Nafplio Street, and the large bus station is on the right about 1km from the centre of town. Frequent buses run between here and Athens (*2hrs*), Corinth (*1hr*) and Megalopoli (*40mins*), and there are two–three daily to/from Olympia (*2–3hrs*), Argos and Nafplio (*1hr*), Levidi (*30mins*), and various mountain villages.

The **other bus station** (✆ *27102 42086*) is in a café at the end of Lagopati Street, opposite the train station. It is about 400m from the centre of town, and 800m west of the other bus station – ask for directions if you need to transfer. At present it serves Kalamata (*frequent; 1hr*), Sparta (*3–4 daily; 1hr*), Patra (*2 daily; 3hrs*), and Kalavryta (*1 daily; 1hr 45mins*).

WHERE TO STAY AND EAT *Map, opposite*
Should you get stuck in Tripoli, eating and accommodation options are plentiful in the city centre, albeit mostly uninspiring.

🏠 **Hotel Anaktorikon** (23 rooms) 48 Ethnikis Antistasis; ✆ 27102 26545; e anaktorikon@ otenet.gr; w anaktorikon.gr. Centrally located on a pedestrianised road around the corner from the town hall, this standout hotel underwent extensive renovations in 2017, & combines Classical architecture with tasteful modern décor & top service. Good discounts offered to walk-ins. €€€€

✖ **Olive Green** 5 Dimitrakopoulou; ✆ 27102 37971; f OliveGreenBar. Spilling out on to a pedestrian walkway opposite the town hall, this is a coffee shop by day, wine & cocktail bar by night, & serves a great selection of well-priced light meals & snacks throughout the day.

OTHER PRACTICALITIES However you arrive, find the central **Platea Agios Basilikos**, recognisable by the large, Western-style church dedicated to the same saint. A short street running to the southeast past the church connects it to the circular **Platea Kolokotroni**. Everything you need, including banks and ATMs, can be found near here. Taxis congregate around the squares.

WHAT TO SEE AND DO
Archaeological Museum of Tripoli ✆ *27102 42148;* ⏰ *08.30–15.00 Tue–Sun; €2*) The town museum is located in a large Neoclassical building signposted just to the right of the road between Vasileos Georgiou Square and Platea Kolokotroni. The collection is surprisingly large and good, but visitors are few and the museum is sometimes inexplicably closed.

AROUND TRIPOLI

Tegea (Τεγέα) The best-preserved and most interesting of the 'three cities' to which the name Tripoli alludes is Tegea. Named after its mythical prehistoric founder Tegeates (the son of King Lycaon), it was one of the most important cities in the area in its ancient heyday, and the arch rival of Mantinia, only 20km to the north. It only goes to show how localised some of the Greek city states could be. It lies to the south of Tripoli on the road towards Sparta. After 7km look out for the signposts to the left. The scanty remains cover a large area. You first come across the little **museum** (⏲ *should be 08.30–15.00 Tue–Sun, but often erratic*) in the village of Alea (Αλέα), which contains a few of the finds from the nearby temple and other surrounding sites.

The **Temple of Athena Alea** (⏲ *often locked, but viewable through the fence*) itself is a few minutes' walk away: head along the road to the right of the museum. It is easy to make out the plan of this 4th-century BC temple, and it was clearly rather large. Pausanias ranked it first in his league table of temples of the Peloponnese. Considering it was competing against the Temple of Apollo at Vasses and the great Temple of Zeus at Olympia, this is pretty good going.

From the temple follow the signs towards the Folk Museum, which is in the nearby village of Episkopi (Επισκοπή), 10 minutes' drive away. Here, next to a pleasant, shady green park, you will come across one of those sites where the layers of history are literally piled up before you. A large **18th-century church** rests on the foundations of a **10th-century Byzantine church**, which in turn sit on top of an **ancient theatre** from the 2nd century BC. The 10th-century remains commemorate that this was the site of **Nikli**, an important centre in Byzantine times. In the park is a commemoration of the fact that it was here, in 1934, that the IOC hit on the idea of the modern **Olympic Flame**, with the torch being lit by the sun at Olympia and carried by relay to wherever the games are taking place (page 229).

The **Folk Museum** (⏲ *seems to only open on weekends & holidays*) is on the other side of the agreeable-looking taverna, and is housed in an upper floor of an impressive 19th-century edifice that used to be a school. The displays on everyday life in pre-industrial times are interesting, but are labelled only in Greek. A side room has a collection of the last few **Olympic torches**, proving that the one for Athens 2004 was by far the most elegant in recent times.

Carrying on past the museum and church, and then going left at the next junction, will bring you back on to the Tripoli–Sparta road.

Mantinia (Μαντίνεα) (⏲ *both the ancient site & the next-door church seem to be kept unlocked at most times*) The ruins of Tegea's great rival are to the north of Tripoli. Head up the national road in the direction of Corinth and Athens for 10km and take the junction towards Olympia. After 4km along this road take the signposted right turn towards Mantinia.

The site entrance is easily spotted as it is opposite the truly bizarre church of **Agia Fotini**. This is a highly curious mixture of architectural styles, and bits of it look like they were scavenged from the nearby ruins (although this was a common practice in medieval times, one hopes that it wouldn't have been allowed in the 1970s when this church was built), while other parts take their inspiration from the medieval and Mycenaean periods. Inside, the floor is made up of a fetching pebble mosaic. One can only presume that the architect felt that worshipping God didn't preclude having a bit of fun as well.

The remains of Mantinia are reached through the gate on the opposite side of the road. They are set in a marshy and overgrown area so good shoes and long trousers are recommended, especially in the winter and spring, if you want to explore fully.

A path takes you from the road about 300m to the most obvious remains, that of a small Classical **theatre**. From here you can spot the other sparse remains, which are mostly Roman (look for the brown signs in English). Mantinia was well known for its walls, which had a circuit of 4km. Much of this can be traced around the site.

If you are following the trail of the 'three cities' of Tripoli then you would expect the ruins of Palantio to be next. These are 5km to the south of Tripoli near a modern village of the same name, but are frankly too sparse to be bothered with. A more interesting onward option would be to continue driving north, past a low hill on the right where Mantinia's acropolis once stood, through countryside full of vineyards, then take a left turn just before the village of Artemisio (Αρτεμίσιο) and a right at the junction 7km beyond to take you to the ancient city of Orchomenos (see below).

LEVIDI (ΛΕΒΊΔΙ)

This small but prosperous-looking town stands at an altitude of 860m on the northeastern slopes of the conifer-swathed Mainalo Mountains. It has a fabulous setting overlooking a large fertile plain punctuated by hills and enclosed by taller mountains. Centred on a pretty central square lined with tavernas, cafés and craft shops, Levidi lies within easy striking distance of two quiet but worthwhile attractions: the hilltop ruins of Orchomenos and atmospheric Kapsia Cave. It also makes a useful base for exploration further afield, lying within 60–90 minutes' drive of Nafplio, Ancient Mycenae, Ancient Olympia, Lousios Gorge and Stymfalian Lake.

GETTING THERE AND AWAY Levidi lies about 25km north of Tripoli, and 20km northeast of the national highway from Athens to Kalamata along the main road to Olympia, for self-drivers.

WHERE TO STAY AND EAT

✴ 🏠 **Villa Vager** (9 rooms); 📞 27960 22073; e info@villavager.gr; w villavager.gr. Situated 200m uphill of the central square, this old mansion was falling down when Nikolaos & Marina started to restore it. They have done a fantastic job & it mixes homely comforts with top-notch design & architecture. The individually styled suites are all spacious & characterful, & most offer huge views over the plains towards Orchomenos. Nikolaos also runs tours on Polaris ATVs (basically enormous quad bikes) on more than 500km of trails that he has developed in the surrounding mountains. Rates include a superb & leisurely b/fast. Winery visits & cooking lessons can also be arranged. Call for directions – it's rather hidden. €€€€€

🏠 **Artemis Traditional Hotel** (16 rooms) 📞 27960 22600; e artemislevidi@gmail.com; w artemis-levidi.gr. Situated a few doors up from Villa Vager, this small, attractively decorated &

well-priced family-run guesthouse offers similarly splendid views to its more upmarket neighbour. €€

✴ ✕ **Taverna Skourkos** 📞 27960 22231. The pick of the eateries dotted around the main square, this friendly taverna is notable for its engaged staff & competitive prices & it also offers a refreshing break from the usual oil-heavy cooking style. A varied menu of Greek dishes is supplemented by pizzas, pasta & burgers.

✕ **To Hani tis Kandilas** 📞 27960 22004; e info@taverna-hani.gr; w taverna-hani.gr. A local favourite, this is in the small hamlet of Kandila (Κανδηλα), 8km north of Orchomenos; look out on the left-hand side for a stone building with lots of windows. Established in 1950, it is an absolutely traditional mountain taverna, where tables full of hunters jostle elbows with families of 3 or 4 generations. You are best to take advice on what is cooking that day rather than rely on the menu.

WHAT TO SEE AND DO
Orchomenos (Ορχομενός) (*see box, page 52; free entrance*) The little-visited ruins at Orchomenos reward the intrepid with the best setting of any of the

plethora of ancient cities that seem to have sprouted in this historically fertile area. The spectacular views emphasise the strategic importance of the old city, which could control several important routes around it. The most obvious ruin is that of a theatre, which must have had one of the most dramatic backdrops going; it's surprising that the audience could spare any attention for the actors. The footpath from the entrance gate to the theatre leads past some more remains, including an agora, and a temple, all with informative English display boards. Again, the chief rewards are the views and the solitude; your only likely companions being an occasional grass-munching tortoise or a flock of goats or sheep (Homer called the area 'rich in sheep' and it seems the tradition is being kept alive).

Orchomenos lies about 8km northeast of Levidi. To reach the site, which is signposted from the main square, take the road downhill to Nemea and follow it for 6km until you see the ruins signposted road to the left. From here, follow the narrow road that snakes above the modern village of Orchomenos for 2km until you reach a car park, then walk uphill for another 200m or so to the entrance gate, which is usually manned and has toilet facilities.

Kapsia Cave (Σπήλαιο Κάψια) (m 69510 03299; w spilaiokapsia.gr; ⊕ 09.00–15.00 Mon–Fri, 09.00–16.00 Sat & Sun; €4)

This small but very beautiful cave system was first explored by engineers who came to investigate the sinkholes outside it in 1887, but it has only been open to the public since 2010. Guided tours take 20–30 minutes and lead through eight chambers whose spectacular array of stalactites, stalagmites, and waterfall-like dripstone formations have formed over something like 15 million years. You'll most likely have the place to yourself and the guided tour is enhanced by some interesting lighting (but rather less so by an accompaniment of cheesy mood muzak). It is thought that the cave was used as a pagan temple in ancient times, and it contains the skeletons of around 50 people who drowned or starved to death when it flooded a few thousand years ago.

To get there from Levidi, follow the Tripoli Road south for 6km to the village of Kapsia, then turn left along a signposted feeder road that leads you to the car park after another 1.5km. A decent café is attached to the ticket office.

MEGALOPOLI (ΜΕΓΑΛΌΠΟΛΗ)

The 'Great City' does not really live up to its name. The setting is dramatic enough, surrounded by mountains on all sides; whichever way you approach involves a long descent on winding roads with the town laid out below you. However, the view is dominated by two 'great' power stations that spew their smoke and steam into the air. Modern Megalopoli owes its existence to them, and the lignite deposits in the valley that fuel them, and the rest of the Peloponnese owes them its bright lights and air conditioners. Actually, if you ignore their pollution, the power stations can take on a certain dramatic aspect, but it is not the image one really expects of Arcadia.

HISTORY Megalopoli was handicapped right from the start, as it was more of an idea of a city than an organic settlement. Following Epaminondas's defeat of Sparta in 371BC, he encouraged the various Arcadian city states to band together in a defensive league against their humbled neighbour. None of the existing cities, due to their rivalries, could be chosen to lead this confederation, so Epaminondas promptly founded a new city, Megalopoli, which was built between 371BC and 368BC and populated by inhabitants of the surrounding villages.

It was an optimistic plan at best, and the league of cities soon broke up; half of them actually sided with Sparta in 362BC. Megalopoli itself managed to survive Spartan attacks until it finally fell to the Spartan tyrant Cleomenes III in 223BC. He was himself defeated three years later, but Megalopoli never recovered.

GETTING THERE AND AWAY
By car Now that the two-lane national toll road from Athens to Kalamata via Corinth goes past Megalopoli, driving here involves less winding roads, but the spectacular mountain scenery remains the same. The main road goes north to Tripoli or south towards Kalamata, and bypasses the centre of the town. To get to the ruins of the ancient city, or up to Karitena in central Arcadia, you need to get into the town and make your way round its central square. The route is signposted. A newly opened 50km national toll road to Sparta branches southeast from the Athens–Kalamata highway at Gefyra, about 5km south of Megalopoli.

By bus The main north–south route is well served with at least eight buses a day in either direction. There are only two a day up to Karitena (*40mins*) and the Arcadian mountains – if you miss them you might want to consider a taxi. The bus station is just by the main square.

OTHER PRACTICALITIES There's really no reason to stay in Megalopoli. If you do miss a bus connection and are stuck here then there are a couple of anonymous hotels near the main square, which also have tavernas. This is also where the banks, post office and taxis are.

WHAT TO SEE AND DO While most people will simply want to pass by Megalopoli on their way to somewhere more appealing, there are actually a few interesting spots in the surrounding countryside. You will probably need your own transport, but they are worth the effort.

Ancient Megalopolis (✆ *27910 23275;* ⊕ *see box, page 52; free entrance*) The ruins of the old city of Epaminondas straddle the Elisson River, about a kilometre outside the modern town on the road towards Karitena. The main entrance is on the left, just before you reach the bridge over the river.

There is something slightly melancholic about the remains of Megalopolis, especially if you know its history as a city that never quite made it. Nowadays the atmosphere is further dominated by the looming power station. It started ambitiously enough, however, and was laid out on a grand scale. Two notable buildings remain. The **theatre**, built into a hillside, was the largest ever constructed in Greece and could hold 20,000 people. Now only the first few tiers of seats remain. In front of this is the almost square remains of the **Assembly Rooms**, where the pan-Arcadian League met. It was built to hold at least 10,000 people. The surrounding area, on both sides of the river, has other scant remains of this briefly great city.

Lykosoura and the Church of Trees (Λυκόσουρα) To the west of Megalopoli, on the slopes of **Mount Likeo** (Λυκαιο), 1,420m, are a couple of quirky, small sights. Head 8km down the main road south to take the (signed) right-hand turn, which will take you up, after 12km, to **Lykosoura** (⊕ *08.30–15.00 Tue–Sun*). This was said to be the oldest settlement in the world, although nothing earlier than the 5th century BC has been found. Beyond the museum building, and down the slope, is the **Temple of Despoina** ('The Mistress'). The stepped seats to its left were originally thought to be merely a retaining wall, but it is now speculated that they formed a theatre in front of a side entrance to the temple (like the one at the Temple of Apollo, page 109), where an unknown sacred rite would be performed.

The setting is fantastic, with sweeping views down to the valley of Megalopoli and its power stations (which look much better from up here). The **museum** contains copies of the statuary found on the site; it's usually kept locked, but try your luck with the custodian if they are around. The same applies to the remains of a **bathhouse** on the other side of the access road.

From here the adventurous could continue to the summit of Mount Likeo. In ancient times this was the site of a Zeus cult involving rainmaking, human sacrifice, athletic games and werewolves (the name translates as 'Wolf Mountain'). It is about 16km away, above the village of Ano Karies (Άνω Καρυές), and the road is paved for most of this, but gives out before the summit. This last section should not be attempted in the wet. At present the summit can be reached by turning left at the two junctions on the dirt road. According to Pausanias, the columns here were topped by statues of golden eagles. On a clear day the views are stupendous.

On the way back to the main road a turn leads past the villages of Isaris (Ισαρης) and Vastas (Βαστάς) to the little Byzantine church of **Agia Theodora** (over 20km), which occupies a beautiful spot by a river, not even spoiled by the stands selling religious knick-knacks. The remarkable thing about the church is that it seems to have been possessed by a grove of oak trees, at least 15 of which poke out of the walls and roof. Even weirder is the fact that there is no sign of them inside the church. Various miraculous stories are associated with it.

If you are returning to Megalopoli it is tempting to head straight down to the valley floor, rather than back to the main road, but be warned that the various roads are confusing and involve a close introduction to power station architecture and slag heaps.

KARITENA (ΚΑΡΙΤΑΪΝΑ)

Karitena is often the first experience that people have of the mountain villages of Arcadia, especially if they have come up from Megalopoli, and it is as good an introduction as any to this fantastic region. The solidly built stone houses with wooden balconies are characteristic of the area. The attractive village is above a gorge through which the Alphios River runs, and is laid out on a saddle between two hills, one of which is occupied by the famous castle. It is from here that Kolokotronis defied the army of Ibrahim Pasha during the War of Independence. So closely is the Greek general associated with the place that it formed the background to his bewhiskered face on the old 5,000 drachma note.

HISTORY The story of Karitena really begins in the medieval period, when, in 1209, the Franks made it the capital of a barony. The castle was built by Hugh de Bruyères in about 1254. His son, Geoffrey, is often held up as the epitome of chivalry. There is no denying his prowess in battle – enemies were said to fall before him 'like meadow grass before the scythe' – but with this came the other side of the chivalric code: an eye for the ladies, especially other men's wives. Because of his immense charms he seems to have generally got away with it.

In 1320, the castle was sold to the Byzantines by a treacherous general, and then was taken by the Turks in 1460. After being occupied by Kolokotronis it saw its last warlike use when the Germans occupied it during World War II.

GETTING THERE AND AWAY

By car Whichever way you approach Karitena you will be faced by the somewhat bizarre junction beside a petrol station below the village. This is where the winding 2km-long feeder road to Karitena intersects with the road up from Megalopoli and the main road between Stemnitsa and Andritsena. Don't even try to make sense of this junction; just take it slowly and try and end up on the right road.

By bus A couple of buses a day come up from Megalopoli (*40mins*). Several a day go back and forth along the main road below the village, but do not always go up to the village itself.

WHERE TO STAY AND EAT

🏠 **Hotel Pelasgos** (15 rooms) ☏27910 31490; m 69730 12459; e info@pelasgoshotel.gr; w pelasgoshotel.gr. Boasting an attractive sloping location alongside the feeder road to Karitena, this family-run out-of-town hotel has specious & comfortable rooms with stone walls, wooden floor & fireplace, & a good restaurant. €€€€

🏠 **Guesthouse Vrenthi** (6 rooms) ☏27910 31650; e info@vrenthi.gr; w vrenthi.gr. Very friendly family-run inn in the heart of the village. A decent café is attached. €€

✗ **Kastro Taverna** ☏27810 31113; m 69732 90998. The pick of a few small tavernas & cafés on the pedestrian road below the main square.

WHAT TO SEE AND DO

The castle (🕒 *daylight hours*) The main reason for climbing for 10 minutes up the steep path to the castle is for the views, especially the stunning drop down into the gorge. The building itself is almost triangular, with a rectangular structure inside that may have been the main hall. Experts believe that the walls, for the main part, date all the way back to the castle's foundation in the 13th century, although additions must have been made. Kolokotronis, in his autobiography, claimed to have built the whole thing 'at my own expense'!

Three churches Karitena boasts three attractive churches. The first, **Panagia tou Kastro**, is reached by following the path to the left, rather than right and up to the castle. It is probably 15th or 16th century, but just might date back to the 11th, and has fine views over the gorge. Back down near the start of the path up to the castle, follow the sign under an archway to the church of **Agios Nikolaos**, a fine 14th-century building with five cupolas. The church of **Zoodochos Pigi**, at the bottom of the village, is chiefly notable for its separate 13th-century bell tower, a very Italianate/Frankish feature given a distinctive Byzantine twist with its tile and brickwork finish.

A medieval bridge It is hard to spot now, but under the modern concrete bridge over the gorge on the way towards Andritsena lies its medieval predecessor, which is an absolute gem. To see it properly look out for the lay-by on the left just past the modern bridge. From here it is a short walk down to the old bridge, which is still crossed by a dirt road. It is amazing to think that the main route to Karitena led over this until well into the 1960s. To get the best views cross over to the other side.

The bridge originally had six arches, three either side of the chapel that is built into a central pillar. Unfortunately two collapsed after the Germans drilled into the foundations during the war in order to mine the bridge. What remains is still beautiful and is a unique survival of Frankish architecture. It is certainly older than the 15th century, as a now lost inscription told of its renovation in 1439, but its exact date is unknown.

Alfeios and Lousios rafting The longest river in the Peloponnese, emptying into the Ionian Sea near Pyrgos, the 110km Alfeios rises near Megalopoli and flows through the lush valley immediately south of Karitena about 2km upstream of its confluence with the Lousios. Most easily accessed from Karitena, a 5km stretch of the two rivers including the confluence offers fine rafting and excursions can be arranged through two specialist operators: **Peripetia** (↘ *21096 46366;* m *69449 48487;* e *info@peripetia.com;* w *peripetia.com*), and **Trekking Hellas** (↘ *21033 10323;* e *info@trekking.gr;* w *trekking.gr*).

ANDRITSENA (ΑΝΔΡΙΤΣΑΙΝΑ)

This is another pleasing mountain village, with plenty of wood used in its houses. Its past, represented by a few remaining monuments, is more illustrious than its modern, slightly dishevelled and sleepy aspect would have you believe. Most people pass through here on the way to the Temple of Apollo, but it's worth stopping off in the village first. Indeed, it's the traditional approach.

HISTORY Andritsena only really entered the Western consciousness with the 'discovery' of the Temple of Apollo by Joachim Bocher, a French architect, in 1765. The locals, of course, always knew it was here. In fact the locals were not as ill-educated as might be supposed. The village was the site of one of the schools that legend says kept Greek culture alive during the Turkish occupation. One of its graduates was Panayotis Anagastopoulos, a key member of the independence movement. There is a monument to him in the village square. Another prominent citizen was the founder of its excellent library (see opposite).

Meanwhile the village people had realised that a trade was to be made in guiding interested foreigners up the mountain to the temple on foot and muleback. Bocher, after his discovery, was killed by bandits, who mistook his brass buttons for gold, and bandits remained a problem for travellers. The people of Andritsena, realising they were bad for business, often co-operated in trying to get rid of them. A worse enemy was to come in the shape of the road up to the site. Once this was tarmac the coaches arrived and swept up to the temple without pausing at poor little Andritsena, which settled back into being a backwater. Nowadays, the tourist coaches are a rare occurrence, and the only visitors are independent travellers. Some of them might well enjoy a mule ride. It's an instructive tale for modern tourism planners.

GETTING THERE AND AWAY
By car Andritsena is on the main route between Karitena and the coast, a beautiful stretch of road. It can also be reached from Messinia to the south along back roads.

By bus A couple of buses a day pass through the village in either direction along the main road. An occasional bus does head in the direction of the temple, but does not return the same day.

WHERE TO STAY AND EAT
 Theoxenia Hotel (28 rooms) ↘ 26260 22219. This modern hotel at the east end of Andritsena is the standout among a few modest lodgings in the small village. A restaurant is attached. €€

OTHER PRACTICALITIES Most things in Andritsena are based on, or near, the main road, including a bank, post office, and a couple of basic food shops. Cafés and tavernas can be found in the village's two squares.

WHAT TO SEE AND DO The Temple of Apollo is very much the main event here, but the ancient town of Figalia, whose inhabitants built it, is worth a look as well, especially as it provides the easiest access to the dramatic Neda Gorge. The village has a surprisingly good folklore museum, and a fantastic library. If you travel along the road to and from the coast, the Sepetos Monastery is also a good diversion.

The Nikolopouleios Library (⏲ 08.30–14.30 Tue–Sat) This collection of 4,000 rare books, donated in 1840, has been housed in the old school building since 1875. You can find this to the left on the way into the village from the direction of Karitena; it is just above the prominent modern school. The custodian can show you a 10-minute video, in English, which describes the library's history. The books themselves are in glass cabinets, with some of the finer volumes on display. The oldest title dates back to the early 16th century, and the collection is strong on the classics, archaeology and travellers to Greece. Anyone with an interest in these could while away a happy few days here.

The other joy of the library is that it contains a cast of the **frieze** from the Temple of Apollo. The original was carted away by a party of British and German 'archaeologists' in 1811–12 and sold to the British Museum, where it resides to this day. It depicts two mythological battles: between the Greeks and the Amazons, and between the Lapiths and the Centaurs. The Amazons were, of course, the all-female tribe of warriors who lived to the east of Greece. Their attempted invasions were a common subject of Greek art. The fight between the Lapiths and the Centaurs was also often portrayed (notably at Olympia; page 239), and represented the struggle between civilisation and barbarity.

Folk Museum (m 69830 98883; w andritsainamuseum.gr; ⏲ noon–15.00 Wed, Fri, Sat & Sun; €2) This is in a large, old stone building just up from the main road in the centre of the village. Downstairs there are various rooms set up to look like they did in the 18th and 19th centuries. Don't miss the upstairs, which is reached by going outside again. This large room contains a plethora of fantastic old costumes, as well as a dentist's chair along with some disturbing-looking dental instruments.

Temple of Apollo (☎ 26240 22529; ⏲ timings & entrance fees, see box, page 52) This fabulous temple is one of the best preserved in all of Greece, and has what must be the most dramatic location. It seems to go under a variety of names: Pausanias calls it the **Temple of Apollo Epikourios** (Apollo the Helper); **Vassai**, or in old-fashioned transliteration **Bassae**, properly refers to the area it is found in, and translates, appropriately enough, as 'Ravines'; the locals often still refer to it as simply the 'stylous' – the 'pillars'.

There is also some confusion as to its date. Pausanias, whom scholars have learnt to place a great deal of trust in, says that it was called Apollo the Helper as the god saved the inhabitants of Figalia from a plague, and also that it was built by Iktinos, the architect most famous for the Parthenon in Athens. The problem is that this temple appears more primitive than the Parthenon, but the plague that he mentions dates its building as later. The somewhat fudged solution is to say that the temple was begun about 450–440BC, before the Parthenon, but not fully finished until 425BC, after it was built.

The site is wonderfully isolated, set in dramatic mountains at a height of 1,131m. This means that it can be hard to get to without your own transport. Taxis can be arranged for the 14km ride from Andritsena (about €35 there and back with a wait), or you could try the old mule path (ask for local advice). The walk is said to take around 3 hours.

It should also be pointed out that the temple is still under wraps. It was covered in 1987 by a cleverly constructed **tent** to preserve it from the mountain elements while restoration work continues. There is, as yet, no sign of it being removed. While this obviously detracts from the temple's impact, the tent itself is a pretty impressive structure. Arriving by road it seems to pop out at you by surprise; to get the full impact you need to climb the hills above and look down. An inspiring sight now, one can only imagine what it was like before the tent and the tarmac road existed. Old photos, available on the internet (putting 'Bassae' into a Google Images search will bring up several), give you some idea.

Inside the tent the space is dominated by the great pillars, and it is hard to get an accurate impression of the great scale of the temple. It is surrounded by a colonnade of Doric pillars, 6 x 15, and is 14.6m wide and 38.3m long. The orientation is roughly north–south, rather than the more usual east–west, possibly due to the constraints of the ridge it is built on.

The central, enclosed, part of the temple has a series of five half-columns that project out from the wall – the first four pairs at right angles and the fifth at a diagonal. A final marble column used to stand on its own between this last pair, and was the earliest-known example of the Corinthian order. Some experts think that this column represented Apollo, and that the temple had no actual statue of the god (no base to one has been discovered). Pausanias, however, insists there was one. Perhaps it sat opposite the door in the side of the central enclosure, facing east as befits the sun god, but this would be an unusual arrangement in a Greek temple.

Figalia and the Neda Gorge
It's hard to imagine now, but the little village of Figalia (Φιγαλεία), 10km further along the tarmac road, was once an extensive city, rich enough to build the impressive Temple of Apollo. Pausanias describes it at some length.

Little of this former glory now remains. Next to a map board, underneath a plane tree in a small square, are the remains of a **fountain house** dating from the 4th–3rd century BC, which still provides the village with its spring water. Above is an 11th-century **Byzantine church** that has frescoes inside if you can find a key. The map board details various footpaths in the area, most of them leading down into the **Neda Gorge** (Νέδα). One path skirts the ancient walls, near to the remains of tombs and a temple, before also descending into the gorge where the cave of Black Demeter was probably located (mentioned by Pausanias). To explore the gorge more fully, it is worth contacting Trekking Hellas (page 30).

The gorge stretches from here to the sea. There is a spectacular view of it from above the pretty village of **Platania** (Πλατανιά), where a local philanthropist has built a modern viewing tower by an open-air theatre. To get here follow the gravel road from by the fountain house; it soon becomes tarmac, snaking down and up the other side of the gorge, and is driveable, although not for the nervous. The attractive village square at Platania has a couple of tavernas.

Sepetos Monastery
Driving towards the coast from Andritsena look out for the signs pointing to the right for the Sepetos Monastery, which is near the tiny village of Alifira (Αλίφειρα). The monastery dates back to the 12th century, but much of it is modern as it burned down in 1915. The setting, as it hangs above the gorge, is dramatic. If you want to visit inside then note that the dress code is strict and that it closes in the afternoons.

THE LOUSIOS GORGE (ΛΟΎΣΙΟΣ)

The Lousios is said, by Pausanias, to be where Zeus was bathed as an infant (hence the name, which means 'Wash'). He also claimed it was the coldest river in the world, which on a hot summer day is well worth checking. Sometimes also known as the Gortys, it is not a long river, beginning only 26km north of Karitena, near to which it merges with the Alphios. For almost all its length, however, it flows through an impressive gorge, with red limestone cliffs rising to 100m above the tumbling river, which is surrounded by prolific plant life even in the summer. Right up to the 20th century the river's power was harnessed by countless watermills, while the cliffs above provided the home to hermits and monks in caves and cliff-hugging monasteries, the latter of which are still inhabited. The gorge is becoming more accessible as the various dirt roads to its attractions are asphalted, but most of it is still only reachable by paths. Walking along these, with the clear waters of the river running beside you, it is easy to see what an Arcadian idyll really is.

Above the gorge are the two villages of Stemnitsa and Dimitsana, which are perhaps the most beautiful of all the Arcadian mountain settlements. Not so long ago these were rustic backwaters with basic, if any, accommodation. Now they have become trendy weekend getaways for Athenians, but with strictly enforced preservation orders they have lost none of their charm.

GETTING THERE AND AWAY

By car The road that links Stemnitsa and Dimitsana continues north and then branches towards either Tripoli or Olympia. To the south it continues past Andritsena to the sea. It is one of the most consistently scenic routes in the Peloponnese, with over 100km of gorgeous mountain views.

Parking in Dimitsana can be problematic; you are best to stick to the outskirts, or head up the little alleyway next to the viewing platform/village square, where there is a small parking area. Stemnitsa is a little easier.

By bus You are best to approach the villages from Tripoli. There are two or three buses daily (*1hr 20mins*).

WHERE TO STAY   *Map, page 112*

Thirty years ago, the only options up in these mountains were the Xenos in Stemnitsa, a dirty, comically badly run 'hotel', and whatever the local kafenion could knock up for you (mainly omelettes, but roast goat or lamb if you were lucky). Keep reading, because things have improved dramatically. This has also seen a rise in prices of course, but high season in the mountains is in the winter; come at other times of the year and you can often negotiate a bit of luxury at a bargain price. During the winter season, and at weekends and holidays, making reservations is recommended. Dimitsana is the more obviously dramatic village, but verges on the touristy, so I tend to prefer Stemnitsa, which remains a delight.

Trikolonion Country Hotel (18 rooms) Stemnitsa; ＼27950 29500; e info@ trikolonioncountry.gr; w trikolonioncountry. gr. Slightly unbelievably this used to be the old doss house hotel of Stemnitsa, which once held my rucksack for ransom over a bill dispute. Now, it is a 'country house' in the 'English style'. The atmosphere is authentically snobby. It's on the right as you enter Stemnitsa from the south. €€€€€

Elaion (7 rooms) Elliniko, 10km south of Stemnitsa; m 69369 08517; e dimlyko@yahoo.

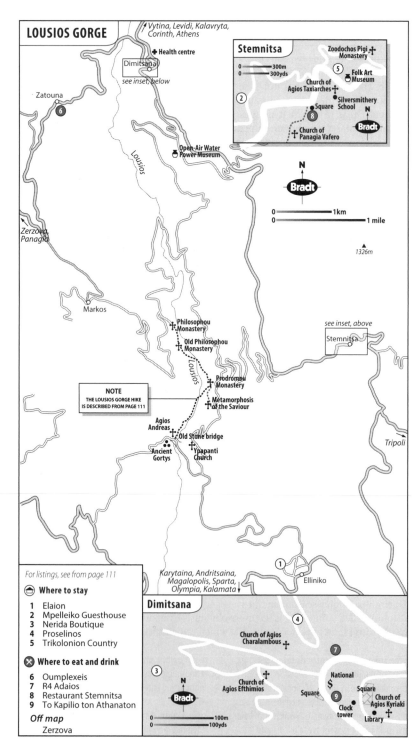

LOUSIOS GORGE

↑ Vytina, Levidi, Kalavryta, Corinth, Athens

+ Health centre

Dimitsana
see inset, below

Zatouna
6

Stemnitsa

Zoodochos Pigi Monastery +

5 Folk Art Museum

0 ——— 300m
0 ——— 300yds

Church of Agios Taxiarches +

2

Silversmithery School

■ Square

8

Bradt N

+ Church of Panagia Vafero

Lousios

Open-Air Water Power Museum

↗ Zerzova, Panagia

Bradt N

0 ——— 1km
0 ——— 1 mile

▲ 1326m

Markos

Philosophou Monastery †

Old Philosophou Monastery †

see inset, above

Stemnitsa

Lousios

Prodromou Monastery †

NOTE
THE LOUSIOS GORGE HIKE IS DESCRIBED FROM PAGE 111

Metamorphosis of the Saviour †

Agios Andreas †

Old Stone bridge

Ancient Gortys ●●

Ypapanti Church †

→ Tripoli

↓ Karytaina, Andritsaina, Magalopolis, Sparta, Olympia, Kalamata

1

Elliniko

For listings, see from page 111

🏠 **Where to stay**

1 Elaion
2 Mpelleiko Guesthouse
3 Nerida Boutique
4 Proselinos
5 Trikolonion Country

❌ **Where to eat and drink**

6 Oumplexeis
7 R4 Adaios
8 Restaurant Stemnitsa
9 To Kapilio ton Athanaton

Off map
   Zerzova

Dimitsana

4

Church of Agios Charalambous +

7

3

Church of Agios Efthimios †

Square

National $

Bradt N

Square

Clock tower

9

Church of Agios Kyriaki †

Library

0 ——— 100m
0 ——— 100yds

112

gr; w innelaion.gr. Dimitris & his wife Giota have renovated his old family house (1886) into a guesthouse with well-decorated rooms in a rustic style. They also have a pool. €€€€

🏠 **Proselinos** (5 rooms) Dimitsana; 📞27950 31675; m 69733 51128; e info@proselinos.gr; w proselinos.gr. The 'Tower of the Stranger', as it was once known, was built by an outsider, a raisin magnate would you believe, in 1850. It now luxuriates in 4-poster beds & hand-painted walls & ceilings. Find it by going up the alley off the sharp bend on the main road. €€€€

✳ 🏠 **Mpelleiko Guesthouse** (6 rooms) Stemnitsa; 📞27950 81286; m 69766 07967; e info@ mpelleiko.gr; w mpelleiko.gr. Some places are absolutely made by their hosts, & this is the case here. It would be pretty nice anyway; the rooms, set in a renovated stone house built in 1650, are comfortable & cosy, the views, from its perch above the village, are great. But it's Nena who sets the place apart. Her local knowledge, particularly about hiking, is superb, & the home-cooked breakfast, which changes every day, is the stuff of legend. €€€

🏠 **Nerida Boutique Hotel** (22 rooms) Dimitsana; 📞27950 32700; e info@nerida-hotel. gr; w nerida-hotel.gr. This attractive new owner-managed hotel is built with stone & split over 3 levels on the slopes immediately below the village centre overlooking the Lousios Gorge. Cosy well-equipped rooms have a wooden floor & fireplace. €€€

WHERE TO EAT AND DRINK *Map, opposite*

As with accommodation, eating out prospects have taken a turn for the better in recent years. A fair choice is now available in the main villages, although prices can be rather inflationary, reflecting the mainly Athenian clientele. It is worth checking out whether these tavernas are open before heading for them.

✕ **Oumplexeis** m 69733 06226; w oumplexeis.gr. This is another good bet. In Zatouna, a village that also boasts superb views down into the gorge.

✕ **R4 Adaios** 📞27950 31550. The latest addition to Dimitsana's burgeoning culinary scene is also perhaps its busiest eatery & seems to be very popular with visitors from Athens. Ostensibly a coffee/wine bar but more like a taverna in feel, it serves tasty Greek fare at reasonable prices with traditional music playing in the background.

✕ **Restaurant Stemnitsa** 📞27950 81371. Reliably open all year, this friendly family-run taverna on the central square in Stemnitsa serves excellent traditional Greek fare (oven-baked lamb in lemon sauce is a speciality) & is heated by a log fire in winter. Portions are generous & prices very reasonable.

✕ **To Kapilio ton Athanaton** m 69774 22578. Situated on the main road through Dimitsana, this family-run stalwart has limited seating in the cave-like interior, but there's a lovely outside space overlooking the gorge. Good salads & steak, as well as traditional fare such as oven-roast wild boar.

✳ ✕ **Zerzova** m 69328 47358. This is the village taverna at Panagia & is one of the area's best (follow the west road out of Dimitsana past Zatouna).

OTHER PRACTICALITIES Dimitsana is better provided for than Stemnitsa, and has a bank, ATM and post office by the little square, as well as a couple of adequate mini markets. Dimitsana also has a health centre (📞27950 31401). Each village has a local taxi or two – ask hotel owners to contact them for you. Many of the hotel owners are enthusiastic and knowledgeable about the area, and can prove to be a useful mine of information.

WHAT TO SEE AND DO Just being up in the mountains of Arcadia is pleasure enough, and it is sometimes enough just to let it all soak in, but there is plenty to do for all tastes, from a gentle wander around the back streets of its handsome stone villages, through exploring the monasteries in the gorge, up to rafting the cold waters of the Lousios itself. To get to know the area well you should invest in the Anavasi *Lousios* map, which is available from village shops. Trekking Hellas ✳ no longer maintains an office in Dimitsana, but is still very active in the area, offering trekking, rafting and even cooking courses (📞21033 10323; e info@trekking.gr; w trekking.gr). Highly recommended.

If you fancy exploring the area on horseback, there is a **riding stable** 3km outside Stemnitsa on the road to Elliniko; look out for the sign that says 'pros Ippostaio' on the right, but you are best to call first (m *69805 28647*). Another horseriding stable can be found at Elati, which lies about 20km northeast of Stemnitsa along a little-used surfaced backroad that passes through some lovely pine-covered slopes; contact Christos (m *69770 22173*) for details.

Stemnitsa (Στεμνίτσα)

The first building you notice on the way into Stemnitsa from the south is the large, pentagonal **Silversmithery School** (✆ *27950 29502*), on the left-hand side. The village has long been known for its craftsmanship in gold and silver, and there are shops that still specialise in its wares. To get a sense of the history of this, and other crafts, visit the **Folk Art Museum** (✆ *27950 81252*; ⊕ *10.30–14.00 Wed–Mon; €1*), which is opposite the college. The nearby church looks distinctly Byzantine, but in fact was built in 1715, a reminder of the continuing traditions that often make dating these buildings so difficult.

To see a real medieval church head to the central square and go up the lane by a free-standing 19th-century bell tower. This leads up to the **Panagia Vafero** whose earliest bits date back to 1185. Its newest bits are the dozens of incongruous green hosepipes that poke out of one wall, there to drain the damp away.

There are several **craft shops** in the village (and in Dimitsana) that sell mountain herbs and honey, and carved, wooden shepherds' crooks and the like. These are mostly aimed at the Athenian tourists, but it's not hard to find where the locals shop, where you will find the same products a fair bit cheaper.

Dimitsana (Δημητσάνα)

This village feels like it is on a balcony overlooking the gorge below, particularly its small square, which has great views. It was an important centre in the 18th and 19th centuries, and came into its own during the War of Independence. Kolokotronis called it his 'arsenal', due to the 14 water-powered gunpowder mills, hidden in the gorge, which provided his army with ammunition.

Head up the alley to the right (if coming from Stemnitsa) on the sharp bend in the main road and you will come to a small square dominated by a statue of Grigoris V. Born and educated here, he rose to be Patriarch of the Orthodox Church (roughly equivalent to the Pope). Another locally bred priest was Archbishop Germanos, who raised the banner of Greek freedom at Kalavryta in 1821 (page 16). Near the statue is the impressively large town **library** (⊕ *weekday mornings*) which, as the *Blue Guide* points out, contains 'some *incunabulae*' – books published before 1500, just in case you didn't know.

The grandly named **Mansion of the Patriarch** (⊕ *weekends & holidays*) is Grigoris V's old house, and now contains a small museum of religious items. It's on the alley to the left just past the small square. Just outside Dimitsana, on the way south toward Stemnitsa, is the 1km road towards the **Open-Air Water Power Museum** (✆ *27950 31630*; w *piop.gr*; ⊕ *Mar–mid-Oct 10.00–18.00 Wed–Mon, mid-Oct–Feb 10.00–17.00 Wed–Mon; adult/concession €3/1.50*). This outdoor museum is well worth an exploration, and gives a real insight into early industrial life in the Peloponnese. It is also very attractively laid out and a pleasure to wander around. The signage is all translated and even the video presentations have English subtitles. Perhaps the most interesting exhibit is the powder mill – try to get one of the custodians to get it running.

Menalon Trail

The Menalon Mountains around Stemnitsa and Dimitsana have long been one of the most popular hiking destinations in Greece, and in 2015 the many footpaths and old mule tracks in the area were semi-formalised, with the

(At least 2hrs one way; easy one way, medium if you have to return; water at both monasteries)

This short, reasonably easy, walk takes you right into the heart of this beautiful gorge, visiting two monasteries, criss-crossing the river, and ending up by an ancient site that is the perfect picnic spot. It is a one-way walk – you might be able to arrange a taxi to pick you up, but it is not too hard to reverse it to get you back to your starting point. If you need to do this it is worth considering shortening it by starting from the Prodromou Monastery. You can also walk down to Prodromou from Stemnitsa on a lovely path that begins in the village itself (see the Anavasi map or ask locally). All the junctions listed below are now well signposted as part of the Menalon Trail (page 114). See the walking guide on page 42.

0mins The walk begins at the Philosophou Monastery, where you can fill up your water bottle from spring taps. A gate leads from near to the church down into the gorge, and is signposted toward the old monastery, 800m away. The path is stone all the way.

10mins After reaching the old monastery, tucked against the cliffside, and exploring, backtrack a little and head down a gravel path, which you will have noticed previously, through the woods.

22mins You cross over the river on a new, but tastefully done, bridge, above some pretty impressive rapids, and head up the path on the other side.

42mins You reach the monastery of Prodromou, where you can refresh your water bottle. After having a look inside, head back down the path. The first, large, turn to the left leads up to the car park and tarmac road. Head a little further down the path you arrived on and turn down the next, small, path to the left, which takes you steeply downward.

1hr Crossing the river again you will see one of the old water mills, which used to be numerous along the river. Head up a stepped path which soon levels out.

1hr 14mins You emerge on a dirt track; turn down and left passing the Byzantine chapel of Agios Andreas to the left. The ruins of Gortys are up to the right, the inviting riverside ahead. A tarmac road comes to here, stopping just the other side of the narrow, stone bridge.

help of local volunteers, to create the 75km Menalon Trail (e *info@menalontrail.eu*; w *menalontrail.eu*). The first trail in Greece to be certified by the European Ramblers Association, it connects nine villages, starting in Stemnitsa and ending at Langadia, which is famous for its stone housebuilding tradition. The trail is divided into eight sections, each of which connects two villages, all with accommodation of some sort, allowing you to hike it in its entirety or to tackle any single section or succession of sections. Sections range in length and difficulty from the 4.2km leg between Dimitsana and Zygovisti, which can be covered in 2 hours, to the 15km trek between Zygovisti and Elati, which might require 6 hours. The hike is well signposted from start to finish and the website is a mine of useful information. A superb foldout map of the entire hike can be bought in Stemnitsa, and there is even an app available for downloading to Android phones.

The monasteries The area around the Lousios is rich in monasteries, perhaps because the landscape allowed them to remain isolated and unmolested during centuries of turmoil and occupation. The first inhabitants of the gorge would have probably been hermits, making use of the plentiful caves as shelter; you can still see where they lived, although it is sometimes hard to fathom how they reached their cliffside residences. Over time some of them would have banded together into small communities, the precursors of the monasteries you see today. Since their inception, the buildings have been constantly added to and improved; these are living communities rather than museums, which often makes dating them a speculative process. Nonetheless, they all exude an air of a palpable history and tradition, stretching well back into medieval times, but also continuing into the future. The monks, although not as numerous as in previous centuries, are still active, and some are surprisingly young.

Many of these monasteries are now accessible by car, if only by long and winding roads, but these all stop above the buildings themselves, leaving them in glorious isolation. Visiting working religious communities is not everyone's cup of tea, but the monks are very hospitable, and the beauty of the surrounding landscape is enough to lift anyone's spirit. Several monasteries in the area are worth visiting but the main two are Philosophou and Prodromou. These are linked by a lovely path through the gorge, which continues to the site of Gortys (see box, page 115).

Philosophou (Φιλοσόφου) (☉ *sunrise–sunset daily*) The easiest way to reach the monastery of Philosophou by car is to take the road at the north end of Dimitsana that drops down into the gorge (crossing it by an old stone bridge with good views) and continues via the villages of Zatouna (Ζάτουνα) and Markos (Μάρκος). This route is tarmac all the way to the car park just above the monastery. The attractive monastery complex sits right at the edge of the gorge and there are some well-restored frescoes in its church, the earliest dating back to the 1690s. This is, in fact, the New Philosophou, founded in 1691 (not 1961 as the self-published guide to the monasteries proclaims). To visit Old Philosophou, follow the signposted path into the gorge (this diversion is particularly recommended if you aren't going to do any other walking in the area). The old monastery is 800m away (about 10–15 minutes' walk); head up and right when you come to a fork.

The walled ruins of the monastery seem to almost disappear into the rock face, and it is barely visible from across the gorge (try and spot it from Prodromou, which is opposite). This was no bad thing during the years of Ottoman occupation. Apparently a 'secret school' was founded here in 1765, where the Greek language and culture were taught in defiance of the Turks. However, modern scholars rather dismiss the notion of these schools. You can walk through the remarkably narrow interior up to the old church, which has a few fresco fragments remaining.

The monastery was founded by John Lambardes from Dimitsana in around AD960. He had risen to become chief secretary of the Byzantine emperor Nikiforos Fokas, known as the 'Philosopher' and hence the name. There is no other written record of its existence until the 16th century, when its charter was renewed.

Prodromou (Προδρόμου) (☉ *sunrise–13.00 & 17.00–sunset daily*) This is just across the gorge, but to reach it by car you need to take the road that switchbacks down into the gorge from 2km outside Stemnitsa, on the way to Dimitsana. The

PRODROMOU MONASTERY: A MODERN MYTH

This story was told to me in the late 1980s by a youngish monk, while leaning over the balcony of the Prodromou Monastery, staring down into the gorge below. Make of it what you will.

During the Turkish occupation a nearby village was known for its population's resistance to the occupying forces, using their hidden position as a refuge, while descending from the mountains to attack and harry the enemy. Finally the Turks had had enough and the word spread that they would be sending a large force up into the gorges and crags of central Arcadia with the express purpose of finding and wiping out the troublesome villagers.

Upon hearing of the coming danger the village was abandoned and the inhabitants, including the women and children, took refuge at Prodromou, hoping that the Ottomans' respect for the Greek religion would ensure their safety. Soon enough, the frustrated Turkish troops approached the monastery and their commander questioned the abbot about the villagers' whereabouts, while they tried to keep silent, hidden in the upper storeys of the building.

The abbot denied all knowledge of the rebellious village and asked the troops to depart, reminding them of the traditional inviolacy of the Church. The Ottoman commander, at an impasse, ordered their withdrawal, but before they could leave disaster struck.

Upstairs in the monastery a young bride, married to the bravest warrior in the village, was trying to nurse her newborn child, but fear had dried her up. Just as the Turks began to depart the baby began to wail. Seeing the danger, and wishing to protect the majority, the selfless father seized his son from his wife and flung him down the cliffside. It was too late; the Turks, hearing the unaccustomed noise emanating from the monastery, opened fire, and soon a general engagement broke out, with the Greeks firing down on them from above.

The villagers had a plentiful supply of gunpowder, garnered from the secret mills of the gorge, and they could make cartridges from the paper torn from the old books of the monastery, but they were short of the lead needed to make the actual bullets. Soon the Greek guns fell silent.

The Turkish commander, realising what the situation must be, approached the monastery door, expecting to receive the abbot's surrender. Upstairs the same warrior who had just sacrificed his only child suddenly noticed that the button that fastened his wife's shawl was made of lead. Quickly forming it into a ball he loaded his rifle and with the last shot available to the Greeks took aim at the approaching Turk. The bullet took him through the head and his troops, unnerved by this sudden turn of events, beat a hasty retreat, allowing the villagers to make their escape.

One more thing. As the Greeks descended into the gorge they heard crying from above them. There, lodged in the fork of a fir tree, was the young babe, distressed, but entirely unharmed.

So, obviously a much-embellished story, handed down by word of mouth. Well, maybe. Take a look at the old wooden door that leads into the monastery. It is riddled with bullet holes that bear witness to the attack on 16 April 1779 by Albanian troops under Ottoman command. At the time the monastery was full of women and children but, for some unknown reason, the attack failed…

4

monastery is a 5-minute walk from the parking place. It is the most visually stunning of all the monasteries, with its stone buildings and ramshackle wooden balconies seeming to hang precariously from the overhanging cliffside.

It is dedicated to John the Baptist; Prodromou literally means the 'Forerunner', meaning the one who came before Jesus. Its foundation is said to date back to 1167, and it was originally an extremely rich establishment. Unfortunately, it was dissolved in 1834, seemingly by mistake, and all its relics and records were carted off – it took 16 mules to achieve this. After this the monks pulled themselves up by their bootstraps and rebuilt the monastery's wealth through hard work, building mills and keeping livestock.

It is the most active of the monasteries, particularly on its feast days, 17 May and 29 August, and it is fascinating to look around. The church is dug into the cliffside and has 16th-century frescoes, and the balconies are a prime spot to contemplate the beauties of the gorge. For an interesting story about Prodromou see box, page 117.

Gortys (Γορτύς) The same road that goes to Prodromou carries on past the site of Ancient Gortys, and then on to join the main road at the village of Elliniko. Again, it is now paved all the way.

One of the main reasons for visiting here is that it is such a beautiful spot, and is also perhaps the most accessible part of the river, where ice-blue waters rush under a narrow, old stone bridge. You could picnic here, and in hot weather even swim. The main ruins are on the other side of the bridge and up the slope. These are the remains of a 4th-century AD healing centre and associated bathhouse. The most obvious feature, a circular construction, was a dry sauna. Traces of the city walls can be found in the hills above. The nearby chapel of Agios Andreas possibly dates back to the 11th century.

VYTINA AND AROUND (BYTINA)

Vytina was the first of the Arcadian mountain villages to be developed for visitors, mainly due to it being on the way from Athens (only a 2½-hour drive away) to Olympia. Consequently it can seem more touristy than the villages to the south, and it also doesn't have quite as pretty a setting. It's a pleasant place nonetheless, and it, along with nearby Langadia (Λαγκάδια), can provide a good fallback if the other villages are all booked, as well as a reasonable base from which to head on to Olympia (80km away).

GETTING THERE AND AWAY Two to three buses run here daily from Olympia in the west (*2hrs*) and Tripoli to the east (*1hr*).

WHERE TO STAY AND EAT Vytina is a good base for exploring the area. The village is also famous for its bread, which is available from two bakeries near the square.

Chalet Elati (18 rooms) Elati; `27950 22900; m 69473 79401; e sale-elati@hol.gr; w sale-elati.gr. Located in the hillside forests about 10km south of Vytina, this is a place to get away from it all. It has comfortable, rustic rooms & the luxury, this far from the sea, of a swimming pool in the summer. €€€€€

Art Mainalon Hotel (47 rooms) Vytina; `27950 22217; m 69463 66456; e mainalon@gmail.com; w artmainalon.gr. Centrally located a block away from the main square, this modern boutique hotel has rooms decorated with original artworks (mostly by Greek painters), & the swimming pool is welcome in summer. €€€€

🏠 **Thea Mainalou** (20 rooms) Vytina; 📞 27950 22190; e info@thea-mainalou.gr; w thea-mainalou.gr. About 1km outside Vytina, this stone-built chalet is smart & comfortable. €€€

✖ **Kokkina Pytharia** 📞 27950 22450; m 69738 27555; e pitharia@gmail.com; w kokkinapitharia. gr. The most stylish of several tavernas in Vytina, & priced accordingly, this lies just off the square on the road to Dimitsana.

OTHER PRACTICALITIES The main square of Vytina surrounds a large, modern church. Opposite this is the municipality office, which has an ATM, and a rarely open ethnographic museum. Past the Art Mainalon Hotel is a post office.

WHAT TO SEE AND DO

Vytina The village, while pleasant, does not reward wandering as much as Stemnitsa and Dimitsana. It is well provided with craft shops, however, and is a good place to get mountain honey on your way to Olympia. One curiosity to look out for is the statue near the church, with its maps of Africa and Asia. It depicts Panagiotis Potagos (born 1838 in the village), a Greek explorer who found traces of ancient Greek settlements in Afghanistan.

Libovisi (Λιμποβίσι) If you have your own transport an interesting excursion takes you up into the pine forests south of Vytina, past the village of Elati (Ελάτη), then round a long loop through pretty countryside that ends up back on the main road just south of Stemnitsa. About halfway round look out for a left turn up to the old village of Libovisi, which was abandoned in 1880. Before that, it was the ancestral home of the Kolokotronis family, whose most famous son, Theodoros, was not the only one of them to be a thorn in the Turks' side. In fact they settled here, in 1536, in order to hide from the Ottomans, who were hunting them. A flavour of this warlike family comes from a contemporary folk song, which talks of how they never dismounted:

Ahorse they go to church,
Ahorse they kiss the icons,
Ahorse they receive communion
From the priest's hand.

Certainly most of the statues you see of Theodoros have him mounted, and he is said to have lived in the saddle, but there are scurrilous rumours that this was to hide his short stature.

Not much remains of the village save the church and the Kolokotronis's house, which was restored in 1988. If it is open, which it is erratically, there are paintings and old costumes inside. You can get back on the main loop by driving on and turning right at the junction.

MOUNT PARNONAS (ΠΑΡΝΩΝΟΣ) AND THE ARCADIAN COAST

The little-visited 50km-long extension of the administrative region of Arcadia that runs southeast from Tripoli was home to a tribe called the Cynurians in ancient time, and is still often referred to as Cynuria (Κυνουρία) and split between the municipalities of North and South Kynouria. Cynuria is a lovely area, incorporating the only stretch of coast in Arcadia, as well as the 1,934m peak of Mount Parnonas. Full of inviting coastal coves, pine forests and sweeping views, it could be explored as a slow and scenic alternative to the main road between Nafplio and the Laconian towns of Sparta or Monemvasia.

Coming from the north, the urban gateway to the Cynuria is Astros, some 35km southwest of Nafplio. Two main routes connect Astros to Laconia via Cynuria. More northerly and direct is the 85km route running inland from Astros to Sparta via Kastanitsa and the northern slopes of Mount Parnonas. Longer and more southerly is the route that follows the coast south from Paralio Astros for 50km to the port of Plaka, than runs inland for 45km to Geraki via Leonidio and Kosmas. From Geraki (page 144), you could either continue west to Sparta, southwest to Gythio and the Mani, or southeast to Monemvasia.

Both driving routes are described below from the northeast to southwest, which is how one would follow them travelling from Nafplio towards Laconia. But you should be able to follow either in reverse if desired. Either route is doable in half a day, but it is worth lingering; there are plenty of places to stop for some sightseeing, a leg stretch, a picnic or a taverna lunch.

You could also base yourself in the area for a few days. Some attractive lodgings are mentioned in passing below, and discreet wild camping, though technically illegal, is possible too. If you are thinking about the latter option, bear in mind that it is a fair bit cooler up here in the mountains, even in summer, and that campfires, and even gas burners, are a very bad idea up in the forests – even if you are boy-scout careful, you could get a hefty fine if caught.

Without your own transport getting around this area is hard, involving hitching or the infrequent buses (maybe one or two a week).

ASTROS (ΆΣΤΡΟΣ) Nestled within a river valley 2km inland of the Argolic Gulf, the small town of Astros was the site of the second Greek National Assembly in the wake of the war of Independence, and it is where the country's first modern constitution was drawn up under President Mavromichalis in 1823. It lies about 35km southwest of Nafplio along a road that hugs the coast for most of its length. Situated at the base of a hilly headland only 4km to the northeast of Astros, the tiny port of **Paralio Astros** (Παράλιο Άστρος) was once a popular package holiday destination. Paralio Astros is worth a second glance, boasting a Frankish castle, an attractive traditional fishing harbour that was renovated in 2015, and access to some good beaches with views across to Nafplio.

ASTROS TO SPARTA VIA NORTH PARNONAS Only 85km in length, but requiring at least 2½ hours to drive without stops, this back route leads through a mountainous area characterised by small winding roads that might vary greatly in condition from one year or season to the next. Maps struggle to keep up, and you might be surprised to find what appears to be an old track is a perfectly driveable road, while a 'major' route has degenerated into a mass of pot-holes, or is interrupted by short dirt passages under repair. You should be able to follow the route described below just by the aid of the directions given, perhaps with the help of a good Peloponnese map (page 42) to give you your general bearings. For those who want to explore further, their more detailed map of the area is useful, and it comes with a booklet that describes 4x4 routes.

Towards Mount Parnonas Starting in Astros, look out for signs towards **Platanos** (Πλάτανος) and follow them on to a road that soon heads upward. You climb slowly up and up, with increasingly good views back down to the coast. This is one of those roads that seems to be on top of the world, and it takes you into the heart of the mountains. At a junction, ignore the left turn towards **Haradros** (Χάραδρος), and turn right and down towards a river gorge. At the bottom of the gorge, as you cross to the other side, is a lovely rest stop, with information boards in Greek detailing the local wildlife.

Carrying on up the other side, there is a fork down to the left to Platanos. This village is worth a diversion, and has a pretty setting with streams and a waterfall running through it. There is a café and a taverna here.

Carrying on from Platanos, after about 6km, you come to the outskirts of the village of **Sitena** (Σίταινα), where there is another pleasant rest stop beside a spring. A path, apparently accessible to 4x4s, leads through the Sitena Fir Forest from here. In a normal car you can safely ignore this; you will be passing plenty of firs soon enough. The way through the village takes you straight past its two handsome churches; you will feel as if you are driving straight through the churchyards, but be assured that this is the main road.

Kastanitsa (Καστάνιτσα)

The next section of road is perhaps the loveliest in the area: the slopes of Mount Parnonas rise to your right, while Tripotamia Gorge drops away. Soon you see the village of Kastanitsa ahead, and after a corner, it appears perched across the gorge from you. For a short while it seems you are going past it, but then you cross the gorge and reach a junction. Turn left to go back and explore the village. If you are looking for somewhere to stay over, **Antoniou** (*5 rooms;* \ *27550 52255;* m *69790 03530;* e *info@sun-mountain-snow.gr;* w *sun-mountain-snow.gr;* **€€€**) has plain and simple rooms based around a wood-and-stone mountain aesthetic.

To explore Kastanitsa, it's best to park in the space outside the village, although be warned that this is where the bus turns, so keep to the side in case this is one of the occasional times it visits. Walking into the village you can either go down and right, and then up past a local produce shop, or down and left and straight along. Either will bring you out by the central square with its tavernas. It is a good-looking village to explore, with stone houses and wooden balconies overlooking the gorge.

Agios Petros (Αγ Πέτρος) and Vamvakou (Βαμβακού)

From Kastanitsa, go back to the junction just after crossing the gorge, and head in the other direction, switchbacking up through the fir trees for about 10km until you reach a surprisingly large crossroads bang in the middle of nowhere. Straight ahead is a dead end. Right would take you north along the other side of Mount Parnonas towards **Agios Petros**. For the purposes of this tour, you want to turn left. Ignore the first left-hand turn you pass (after 1.5km) but take the next one (after another 4km).

Going straight ahead here would lead to the village of **Vamvakou**, where the **Vamvakou Guesthouse** (*8 rooms;* \ *27310 27492;* m *69447 86798;* w *xenonasvamvakou.gr;* **€€**) comprises an old 'manor house' that was donated to the village by an émigré to South Africa, and combines good views and affordable rooms with a friendly atmosphere.

Polidroso (Πολύδροσο)

Assuming you turned left before Vamvakou, then not much further on you'll reach another signposted left turn that leads down towards the village of **Polidroso**, which you will see ahead. As you reach Polidroso you will arrive at a junction. Left takes you onward past the hotel, but the village is well worth a stop. To explore it turn right; this road leads to the village square. You may be able to park here; if not, turn around and look elsewhere, as driving further will give you a probably unwelcome crash course in extreme Greek village driving (impossibly narrow alleys, streams to ford, 45-degree slopes, etc). There are a couple of places to eat and drink here and it would make a lovely rest stop.

Polidroso is also known by its old name of Tzitzina, but its modern name translates roughly as 'Much Coolness', and it's a fairly accurate description. The surrounding countryside can be explored via an excellent selection of well-marked hiking trails. You can also stay at the **Pritanio** (*11 rooms;* **℡** *27310 26982;* **m** *69740 74340;* **e** *info@pritanio.gr;* **w** *pritanio.gr;* **€€€**), which stands in a handsome new cluster of buildings overlooking the village, and has a good restaurant and enthusiastic owners who can offer good advice on local hiking.

Agriani (Αγριάνοι) and Hrysafa (Χρύσαφα)
The onward route curls around Polidroso until it reaches another junction; go straight on over the stream. Ignore the first turn to the right and continue to the next junction, where you need to turn right towards Agriani, only 3km away. It is a good-looking village, with a large, modern church, but it is hard to know where to stop without blocking the road. Continue straight on, and on the road beyond it ignore a sharp turning to the left. You will soon emerge on another stretch that feels like you are on top of the world. At least it would do if the mighty bulk of the Taygetos could not be seen rising up before you in the distance.

You see the next village, Hrysafa, from high above, and then descend towards it in a series of switchbacks. On the outskirts turn right and down into the village. Hrysafa is famous for its Byzantine churches, one of which you will spot up to your right. From here on in, it feels like you have left the mountains behind you. A generally wide and easy road continues down (13km) to the plain of Sparta. When you reach a main road, turn right and then left on to the main highway to Sparta.

ASTROS TO GERAKI VIA THE COAST AND KOSMAS
The Arcadian Coast The 50km road from Argos to Plaka actually runs about 2km inland of and parallel to the coast for its first 12km, before arriving at the beautifully located but rather contrived resort village of **Arkadiko Chorio** (Αρκαδικό Χωριό). South of here you follow a beautiful cliffside road above an intriguing mixture of inviting coves and some rather overdeveloped resorts, varying between the sublime and the dreadful. Another 12km to the south, **Camping Zaritsi** (**℡** *27570 41429;* **e** *campingzaritsi@gmail.com;* **w** *campingzaritsi.gr;* **€**), on another beach, is the best of a handful of beachside campsites along this coast. Golden Beach, 4km to the south, is a great spot if swimming is on your agenda. It abuts the large resort of **Tyros** (Τυρού), which is not even redeemed by its thin and pebbly beach.

Far more tempting is **Plaka** (Πλάκα), which stands on the coast at the junction of the road running inland to Leonidio. Plaka has a long, sandy beach and a few places to stay; try the **Dionysus** (**℡** *27570 23455;* **m** *69708 04050;* **e** *info@dionysos-leonidio. gr;* **w** *dionysos-leonidio.gr;* **€€**). You could also divert 4km south to **Poulithra** (Πούλιθρα), which forms the southern terminus of the coastal road through Arcadia, and forms a good option for a rest stop or even a few days of relaxation.

Leonidio (Λεωνίδιο)
Surrounded by a fertile plain flowed through by the River Dafnon, the town of Leonidio, which runs almost immediately inland of Plaka, is named after a saint, rather than the ancient Spartan hero. This is the capital of the area, inhabited by the Tzakonian people. You won't find much evidence of them here, but some of the older folk in the mountains still speak the old language, much studied by linguists. They were probably a mix of Slavic tribes and the various

existing 'Greek' people, who preserved their local dialect because of their isolation. Don't mention this, however, as the locals trace their roots back to the Dorians.

Leonidio is famed for its aubergines, which grow in profusion in the fields around the town, and have a distinctive long and narrow shape, as well as light purple stripes. There is even an **aubergine festival** here in late August. It used to be a difficult town to drive through, but now you can follow the signs to a riverside boulevard that bypasses the centre of town. There are a few **buses** a day that go up the coast from here towards Argos and beyond.

Panagia Elonis (Παναγία Ελώνης)
The road inland of Leonidio runs through the gorge formed by the seasonal Dafnon for another 12km or so to the nunnery of Panagia Elonis, which is signposted to the left. While none of the nunnery's buildings are particularly old (it's been rebuilt too many times), the setting is fabulous. You follow a stepped path around the cliffside until you reach the surprisingly extensive monastic buildings, which seem to be on the verge of being crushed by the overhanging rock face and tumbled into the gorge far below. It is usually open to visitors throughout the day, although the silent nuns always seem to look at you with a slight air of disapproval; try to dress as respectfully as possible, and leave a few coins in the collection box.

Kosmas (Κοσμάς)
After another bendy 16km passing through the fir forests to the south of Mount Parnonas, you arrive at the village of Kosmas, perched at a lofty altitude of 1,150m on the southern slope of Mount Parnonas. The village's attractive central square wraps around the church, and it is fringed by a couple of excellent tavernas round the square, notably **O Navarchos** (↘ *27570 31489*) and **Maleatis Apollon** (↘ *27570 31494*; e *xatzpanos@gmail.com*), with the latter also offering agreeable and affordable accommodation (**€**). You could also drop into the shop called **Traditional Products Kosmas**, which stocks excellent honey, dried wild herbs collected in the mountain forests, and other such goods. An enjoyable 30-minute walk out of Kosmas leads through a large chestnut forest on the slopes below the village.

It's another 16km from Kosmas to Geraki, whose recently reopened hilltop archaeological site (page 144) is emphatically worth a stop.

5

Laconia
(Λακωνία)

Laconia, homeland to the Spartans, is a name redolent of the ancient world, but it is for more modern remains that most visitors will remember it. After visiting modern Sparta, many are attracted by the side trip to Mystra and are then captivated by the architecture and art of Byzantium. Further delights await at Geraki, and the heartbreakingly lovely Monemvasia.

Above all these are the mountains, which look forbidding, but with a bit of time and effort are surprisingly accessible.

SPARTA AND MYSTRA (ΣΠΆΡΤΗ (SPARTI) & ΜΥΣΤΡΆΣ (MYSTRAS))

Thucydides, the historian of the Peloponnesian War, famously commented that future generations would look for the evidence of Sparta's greatness and would be unable to find any. The Spartans themselves commented that they had no need to build city walls, as the fearsome reputation of their warriors was defence enough. All this is leading up to say that if you come here expecting to find Classical remains such as can be found in the city's great rival, Athens, you are going to be sorely disappointed. In fact little in the modern town dates back to before 1834, when it was refounded after the Greek victory in the War of Independence.

It is worth being persistent, though; Sparta, after initial first impressions, may well surprise you. There are still some remains to be seen, made more interesting because they are so little visited, and the city itself is well laid out and handsome, with wide boulevards and large squares, and it is decidedly untouristy. Moreover the setting is superb. Part of the reason that the Spartans needed no walls is that their natural defences were so good. To the west are the mighty Taygetos Mountains, a dramatic wall of rock whose peaks remain snow-capped well into May. To the east is the Parnonas range, here playing second fiddle, but anywhere else an impressive collection of mountains. Between them, with Sparta in its centre, lies a fertile plain, watered by the River Evrotas, its lushness contrasting with the bare rocks of the mountains.

All this, combined with the ancient fame of Sparta, would be enough to encourage a visit, but one last jewel in the crown remains: Mystra. The name of this medieval city is little known outside the ranks of Byzantine historians, but its remains are one of the highlights of the Peloponnese. So, too, are the less extensive but far quieter Byzantine ruins at Geraki some 40km east of Sparta; indeed the painted medieval churches at this little-visited site rank among the most atmospheric anywhere in the Peloponnese.

MYTHOLOGY Homer called this area 'hollow Lacedaemon', a reference to its bowl-like geography. The story goes that Lacedaemon married the maiden Sparta, daughter of Evrotas, and named his city after his wife. His territory he

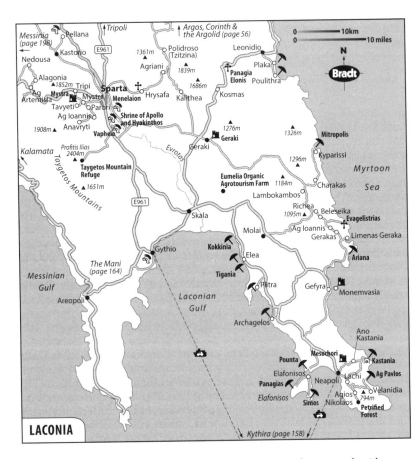

*Argos, Corinth &
the Argolid (page 56)*

*Messinia
(← page 198)*

Kythira (page 158)

*The Mani
(page 164)*

LACONIA

named Lacedaemonia, after himself. Ever since confusion has reigned, with many authors using the two names interchangeably. The ancient Greeks seemed to prefer Lacedaemonia, while the Romans plumped for Sparta. Nowadays the town is once again Sparta, or more authentically Sparti, and the region is Laconia.

The great myth of the region revolves around the outbreak of the Trojan War, and is mainly related in Homer's two epics, the *Odyssey* and the *Iliad*. The story starts with three rival goddesses: Hera, queen of the gods and Zeus's long-suffering partner; Athena, goddess of wisdom; and Aphrodite, goddess of love. They decided to have a competition to determine which of them was the most beautiful. To judge this they chose a mortal, Paris, a young prince of the city of Troy in Asia Minor (modern Turkey).

They were typical goddesses, however, and none of them had any intention of playing fair. Hera offered Paris great power if only he would choose her, while Athena offered him great wisdom. Only Aphrodite knew the best way to a young man's heart – she promised him the love of the most beautiful woman in the world, and duly won.

Unfortunately there was a bit of a problem: the most beautiful woman in the world at the time, Helen, was already married to King Menelaus of Sparta. Still, trifling details like this were not going to get in the way of a goddess's promise. Paris went to Sparta and was received with due hospitality by Menelaus. During a feast in his honour Aphrodite caused Queen Helen to become enamoured of the handsome youth and that very night they conspired together and escaped Sparta, spending their first night together at Gythio (page 165), before fleeing by boat back to Troy (possibly enjoying a 'honeymoon' on Kythira – page 157).

These events precipitated the ten-year siege of Troy, with the combined Greek armies led by the Great King Agamemnon of Mycenae (page 11). It only ended due to Odysseus's cunning ruse with the wooden horse. One of the most remarkable aspects of the tale is that, after all the bloodshed, a contrite Helen was welcomed back as Menelaus' queen. The historian Bettany Hughes, despite calling her book on the subject *Helen of Troy*, makes a convincing case that she should be known as Helen of Sparta (page 273).

Unlike at Mycenae or Pylos no Mycenaean palace complex has been discovered that we can link to the Homeric myths. Perhaps it lies somewhere under the modern town or was attached to one or other of the Mycenaean sites found in the surrounding countryside – a number of options are discussed in the text.

HISTORY As well as not being great builders of monuments, the Spartans were also averse to writing (one of their few poets, Tyrtaeus, wrote cheerful ditties about the joys of dying in battle), so we are reliant for their history on what others thought of them. There is an obvious danger in this, and it is often hard to separate the truth from the 'Spartan myth'. What is true is that they were, and still remain, the ideal of the warrior state: a whole society geared towards war (see box, page 133, for a description of how this worked).

Unsurprisingly, given the city's reputation, its history is dominated by conquest. The Spartan people first set about gaining control of Laconia itself, before turning their attention to fertile Messinia on the other side of the Taygetos Mountains in the 8th century BC. Around the same time they founded their only overseas settlement, Tarentum in southern Italy. Unkind outsiders said that this came about when the Spartan warriors, always away at war, were surprised to find their wives were still producing children, and exiled the dubious offspring.

By the 5th century BC, the Spartans entirely dominated their neighbours and were the head of the Peloponnesian League, an organisation of their own devising. A reckoning with Athens, the other great power of the time, was inevitable, but in 480BC the Persians, under Xerxes, invaded Greece and Sparta had the chance to cement the reputation of her warriors forever.

King Leonidas and his band of 300 warriors have once again entered the public consciousness, because of a rather fantastical 2006 film, *300*, that was adapted from a graphic novel, and its 2014 sequel. The true story of their last stand against unbeatable odds in the Pass of Thermopylae really doesn't need much embellishment. While it is true the odds were probably closer to 1,000 Greeks versus 150,000 Persians, rather than Herodotus's rather precise estimate of 300 versus 5,283,320, there is no getting away from the impact of the Spartan actions. When Leonidas realised that the Greek position was untenable he sent away most of the other Greek forces, thinking that a small force, although doomed, could sufficiently delay the Persian advance so that the rest of the Greeks could regroup. The Spartans knew that they were soon to die and started to ritually prepare themselves. A watching Persian spy was flabbergasted, believing the warriors to be merely combing their hair. It was said that two Spartans, to their shame, survived the encounter. One achieved a noble sacrifice in a subsequent battle, the other quickly committed suicide.

The Peloponnesian War (413–404BC) against Athens (page 14) saw Spartan victory over the rest of Greece and the summit of their powers. It didn't last long. First the Spartans suffered a decisive defeat by the Thebans under Epaminondas at the Battle of Leuctra in 371BC, and then fell successively under Macedonian control and, in 195BC, Roman. Subsequently Sparta was burnt by Alaric the Goth and invaded by Slavs. By the early medieval period it was little more than a village, huddled around the old acropolis.

In 1249, partly to counter the Slavic incursions, the Frankish prince William de Villehardouin built a castle on a rocky outcrop of the Taygetos. This pyramid-shaped spur, 5km from Sparta, was known to the local Greeks as Myzithra, after a local, soft cheese which was often formed into a similar shape. Over the years this became Mystra. Frankish control did not last for long, and in 1259 William was captured in the Battle of Pelagonia by the Byzantines. He tried to hide, but it is said he was recognised by his prominent front teeth. William was forced to cede the castle, among others, and thus began the Byzantine domination of the Peloponnese. Initially they based themselves at Monemvasia (page 146), but in 1348 Mystra was made the seat of the despot of the Morea.

The next 162 years saw one of the finest flowerings of Byzantine culture. While it couldn't rival Constantinople in scale, Mystra could certainly compete on the quality of its artistry and intellectual life. The despot (the word was yet to have any negative connotations) was ruler of the Peloponnese and was usually a son or brother of the emperor himself, and often his presumed heir. This made Mystra the de facto second city of the Byzantine Empire. As such it attracted the cream of cultural life, including artists (just look at the frescoes that survive in the city's many churches) and scholars. Perhaps Mystra's most famous inhabitant, bar the presumptive emperors themselves, was the philosopher Gemistos Plethon, who did much to revitalise Greek intellectual life, and was thus precursor and influence on the events of the Western Renaissance.

Plethon died in 1452 and so, mercifully, did not live to hear of the Ottoman conquest of Constantinople on 23 May 1453, nor yet the capture of his own beloved city in 1460, although he surely saw the writing on the wall. The city did live on through Turkish occupation and even had a resurgence under Venetian rule (1687–1715), when it reached its peak population of just over 40,000 people – not far under the population of Kalamata today, and double that of modern Sparta. After independence the need to huddle behind its walls lessened, and the population began to migrate to the refounded Sparta down on the plain, as well as to the modern village, just below the old walls. The city saw its last fighting in 1944, an action between resistance groups that presaged the civil war, and in 1952 the last few families were moved out and the Greek Archaeological Service started the long, and ongoing, task of restoring the city to its former glory.

GETTING THERE AND AWAY

By car Coming from Athens or elsewhere to the north, there are two main routes to Sparta. You can either take the national multiple-lane toll road the whole way, diverting southeast from the Corinth–Kalamata highway on to the newly opened last 50km stretch at the Gefyra interchange a few kilometres south of Megalopoli, or leave the toll road at Tripoli and head directly south on the old road. The new toll road is about 30km longer than the old road, and less scenic, but many people favour it as being faster and more hassle-free. Also worth considering if you are heading to or from Nafplio and the Argolid is the back route through Kastanitsa (page 121).

The route from Gythio to the south, while not a two-lane national road, is reasonably straight and fast. The fastest route to Kalamata entails following the toll roads all the way, via the Gefyra interchange, but this is about 40km longer than the more direct but slower route through the Langada Pass and Taygetos Mountains – the latter also being one of the most scenic drives in the Peloponnese (page 140).

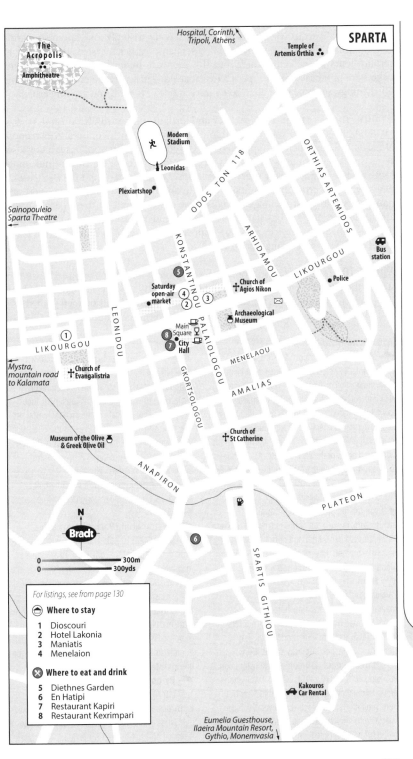

SPARTA

The Acropolis
Amphitheatre

Hospital, Corinth,
Tripoli, Athens

Temple of
Artemis Orthia

Modern
Stadium

Leonidas

Plexiartshop

*Sainopouleio
Sparta Theatre*

ODOS TON 118

ARHIDAMOU

ORTHIAS ARTEMIDOS

LIKOURGOU

Bus
station

KONSTANTINOU

Saturday
open-air
market

⑤

④
② ③

Church of
Agios Nikon

Police

Archaeological
Museum

①

LIKOURGOU

*Mystra,
mountain road
to Kalamata*

Church of
Evangalistria

LEONIDOU

Main
Square

⑧
City
⑦ Hall

PALAIOLOGOU

MENELAOU

GKORTSOLOGOU

AMALIAS

Museum of the Olive
& Greek Olive Oil

Church of
St Catherine

ANAPIRON

PLATEON

N

Bradt

0   300m
0   300yds

⑥

SPARTIS GITHIOU

Kakouros
Car Rental

*Eumelia Guesthouse,
Ilaeira Mountain Resort,
Gythio, Monemvasia* ↓

Laconia   SPARTA AND MYSTRA

5

For listings, see from page 130

🛏 **Where to stay**

1   Dioscouri
2   Hotel Lakonia
3   Maniatis
4   Menelaion

✖ **Where to eat and drink**

5   Diethnes Garden
6   En Hatipi
7   Restaurant Kapiri
8   Restaurant Kexrimpari

Parking in Sparta, owing to its wide streets, is surprisingly easy, and it shouldn't be too hard to find a spot somewhere. A scratch card ticket system is operated at certain hours in the central area, but this seems to be fairly laxly enforced. The tickets are purchased at local *peripteros* (roadside kiosks selling cigarettes, among other things; see box, page 202), so enquire at one of these if you are concerned.

By bus There are frequent buses back and forth north towards Tripoli and Athens (*3–4hrs*). Six a day go south to Gythio (*1hr*), four of which continue to Areopoli (*1hr 30mins*), and then a couple go on to Gerolimenas (*2hrs*). Six buses a day also serve the eastern route as far as Molai (*1hr 20mins*), three of which continue on to Monemvasia (*2hrs*). During the week four buses a day go to Neapoli (*2hrs 20mins*). Only two buses cross the mountains daily to and from Kalamata (*2hrs*). There are hourly buses to Mystra village (*15mins*), but only a couple of these go up to the archaeological site. The bus station is at the east end of Likourgou, about 500m past the museum. Some services also stop opposite the museum, which is a good place to get out if you are coming into town.

WHERE TO STAY Sparta has a range of good hotels, but there is no real reason to stay in the city. Even for those using public transport it is easy enough to head for the modern village of Mystra, where there are options for all budgets. For those with their own transport there are tempting choices in the mountains.

Sparta *Map, page 129*

🏠 **Menelaion** (48 rooms) 91 Konstantinou Palaiologou; 📞27310 22161; e info@menelaion. gr; w menelaion.gr. Bang in the centre, this large elegant Neoclassical hotel is easily the smartest in town. Inaugurated in 1935, it was requisitioned by Italian, German & later Greek troops during World War II, but reverted to being a hotel shortly after. The swimming pool, for the exclusive use of hotel guests, is a welcome addition this far from the sea. €€€€€

🏠 **Dioscouri** (30 rooms) 182 Likourgou; 📞27310 28484; e info@dioscouri.gr; w dioscouri. gr. If you can get past the 1960s Brutalist architecture, or are a fan of this outmoded concrete genre, this is a decent enough option for those on more of a budget. It overlooks a park about 500m along the road out towards Mystra. €€€

🏠 **Maniatis** (80 rooms) 72 Konstantinou Palaiologou; 📞27310 22665; e info@ maniatishotel.gr; w maniatishotel.gr. Just down the road from the Menelaion, it counters its Neoclassical charm with modern chic & is significantly cheaper, but lacks a pool. €€€

🏠 **Hotel Lakonia** (30 rooms) 89 Konstantinou Palaiologou; 📞 27310 28951; e info@lakoniahotel. gr; w lakoniahotel.gr. This comfortable & central hotel probably represents the best overall value in Sparta, with modern well-equipped rooms & a great buffet b/fast. Streetside rooms can be noisy. €€

Mystra *Map, page 135*

☀ 🏠 **Guesthouse Mazaraki** (11 rooms) 📞27310 20414; m 69377 13078; e info@ xenonasmazaraki.gr; w xenonasmazaraki.gr. Situated in the tiny village of Pikoulianika about 1km past the upper gate to the archaeological site, this exquisite boutique hotel has a superb location with views towards the fortress & Sparta. Rooms are in 2-storey stone cottages & have a light, airy ambience, fireplace, kitchenette & wooden balconies. Amenities include a swimming pool, an excellent traditional restaurant & a wine bar. €€€€€

🏠 **Mystras Grand Palace Resort & Spa** (29 rooms) 📞27310 21111; e info@mystraspalace. com; w mystraspalace.com. Focused around a massive swimming pool, this 5-star resort 2km from Mystra along the Sparta Rd positions itself as the most luxurious hotel in the Peloponnese. The spacious wood-&-stone rooms, complete with large marble-surfaced bathroom & standing tub, more-or-less live up to the hype (as do the prices), but it lacks the personality of the smaller boutique hostels listed elsewhere. €€€€€

🏠 **Pyrgos Mystra** (7 rooms) 3 Manousaki; 📞27310 20770; e info@pyrgosmystra.com; w pyrgosmystra.gr. Built in 1850, the stone 'Tower of Mystras' was once the social hub of the village & played host to the great & the good. It has been superbly converted into a special, if expensive, small hotel, one whose individually styled rooms are characterised by an exquisite eye for detail. In a quiet corner of the village, at the start of the road up to the Taygetos. €€€€€

🏠 **Byzantion** (26 rooms) ☎27310 83309; e byzanhtl@otenet.gr; w byzantionhotel.gr. This hotel, with its superb views up to the old city, has been housing travellers to Mystra for many years. It now has a nice garden pool & remains very good value. On the main road coming into the village. €€€

✳ 🏠 **Mystras Inn** (6 rooms) ☎27310 82666; m 69777 18068; e info@mystrasinn.gr; w mystrasinn.gr. Situated in the centre of the village alongside the Ellinas taverna, the budget ground-floor rooms here have windows looking directly into the square to make you feel like an integral part of village life. €€

⛺ **Camping Castle View** ☎27310 83303; w castleview.gr. Of the 2 campsites on the road between Sparta & Mystra, this is closer to the new village & the ruins, with a pleasant location among the olive groves about 200m to its east. It has a swimming pool & a couple of simple bungalows to rent. Buses will stop here on request. € (camping) or €€ (bungalow)

⛺ **Camping Paleologio** ☎27310 22724; e demikap@hotmail.com; w campingpaleologio. com. This campsite is located behind a petrol

station about 2.5km from Mystra on the road towards Sparta, & has less of a rural atmosphere than Castle View. However, it is pleasant enough, it also has a pool, & the welcome is friendlier. €

Further afield

🏠 **Eumelia Guesthouse** (5 rooms) Gouves; m 69471 51400; e info@eumelia.com; w eumelia.com. Set in the eponymous organic farm 50km southeast of Sparta (page 145), this friendly owner-managed guesthouse comprises 5 spacious cottages with fully equipped self-catering kitchens, a large lounge with a fireplace & a large bedroom. Stylishly decorated with warm colours, the cottages are designed in an eco-friendly way to stay cool in summer & to be heated hydrothermally in winter. Activities include farm tours, cooking lessons, wine & olive oil tasting, cycling & walking, & it is a useful base from which to explore most sites of interest in Laconia & the Mani. €€€€€

🏠 **Ilaeira Mountain Resort** (15 rooms) Toriza; ☎27310 35515; e info@ilaeira-resort. gr; w ilaeira-resort.gr. A very smart selection of hillside suites & villas on the way up to the Taygetos Mountain Refuge about 20km south of Sparta by road. Amenities include a stunning swimming pool with a view & 2 restaurants. €€€€€

🍴 **WHERE TO EAT AND DRINK** Spartan restaurants tend to be down-to-earth and untouristy, although coach tours do sometimes stop at the more accessible ones. Despite the stereotype of 'Spartan' food, they also tend to be very good. The main cluster of restaurants in Sparta itself is set around the central square immediately southwest of the junction of Likourgou and Konstantinou Palaiologou.

In Mystra, most of the restaurants are primarily catering to the lunchtime tour bus trade. The ones around the small square tend to be the most authentic.

Sparta *Map, page 129*
🍴 **Diethnes Garden** 105 Konstantinou Palaiologou; ☎27310 28636. Popular both with locals & guests staying at the trio of tourist hotels a block to its south, this well-priced family-run restaurant specialises in traditional Greek dishes. The cosy interior is decorated with old black-&-white photos of Sparta, & there's also shaded pavement seating.

🍴 **En Hatipi** 27 P Hrysikou 27; ☎27310 26677; f enhatipi. Tucked away 200m along the Gythio Rd, this family-run restaurant serves some of the

best traditional Greek food in Laconia, & is very reasonably priced. There's occasional live music too.

✳ 🍴 **Restaurant Kapiri** ☎27313 00520. Boasting a soothing interior of pastel greys & blues, & plenty of terrace seating, this relatively pricey option on the central square offers the closest thing in Sparta to fine dining. Strong on seafood & salads, but also a good choice of grilled & oven-baked meat dishes.

🍴 **Restaurant Kexrimpari** ☎27313 02440. The pick of the more affordable restaurants clustered around the central square, this friendly restaurant serves a fairly typical set of Greek taverna staples, but it's all tasty & affordable, & there's live music some evenings.

Mystra *Map, page 135*

✕ Chromata ✆27310 23995; m 69766 83050; f Chromata.Mystras. Boasting a stunning setting in Pikoulianika 1km uphill from the upper gate, this legendary restaurant is the ideal spot for a relaxed meal after exploring the archaeological site. Open for dinner daily but for lunch only over weekends. The cuisine is a contemporary take on traditional Greek cooking, & vegetarians are well catered for.

✷ **✕ Drosopigi** ✆27310 83744. A short 10min walk from Mystra to the nearby village of Parori. This is popular with locals & is the most reliable of the couple of tavernas that have a lovely setting around a spring & group of small waterfalls. It specialises in river trout, which can be chosen still live from the tank. Call first to check they are open.

✕ O Ellinas ✆27310 82666. On the small square, this serves up decent Greek fare.

OTHER PRACTICALITIES The basic geography of Sparta is a fairly simple grid system, based round two intersecting main roads whose names reflect the town's dual history. Likourgou, named after Sparta's mythical king, runs east–west, and Konstantinou Palaiologou, named for the last emperor of Byzantium, crowned at Mystra, runs north–south. Just by where they meet is the large central square, always a hive of activity, and noted for its evening *volta*, where half the town's inhabitants seem to come out for a social stroll.

Konstantinou Palaiologou is the main shopping street, and has banks and ATMs, as well as a couple of places to get foreign newspapers. The large supermarkets are to the south of town on the road to Gythio, but there are good alternatives in the centre. The tourist police (✆*27310 20492*) share offices with the regular police, just off Likourgou, past the museum. The post office is close by. The hospital (✆*27310 28671*) is signposted to the left on the road north out of town.

The town is fairly easy to cope with on foot, but for the outlying sights, bar Mystra, you will need your own transport. Taxis (✆*27310 24100*) are plentiful and easy to find or you can rent a car. The Sparta-based representative of Europcar, Kakouros Rent (*Gythiou 99;* ✆*27310 27784;* e *info@kakouros.gr;* w *kakouros-rent.gr; see ad, page 162*) has a good fleet of cars for rent at competitive rates.

WHAT TO SEE AND DO

Sparta Although the focus tends to be on historical sites, Sparta is not without contemporary interest. A highlight of the weekly calendar is the **open-air market** held on the corner of Vrasidou and Agisilaou every Saturday morning – an excellent place to buy local produce ranging from organic and wild vegetables to speciality cheeses, olive oil, figs and boutique wines. For funky but affordable modern trinkets, drop into the **Plexiartshop** (*143 Konstantinou Palaiologou;* ✆*27310 82635;* w plexiartshop.com), which specialises in colourful silkscreen products decorated with modern variation on ancient Greek patterns. Finally, the **Sainopouleio Sparta Theatre** (✆*27310 82470;* e *idrymaia@otenet.gr;* w *sainopouleio.gr*), 4km out of town along the old Kalamata Road, is a modern open-air venue built in the style of an ancient amphitheatre and used to host modern adaptations of ancient Greek plays during the summer months.

The Acropolis (⊕ *see box, page 52, free entrance*) The sparse remains of the ancient Spartan acropolis are found at the north end of Konstantinou Palaiologou, where a modern statue of Leonidas presides in front of the equally modern stadium; you can park here if needs be. Head up the road by the left-hand side of the stadium, which soon leads up into pleasant olive groves.

There have been few examples of societies as dedicated to waging war as Sparta (the Zulus under Shaka were another). Every male Spartan citizen had only one choice of employment, that of being a soldier, and he started his career at age 20 and carried it on, if he wasn't killed, until he was 60. Of course this lifestyle was only sustainable because there were other people to do all the normal work such as tilling the fields. This was done by *helots*, or slaves, who were often conquered citizens of other states or their descendants.

The story has it that if a Spartan baby was deemed to be feeble in any way, it was flung down a ravine, a rather primitive form of eugenics. While this may be a slander made up by enemies it was true that a Spartan boy only lived with his mother until aged seven, when he left to live in all-male barracks and army training began. They were underfed and stealing food to survive was encouraged, but severely punished if discovered. Another joy of growing up in Sparta was the ritual flogging that the boys endured at the Temple of Artemis. This often continued until they bled, and any sort of flinching or reaction to the pain was frowned upon.

When the boys reached 18 they became reserve members of the army. At this stage the elite were further trained by letting them loose in the countryside with only a knife with which to survive. It was understood that, while out there, they should hunt down and kill a few *helots*. This was not a crime, as Sparta ritually declared war on the *helots* each year.

Aged 20, men became full members of the army and carried on living in barracks, even after they got married. Marriage seems to have been a rather peculiar affair, at least by modern standards. The bride shaved her hair and was dressed in men's clothing before her husband visited her in secret in order to consummate the union. There have been various explanations for this – perhaps Spartan men would have been disconcerted by a normally attired woman, as they didn't come across them in their all-male world.

On the other hand many ancient sources emphasise the scandalous freedoms that Spartan women enjoyed, including owning property, exercising naked, and dancing in public. Many stories are also told of their role in encouraging their husbands into battle. Cowards were publicly humiliated, even by their own wives and mothers, and the men would be sent off to war with their shields and told to return 'either with it or on it', that is either victorious (still carrying their shield) or dead (carried on it).

Perhaps the most obvious legacy the Spartans have left us with are two words: Spartan itself, used to describe a simple and severe lifestyle or aesthetic, and 'laconic', which comes from the Spartan habit of giving pithy responses. One famous example of the latter is when the Persians at Thermopylae said that they would darken the sky with the number of their arrows. 'Good,' the Spartans are said to have replied, 'we like fighting in the shade.'

The ruins are few, and somewhat confusing. By far the best among them are those of the **theatre**, which is mostly Roman. Either head left at the brown sign through the olive groves to reach the few remaining rows of seats, or continue straight on up the cobbled path, and then left at the junction, to reach the top of the theatre, once one of the biggest in Greece, and with magnificent views over to the Taygetos Mountains.

Temple of Artemis Orthia (⊕ *currently kept closed, but easily viewable through the fence*) For those with an interest in Spartan history and culture, the ruins of this temple are an essential, if somewhat macabre, pilgrimage. To reach them follow the Tripoli road out of town, and where it turns sharp left at a large crossroads, go straight over and then right down a signposted track below a school.

This was where the ancient Spartan youth, not allowed to lounge about smoking, underwent a **ritual flogging** until they bled, thus proving their manliness. Back in Roman times, the local Spartans would recreate the ritual floggings for the entertainment of jaded Roman aristocrats. The site used to be almost derelict, and not so long ago was surrounded by a colourful gypsy encampment. It was tidied up, and fenced in, a few years back but do note that recently this has become an area where the homeless of Sparta congregate, and begging is not unknown.

The Archaeological Museum (↖ *27310 28575;* ⊕ *see box, page 52; €1*) Sparta's town museum is just along Likourgou from the central square, and has a reasonable collection of finds from the surrounding area although the signage is a little perfunctory. The highlights are some intriguing **clay masks** from the Temple of Artemis, some fine **Roman mosaics**, and, above all, the famous **bust of a Spartan hoplite** thrusting his chest forward beneath his well-plumed helmet. In modern times there has been some controversy over whether this is actually a statue of the noble Leonidas, hero of Thermopylae. Ignore this – of course it is.

Museum of the Olive and Greek Olive Oil (*129 Othonas-Amalias;* ↖ *21032 56922;* w *piop.gr;* ⊕ *summer: 10.00–18.00, winter: 10.00–17.00, closed Tue & public holidays; €3*) This excellent museum is part of a group of industrial museums set up by the Piraeus Bank Group Cultural Foundation that also includes the water mill museum at Dimitsana (page 114) and the environment museum at the Stymfalian Lake (page 257). It is housed in the generator rooms of the old electrical company, which have been renovated over two floors, and some outside space, to create a light and airy museum of a type that used to be rarely seen in Greece. The exhibits, which are labelled with extensive English commentary, follow the use of the olive throughout history, and include an interesting array of olive presses. Apparently the ancient Greeks used olive oil for cleaning, for lathering athletes and for sex, although the last goes unelaborated.

The museum is in the southwest of the town, and has a large car park if you are driving. It is signposted throughout Sparta, and for a surprising distance surrounding it, but these signs often seem to lead you around in a circle; refer to the map, page 129, to find it.

The Old City of Mystra (Μυστράς) (↖ *27310 83377;* ⊕ *summer: 08.00–20.00 daily, winter: 08.00–15.00 daily; €5*) Nowhere else does the medieval, and especially the Byzantine, world seem to come alive as it does at Mystra. The setting itself is breathtaking enough. The *Chronicle of the Morea*, the romanticised account of the Franks in the Peloponnese, calls it a 'strange hill, as though cleaved from the mountainside'. On this spur of the Taygetos are the ruins of an entire city, the old Byzantine capital of Morea, with its lanes and alleyways, palaces, castle and, above all, churches calling out for exploration. Even on the site's busiest day it is not hard to find a quiet corner where you can drink in the combination of natural and manmade beauty, and try to commune with the ghosts that walk the streets of this once-great city.

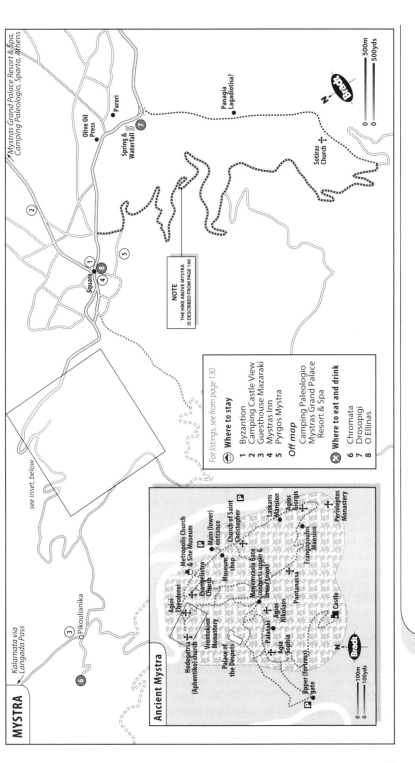

MYSTRA

Kalamata via Langada Pass

③ Pikoulianika

see inset, below

②

⑤ Square

① ④ ⑧

Olive Oil Press

● Parori

Mystras Grand Palace Resort & Spa, Camping Paleologio, Sparta, Athens

Spring & Waterfall ⑦

Panagia Lagadiotsa?

Sotiras Church ✝

NOTE
THE HIKE ABOVE MYSTRA IS DESCRIBED FROM PAGE 140

N

500m
500yds

0
0

For listings, see from page 130

ⓘ **Where to stay**

1 Byzantion
2 Camping Castle View
3 Guesthouse Mazaraki
4 Mystras Inn
5 Pyrgos Mystra

Off map
  Camping Paleologio
  Mystras Grand Palace
  Resort & Spa

✖ **Where to eat and drink**

6 Chromata
7 Drosopigi
8 O Ellinas

Ancient Mystra

Agioi Theodoroi ✝

Metropolis Church & Site Museum

Evangelistria Church ✝

Main (lower) entrance

Church of Saint Christopher ✝

Museum shop

Hodegetria (Aphentiko) church ✝

Vrontokion Monastery

Palace of the Despots

Monemvasia Gate (connects upper & lower town)

Laskaris Mansion

Agios Giorgis ✝

Frangopoulou Mansion

Pantanassa ✝

Perivleptos Monastery ✝

Palataki ✝

Agios Nikolaos ✝

Agia Sophia ✝

Upper (fortress) gate

Castle

N

Bradt

0   100m
0   100yds

Exploring Mystra Mystra lies 5km to the west of Sparta. From Sparta you can reach the modern village by a frequent bus (page 130), or reasonably priced taxis (*around €12*). Unfortunately the walking path, part of the trans-Europe E4 hiking trail, that runs between Sparta and Mystra has fallen into disrepair and is impassable in certain places.

Mystra is a large site, and can be tiring to visit, especially on a hot summer's day. At the very least you will want to spend a couple of hours here, but ideally you should set aside a half, or even a full day, for exploration. Wear good shoes, as some of the paths are rocky, and bring some water (you can refill your bottle at a few places, most notably at the convent at Pantanassa). Bringing a picnic is an excellent idea, although officially against the rules, and there are numerous quiet spots where one could be enjoyed. The only toilets at the site are just below the main entrance (your ticket remains valid if you leave and re-enter the site). There is a canteen selling drinks here in summer (the fresh juices are excellent) and on a loop of the road below there's a tourist café/restaurant. There are currently no facilities at the upper gate.

Mystra is approached through the 'new' village, from where the road winds up to its walls and the main entrance. This road then continues up past a turn for the upper, or fortress, gate, and then on to join the Sparta to Kalamata road. If possible, the best way to explore the site is by going in at this upper gate, climbing up to the castle, and then descending down the hill to leave by the main gate (perhaps sending the fittest member of the party back up to fetch the car?). This approach is assumed for the description below, but the map (page 135) will allow you to plan other routes. The signage around the site is pretty good, with English text describing various aspects of Byzantine life. Be aware that out of high season one or two of the churches may be closed owing to restoration or just lack of staff.

The city's fortifications, and therefore the city itself, are divided into three. The outer walls surround the **Lower Town**, where most people lived and ran their day-to-day lives. Another line of walls, with just a single gate leading in and out, divided this from the **Upper Town**. This was the imperial centre of the city, where the despot had his palace, and some of the more prominent citizens built their mansions. The final line of defence was the **castle** itself, high above the rest of the city.

The castle Entering through the **upper (fortress) gate** quickly brings you to a ticket kiosk, just past which the path forks. Down to the left is the Upper Town, but you would be wise to head up and right first, towards the castle, while your legs are still fresh. It is not a huge ascent, maybe 15–20 minutes, but is the steepest part of the site and can be exhausting on a hot day. It is well worth the effort.

At the top of the path a gateway leads into the outer wall of the **castle**. This was first built in 1249 by the Franks but has seen a fair few alterations over time, primarily by the Turks. An inner gateway leads to the keep and the highest point of Mystra (621m). Odd though it is for Greece, it is important to imagine that this was once, if only briefly, a centre of knightly chivalry, having more in common with King Arthur and the Round Table than the myths and gods of Classical times.

The views from here are simply superb. On one side you can see down to the city below, which is laid out like a map, the domed roofs of the churches waiting enticingly for your exploration. Beyond stretches the fertile plain of Laconia, full of the citrus orchards that are the main agriculture here, and the white splash that marks the modern town of Sparta. Beyond lie the mountains of the Parnonas range. On the other side the cliffs drop away, forming an impregnable defence to the south and west. From the ravine the sound of goat bells often drifts up to the ramparts. Above rise the mighty peaks of the Taygetos, often lined with snow from November to May.

above right The village of Limeni, in the southern corner of Itylo Bay, is a great place for swimming (PK/S) page 178

below right Working fishing boats line the Neoclassical harbour of Gythio (AB) page 165

bottom The island of Elafonisos is just a short ferry ride from Pounta (SS) page 153

top and above **Although difficult to reach with its spectacular position, Acrocorinth is most definitely worth the effort** (T/S and W/S) page 62

below **Epidavros theatre is one of the finest examples of Classical architecture in the world** (JK/DT) page 90

top The relatively undiscovered site of Ancient Messene contains an entire city, with everything from towering walls to a marketplace, stadium and tombs (PK/DT) page 203

above The monumental palace of Mycenae was already old at the time of the ancient Greeks (H/AWL) page 73

right The famed ruins of Olympia lie in a peaceful river valley (AVZ) page 229

top and above left   The ghost town of Mystra, in the foothills of the mountains, is full of beautiful Byzantine churches, including Perivleptos Monastery (F8/S and AVZ) page 139

above right   The Peloponnese is littered with exquisite medieval buildings like the convent at Pantanassa (AB) page 138

below   The beautiful views mask a past of battles and massacres at Methoni Castle (e/S) page 214

above   The Lousios Gorge is the quintessential Arcadian idyll, with its river flowing beneath red limestone cliffs and perilously perched monasteries (O/DT) page 111

below   The Bourtzi, a mini Venetian-built castle, was once an executioner's house, and can be seen from the waterfront at Nafplio (OM/DT) page 84

left	Village life often centres on the *kafenion*, which was until recently an all-male preserve (H/AWL) page 49
above	Various types of grapes, both red and white are grown around Nemea (LV/S) page 66
below	Kalamata's market is held twice-weekly and is one of the best in the Peloponnese (SS) page 201

above   A local preparing the regional speciality of *pasto* (smoked ham) (HM/A) page 46

below   Patra has one of the biggest carnivals in Europe in the weeks leading up to Lent
(sv/S) page 245

Annìska & Liakotò
Unspoilt Greece

Join Ilia and Geraldine Paliatseas in their seafront apartments - Anniska and Liakoto - the tranquil setting of the beautiful village of Kardamyli where the crystal blue waters o the Mediterranean meet the Taygetos mountains.

• enjoy the flexibility of apartment catering or eat in Kardamyli's many lovely tavernas
• swim in Liakoto's pool looking out on the Messinian bay
• relax on Anniska's seafront terrace
• taste the very best Peloponnesian wines

All rooms have fully equipped kitchenettes, balconies and air-conditioning.

Come and see us soon !

Google-earth us and visit our website: www.anniska-liakoto.com

BYZANTINE CHURCHES

When thinking of distinctive Greek architecture it is the white columns and theatres of the Classical world that spring most readily to mind, but it's often the legacy of the Byzantine Empire that most obviously faces the traveller. Not only do modern Orthodox churches follow a pattern set down by the styles of Constantinople, but there are also many churches from this era that still survive, most notably in the Mani region and in the abandoned city of Mystra.

Many of these churches are tiny, built by a single family, and they range in shape from a simple barrel vault to many-domed extravaganzas. The older, medieval churches, can often be spotted by their cloisonné brickwork, reddish-orange layers set in repetitive designs, although this style has also been carried on through the ages. They are also often notable for their re-use of older building material, including carved marble from the Classical period.

While they are beautiful from the outside it is also worth taking a peek inside some of these churches. The frescoes, if they have survived, can offer a stunning display of religious art. They usually follow a fairly set pattern, with the main dome, or centre of the ceiling, dominated by the Pantocrator, or Christ in His Majesty, holding up one hand in blessing. Surrounding him are the evangelists – Matthew, Mark, Luke and John – usually painted on the four squinches (the four curved triangles that connect the square church to the round dome). Below them are various saints, martyrs (often shown in rather gruesome detail at the event of their deaths) and various gospel stories. The screen separating the main body of the church from the altar is the iconostasis (or templon if it is made of stone not wood). Only priests are allowed past this threshold. On this are depicted (left to right) the Virgin Mary, Christ and, sometimes, John the Baptist – dressed rather scruffily, he carries his own severed head on a tray, even though he still has one attached to his neck. Above the altar, on a half dome, are the Virgin Mary and Child. Facing them, on the back wall, there is often the Crucifixion and below that the Last Judgement, with the blessed to the left (as you look at it) with halos, and the damned falling into the gaping jaws of a monster to the right.

Byzantine art can often seem staid and unemotional to western eyes, but look beyond the set formulas and traditions and it is often incredibly powerful, and even quirky and amusing on occasion. There is also nothing to compare with coming across a tumbledown church in the middle of nowhere, only to find its interior still emblazoned with frescoes.

A word of warning, however: these old churches used to be left open for any passing traveller or worshipper. Unfortunately this privilege was occasionally abused and they are increasingly kept locked. Local enquiries might produce a key holder (try the nearest kafenion), but may not. If you do gain access, dress respectfully (cover shoulders and knees), and leave some coins for the church's upkeep.

The very highest point of the castle walls forms a throne-like seat where, if you are brave, you can sit in isolated splendour with the landscape stretching out below in an unbroken sweep. It is a magical spot.

The Upper Town From the castle you need to head back down the way you came, before taking the downward fork in the path near to the ticket kiosk. The first building of note that you pass is the church of **Agia Sophia**, built from 1350 to 1365. Its frescoes are not as well preserved as those of some of the other churches in Mystra, but the building is handsome enough, unusually tall for its size. It was the official church of the palace, and several emperors' wives were buried here.

Beyond the church you reach another main fork in the path. The left-hand path leads down to the two-winged **Palace of the Despots**. Twenty years ago only the walls and a hollow shell stood, but painstaking reconstruction work has returned it to some of its former glory. This work is ongoing and you can't currently enter the buildings. It is hard to determine when the restoration might be completed, and how the buildings would then be used, but we live in hope. The larger of the two wings was clearly the **Great Hall**, which was heated by no fewer than eight large fireplaces. The area in front of the palace was open and probably served much as a modern town square does.

These are the best-preserved imperial buildings from Byzantine times in existence, and give some idea of the majesty of their contemporaries in Constantinople, now Istanbul, which sadly no longer exist.

Below the palace the two forks in the path rejoin each other. The other path passes by the **Palataki**, 'Little Palace', and the church of **Agios Nikolaos**. The Palataki was so named because of its size, but it was more probably a large mansion, belonging to a prominent merchant or government official. Agios Nikolaos is a youngster among the churches of Mystra, dating back only to the 17th century.

Down from here the path passes through the **Monemvasia Gate** into the Lower Town. This road used to reach all the way to Mystra's sister city of Monemvasia, in the far southeast of the Peloponnese (page 146).

The Lower Town   The lower section of Mystra lacks the spectacular views to be had from above, although they're still nothing to be sniffed at, but does contain the most exquisite of the city's churches. The first of these, **Pantanassa**, dedicated to the Virgin Mary, is arguably the most beautiful. It is reached by turning right at the first major fork in the path down from the Monemvasia Gate. The church is surrounded by a still-working convent, with around half-a-dozen nuns in residence. This means that before entering you should make sure you are respectfully dressed (knees and shoulders covered). The nuns thoughtfully provide garments that you can pull on, although these won't please the fashion-conscious! Many tourists in the summer choose to ignore the nuns' polite notice about dress code, but please don't join them.

The church itself (1428) is one of the last ever Byzantine buildings, and marks the final flowering of their style. It is a delight from start to finish, with a handsome bell tower adjoined to an arched portico providing framed views down to the Spartan plain. A close examination of the exterior shows a marked Western influence (such as pointed, Gothic arches over windows). Inside, the frescoes are stunning. The upper ones date back to the church's building. Look out especially for the Virgin herself, in the half dome above the altar, Christ's ascension into heaven on the ceiling above her, and the raising of Lazarus to the left (the bystanders are shielding their noses from the recent corpse's stench). The vibrant use of colour and the humanity in these paintings show that the Byzantines, had they survived longer, would have easily kept pace with the Renaissance in the West. The paintings lower down are later and less distinguished, but include some good, gruesome martyrdoms, including a flaying and a nailing to death.

At the back of the convent a path leads on, and down. This is often the quietest and most peaceful part of the site, out of reach of most tour groups. The path leads past the **Frangopoulos Mansion**, another rich residence, to the monastery of the

Perivleptos (late 14th century), tucked into the lower corner of the city. It is also tucked into the cliffside, and is half built into it. You get the impression that this was a quiet enclave of Mystra, even in its heyday. The frescoes inside are again magnificent, and include the only full representation at Mystra of Christ in his Majesty on the main dome, and an excellent Dormition of the Virgin (her 'falling asleep' – in the Monty Python sense of the words).

Another peaceful path runs from the monastery along the lower wall of the city. On the way it passes two small chapels which were probably private, family churches. The first of these, **Agios Giorgios**, is tiny and contains no frescoes, but there is something extremely attractive about the mixture of its tiled roof and intricate brickwork. The path also passes beneath another mansion house, that of the **Laskaris** family, which is also seeing some restoration work, before reaching the main **entrance gate**, set in the old, fortified gateway.

Continuing past the entrance gate you soon come to the **Metropolis** (1291) which was designed as the main cathedral of the city. It was originally not domed, but in the 15th century this was deemed unfitting for such an important church, so the top was sliced off and domed and a women's gallery added. Unfortunately this left many of the interior frescoes headless, and the architecture of the church a mite confusing. Nonetheless the interior is impressive, and in the floor a carving of the Byzantine double-headed eagle marks the spot where Constantine XI Paleologus, the last emperor, was crowned. He died not long afterwards, fighting the Turks on the walls of Constantinople.

The church is surrounded by beautiful colonnaded courtyards which, as always, have lovely views down to the plain. On the upper floor of these is the small site **museum**, blissfully air conditioned in the summer months, which contains various bits of sculpture and fresco. Perhaps the most intriguing exhibit is the fragments of silk dress recovered from a noblewoman's grave, along with a lock of her hair. The museum was originally set up by the French Byzantinist Gabriel Millet (1866–1953), who deserves mention as he devoted much of his life to preserving the treasures of Mystra.

On the outside wall of the courtyard, viewable from the path, is a metal grille protecting a stone splashed in spots of what is said to be blood. This marks the spot where the Turks, in 1760, executed Ananias Lambardis, Bishop of Lacedaemonia, for plotting with the Russians against them.

The next church along is the well-proportioned, 14th- or 15th-century **Evangelistra**. Inside there are some intricate, patterned carvings, particularly on the iconostasis and the capitals on the columns.

The path now turns left and uphill towards Mystra's final glory, the monastery complex of **Vrontokion**. Still surrounded by walls, and containing the ruins of many of its buildings, this monastery was once the richest in the Peloponnese, and it contains two churches that were built to rival those of Constantinople itself. The first of these is **Agioi Theodoroi** (late 13th century), the oldest church in Mystra. Its beauty is chiefly external, with its patterned tilework and huge dome. The price of the latter is that it needs eight columns to support it rather than the usual four, making the interior of the church notably darker than most.

The main church of the monastery goes under two names, either **Hodegetria** or **Aphentiko** (1322). Either way its beautiful roof is a harmonious mixture of domes and barrel vaults that come together in an almost organic whole. It is a masterpiece of architecture that, unlike its companion church, allows the interior to be light and airy. The frescoes are excellent and include a selection of Christ's miracles, such as turning the water into wine. One of the side chapels contains the tomb of the

(2½hrs; easy, but precipitous at one spot; spring water available at several spots)
This short, circular walk gives you an insight into the Taygetos Mountains without you having to do too much climbing (the ascent is about 300m). Despite its brevity, the walk passes some spectacular scenery and several diverse landscapes, starting in a dramatic gorge, passing through a forest, and finishing with splendid views across to Mystra itself.

There is drinking water at the Sotiras church, a bit over halfway through the walk. The last section of the walk, and its very beginning, are on tarmac roads, but they see hardly any traffic. See the walking guide on page 42.

0mins Start in the square of the modern village of Mystra. With your back to the main road up to the site, head out on the 1km road ahead to the village of Parori (Παρορι). Shortly before entering Parori, you pass an olive-oil press on your left. Shortly after this, ignore a fork to the left, and curl right up into the village. You will see the gorge ahead.

10mins Passing the Taverna Drosopigi and a spring and waterfall, you cross a small bridge over a river. Immediately after crossing the bridge, turn right on to the wide path into the gorge indicated by brown sign. The gorge quickly becomes dramatic. After a quarry on the left the path narrows.

18mins Shortly after the path's first switchback, it forks. It is emphatically worth detouring down the path to the right for 100m to the cave church of Panagia Lagadiotisa. It's an inspiring spot, decorated with traces of frescoes dating back to the 14th century, and you can hear, and just see, a waterfall up the gorge.

Byzantine emperor Theodore II, who abdicated the throne in order to return, as a monk, to his beloved Mystra. He is depicted above the tomb in both imperial and monkish garb. Another side chapel has walls covered with written imperial edicts listing all the monastery's many possessions, which included land all over the Peloponnese.

From the monastery you can either backtrack to the main entrance or carry on through the interior of the city, where various little paths can take you down again.

Around Sparta and Mystra

Langada Pass (Λαυγάδα) This route – above Mystra, between Sparta and Kalamata – is one of the most dramatic in the Peloponnese, and traces the route Telemachus, Odysseus's son, took between the palace of Nestor at Pylos, and that of Menelaus at Sparta. The gorge at its beginning is one of the candidates for where the ancient Spartans might have exposed their unwanted babies. As you climb up the gorge the road passes through the small village of **Tripi** (Τρύπη) which clings to its side. There is a spring here, and opposite a popular taverna with a balcony overlooking the gorge.

The road crests its peak at about 1,600m. It is worth noting that you are now a good 250m above the top of Ben Nevis, Britain's tallest peak, yet mountains still tower above you. There is a good coffee stop here that looks like a Swiss ski chalet; it is noted for its hot chocolate, and good yoghurt and mountain honey. The road now descends and passes through the isolated village of **Artemisia** (Αρτεμισία). There

22mins Return from the cave church to the junction, but this time take the left fork to climb up above the waterfall, and then cross another one over an old stone bridge. Shortly after, a concrete lid covers a water pipe and the path continues along on top of it. This makes for easy walking and you almost feel you should be rollerblading along. This is not recommended! Although one section of it clings to an overhanging cliffside, it is now hemmed in by a fence that should reassure even the most nervous of vertigo sufferers.

45mins When the concrete ends you enter a forest, cross the river, and arrive at the modern church of Sotiras. It's an idyllic place, made even more so after the hot climb by the availability of drinking water from spring taps. The cross-European hiking trail E4 passes the church here. You can also walk along this near Kalavryta (see box, page 250). Turn right on to the E4, heading slightly uphill and away from the church. (A left turn, past the church, leads you in the direction of Anavryti; page 142.) The wide track soon levels out and, just past some shepherd huts, gives you views down to the gorge, and the path you came up, far below.

1hr 10mins When you reach the tarmac road you are rewarded with views across to Mystra. Turn right and down. After about 10 minutes, look out for a red shrine on the right where a path (30m) leads to a small spring. This does not run every year, but when it does villagers have been known to drive 30km to fill up a carload of its sweet waters.

1hr 50mins You come into the back streets of Mystra from where you can quickly make your way back to the square.

are two excellent **grill tavernas** on either side of the village. The first is the **Taverna Koupitsa** (✆ 27210 76117; m 69721 34953; w *koupitsakalamata.gr*), which stands under the trees on a sharp bend some 500m before entering the village. The second is the **Taverna Theotokos** (✆27210 76219), which stands opposite a mountain spring about 500m past the village centre, and enjoys great views. Both serve excellent lamb and other Greek dishes, and either would make for a great place to stop and have lunch as you cross the mountains, but my nod goes to Theotokos, if only for the views. Roadside stands and one shop sell superb mountain honey and dried herbs.

You could carry on from here directly towards Kalamata, and if you do so the scenery remains dramatic. However, there are two diversions on either side of the road if you have the inclination. Both will take you deep into the mountains through hidden villages. The routes are tarmac, but mainly single track and fairly serpentine (although you will meet little other traffic, if any). One big surprise is that these villages are not entirely abandoned; after all, they are often cut off by snow.

The first diversion off the main route leads to the north from Artemisia via Alagonia (Αλαγονία), Machalas (Μαχαλάς) and Nedousa (Νέδουσα). The last of these is noted for the unusual **carnival** that takes place here on Clean Monday (the first day of Lent; page 50). The villagers, and often visitors, dress up as goats and perform various dances and rituals. It's all rather mysterious and pagan, and indeed similar events are described by Hesiod back in the 7th century BC. If you want to attend the festivities be warned that many Greeks have the same idea and it is often tough to get near the village – you will need to be persistent, but it is highly recommended. Even out of carnival time this route offers an interesting insight into mountain life. Carry on from Nedousa to rejoin the main road to Kalamata.

There is another loop off the main road to the south that also offers terrific views among hidden valleys and villages. This route starts shortly after the café at the main road's highest point and heads south through Ladas (Λαδάς) and Karveli (Καρβέλι). It would be possible to explore both these diversions (with a bit of backtracking on the main road and a few stop-offs) in about half a day.

Anavryti (Αναβρυτή) A good bet for those who want to hike in the Taygetos, or simply just get a closer view of the mountains and life among them, this village is perched at an altitude of 800m high above Mystra. Heading out from Sparta you can spot the rather startling 15km road to Anavryti switchbacking up the mountains to the south of Mystra. Unfortunately there are no longer buses running to the village. A taxi up here from Sparta costs about €25. If you are driving, head south out of modern Mystra through the villages of Parorio (Παρόριο) and then Agios Ioannis (Αγ Ιωάννης). The road snakes up just beyond the latter – look out for the signs. It is an exhilarating drive, seemingly straight up a cliffside, and you complete no fewer than ten switchbacks before you reach the top. A low concrete wall now edges the road all the way up, making it feel a bit safer than it once did. At the top the road crosses over into a lush mountain valley, a landscape that is hidden from the plains below, before reaching the surprisingly large and prosperous village of Anavryti.

When Sir Patrick Leigh Fermor (see box, page 188) was in Sparta in the 1950s, he was warned, half-jokingly, to be wary of the villagers of Anavryti, who apparently were all Jews, exiled by Agios Nikon, a warrior saint of the 9th century. The story is still told today, although Nikon sometimes seems to have transmuted to the better-known Nikolaos. Sir Paddy, always a romantic scholar, did manage to uncover some evidence of a link between the Jews and ancient Sparta, but the story has more to do with jealousy of the business acumen of the villagers and old-fashioned stereotypes.

That they have done well for themselves is pretty evident. The villagers built their fortunes as wool and leather merchants, but now, apparently, most Anavryti families are millionaires and spend much of their time in the US. It is not hard to believe – this inaccessible mountain village is full of locked-up but beautifully maintained mansions.

The village is well set up for **walkers**, with map boards showing the several trails that start here – head north out of the village on the E4 hiking trail and you will intersect with the walk described on page 250. There is also a grand-sounding **Museum of Geology and Botany**, next to the now-closed school (this had almost 300 pupils not so long ago), but unfortunately it is rarely open. For simple traditional Greek food, try the **Taverna Soumaki**, 200m from the village on the road back towards Sparta. A good overnight option in the heart of the village, the family-run **Guesthouse Arhontiko** (*5 rooms;* m *69871 28554;* w *kaneltrekking.gr;* €€€) can also offer advice about hiking in the vicinity.

The Menelaion (Μενελαιον) (⊕ *nominally 08.30–15.00, but actually always open*) This is the remains of a shrine to Menelaus and Helen, but could also be the site of their palace itself. To find it head out of Sparta on the Tripoli road, and immediately after crossing the Evrotas River turn right on to the road towards Geraki. After 3km look out for the large shrine on the left and the sign pointing up a small road to the Menelaion. This starts out somewhat rough and soon degenerates badly. Unless you are in a 4x4 and know what you are doing, it is best to park by the chapel 200m up the road and walk the last 1km (*15–20mins*). The road currently has been partially repaired so that it looks as though you can carry on past the chapel. Don't be fooled – after two tight hairpins it gives out again.

The ruins are a squarish structure of large blocks on what appears to be three levels. The main reason for coming here, however, are the views, which stretch across the Evrotas and Sparta towards Mystra and the Taygetos. It certainly feels right as the site of a Mycenaean palace, but unfortunately few remains have been found. Head back down the path a little, and slightly to the right towards another flat area, to see the remains of a 15th-century BC dwelling whose size led to it being proclaimed a 'mansion', not a palace.

Recent scholarship, however, has offered a tantalising possibility. The area is highly prone to earthquake activity, and geological evidence points to this hill once being far more extensive than it now is. Could the rocks, and the palace with it, have tumbled into the river below? If so then the 'mansion' would merely have been the storage basement of a far larger structure above.

Pellana (Πελλάνα) (🕐 *gates often unlocked, some ruins visible if not*) Another candidate for the site of Homeric Sparta lies 25km northwest of the modern town. The ruins are not huge, and are less attractively positioned than those of the Menelaion, but the drive through the rural hinterland of Laconia makes the trip worthwhile, and this would make an excellent **back route** towards Megalopoli and Arcadia. Note, however, that the new national toll road also comes this way (page 105). The old road should remain a more pleasant option and can be followed with the directions below.

Once again head out of Sparta on the Tripoli road, but this time take the left turn before the Evrotas, which is signed towards the hospital. The road starts by winding through orange groves before passing the scant remains of a **Roman aqueduct**, then climbing into the foothills of the Taygetos. **Kastorio** (Καστόρειο), a handsome market town, offers promising tavernas around its central square. Soon after, the road crosses the pretty river of Vrisiotino and there is a signed right turn towards Pellana. In the village follow the brown signs between two kafenia, and soon turn right past a church and down a farm track.

On the hill above are scattered remains of Mycenaean origin (2500–1500BC), which could possibly be from a **palace structure**. This supposition is supported by the collapsed **tholos tombs** a few hundred metres further up the road between the two kafenia (only viewable if the gate is unlocked). The largest of these has a diameter of 10m, now covered by a wooden shelter, and is certainly large enough to suggest a royal burial. Is this the tomb of Menelaus, or even Helen, the 'face that launched a thousand ships'? Probably not, but you never know.

Amyklai (Αμύκλες) The final contender most certainly was a large Mycenaean settlement, the largest yet found in Laconia, but doubt still remains over whether it is the palace referred to in Homer. Nowadays the sparse ruins are mostly of the Classical **Shrine of Apollo and Hyakinthos**. The latter was an ancient god, co-opted by the worshippers of Apollo, who made him into a handsome youth whom Apollo loved and accidentally killed. His spilt blood turned into hyacinth flowers.

To get to this shady, church-topped hill, which would make a nice picnic spot, drive 8km south of Sparta on the Gythio road to the modern village of Amikles, and look out for the large sign directing you down the tiny road to the left. Follow the signs 1km straight down this road. There has been some recent excavation work here, so perhaps we'll have more answers soon.

If this was Homeric Sparta then the royal tomb was just to the south at **Vapheio** (Βαφειό). Carry on down the main road another 2km and turn left at another signed road that is easy to miss. Drive another 2km through the modern village and turn right (signed) just after the small platea (village square). When this road turns to a crazy-paving path, park and walk. This tholos tomb is enormous, and two famous gold cups, both adorned with scenes of bull-taming, were found here (now in the museum at Athens), which give credence to a royal interment. However, nowadays it is just an impressively big hole in the ground.

Mount Profitis Ilias (Προφήτης Ηλίας) Given that the Taygetos Mountains, viewed from the plains around Sparta, look like an impassable wall of rock, they are surprisingly easy to get to. The tallest of them, and thus the tallest peak of the Peloponnese, is Profitis Ilias (2,404m), named after the prophet Elijah, like so many other Greek mountains (see box, page 254). It is one of five mountain peaks collectively named the Pendadaktilos, 'the five fingers'.

The best way to reach it, or at least get close, is to follow the prominent sign to the **Taygetos Mountain Refuge** a couple of kilometres south of Amikles. Follow the signs through the two villages of Anogia (Ανώγεια) and Paleopanagia (Παλαιοπαναγιά), before turning uphill and continuing for 9km (with good views of the pyramid-shaped Profitis Ilias) to a small car park and picnic area by a babbling brook. A dirt road leads on from here to the refuge, but it is more pleasantly reached by a well-waymarked trail (*1½hrs*) through the trees. If you want permission to stay at the refuge, or advice on reaching the peak, it's best to make advance contact with the **Hellenic Alpine Club of Sparti** (*97 Gortosologou;* ☏ *27310 22574;* e *eosspa@otenet. gr*). Failing that, contact the 2407 mountain shop on the other side of the Taygetos in Kardamyli (page 193) for advice. It is more romantic, but colder, to sleep at the peak itself, where there is a small chapel and some scant shelter. At sunset and sunrise you will see the mountain's impressive shadow. Hordes make the climb for 20 July, Elijah's name day.

Geraki (Γεράκι) Easily but unfairly dismissed as the poorer, smaller sister of Mystra and Monemvasia, the Byzantine hillside town of Geraki, topped by a Frankish castle, seems to have rather forgotten by the rest of the world, overshadowed by its flashy siblings. In a way this is a good thing, allowing you to explore this site in solitude, and giving a taste of what somewhere like Mystra must have been like in the 1950s or 60s. But it is a shame for the inhabitants of the nearby modern village, whose visions of coachloads of tourists descending on their little community has never materialised. If you have time, pop in and pay them a visit; they'll be delighted and it is well worth the effort (see opposite).

The archaeological site of **Geraki** (⊕ *see box, page 52; free entrance*) stands on the limestone Paliokastro Hill, which rises to 562m immediately east of the modern village. Closed for restoration and enhancement for several years, Geraki has now reopened with a small visitors' reception where you can watch an informative short video about the site before exploring it for yourself. Reasonably extensive, the site itself is a gem, housing the third-most important Byzantine relics in Laconia (after Mystra and Monemvasia), and it is also liberally dotted with interpretative panels. Most of the buildings lie in various stages of ruin, but three main churches are well preserved – a torch would be useful for these, but is not essential. The first is that of the 13th-century cross-vaulted **Agia Paraskevi**, which was clearly founded as a family chapel; you can see the family members frescoed on the church's back wall, along with the saint herself in a niche on the left-hand wall. A stepped path leads up the hill from here, through the ruined buildings, before reaching another larger church, that of **Zoodochos Pigi**. Inside it contains frescoes of impressive colour, including a fine Virgin and Child in the half dome, and a depiction of Christ carrying the cross to Calvary on the back right wall as you enter. This single-vaulted church was constructed in the 13th century, but its paintings date to 1430–31.

At the top of the hill the path crosses through the arched main entrance of **Geraki Castle**, which was built in the mid 13th century by Guy de Nivelet, a Frankish knight. It soon passed to the Byzantines, its history closely mirroring that of Mystra. The 10m-high castle walls, whose irregular shape follows the hill's contours, are still well preserved in parts, and enclose an area of 5,000m². Protected within them is the church of **Agios Giorgios** which was built at the same time as the castle. An unusual feature of the church interior is the stone shrine to the left, surrounding a fresco of St George himself. It has clear Western influences, and is carved with the coat of arms of Guy de Nivelet and a Frankish fleur-de-lis. The church also contains several well-preserved medieval paintings.

The views from the hilltop castle to the modern village and ancient olive groves that swathe the Laconia Plains are truly breathtaking. On a clear day you can see all the way from the Taygetos and Mystra, 33km to your right, to the rock of Monemvasia, poking into the sea 45km to your left. It is said that the Byzantines had a system of signal fires that passed messages between the three castles.

Founded in the late 15th century after the ancient hilltop citadel of Geraki was abandoned, the eponymous **modern village** is delightful, and something of a throwback, seemingly barely changed since the 1950s, with narrow alleys filled with old-fashioned shops. It is a friendly place as well, and the locals, mostly of the older generation, greet strangers warmly. **Cafés and tavernas** can be found around its central square. The village women have formed a co-operative called **Ergani** (✆ 27310 71208) to revive the art of **carpet and rug weaving**, for which the village was once renowned; it has a showroom on the main square. To top it all, it is also the site of the ancient city of **Geronthrai**, and some (Mycenaean?) walls can be seen at its highest point.

Geraki lies about 40km east of Sparta by road. Self-drivers should first head to the village of Geraki, then follow the Agios Dimitrios road southeast for 1km past the striking double-vaulted church of Agios Athanasios (and adjacent cemetery), before turning left on to the signposted 1.5km feeder road that winds uphill to the entrance. Without your own transport, visiting Geraki can be difficult. Buses run from Sparta to the village (*2–3 daily; 45mins*), and you might be able to organise a taxi or another lift from here to the ruins (*10mins*). You could also walk – it's less than 3km in either direction, albeit rather steep towards the summit.

Eumelia Organic Agrotourism Farm (m *69471 51400*; e *info@eumelia.com*; w *eumelia.com*).

This 20ha family farm on the Laconia Plains 50km southeast of Sparta and 12km from Geraki is run by a husband-and-wife team dedicated to organic methods and permaculture. It incorporates a 2,000-year-old olive grove, organic fruit orchards and vegetable gardens, and newly planted vineyards of rare traditional Greek grapes used to make its own organic wines. The couple who run it are enthusiastic hosts and speak fluent English, and they offer fascinating tours of the farm, as well as cooking lessons (how to make super-thin phyllo pastry), wine-tasting sessions focused on locally grown organic wines, olive oil tasting and yoga retreats. These activities were initially aimed mainly at overnight visitors staying at the farm's delightful boutique guesthouse (page 131), but they are also open to day visitors by appointment.

TOWARDS MONEMVASIA

The approach to Monemvasia is made either from Sparta, via a large interchange 17km along the road south, or from Gythio. The latter route starts very pleasantly, meandering along a coast lined with **sandy beaches and coves**. One of the best of them is Valtaki Beach, which has a shipwreck on it that deserves a photo stop, even if you are not swimming. This is the wreck of the *Dimitrios*, and it has been stranded here since 1981; the rumour is that it was involved in cigarette smuggling between Turkey and Italy, though how it ended up here is shrouded in mystery.

The two routes join at the provincial town of Skala (Σκάλα), and from here on to Monemvasia the direct route passes a string of similar towns. The only one that need detain the visitor is **Molai** (Μολάοι), where you might need to change buses if going to or from Monemvasia to Neapoli or Gythio. If you've a couple of hours to kill in Molai, the 30-minute hike from the town centre west through the Lanarka Gorge to the church of Panagitsa Mary offers some fine views back over the town.

South of Skala is the drainage basin for the Evrotas River, which flows south from Sparta. It forms a large **wetlands** area, which is important for migratory birdlife, but often uncomfortably mosquito-infested for humans.

On the coast south of Molai there are a few **beach resorts**, mainly aimed at the Greeks. They are all pleasantly low key, at least outside of August and the holidays. However, the beach at **Kokkinia** (Κοκκινιά) is not up to much. **Elea** (Ελιά) is a better bet; a pleasant enough little place with a tiny town beach, and a bigger one just to the south. The beach in **Tigania** (Τηγάνια), a bit farther on, is nicer still.

Plitra (Πλύτρα) is a larger resort that is probably heaving with Greeks in season but is pretty laidback the rest of the time. The sandy beaches, below a pretty headland, are Blue Flag-winning, and there are cheap, basic rooms available. Finally **Archangelos** (Αρχάγγελος), 'Archangel', is also worthy of a swim stop.

MONEMVASIA (ΜΟΝΕΜΒΑΣΙΆ)

It's impossible to avoid the hackneyed comparison between Monemvasia and Gibraltar, and it does bring up an image that is, in large part, accurate. Monemvasia is a great rock that rises up out of the sea, with only a thin connection to the mainland, but it doesn't convey the place's main feature, which is an enormous dollop of romance. Above all Monemvasia is for couples: to wander, hand-in-hand, down the cobbled lanes; to browse the small boutiques in search of art or jewellery; to sip cocktails on terraced platforms above tiled roofs. It is still a place of beauty for those on their own, but if you are in love, you have found your Mecca.

Monemvasia is basically a Byzantine settlement, much like Mystra. The major difference is that it was never abandoned, and people still live here. Anywhere else this would have led to modernisation and the loss of the old town, but Monemvasia had one advantage going for it, and the clue is in the name: it means 'Single Entrance'. Like Mystra the town was surrounded by walls, and there is only one gateway that leads through them towards the causeway and the mainland. Crucially it was, and remains, too small for cars. The villagers probably cursed this, and many of them moved to Gefyra (Γέφυρα), the mainland settlement opposite the rock, but it meant that the old style of the town endured. For a long while this historical survival was its main interest, but about 20 years ago people started noticing Monemvasia's other virtue: its breathtaking, heart-stopping, beauty.

Fortunately the locals, and others who bought property, realised that they must preserve the nature of the place, meaning that development has been careful and

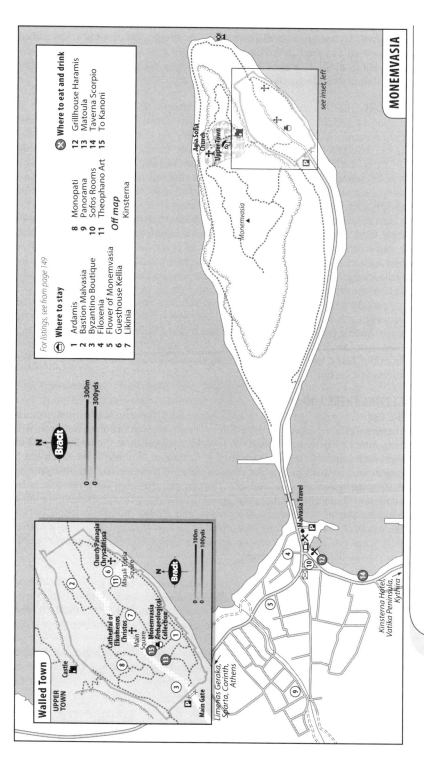

For listings, see from page 149

Where to stay
1 Ardamis
2 Bastion Malvasia
3 Byzantino Boutique
4 Filoxenia
5 Flower of Monemvasia
6 Guesthouse Kellia
7 Likinia
8 Monopati
9 Panorama
10 Sofos Rooms
11 Theophano Art

Off map
Kinsterna

Where to eat and drink
12 Grillhouse Haramis
13 Matoula
14 Taverna Scorpio
15 To Kanoni

MONEMVASIA

Walled Town

UPPER TOWN
Castle

Church Panagia Chrysafitissa

Cathedral of Elkomenos Christos

Monemvasia Archaeological Collection

Magali Tsipia Square

Main Square

Main Gate

Limenas Geraka, Sparta, Corinth, Athens

Malvasia Travel

Agia Sofia Church
Upper Town

Monemvasia

see inset, left

Kinsterna Hotel, Vatika Peninsula, Kythira

measured. Hotels are in well-restored old buildings, and the town has gained a reputation as an artists' colony. The atmosphere of the old town has actually benefited from this new lease of life, and as long as nothing bigger than a donkey can get in, it should long continue.

HISTORY The first extensive Byzantine settlement of Monemvasia was set in motion by Emperor Maurice in AD580, but its defensive advantages must have been noticed a long time before that. They were put to the test in 1147, when the city survived an attack by the Normans of Sicily. It eventually succumbed, if only briefly, to the Franks. William de Villehardouin laid siege to Monemvasia in 1246. It is a testament to its unassailable position that this lasted for three years, and the population only surrendered when they had absolutely no food left; they had already gone through the cats, dogs and rodents.

In 1260, after William's defeat, the city returned to Byzantine hands, and became their most important settlement in the Peloponnese. In 1348, Mystra overtook it, but it remained an important strategic site, as well as a centre for trade: it was best known for its fine wine, Malmsey or Malvasia, which was celebrated by Shakespeare. Famously Richard III's younger brother, the Duke of Clarence, is said to have drowned in a 'butt' of it (a large cask, in case you were wondering).

After the fall of Constantinople the city's rule, like many other places, alternated between the Venetians and the Turks. It was even briefly ruled by the Pope at one stage. After a Turkish victory in 1570, much of the Greek population fled, taking their wine-growing skills with them. In 1821, it was the first fortress to be liberated from the Turks, but then fell into a long decline that was only reversed with the advent of tourism.

GETTING THERE AND AWAY

By car The route from Sparta and Gythio (and, for that matter, pretty much anywhere else in Greece) is described on page 146. The main problem you will encounter on arrival in Monemvasia is parking, especially at the weekends and in the Greek holidays. This is not so bad in Gefyra, on the mainland, which has a largish free car park just by the causeway over to the rock. But on Monemvasia itself it can be very difficult. You can drive over the causeway, and around the rock all the way to the gateway, but there is only a turning space here. Parking is on the left-hand side of the road as you approach, and is often full of cars practically all the way back to Gefyra. Don't be tempted to park on the right, even if others have done so, as you are likely to pick up a ticket. Walking will take 20 minutes at most, however, so don't worry too much.

By bus There are around five connections a day to Sparta (*2hrs*) and you can change at Molai for Neapoli and Gythio. In summer, a bus service takes you from Gythio over to Monemvasia from the start of the causeway, which leaves every 15 to 20 minutes during the day. The Malvasia Travel tourist agency serves as the bus stop (page 150).

By ferry The brief reawakening of the ferry service from Athens and the east coast of the Peloponnese to Monemvasia seems to have died off again, and the route has not run since 2014.

 WHERE TO STAY *Map, page 147*
This is a place to save up for. There is nothing quite like staying on the rock itself, and you do have to pay for the privilege. Even if you camp for the rest of your holiday,

you might consider splashing out at Monemvasia (in any case there is currently nowhere to legally camp in the area). If your budget won't stretch to a room in the old town, there are plenty of more affordable options in Gefyra, although it is everything Monemvasia is not; a typical seaside resort with fast-food joints, noisy roads and a relatively tacky feel.

Old town

All the recommendations below comprise converted old buildings within the walls of Monemvasia, & staying at any of them normally requires a bit of forward planning. Come in August, or on a holiday weekend, & you can forget it unless you booked last year or the year before that. On weekdays in off-peak times you should have more luck, but it is still worth making reservations ahead of time to ensure you get what you want.

The hotels within the walls all share 2 unique problems – try to regard them as part of the 'medieval experience'. The first is parking (page 148), & the second is actually finding where you are staying in the maze of alleys & then getting your luggage there. Get good directions when you book &, if you are driving, consider leaving suitcases in the car & packing an overnight bag. A couple of the hotels have receptions by the gate & will show you to the actual buildings from there, & some of the classier ones will arrange to meet you & porter any luggage.

🏠 **Ardamis** (10 rooms) 📞27320 61887; e info@ardamis.gr; w ardamis.gr. Perhaps the nicest place on the rock, although the competition is steep. The eponymous owner, first name Vasilis, has made a point of keeping as many of the old architectural features as possible: 1 room contains an 800-year-old well; another a Turkish bath; & 1 is inside a 14m-high tower. Its large mosaic terrace over the sea is a delight. €€€€€

🏠 **Bastion Malvasia** (40 rooms) 📞27320 63007; m 69732 49607; e info@bastionemalvasia. gr; w bastionemalvasia.gr. Similar to the Byzantine & spread over several different buildings. The ground-floor café has lovely terrace seating overlooking the city walls. €€€€

🏠 **Byzantino Boutique Hotel** (38 rooms) 📞27320 61351; e info@hotelbyzantino.com; w hotelbyzantino.com. 1 of the 2 larger hotels within the walls. It is housed in a variety of different buildings & the rooms come in different styles & sizes. A small one without a view can be reasonable & is just as stylishly decorated as its fellows. €€€€

🏠 **Guesthouse Kellia** (11 rooms) 📞27320 61520; e info@kelliamonemvasia.com; w keliamonemvasia.com. This used to be the monastery next to the church of Panagia Chrysafiotissa (page 151) & you will be sleeping in the monks' old cells. They are much more comfortable nowadays, & the large, tree-lined courtyard provides a welcome sense of space in sometimes claustrophobic Monemvasia. €€€€

🏠 **Likinia Hotel** (16 rooms) 📞27320 61939; e info@likinia.gr; w likinia.gr. Situated on Chrysafiotissa Sq, at the quieter east end of the walled town, this beautifully furnished hotel has been reconstructed from older buildings whose original architectural elements – arches, cisterns, etc – have been lovingly preserved. A characterful gem. €€€€

✳ 🏠 **Monopati** (2 rooms) 📞27320 61772; m 69748 32818; e info@byzantine-escapade. com; w byzantine-escapade.com. This house & apartment are now only open for long-term rents of 2 weeks or more, but it's well worth thinking about. Isabelle & Christos, the owners, have put a lot of love into this place & it shows & chatting to them is worthwhile both for their local knowledge & interesting pasts. €€€€

🏠 **Theophano Art Hotel** (14 rooms) 📞27320 61212; e reservations@theophano.gr; w theophano.gr. Situated on Chrysafiotissa Sq alongside the Likinia Hotel, this calm & beautiful owner-managed boutique hotel has individually styled rooms decorated with remarkable taste. €€€€

Gefyra

🏠 **Flower of Monemvasia** (20 rooms) 📞27320 61395; e info@flower-hotel.gr; w flower-hotel.gr. Though it lacks a waterfront location, the smartest hotel in Gefyra has comfortable & well-equipped rooms, & those on the upper floor have a sea view. €€€€

🏠 **Filoxenia Hotel** (18 rooms) 📞27320 61716; e info@filoxenia-monemvasia.gr; w filoxenia-monemvasia.gr. This unpretentious & well-priced hotel has a useful location 100m from the causeway & offers grand views over to the rock. It underwent extensive renovations in early 2018. **€€€**

🏠 **Panorama Hotel** (27 rooms) ☎ 27320 61198; e info@panoramahotel-monemvasia.gr; w panoramahotel-monemvasia.gr. Situated on a slope about 500m inland of the causeway, this presentable midrange hotel has good views to the rock & the family rooms are particularly good value. **€€€**

🏠 **Sofos Rooms** (8 rooms) ☎ 27320 61202; w sofosrooms.gr. Just up from the taxi rank beside the National Bank, this seems to be the cheapest option in town for a basic AC room with fridge & TV. **€€**

Further afield

✳ 🏠 **Kinsterna** (41 rooms) ☎ 27320 66300; e info@kinsternahotel.gr; w kinsternahotel.gr. It would take something pretty special to persuade you to not stay on Monemvasia itself, especially at this end of the budget scale. Remarkably, the Kinsterna, set on an isolated olive farm & winery 10mins' drive south from the rock, comes up with the goods. The main building is a superbly renovated mansion constructed by an Ottoman judge in the late 17th or early 18th century, built in a U-shape around the spring-fed cistern for which the hotel is named. Accommodation is in luxurious & expansive bungalows with wooden floor, king-size bed, flatscreen TV built into the wall, separate lounge with coffee-making machine & minibar, & large balcony with a view to the sea below. The property also includes a wonderful swimming pool, a world-class spa & the classiest fine-dining restaurant in the vicinity of Monemvasia. Activities range from wine-tasting & farm tours to carriage rides or hiking & cycling on an extensive network of local footpaths. The buffet b/fast is astonishing. Rates are steep, but it's well worth it. **€€€€€**

✗ WHERE TO EAT AND DRINK *Map, page 147*

Monemvasia

✗ **Matoula Restaurant** ☎ 27320 61660; w matoula.gr. Established as a coffee house in 1950, this is the oldest eatery in the old town, & still arguably the best, serving traditional Greek fare on a vine-shaded terrace that looks over the castle walls to the sea below.

✗ **To Kanoni** ☎ 27320 61387; w tokanoni.com. Situated on the main square, this stylish restaurant serves good seafood & traditional dishes associated with the Peloponnese, supplemented by pasta & pizza. It has an extensive wine list.

Gefyra

There is plenty of choice over in Gefyra, with the advantage of a view of Monemvasia during the day, but quality & service can be variable.

✗ **Grillhouse Haramis** ☎ 27320 61010. This waterfront grillhouse doubles as a giros joint (see box, page 47); it's the place to chow down on cheap pitas & chips, & the Greek salad is also OK.

✗ **Taverna Scorpio** ☎ 27320 62090. The pick of Gefyra's smarter seafront options serves excellent seafood as well as meat-based grills & stews. Although it stands at the opposite end of the harbour to the car park & bridge, it has conspicuous blue-&-purple décor & a gazebo-like outdoor sitting area.

OTHER PRACTICALITIES A must-visit for eager shoppers, the super-friendly **Edodimopolio Honey Shop** (☎ *27320 61303*) is a good place to try local produce such as mead, olive oil, liqueurs and Malvasia wines within the castle walls. That aside, there is nothing 'practical' about Monemvasia. For that kind of thing, you need to cross the causeway back to the real world in Gefyra. Your first port of call for information and help with rooms and car hire is **Malvasia Travel** (☎ *27320 61752;* e *malvtrvl@spa.otenet.gr*), on the right just before the causeway to Monemvasia. Taxis (☎ *27320 61888*) can be found just along the road inland. Along the road towards Sparta is the National Bank with an ATM, a post office and, farther along, a doctor. There are also a couple of small supermarkets, which are where to stock up before heading over to the rock itself. The area around Monemvasia and south into Vatika is served by an unusually good website: w monemvasia.gr.

WHAT TO SEE AND DO   The main 'point' of Monemvasia is to wander around the town in a fairly aimless fashion. It is at its best at dusk or at night; try, if you can, to arrive at these times. The town is invisible from the land, and even standing in front of the **gateway** you have little idea of what awaits inside. The entrance tunnel includes a sharp right turn, an excellent defensive measure. The result of all this is that when you emerge, blinking, on to the cobbled main lane, it is as if some magical transformation has taken place; perhaps a time portal back to the Middle Ages. The trendy art and craft shops soon put paid to the last notion, but there is something enchanted about the place.

The **main alley** leads straight ahead, past attractive shops, cafés and tavernas, until it reaches the central square with its cannon. There is a map board here, but try to avoid looking at it until you must. One of the pleasures of Monemvasia is getting lost. Its alleyways and lanes seem to twist about with a mind of their own, sometimes bringing you to a small church, sometimes to the sea, and often to a dead-end wall – it doesn't really seem to matter.

That said, this is a guidebook, so here are a few pointers. Just above the main gate, on top of the walls to the left is a small monument to the left-wing poet **Yiannis Ritsos**, a native of Monemvasia. Arrested after the civil war for fighting on the side of the communists, and again under the dictatorship of the Colonels, he seems to have spent half his life in prison. There is something odd, at first, about a lefty radical coming from Monemvasia, but somehow it seems to suit. For the full experience, ask your bar or taverna to put on his poems, which were set to music by the equally renowned Mikis Theodorakis.

At the main square, to the left of the cannon, is the 13th-century **cathedral**. It is more the size of your average English parish church than what you would think of as a cathedral, but is the largest medieval church in Laconia, although it has been heavily altered over the years. Opposite it, the **Monemvasia Archaeological Collection** (✆ 27320 61403; ⊕ *see box, page 52; €2*), housed in an old mosque, contains archaeological finds from all periods of Monemvasia's history. Below the square is the **Portello**, a sea gate that leads on to a quay and rocks from where you can have an atmospheric swim.

There are a number of churches hidden in the back alleys, the most renowned of which is the 17th-century **Panagia Chrysafiotissa**, towards the opposite end of town to the main gate. Local legend has it that its icon flew here from the village of Hrysafa, although the reality may be more prosaic. Whatever the case, the church's celebration day, 2 May, is the town's big festival. Panagia Chrysafiotissa stands in the middle of **Magali Topia**, a cobbled square that forms the largest open area in the old town and stands above a tall fortified wall lapped by the waves below. A 200m cliff path leads from the eastern gate, immediately past the square, to a stone lighthouse built in 1896.

All these are in the Lower Town; if you have the energy you really should climb up to the Upper Town, which is occupied, as in Mystra, by the **castle**. Best attempted as early as possible on a hot day, it is a hard climb up a zigzag path that passes through several arches, and the cobbled stones, worn smooth by centuries of use, could be treacherous after rain. The castle is mostly in ruins, but you can easily see that it was not a place to attack lightly. Inside the walls, the plateau is studded with the remains of old vaulted stone buildings, many built in the 16th century and occupied into the 19th. A riot of wild flowers in spring, the ruins also provide stunning views in all directions, especially back down on Monemvasia itself, and would be a great place to bring a picnic.

The best-preserved building in the upper town is the prominently domed Orthodox church of **Agia Sofia** (⊕ *08.00–15.00 daily; free entrance*), which was built in 1150 and originally dedicated to the virgin Hodegetria according to historical documents. Given its current name in 1821 and extensively restored in the 1950s, the old church still retains some late 12th- and early 13th-century frescoes, despite having been converted to a mosque during both the Turkish occupations, and a Catholic church under the Venetians.

VATIKA PENINSULA

The most easterly of the Peloponnese's three 'fingers', the Vatika (Βάτικα) Peninsula is the least well known. Messinia has famous towns and famous beaches, and the Mani delights in its tower houses and rugged reputation. Meanwhile the Vatika Peninsula carries on in relative obscurity, despite its proximity to Monemvasia, which stands off its northeastern shore.

This is slowly changing. Neapoli, while not a destination in itself, is a stepping-off point to the magical island of Kythira. The island of Elafonisos, practically part of the mainland, was once a jealously guarded secret, but now its beaches, said to rival those of the Caribbean or Tahiti, are well known, at least to the Greeks.

So far it is still mostly Greeks that visit here, and they rarely get past these two places, but further to the south is an area of surprisingly rugged mountains, dotted with villages and the odd secret cove. The discovery of a spectacular cave system here, and its recent access to the public, has opened the region up, but it still feels like the back of beyond.

WHAT TO SEE AND DO

Neapoli (Νεάπολη) The gateway town both to the southern tip of Vatika and to the island of Kythira, the 'New City' is actually little more than a harbourfront strip. During the summer the town can be quite lively, especially when the ferry to Kythira (page 158) comes in, and the town beach is perfectly acceptable for a dip. However, although there are tavernas, hotels, supermarkets and an ATM, you wouldn't really want to hang out here. Four **buses** a day link Neapoli to Sparta via Molai (*2hrs 20mins*) and the bus station is just up the next road (Dimokritios) after the quay.

Elafonisos (Ελαφόνησος)
The island is reached by way of a signposted road to the right, off the main road towards Neapoli. This leads, in 7–8km, to the little harbour of Pounta (Πουντα), from where small **car ferries** (*27340 61122; m 69720 08093; e katonisi@yahoo.gr; €10/car each way, €1pp, pay on board*) make the short run over to Elafonisos. The ferry schedule seems to be decided on a month-by-month basis. They claim to run at least nine crossings a day in either direction, even in winter, between 07.30 and 18.00, but according to some locals this is a bit of an exaggeration. For most of the year they are pretty frequent, often running every hour from early until quite late, making a day trip easy. Ferries to the island tend to leave on the hour, and return at half past, and they may stop for an hour in the afternoon for siesta. The schedule, which changes every month, is posted at the small café, which is the only facility at the quay. Be sure to make a note of the return times. If you do have to wait here, don't despair – the water is lovely and there is a **sandy strip of beach** by the quay. It is also a good opportunity to reflect on lost civilisations and the march of time, as the underwater city of Pavlopetri is just along the coast (see box, page 155).

The ferry lands you just to the left of the island's only settlement, a little fishing port. There are two beaches, both about 5km down the island's two tarmac roads. Be warned that Elafonisos is not the undiscovered paradise it once was and both beaches have seen some development, especially **Panagias** (Παναγίας) to the west. This long sandy beach, facing a cluster of pretty islets, is now backed by several hotels and taverna buildings. It is reached by turning right off the ferry, and then up the road to the left.

Simos Beach (Σίμος), on the east of the island, is a much better bet, and still retains its air of unspoilt beauty. You reach it by turning immediately left off the ferry. When the road forks, go left to reach the prettier section of this twin beach, whose pale sands meet at a small promontory (right leads to the campsite). The low dunes mask the few tavernas and other buildings from the beach itself. Even in June, on a weekday, you will only find a handful of people here. August, as always, is another story, and the collection of pay car parks (just roped-off bits of land) show what hordes must descend. In the summer boat trips to Simos leave from the port each morning.

🏠 ***Where to stay and eat*** If you want to stay on the island the options are numerous, and rooms, outside of the Greek holidays, easy to find. Try **Berdoussis** (↘*27340 61046;* m *69727 74016;* e *info@berdoussishotel.gr;* w *berdoussishotel.gr;* **€€€€**) which is 200m from the port towards town, or just wander the back streets of the fishing port, which are made up of nothing but rooms places. **Simos Camping** (↘*27340 22672;* m *69409 94994;* e *info@simoscamping.gr;* w *simoscamping.gr;* **€**) is expensive for a campsite, but is right behind Simos Beach and also offers bungalows (**€€€**). Your best bets for eating are the **fish tavernas** that line the pretty front of the port. They are faced by a flotilla of obviously hard-working fishing boats, so freshness should not be an issue. There is a pharmacy here, and minimarts, but no other facilities.

The southern tip
To get up into the mountains above Neapoli take the road (Dimokritios) marked towards the Kastania Cave, which soon leaves town and starts upwards, towards the village of **Lachi** (Λάχι), with views across to Kythira and Elafonisos. Be aware that although all these routes are on tarmac, the roads are often narrow, precipitous, and extremely bendy. The curve signs are marked as *synxeis*, or 'constant', and they are not kidding. If you like this kind of driving, then it's great fun; otherwise you have been warned. There are two main routes: south to the village of Velanidia; or a circular drive that takes you past the caves.

Not far after Lachi is an isolated junction where you turn left towards Velanidia. The 10km road takes you steeply up the mountains, and then up and over to the other side with majestic views all the way. About a kilometre before the village, a dirt road (4km) leads off a sharp bend down to the left, ending close to **Agios Pavlos Beach** (Αγ Παύλος), reputedly one of the finest in the area. **Velanidia** (Βελανίδια) is surprisingly large, and attractively arranged on the mountainside. It's best to park at the outskirts and walk down to where there is a café and a taverna. A lot of the houses here are only occupied in the holidays, but there is a year-round population, and the possibility of rooms available; enquire at the café. This would make a great base from which to explore the hiking opportunities of this isolated cape.

For the circular route past the caves, take the signed junction before you reach Lachi, coming from Neapoli. This road also winds up and over the mountains before reaching the pretty village of Kato Kastania (Κάτω Κασταvιά), whose population seems to consist of one old lady. Whatever the maps say, the tarmac road does now continue from here straight towards the **Kastania Cave** (see opposite). A couple of hundred metres before you reach the cave, where the road dead-ends, a large turning to the right takes you down to **Panagia Beach** (Παναγία), which is somewhat gravelly but pretty enough for a swim.

To carry on with the loop, head back along the road and take the right fork for a steep ascent up past **Ano Kastania** (Άνω Κασταvιά), and then down towards Neapoli past **Faraklo** (Φαρακλό) and **Mesochori** (Μεσοχώρι). Soon after the turn to the latter you will see a dramatic **ruined castle** atop a spur of rock below you. It makes a great photo opportunity, but is somewhat difficult to get close to. If you want to make the attempt turn right down a signed concrete track towards the **chapel of Agia Paraskevi** (Αγ Παρασκευή). Park at the chapel and take the path that heads towards the castle through the olive groves. This soon ends and you have to fight your way through the undergrowth round the left-hand side of the castle almost to its opposite corner. From here you can scramble up to a hole in the walls. Watch your footing inside. Unfortunately there isn't a sleeping princess to waken as a reward, but the views are just about worth the effort. The castle's origin is uncertain, but it is probably Frankish (13th century) or Venetian (15th century). The main road continues down to Neapoli.

The underwater city of Pavlopetri, located just off the coast of Vatika, was first discovered in 1967. Early investigations dated the site to the Mycenaean era, around 1600–1100BC. Recently, however, more detailed studies have bumped it back at least another 1,500 years, making it contemporary with the great Minoan civilisation of Crete. By 1000BC the city had disappeared beneath the waves, probably due to earthquakes. While this would have been unfortunate for the inhabitants, it has ensured Pavlopetri's place in the history books. Its submergence meant that no more modern buildings could be built over it, and its ground would never be ploughed over for agriculture, preserving a Bronze Age town in its entirety.

The importance of this site only really came to the fore in 2009, when the University of Nottingham started to survey the area, using 21st-century robotic and mapping technology (see w nottingham.ac.uk/pavlopetri for more details). The site was revealed to extend over at least 9,000m² and computer wizardry allowed a 3D model of the city to be developed. All of this was recorded in a BBC Two documentary that came out in 2011, some of which is still available on YouTube.

As always, talk of a submerged city, especially so close to the Greek mainland, led many newspaper articles to ask whether Pavlopetri had inspired the story of Atlantis. Almost certainly not, is the sober response to this, but the reality may turn out to be even more fascinating than such fanciful stories.

Unfortunately for the casual traveller, there is little to see of Pavlopetri, and developing it into a destination for visitors lies in the future. For the moment what is there should really be left for the archaeologists.

Kastania Cave (℡27343 60100; w kastaniacave.gr; ⊕ 10.30–16.00 Sat & Sun, daily in the summer; last tour leaves half an hour before closing; €7; photography forbidden) A local shepherd who saw bees disappearing down a hole in the rocks apparently discovered this stunning cave complex. Correctly assuming that they were going to an underground water supply, he followed them in. He found the water, but only after a 150m crawl through a fantastical forest of stalagmites and stalactites. The fact that he kept his discovery secret for many years shows you just how important a secure water source could be in this arid landscape. Estimated to be three million years old, the caves are now open to the public, and are particularly known for their unusual rock formations, some of the best in Europe. Tours leave every half hour, and the guides usually speak some English. There is a café/restaurant in which to wait for the next tour.

The opened section of the cave is about 1,500m long and you explore it on a circular concrete walkway of 500m. It is well lit and a torch is unnecessary, but could be helpful.

For keen hikers, an excellent way to reach Kastania would be the 10km hiking trail that connects it to Agios Fokas, to the northwest, via a wild stretch of coastline that traverses a steep gorge.

Petrified Forest Another intriguing geological site on the Vatika Peninsula is the Petrified Forest close to its southern tip. Though it is not nearly as breathtaking as the caves, it does provide a good excuse for some exploration, and is close to some great swimming spots. To find it, head south from Neapoli through the village of Agios Nikolaos (Άγιος Νικολαός). Look out for a sign pointing to the 'Climbing Park' pointing up a gravel road to the left. If you reach the pretty little fishing port of Profitas Ilias (Προφήτης Ηλιάς) you have gone too far. About 2km along this gravel road you will find some concrete signs in front of what looks like, to untrained eyes, a field of boulders. Despite this the setting is superb, and it is worth driving along further. After another 2–3km you will pass a small chapel, from which you will spot a parking area with some more signs near it. There are more interesting rock formations near here, but more enticingly there are also some hidden little swimming spots where, if it is not too windy, you can climb off the rocks and swim round to inaccessible coves. If you fancy a relaxed lunch in the area, Agios Nikolaos is home to the highly-rated **Neraida Restaurant** (\ *27340 31227*), which serves mixed Mediterranean cuisine on a lovely hillside terrace overlooking the sea, and also sells homemade bread, locally produced liqueurs and the like.

THE COAST NORTH OF MONEMVASIA

Heading north from Monemvasia there is a great detour along the coast. Be warned, however, that the road is almost 50km long and finishes in a dead end. It is also only really possible if you have your own transport or a lot of time on your hands, or ideally both. If you like getting off the beaten track it is a worthwhile trip if you can fit it in, as it includes some stunning scenery, pretty villages and, at the end of the road, a great beach.

Five kilometres north of Monemvasia, look out for the heavily signposted road to the right (some of the signs refer to various ancient ruins, but the remains are scant). This follows the coast around, skirting a sandy beach with good views back to the rock of Monemvasia. The road then heads up and inland a bit. At about 6km past the first junction you will pass a turning to the right, which leads down to the little pebble beach with views of the islet of **Daskalio** (Δασκαλίο). Unfortunately this looks much nicer from above, as you continue down the main road, than it proves to be close to – there are better options ahead.

Another 4.5km brings you to the right turn towards **Limenas Geraka** (Λιμένας Γέρακα). This is set on a marshy inlet of the sea that has the air of a Scandinavian fjord, especially as you approach it from above, and is in fact regarded to be Europe's southernmost fjord (glacially created inlet). Protected as a nature reserve, the 400ha fjord provides an important refuge for aquatic birds such as herons and egret. It is verged by **Porto Gerakas** (Πόρτο Γέρακας), a pretty little hamlet known for its handful of fish tavernas, which open most reliably at weekend lunchtimes. A circular 1.8km walking trail to the hill above the port passes through the patchy unfenced ruins of Ancient Zarakos and offers super views to the steep cliffs hemming in the fjord.

The main road continues for 6.5km through the pretty inland settlements of **Gerakas** (Γέρακας) and **Agios Ioannis** (Αγ Ιωάννης), before reaching another right-hand turn, this time to the **Convent of Evagelistrias**. The convent occupies a dramatic spot on the cliffside, with good views, but the initially good road (6km each way) soon deteriorates, and is dangerous in places. This is one for the determined only.

Another 6.5km leads straight through the combined villages of **Beleseika** (Μπελεσαίικα) and **Richia** (Ρειχέα), which has a kafenion, before reaching a junction where you turn right. Turning left would take you towards Molai and the main road towards Sparta. The next 8.5km takes you over some wonderfully dramatic scenery, although better is soon to come. When the road forks around a chapel, just past the village of **Lambokambos** (Λαμπόκαμπος), head right. **Charakas** (Χάρακας), after 5km, is a larger place, with a taverna and a kafenion around a pleasant square.

The last 10km are the most stunning. The road first passes a steep path up to the old village of Charakas, whose ruins and chapel you can see above you to the right, and then suddenly emerges on a spectacular cliffside road, clinging high above the sea. When the road starts to descend you will see the beach and whitewashed village of **Kyparissi** (Κυπαρίσσι) below you. Look up to your left and you will also see some cliff chapels. The congregation must fly up to them. Go down through the first collection of houses until you reach a junction. Right would take you into the seaside village, but parking is difficult. You are better to head left, and then turn right along the shore when you hit the sea.

The village is lovely. Its quiet, pebbled bay, surrounded by a few whitewashed houses, presents a stereotypical view of Greece that rarely exists any more, and which was always more common on the islands. Here, at the end of this long road, it seems to have survived. Who knows for how much longer? There is another, longer beach, just outside the village, but follow the road through another collection of houses and you will come to the end of the line, and the best beach, next to the little port of **Mitropoli** (Μητρόπολη). Its greyish-white sands shelve gently into a crystal blue sea.

Amazingly, the Flying Dolphin hydrofoil service used to call at **Kyparissi**, and as a legacy it's still possible to stay here. As always, the place will inevitably fill up at holiday times, but even in June and July you will have your pick of the few rooms places and tavernas. The best accommodation is the **Kyfanta** (✆ 27320 55356; m 69455 21511; e kyfantahotel@gmail.com; w kyfanta.com; €€€). When you get round to leaving, follow the Molai signs through the somewhat confusing upper village.

KYTHIRA (ΚΎΘΗΡΑ)

Slightly oddly, this island belongs to the Ionian group, despite the fact that it is nowhere near any of the others. It fits in more easily with the Peloponnese, both travel-wise and culturally, although it has a very definite culture of its own. For an island of its size it is unusual, and some would say blessed, in the fact that no package tours come here. In fact, most visitors come from the seemingly huge Kythiran diaspora in Australia. Even the islanders who have stayed here seem to speak English with an Aussie twang. Big enough to have a choice of several unspoilt beaches and great hiking in the interior, Kythira is a bit of a gem.

HISTORY As in modern times, Kythira seems to have been forgotten about for most of history. It was a Minoan and then Phoenician colony before coming under the sway of Sparta in Classical times. It was mainly Venetian-owned in medieval times and was infamously looted by the Ottoman pirate king Barbarossa in 1537. Later it was part of Britain's Ionian possessions before becoming part of modern Greece.

GETTING THERE AND AWAY

By air Between them **Aegean Air** (w en.aegeanair.com), **Sky Express** (w skyexpress. gr) and **Olympic Air** (w olympicair.com) operate at least one flight daily between Athens and Kythira's Alexander Onassis Airport weekly. Prices start at around €60 each way, and direct flights only take 50 minutes.

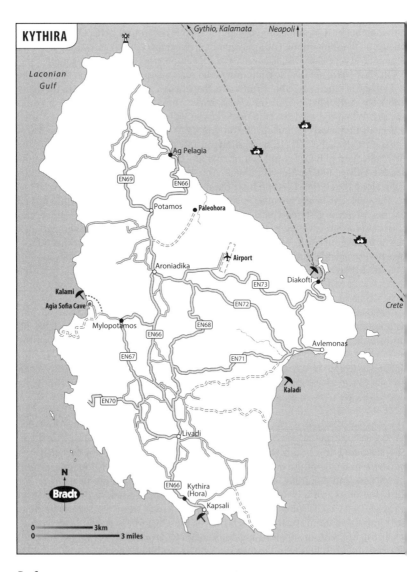

By ferry The easiest approach is from Neapoli. Weather permitting, the *Porfyrousa* sails back and forth six days a week in winter, and once or twice a day in summer (*1hr 15mins; €44.50/12.50 per car/person*). Ferries leave daily from the central quay and tickets can be bought from the mainland shipping agency **Vatika Bay** (\ 27340 24004; e *vatbaydr@otenet.gr;* w *vatikabay.gr*) on the left on the way into Neapoli, or from **Kythira Travel** (\ 27360 31390; e *info@kithiratravel.gr;* w *kithiratravel.gr*) on the island. In August you'd be wise to book in advance, especially for a vehicle, as the ferry is often full.

There are also weekly ferries from Gythio and Kalamata (pages 168 and 199).

GETTING AROUND Buses are pretty scarce on Kythira, and taxis are not much more common. If possible come across with a car on the ferry, or hire one on the island – try **Drakakis** (\ *27360 31160;* e *info@drakakisrentacar.com;* w *drakakisrentacar.com*).

⌐ WHERE TO STAY AND EAT *Map, opposite*
Despite feeling like it gets few visitors, Kythira is not short on accommodation, and you can usually find a place to stay even in the high season. It has lots of old-fashioned 'rooms' places, that can be very good value.

Diakofti (Διακόφτι)
🏠 **Notara Hotel** (10 rooms) \ 27360 38197; w notara.attica-hotels.com. This is pretty much the first place you see as you cross the causeway from the ferry. The best rooms look straight over to the beach. A good place to stay before or after catching the ferry. €€€€

✖ **Minas Café** \ 27360 33243; f minas. diakofti. This trendy beach bar advertises itself, rather unexpectedly, as an ouzeri, but its mixed plates (pikalia) are surprisingly good.

Mylopotamos (Μυλοπόταμος)
🏠 **Giota Studios** (4 rooms) \ 27360 33782; m 69467 53566; e myrtokarydi@yahoo.gr. Giota will welcome you into her house at the edge of the village, where she offers self-catering accommodation in good-sized apartments. €€

✖ **Kafe Kamari** \ 27360 33006; e info@ kafekamari.gr. Set in a 100-year-old building down by the duck pond, this is a good place to retire for after-dinner drinks & dessert. Good coffee & ice cream.

✳ ✖ **Platanos** \ 27360 33397. A good old-fashioned taverna set above the village duck pond & under a huge plane tree (hence the name), as every Greek village taverna should be.

Potamos (Ποταμός)
✖ **Panaretos** \ 27360 34290. This taverna, located on the main square of town, is especially good on a Sunday morning, when it is surrounded by the local market.

Aroniadika (Αρωνιάδικα)
🏠 **Xenonas Fos Ke Choros** (2 apts & 2 studios) \ 27360 31574; m 69807 29399; e info@agreekisland.com; w agreekisland. com. Set on its own outside the village, this is a

stunningly done up traditional house owned by an enthusiastic Dutch couple, Albert & Anita. Out of season they run hiking holidays & yoga retreats, & accommodation can be a bargain. €€€€

Avlemonas (Αβλέμονας)
🏠 **Sotiris Rooms** \ 27360 34374. Nestled above the small harbour with its swimming platforms, this well-known taverna has recently expanded with the construction of a few comfortable & well-equipped rooms on the upper floor. It is renowned across the island & beyond for its lobster pasta, an expensive treat, but other seafood dishes are also delicious. €€

Kythira (Κύθηρα; also known as Hora)
🏠 **Niki Rooms & Apartments** (lots of rooms – not even the owner seems sure how many!) \ 27360 31488; e info@kythirarooms.gr; w kythirarooms.gr. A warren of rooms in several buildings at the start of the road down to Kapsali. Friendly owners will always try to fit you in. Rooms are simple, with no b/fast, but have showers & AC, & are amazing value. €€

✳ ✖ **Zorbas** A little grill house on the main alley of the old town. In summer, they open up a terrace on a nearby rooftop with good views. The waiters run up & down the stairs wearing old-fashioned waistcoats & bearing expertly grilled meats.

Kapsali (Καψάλι)
✖ **Magos** \ 27360 31407. At the harbour end of Kapsali Beach. You can tell this is a good place for seafood as it's where the fishermen hang out.
✖ **Ydragogio** \ 27360 31065. At the other end of the beach, this taverna has a more unusual menu with a slightly eastern feel to it.

OTHER PRACTICALITIES The three main towns of the island are Kythira (Hora), Livadi and Potamos, and although none of them are very big they are where to head for all practical matters such as banks and doctors. They also all have obvious tourist agencies on their main squares where you can book ferries, tours and hire cars.

WHAT TO SEE AND DO You could easily spend at least a week exploring Kythira, but could also whizz through the highlights in a day or two. This would be a shame, however, as this is an island to take things slowly on.

Diakofti Beach (Διακόφτι) Although this is also home to the ferry port, and a rather disconcerting shipwreck, it is one of the best beaches on the island, and one of the few composed of white sand. Popular with the Aussies as it reminds them of home.

Potamos (Ποταμός) A bustling town with lots of character. At its best on a Sunday morning when a market takes over the central square and is a big social event (although parking can be tough).

Agia Pelagia (Αγία Πελαγία) This is where the ferries used to stop, and because of this there are lots of hotels and tavernas. Despite there being nearby beaches, it's not really worth the effort anymore.

Paleochora (Παλιόχωρα) This is the remains of the island's Byzantine capital. The ruins are mainly worthwhile for their dramatic setting, perched above a deep gorge. You can get here by car: look out for the brown sign pointing left as you go south from Potamos, although the last bit turns to dirt.

Mylopotamos Waterfalls (Μυλοπόταμος) Follow the river down from this pleasant village and in under 10 minutes you will arrive at an attractive waterfall. It seems to have two names: Neraida, after the mythological water nymphs; and Fonissa, meaning 'murderess'. Continue down the river past lots of ruined watermills that gave the village its name. One of these has been restored by Phillipis Zervos, and was built by his grandfather of the same name. If he is around, he'll show you around the mill workings, as well as sell you a cold drink. A kilometre further on, just through the arch of another ruined mill, is another waterfall whose cold blue pool provides an excellent swimming opportunity. Reaching here is about an hour's walk. To carry on down the river is difficult, and you are advised to hire a guide from the village, but it would eventually lead you to Kaladi Beach (page 161).

Agia Sofia Cave (Σπήλαιο Αγ Σοφίας) (🕐 summer: 11.00–19.00, enquire in the village at other times of year; €5) Drive on through Mylopotamos past the old village (worth exploring) and follow the signs until the road ends. A path leads down the cliffs to this dramatically situated cave which is surprisingly extensive and impressive. It even includes a chapel with 700-year-old frescoes.

Kalami Beach (Καλάμι) There are more than 30 beaches around Kythira, but this is regarded by many as the best. The catch is that it is rather difficult to get to. After a slightly dodgy dirt road (park near the chapel rather than carry on down it), you still have a hike that ends in a tall cliff. It is rather a scramble, and even though there is a rope to help it's not for the nervous. The reward is a lovely cove occupied only by a few other brave souls.

Kaladi Beach (Καλαδι) If you don't make it to Kalami, don't despair as this beach is almost as nice. It is near the pretty village of Avlemonas (Αβλέμονας) which also offers good swimming from platforms in its cove. To get here also involves a dirt road, but this one ends in steps (although they are steep, and there are quite a few of them). The three pebble beaches have no facilities, but are extremely pretty and have good rocks to swim out to and dive off.

Kythira (also known as Hora) The old whitewashed alleys of the island's capital are exactly what one dreams of in a Greek island. These ones lead up to the old Venetian castle (⊕ 08.30–sunset), which offers fantastic views over to the rock of Hytra (or Avgo – the egg) that rises from the sea and is one of the reputed birthplaces of Aphrodite.

Kapsali (Καψάλι) The little port of Kythira town nestles below it, backed by dramatic cliffs punctuated by the whitewashed monastery of Agios Ioannis. The beach is perhaps the busiest on the island, but is still lovely and especially good for young children. You can head over to Hytra rock from here by contacting Captain Spiro (m 69470 22079), or asking at Magos Taverna. He takes tours out in his glass-bottomed boat, which has a surprising turn of speed, and will lead swims into the large cave in the rock – highly recommended.

Laconia KYTHIRA

5

RENT A CAR AND
**DISCOVER
LACONIA**

*kakouros*RENT

Address: Gythiou , 99 - Sparti - Greece
Web: www.kakouros-rent.gr
E-mail: info@kakouros.gr
Phone: (+30) 27310-27784
Fax: (+30) 27310-29711.

6

The Mani
(Μάνη)

The Mani has always been an area apart from the rest of the Peloponnese. It is often compared to the highlands of Scotland, and there is a resemblance: remote, mountainous and often windswept, with a haunted past full of feuding clans and bitter resistance to invaders.

Occupying the middle prong of the Peloponnese, the Mani is most usefully divided into two parts, a division that is reflected in the borders of the provinces of Messinia and Laconia. Exo (or Outer) Mani stretches from the outskirts of Kalamata to just above Itylo, while Mesa (or Deep) Mani runs south of this right down to Cape Tenaro. Exo Mani is more fertile, more prosperous and closer to 'civilisation', whereas Mesa Mani is barren, rock strewn and, until not long ago, extremely poor. Even 20 years ago it was hard to imagine that this remote corner of Greece belonged in a prosperous EU country. Today, it still retains a very different feel from the rest of the Peloponnese. The landscape, in both Exo and Mesa Mani, is dominated by the Taygetos Mountains, which form the central spine of the region, rising up to 2,404m at their highest.

Until fairly recently this was still a difficult area in which to travel, and an air of being at the end of the world still lingers. Sir Patrick Leigh Fermor kindled some interest in the area with his 1958 book *Mani* (see box, page 188), but it was not until the 1990s, when the holiday companies discovered the sandy coves of Exo Mani, that tourists began to come in any number. Fortunately package holidays are confined to small, set areas in the summer months. Come out of season, or step off the beaten track even slightly, and you will find a Greece that has changed little in the last 20 years.

HISTORY

Legend tells that the Maniats are the descendants of two waves of refugees from elsewhere in the Peloponnese. The first were Spartans fleeing their declining city. The second were Byzantine nobles, who crossed the mountains into safety after the loss of Mystra to the Ottomans in 1460. Whatever the truth of these stories, they do provide a pleasing explanation for the contradictory Maniat character. The Spartan heritage comes out in their taste for warfare and vendettas, while Mystra provides an artistic and religious connection, attested to by the profusion of frescoed churches.

In Classical times the history of the area was indeed tied closely to that of Sparta, firstly under the city state's control, and then, after Augustus, as part of the Free Laconian League that opposed it.

After the Roman Empire split the Mani came nominally under the control of the Christian Byzantine Empire. However, the area seems to have resisted complete conversion to Christianity until well into the 9th century, fairly late

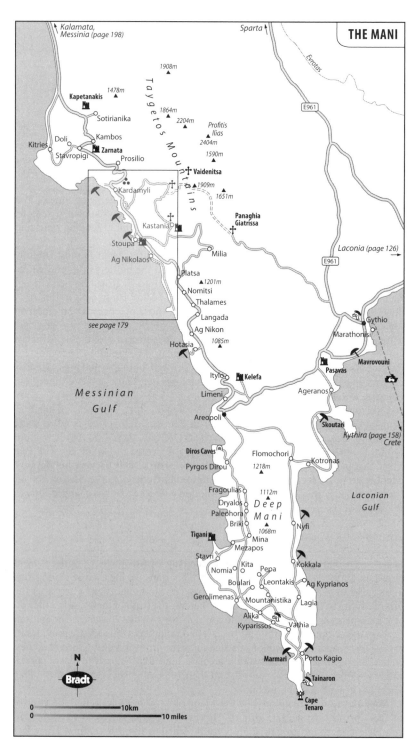

Kalamata,
Messinia (page 198)

Sparta

Evrotas

Taygetos Mountains

1908m

1478m
Kapetanakis

Sotirianika

1864m
2204m

Profitis
Ilias
2404m

1590m

E961

Doli
Kitries
Kambos
Zarnata
Stavropigi
Prosilio

Vaidenitsa

1909m
1651m

Kardamyli

Panaghia
Giatrissa

Kastania

Laconia (page 126)

Stoupa

E961

Ag Nikolaos

Milia

see page 179

Platsa

1201m
Nomitsi
Thalames

Langada
Ag Nikon

Gythio

Hotasia

1085m

Marathonisi

Mavrovouni

*Messinian
Gulf*

Itylo
Kelefa

Limeni

Pasavas
Ageranos

Skoutari

Areopoli

*Kythira (page 158)
Crete*

Diros Caves

Flomochori

Kotronas

Pyrgos Dirou

1218m

*Laconian
Gulf*

Fragoulias

1112m

Dryalos
Palephora

*Deep
Mani*

Briki

1068m

Nyfi

Tigani
Mina
Mezapos

Stavri

Kita
Pepa

Kokkala

Nomia

Boulari
Leontakis

Ag Kyprianos

Gerolimenas
Mountanistika

Lagia

Alika
Kyparissos
Vathia

N

Marmari
Porto Kagio

Bradt

Tainaron

0   10km

0   10 miles

Cape
Tenaro

in the day for Greece. The next 200 years saw an explosion in church building, and many of these still dot the region (see box, page 137). In the 13th century, Frankish invaders built many castles and fortresses that were then passed among the Byzantines, Venetians and Ottomans in the usual confusing manner. Despite all this it is fair to say that the Mani remained at the fringes of the historical record right up until the Greek War of Independence when, in 1821, it suddenly springs into centre stage.

After 1460, the Mani was nominally part of the Ottoman Empire, but the locals will still tell you that the Turks never really subdued the area. While this is an exaggeration it is true to say that the warlike nature of the people made it a difficult place to govern with any surety. Blood feuds were common and these, along with the competition for scarce resources, led to the distinctive architectural feature of the Mani, the tower house (see box, page 176).

When the Ottomans failed to subdue the Mani by force they resorted to a subtler form of coercion, giving nominal leadership to one of the local Maniat warlords under the title of 'Bey'. This only partially worked, with most of the beys secretly plotting against their overlords. It proved a dangerous title – many of its holders were executed, and it was passed from clan to clan in a divide-and-rule policy that, for a while, kept the Maniats busy among themselves. However, the last of the beys, Petrobey Mavromihalis, appointed in 1815, managed to unite the Mani against the oppressor.

When the Maniat rebellion burst out on 17 March 1821, it was Petrobey who led an army north from Tsimova, now Areopoli, to liberate Kalamata on 23 March. Maniats are still quick to point out that this is a full week before the start of the Greek War of Independence as celebrated by other Greeks. Much of the fighting in the following war involved soldiers and generals from the area, but after independence the Maniats discovered that a modern democracy was almost as oppressive to their lifestyles as the Ottoman yoke. The government tried to pull down the towers and even the great Petrobey was thrown in prison. In revenge for this, two of his brothers assassinated Capodistrias, the new president, in Nafplio (page 79).

The Mani sank back into the fringes of Greek life. This, and its ever-present poverty, led to a sharp decline in population as people moved to bigger cities and overseas to make their livings. Only recently has a measure of prosperity returned to the region and certain areas show a rash of new building, both by foreigners and Greeks. The Mani now stands on something of a cusp, and it remains to be seen whether it can benefit from the tourist industry without spoiling what made the area attractive in the first place.

GYTHIO AND AROUND (ΓΥΘΕΙΟ)

Gythio, the modern capital of the Mani, is a pleasant port town with a 19th-century, Neoclassical harbourfront. After the wilds of the Mani this feels like the epitome of civilisation. Compared with some towns, it has a pleasingly low-key air, and its charms are simple. Don't be fooled though – it is also where one of the greatest seductions of all time was consummated.

The main part of Gythio stretches along the harbour from Mavromihali Square in the south to the small triangular park of Perivolaki to the north. This used to be a very busy road but the traffic situation in Gythio has now been much improved by a bypass, meaning that trucks going to and from Sparta and Areopoli no longer have to drive along the front.

6

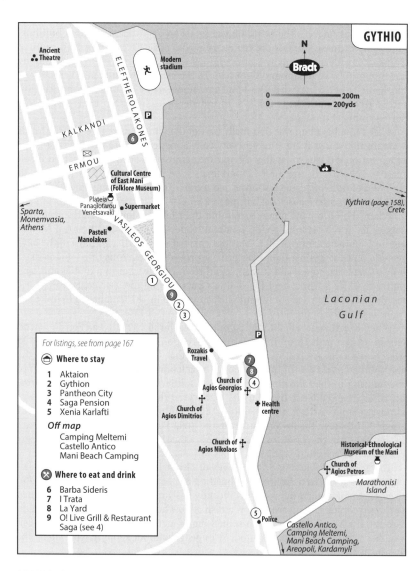

For listings, see from page 167

Where to stay

1 Aktaion
2 Gythion
3 Pantheon City
4 Saga Pension
5 Xenia Karlafti

Off map
Camping Meltemi
Castello Antico
Mani Beach Camping

Where to eat and drink

6 Barba Sideris
7 I Trata
8 La Yard
9 O! Live Grill & Restaurant
Saga (see 4)

MYTHOLOGY AND HISTORY In mythology Gythio was founded jointly by Heracles and Apollo, a seemingly unlikely combination. More famously, the island just off-shore, then called Kranae, is mentioned by Homer as the site of Paris and Helen's first night together after they had run away from her husband, King Menelaus of Sparta. Then, as now, Gythio was the main port for inland Sparta, and after their night of passion the lovers fled by ship to Troy, annoying King Menelaus, but providing ample fodder for epic poetry.

In the Classical Greek period the fortunes of the town were bound to those of Sparta, but under the Romans it made a break and became the most important member of the Free Laconian League. At the same time it became known as one of the best suppliers of *Murex brandaris*, the mollusc from which the purple dye, so beloved by imperial Rome, was obtained. Most of the ancient town now lies beneath the water of the harbour.

GETTING THERE AND AWAY The bus station is located on the square at the north end of the harbour. Buses go to and from Sparta (and further north to Athens) six times a day, Itylo twice a day where you can change for Kalamata (*40mins*), and Areopoli five times a day (*35mins*). There is normally at least one bus a day heading into the Mesa Mani.

WHERE TO STAY *Map, opposite*

There is plenty of accommodation in Gythio, most of it located on the harbourfront. Noise from this road can be a problem, but since the bypass this has improved. There are also **campsites** and a few boutique hotels on Mavrovouni Beach, which starts 2km south of Gythio on the old road out to Areopoli.

Town centre

Aktaion (22 rooms) 27330 23500; m 69747 29001; e aktaiong@otenet.gr; w aktaionhotel.gr. Inside, this hotel doesn't live up to its grand exterior, but it is pleasant enough. Most rooms have balconies overlooking the sea. Located on the northern end of the harbour. It has a sister resort on the sandy beach to the north of town. €€€€

Gythion (7 rooms) 27330 23452; m 69457 77607; e info@gythionhotel.gr; w gythionhotel.gr. A well-done renovation of another 19th-century Neoclassical building in the middle of the harbour. €€€

Saga Pension (14 rooms) 27330 23220; m 69442 67023; e saga@sagapension.gr; w sagapension.gr. Situated in an old-fashioned waterfront 4-storey building above the town's top restaurant, this relaxed family-run pension has pleasant rooms with balconies offering great views to the island. €€€

Pantheon City Hotel (55 rooms) 27330 22289; e info@pantheongythio.gr; w pantheongythio.gr. Situated alongside the Gythion, this smart modern hotel boasts a great

waterfront location & well-priced comfortable rooms. €€

Xenia Karlafti (7 rooms) 27330 22719. This is a real slice of old-style Greek travel – a proper rooms place. Now run by Xenia's stoical & wry daughter, Voula. Simple rooms with fans, but no AC, & shared kitchen facilities. You'll feel like a family guest. The house is on the front, south of the harbour, just before the causeway that goes out to Marathonisi Island. €€

Mavrovouni Beach

Castello Antico (4 rooms) 27330 22601; m 69458 90391; e info@castelloantico.com; w castelloantico.com. This gorgeous beachfront boutique hotel is built around a sparkling swimming pool & garden in the traditional Mani architectural style. €€€€€

Camping Meltemi 27330 22833; e info@campingmeltemi.gr; w campingmeltemi.gr. This has the best facilities of the campsites close to Gythio, including an onsite taverna & swimming pool. €

Mani Beach Camping 27330 23450; e info@manibeach.gr; w manibeach.gr. Friendly campsite with an onsite taverna. €

WHERE TO EAT AND DRINK *Map, opposite*

Beside the fishing boats at the southern end of the harbour, a string of waterfront tavernas, each one with a washing line of drying octopus tentacles outside, do exactly what you'd expect.

Barba Sideris 27330 22476; m 69455 44400; w barba-sideris.com. This seaside taverna to the north of the harbour specialises in roast meat – including piglet souvlakia, spit-cooked lamb & chicken – served on a waxed paper called ladokolla.

I Trata 27330 24429. Easily recognised by its pastel blue exterior & terrace seating on the harbourfront next to the jetty, this down-to-earth

& well-priced taverna also specialises in seafood, & since the owner's husband is a fisherman, freshness is all but guaranteed.

O! Live Grill & Restaurant 27330 22009; OliveGytheio. This popular & stylish seafront restaurant specialises in seafood/fish souvlakia & craft beers.

Saga Restaurant 27330 21358; w sagapension.gr. Gythio's top seafood restaurant has terrace seating looking directly towards the island & lighthouse. Not as expensive as you might fear.

☆ **La Yard** m 69867 78802. This bright & stylish coffee & cocktail bar has a semi-outdoor feel, a relaxed vibe aimed at 30-somethings, & occasional nighttime live music or themed DJ sets.

OTHER PRACTICALITIES There is not much more to Gythio than the road along the harbour. The official tourist office on the road inland to the north of the harbour is a particularly useless example of the genre. Your best bet is to make use of **Rozakis Travel** (✆*27330 22207;* e *rosakigy@otenet.gr*), which is located towards the southern end of the harbourfront. As well as car hire and general info they can also provide information on **ferry services to Kythira and Crete**. These usually run from June to September, but timetables change yearly.

Everything you could need in Gythio is located on or near the harbourfront, including two **supermarkets**, a **health centre** and the **police** (✆*27330 22100*). **Taxis** congregate at the two squares at either end of the harbour (✆*27330 23400/22755*). There is an excellent **tourist shop** underneath the Aktaion Hotel that also sells **English newspapers**, and upstairs, **English books** and local guides and maps. Halfway down the front is a little **antiques shop** – unusual for this part of Greece and well worth a browse. And do pop into **Pasteli Manolakos** (✆*27330 21490;* w *pasteli-manolakos.gr*), a family-run sweet shop founded on the central Plateia Panagiotarou Venetsavaki in 1902, and famed for its sesame bars, but also well stocked with other tempting locally sourced produce, from fruit liqueurs and olive oil to wild honey and homemade preserves.

WHAT TO SEE AND DO
Marathonisi (Ancient Kranae) This island, now connected by a causeway to the mainland, still has a romantic feel to it even though Paris and Helen of Troy are long gone. It is a favourite destination for a *volta* (stroll) in the evenings and there is a café here and a smart(ish) fish restaurant. Should you decide to re-create the couple's first night you'll be pleased to know that the council has planted up the once bare island with fir trees.

Historical-Ethnological Museum of the Mani (✆ *27330 22427;* ⊕ *by appointment only, free entrance*) The one formal attraction on Marathonisi is the small museum, which enjoys a lovely location in the 18th-century tower house of the Grigorakis family. The exhibition inside is short on actual artefacts but is a fascinating insight into the area. The ground floor explores local history and customs through the eyes of travellers over the centuries. The upper floor has plans and architectural drawings of various towers. Best to call in advance, but if you just pitch up and find it closed, try knocking on the office door at the corner of the building.

Ancient theatre This can be found back on the mainland by following the signs into the back streets at the north end of the harbour. There are only a few tiers of seats remaining, but it is an interesting site to wander out to. The fact that it now sits beside an army base and a dusty car park somehow seems to add to its faded grandeur.

Folklore Museum (✆ *27330 23888;* w *kpmanis.gr;* ⊕ *10.00–13.00 & 18.00– 21.00 daily; free entrance*) Housed in the Cultural Centre of East Mani on Plateia Panagiotarou Venetsavaki, the central square two blocks inland of the City Hall, the small but modern installation deals with traditional agricultural and artisanal practices in the Mani, from pottery and stone tools to quail-hunting and terracing methods.

Mavrovouni Beach (Μαυροβούνι) This long stretch of sandy beach is about 2km south of Gythio, on the old road toward Areopoli – just follow the coast along. There are several bars and tavernas dotted along it, as well as some new hotels. The beach has a reputation for windsurfing – equipment for this and other watersports can be hired from the **Ocean Café** (⌕ *27330 24392;* e *info@oceancafe.gr;* w *oceancafe.gr*). There are also some more isolated beaches on the road east along the coast from Gythio towards Monemvasia – see page 146.

Passavas Castle (Πασσαβάς) This is signposted on the main road towards Areopoli, about 4km after Mavrovouni Beach. The castle was originally built by Jean de Neuilly, a Frankish baron, in 1254, but was soon given over to the Byzantines and later occupied by the Ottomans. In 1780, Zanet Grigorakis, later to be a bey of the Mani, massacred the inhabitants of the castle, including civilians, in revenge for the execution of his uncle. There doesn't seem to be a good path all the way up to the castle, but it is possible to scramble through the undergrowth to the impressive walls. They have commanding views of their surroundings but the interior of the castle is very overgrown. The walk up is also longer than it looks so this is probably one for castle freaks only. A good view of the walls can be obtained by driving up the road opposite.

AREOPOLI (ΑΡΕΌΠΟΛΗ)

Areopoli, as you pass it, doesn't look worth a stop. It is surrounded by a sprawl of supermarkets, garages and new houses, but don't be put off. The old town, which lies off the main square to the west of the road, is handsome with its tower houses and winding backstreets, and the shops and services offer you a last bit of civilisation before you head into the Deep Mani. The town's modern centre is the large square just to the west of the main road. The old town is to the west of this and centres on the tiny old square, Platea 17 Martiou – head down the semi-pedestrianised road opposite and to the right of where you enter the large main square.

HISTORY Areopoli, then named Tsimova, had its moment of fame on 17 March 1821, when the Maniat clan leaders united here under Petrobey Mavromichalis in opposition to the Ottoman occupation, raising a banner with the motto 'Victory or Death' (they already considered themselves free so rejected the usual Greek cry of 'Freedom or Death'). This small liberation army then marched north, gaining strength, and captured Kalamata, the first blow in the Greek War of Independence. In recognition of this, Tsimova, where it all started, changed its name to Areopoli – 'City of the War God'. During the fighting in the years to follow the Maniats loomed large: the Mavromichalis family alone lost 49 of its members.

GETTING THERE AND AWAY The bus station is located on the main road next to the school, before you take the turn into the main square if you are heading south. There are two buses a day running to and from Itylo (*15mins*), three that go to and from Gerolimenas (*35mins*) and four to and from Gythio (*40mins*). Taxis are an option for exploring further south, and can normally be found around the main square.

WHERE TO STAY If you're staying in Areopoli, there's no more atmospheric choice than to stay in a tower house. There are a few options at similar prices, each offering something a little bit different.

🏠 **Antares Hotel** (12 rooms) 📞 27330 51700; 📱 69894 88400; e info@antareshotel.gr; w antareshotel.gr. Recently converted from an old tower house, this immaculate boutique hotel dominates the tiny village of Omales 1km south of Areopoli. It now sets the bar for accommodation in the Areopoli area, with the traditional stone architecture & decorative flourish of the artist who oversaw the renovation being complemented by great aerial sea views & modern amenities. Excellent traditional Greek b/fast. €€€€€

🏠 **Areos Polis** (24 rooms) 📞 27330 51028; e info@areospolis.gr; w areospolis.gr. If the tower houses are full, then this option on Athanaton Sq is a good one, with friendly owners & smart rooms. Capping it all is the pleasant roof garden restaurant, which offers views across the square & rooftops of the old town to the protruding upper floors of its tower houses. €€€€

🏠 **Kapetanakos Tower** (7 rooms) 📞 27330 51233. Located off the northeast corner of the old square, this hotel is housed in a solid tower house built in 1826 & renovated as a guesthouse in 1980. €€€€

✗ WHERE TO EAT AND DRINK

✗ **O Barba-Petros** 📞 27330 51205. Just to the east of the old square in an atmospheric setting. Specialises in grilled meats but has good vegetable dishes as well.

✗ **Palaiopolis** 📞 27330 51345. Spilling out into a characterful alley one block west of Athanaton Sq, this above-average central taverna serves a range of national & regional Greek dishes. There is plenty of choice for vegetarians too.

☆ **Spilious Café & Bar** 📱 69774 12222. Situated on the western outskirts of town, this prominently signposted terrace café offers a sensational view down to the coast & sea. The long menu of cocktails & other beverages makes it an ideal sundowner spot.

OTHER PRACTICALITIES If you follow the road from the northwest corner of the main square towards the old town and take the first right by the small church, you will find a bank with an ATM, a pharmacy and the post office. There is another ATM on the main square. Big supermarkets are back on the main road south. On the western side of the square there is an excellent bookshop devoted to the Mani with a few titles in English.

WHAT TO SEE AND DO The new part of town is fairly characterless, although the central Athanaton Square is handsome enough, with its imposing and flamboyant statue of Petrobey Mavromichalis. There is a good **market** every Saturday morning, selling fruit, vegetables and other local products, which takes place just off the main road through the outskirts of town. The normally sleepy town comes to life for this and cars and trucks block the streets all about.

The more sedate old town is well worth an extended wander, with several tower houses about, and is reached by taking the road on the northwest corner of the main square. It is based around the small square where Petrobey hoisted the flag of revolution. There is a plaque commemorating the event and a hole in the paving where the flag apparently stood. A copy of the blue-and-white flag itself normally hangs from the **Taxiarchis** church next door. The whole scene is re-created every 17 March. The church is usually locked, but has some interesting, if primitive-looking, carvings on the outside, including ones of the zodiacal animals.

Another interesting church can be found by taking the road to the southwest of the main square. This is **Ioannis O Prodromos** (John the Baptist, or John the Forerunner in direct translation), which has a set of comic book-style 18th-century frescoes of the Easter story, including one where Jesus seems to be about to float away.

Just next to this church is the new **museum** built in the **Pikoulakis Tower** (📞 27330 29531; ⏰ 08.30–15.00 Tue–Sun; €2), which is part of the Network of Mani

Museums. It is dedicated to religious custom and has well-crafted displays that are captioned in English. It includes several unusual church artefacts dating to the early years of Christianity in the Mani, most strikingly perhaps a beautiful 6th-century oil lamp adorned with a male figure in prayer. There are also several engraved marble basilicas, while the first floor is dominated by ancient icons and paintings salvaged from abandoned Byzantine churches.

INTO THE DEEP MANI

Heading south from Areopoli takes you into the Mesa Mani. Although initially the surroundings look deceptively benign, don't be fooled – this is *Kakavoulia*, 'the Land of Evil Counsel', or alternatively *Kakovounia*, 'the Bad Mountains'. Either way it is a place of ill repute. Evliya Celebi, a Turkish travel writer, came this way in the 1670s and described the land and the people:

> It is in truth an unpitied place. There are no vineyards, gardens, trees, fruits, plants and grass. The place is covered with stones. There is no soil at all. [The inhabitants] are dark skinned, small in stature, with large heads, round eyes, with voices like sheepdogs . . . shoulder length thick black hair, wirily built with large feet they leap from crag to crag like fleas.

None of this is made any better by Sir Patrick Leigh Fermor's flight of fancy/ terrific etymology which has the area's nickname deriving from *Kakovouliotes*, or 'the Cauldroneers'. Apparently the Deep Maniats used to go into battle wearing upturned, tripod-based cauldrons on their heads. A place to be wary of, then.

All of this is in the past of course, but the Deep Mani still has its own special atmosphere, despite the slow incursions of tourism. It is a barren and desolate landscape, but one that still inspires, much as deserts do. The villages with their outcrops of tower houses and the isolated medieval churches seem to blend into the land around them, hidden gems in the rocks. The region also hides other treasures: only 6km after Areopoli you see just how 'deep' the Mesa Mani can get.

DIROS CAVES The village of **Pyrgos Dirou** (Πύργος Διρού) announces itself with a line of tourist shops. There's little of interest in the settlement itself, and no real reason to stay here, but unless the very idea of caves gives you the complete heebie-jeebies, the turn-off towards the coast should not be ignored. The Diros cave system is one of the finest in the world, with its magical combination of stone and water.

History The caves that can be visited are just one part of a warren of caverns in the area (the locals will tell you they stretch as far as Sparta!), and they have yielded important evidence of early human and Neanderthal habitation. Remains of the latter, dating back from 40,000 to 100,000 years ago, have been found near Limeni. The most extensive finds, however, have come from the Alepotrypa Cave. This cave, whose name means 'Fox Hole', was discovered in 1958 and has yielded pottery, fossils and human remains from the Late and Final Neolithic periods (5400–3200BC).

The main sea caves at Diros were known to locals from at least 1895 but weren't explored properly until 1949, when the married team of Yiannis and Anna Petrocheilou, founders of the Hellenic Speleological Society, began to investigate the system. This cave was opened to the public in 1967.

Pyrgos Dirou was also the site of an important battle in the Greek War of Independence. In June 1826, Ibrahim Pasha launched an attack from Kalamata.

All the men of the region rushed northward and defended the Mani at Verga (just south of Kalamata). However, in a brilliant outflanking move Ibrahim also sent a force of 1,500 Egyptian Ottomans south by ship. They landed near Pyrgos Dirou with the intention of capturing Tsimova (Areopoli), which would be undefended. Or so they thought. When the Egyptian troops landed the Maniat women were out harvesting their crops and, armed with their sickles, sticks and stones, they quickly set about repelling the invading force. The Egyptians seem not to have known what had hit them and were soon forced back into their ships, having lost a full 1,000 men. There are two monuments commemorating the brave women of the Mani: one in the small square of the village itself, and one by the entrance to the caves.

Vlychada Caves ☎ 27330 52222; ⊕ May–Oct 10.00–18.00, Nov–Mar 08.30–15.00 daily; adult/concessions €13/7) These caves are the most spectacular of all the ones in and around Diros, and this is where most of the tourists that get this far are heading. Their name comes from the Maniat word for a 'fresh water spring'. While they can be crowded, it is worth persevering, as the caves are truly stunning, with countless stalactites reflected in crystal clear pools of water.

The ticket office is at the top of the cliffs at the end of the road from the village, which then sweeps down past a small museum (see below) to the cave entrance. The tours take place on small punts, which each take about ten adults and are guided through the warren of tunnels and chambers by skilled, but usually unresponsive, ferrymen. After buying your ticket you wait until the next available punt is free, which can be an hour or two on a high-season weekend. There is a small pebble beach and a café to help while away the time. While the cave itself is spectacular, no traces of human habitation have been found. Animal remains abound, however, with fossils of panthers, hyenas, lions and hippopotami all turning up. It must have been a very different Mani once…

Whatever the temperature outside, inside the cave remains about 16–19°C, so an extra layer might be worth it. The tour is 1,300m long and takes about 25 minutes; at the end there is a 200m walk to the exit.

Museum and Alepotrypa Cave ☎ 27330 52233; ⊕ 08.30–15.00 Tue–Sun; €2) The small museum is halfway between the ticket office and the entrance to Vlychada and contains pottery and jewellery, as well as the skeleton of a buried female. The Alepotrypa Cave is accessed through the back of the museum; it is closed to the public at present, although plans are afoot to open it up. The latest news from here is the discovery of a whole Neolithic settlement around the cave, including the intriguing burial of a Stone Age couple still locked in an embrace – 'they're totally spooning', as one eminent archaeologist put it!

SOUTH TO GEROLIMENAS Nowadays the main route south into the Mesa Mani is getting reasonably well travelled upon, and you're more than likely going to spot a few caravans, hire cars and even coaches. It's much more rewarding to get on to the secondary roads and explore, where you'll probably find yourself entirely alone.

Pyrgos Dirou to Mezapos An opportunity to get off the beaten track comes just 2km south of Pyrgos Dirou, where a left fork is marked (in Greek) to Fragoulias (Φραγούλιας), Dryalos (Δρύαλος) and Paleohora (Παλιόχωρα). This road continues south, parallel to the main road, but offers much more scope for the discovery of **tower houses** and **Byzantine churches**, particularly at Dryalos, Briki (Μπρίκι) and Mina (Μίνα), all of which warrant a stop and a wander around. As

you proceed southward the peninsula of Tigani comes into view and the reason for its name, 'Frying Pan', becomes obvious.

After Mina the road turns down towards the coast, crossing the main road, and going past the fortified complex at Agios Giorgios (Αγ Γεώργιος) to the sleepy little harbour at **Mezapos** (Μέζαπος). A concrete road to the right here leads to a small pebble bay with another fine view over to Tigani. The harbour itself is down the cliffs to the left and has a couple of tavernas above it. It's sometimes possible to persuade the fishermen here into boat trips out to Tigani – try asking in the tavernas.

Stavri and Tigani
Despite what maps may say, this road then continues on to **Stavri** (Σταυρί), although the initial climb out of Mezapos is rather steep. There are two well-known Byzantine churches along the way, both set in beautiful locations: Vlacherna is signposted below the road and Episkopi is above it. Stavri is a surprisingly large village, but the only real sign of life is the **Tsitsiris Castle** (*23 rooms;* \27330 56298; w *tsitsiriscastle.gr; closed Nov–20 March;* €€€€), a large hotel that has been tastefully added on to a restored tower house. It would make a great base for exploring the local area and has a restaurant in a barrel-vaulted basement.

Heading north out of Stavri brings you to the edge of **Tigani** (Τηγάνι). This hunk of rock, tethered to the Mani by a low-slung ribbon of land, has often been said to be the site of the castle of Grand Maina, built by William de Villehardouin, Frankish prince of the Morea, in 1248. However, recent scholars are unsure and have started to favour the site of Kelefa Castle, to the north near Itylo. What is certain is that there was some sort of fortification on Tigani going back into antiquity, and plentiful, if somewhat scattered, remains can still be seen. Also obvious is the site of an early Christian basilica, 22m x 15m, which has been dated to the 6th century. The walk over the old salt pans to the site takes about 40 minutes and can be hot and uncomfortable underfoot; allow 2½–3 hours for the round trip, including time for an explore.

South of Stavri
Travelling south from Stavri brings you into the plain that bulges and rises up to the cliffs of **Cavo Grosso** (Κάβο Γρόσσο) or 'Great Cape'. It is a fascinating part of the Mesa Mani, studded with towered villages and the ubiquitous churches. There doesn't seem to be an accurate map of the area and it is easy to get lost in the labyrinth of roads connecting village to village. However, it is hard to totally lose your way, with the bluff of the cliffs to one side and the mountains to the other, and it is a fantastic place to nose around, soaking in the atmosphere of the Deep Mani. With a bit of luck you will eventually find yourself winding down the cliffs of Cavo Grosso to Gerolimenas.

The main road south passes through the twin villages of **Kita** (Κοίτα), on the left, and **Nomia** (Νόμια), on the right, once bitter rivals. It was here, in 1870, that the last great Maniat feud was put down by 400 government soldiers. The villages sprout an interesting collection of tower houses.

GEROLIMENAS (ΓΕΡΟΛΙΜΈΝΑΣ)
The little harbour of Gerolimenas comes as a welcome oasis in the barren land of the Mesa Mani. Lying below the great bluff of Cavo Grosso, it offers a row of tavernas and cafés by a pleasant pebble beach, along with some surprisingly swanky hotels. This is due to a return to form for the village: it was founded as a commercial port in the 1870s and at one point was exporting 7,000 quails a month to France. The last century saw a decline in fortunes as it and the rest of the Mani turned into a backwater. Improved roads mean that Athenians can now come to the pretty port for weekend getaways, and Gerolimenas has taken on quite a trendy vibe. The only thing that's currently

missing is a reasonable shop; the dusty little village store tries hard, but has minimal fresh goods.

Getting there and away

You really need your own transport to explore the Deep Mani, but buses do come here from Areopolis (*2–3 a day*; *35mins*).

🏠 Where to stay

Twenty-five years ago the only options in Gerolimenas were a few rooms above a basic taverna, or the beach. Now boutique hotels vie with each other as romantic getaways for moneyed Greeks. Come off-season, though, and you might be able to grab a real bargain.

🏠 **Guesthouse Laoula** (8 rooms) ✆27330 54269; e info@laoula.gr; w laoula.gr. Just a few doors along from the Kyrimai, this also has nicely done-up rooms & the same view over the harbour to Cavo Grosso. €€€€€

✳ 🏠 **Kyrimai** (22 rooms) ✆27330 54288; e info@kyrimai.gr; w kyrimai.gr. Owned by the descendants of the family who built up the port in the first place, & situated in their original 19th-century warehouses, this hotel is a bit special. Beautifully done throughout, with an eye for detail & a sense of history. It also boasts a pool &

an award-winning chef (the restaurant is open to non-guests). Stay here if you can. The hotel is at the end of the left-hand arm of the harbour if you are looking at the sea. €€€€€

🏠 **Akroyiali/O Gerolimenas** (30 rooms & 4 apts) ✆27330 54204; m 69464 59844; e info@ gerolimenas-hotels.com; w gerolimenas-hotels. com. At the right-hand edge of the harbour, this hotel offers simple rooms & apartments in a converted tower house, or rather more swish accommodation in its newer extension (more expensive). €€€

✗ Where to eat and drink

If you want something special, try the excellent restaurant at the Kyrimai hotel (see above). Alternatively, a few tavernas along the harbour serve standard Greek fare, while the restaurant at the Akroyiali serves fresh local seafood right by the beach, so you can have a dip between courses.

What to see and do

Gerolimenas is a perfect base for a few days' exploring, its comforts providing a stark contrast to the surrounding harsh landscape. This contrast can be seen by going up to the villages of Kato Boulari and Ano Boulari (Μπουλαριοι), Lower and Upper Boulari, on the mountains just to the east of Gerolimenas. Nestled among the rocks and cacti is a wonderful collection of towers and churches. The road loops through the villages and walking up and down from Gerolimenas would take 2–3 hours. This could be extended with an off-road walk that takes you up to the villages of Pepo (Πέπο) and Leontakis (Λεοντάκης), another 2 hours, high above, for good traditional architecture and amazing views.

Perched at an altitude of 600m some 3km inland of Gerolimenas as the crow flies, **Mountanistika** (Μουντανίστικα) is one of the Mani's highest villages, and has some huge views. The village itself is full of ruined tower houses, but almost no-one lives there anymore. To get there, follow the coastal road southeast of Gerolimenas to **Alika** (Άλικα), then turn left on to a road that crosses to the east coast of the Mani via **Tsikkalia** (Τσικκαλιά). About 2km along the road to Tsikkalia, by a large eucalyptus tree, turn left on to the signposted but narrow and vertiginous road that winds 4km northward and uphill to Mountanistika. You are unlikely to meet another car on the way up, unless there's been a funeral at the cemetery, in which case you could meet a whole train of vehicles and have to do some rather tricky driving!

DOWN TO CAPE TENARO South from Gerolimenas, the already parched vegetation seems to give up the ghost entirely and the land is completely covered in rocks. The fact that there are still terraces on the mountainsides is a testimony to the fortitude of the people who once lived here. It is a brutal and beautiful terrain, fitting to the cape's ancient reputation as a gateway between the lands of the living and the dead.

The road south splits among the towers of Alika, with one branch heading up to Mountanistika (see opposite) and the east side of the Mani, while the other continues down through **Kyparissos** (Κυπάρισσος). There are a couple of nice pebbly coves here, as well as the scattered remains of a Roman city. These can be found by parking by the brown sign and following the path to the beach. The next cove can be reached from the road that turns right down to Kyparissos' harbour.

Vathia (Βάθεια)

Just past Kyparissos the road starts to wind up into the mountains and the towers of Vathia appear above. Vathia is the most famous of the towered villages of the Mani and will already be familiar from postcards. Despite this there is little development in the village. In the 1980s, the Greek tourist board tried to open a hotel here but the plan stagnated. More recently a few of the towers have been restored. Most of them are still ruins, however, and only a handful of people live here permanently. Occasionally, in the summer, a café will open up.

The dereliction actually adds to the atmosphere of the village and its forest of towers. It is hard to imagine how these could have housed feuding clans when they sprout up so close to each other, but one account, from 1805, tells of a war in the village that lasted 40 years and cost 100 lives. You can wander freely around the village and carefully poke about the ruins. To get the 'postcard' photo follow the main road up to its next bend.

Porto Kagio (Πόρτο Κάγιο)

Heading still farther south, the peninsula narrows to only a few hundred metres across then flares out again in one final bulge before disappearing into the sea. Just before this, the road forks. The left-hand turn almost immediately forks again: to the left the road climbs into the mountains, with spectacular views back down to the cape, before joining the main road to Lagia (it is asphalt all the way); the right turn leads round the north side of **Porto Kagio Bay** to the castle built by the Turks in 1570. Only the walls remain, sheltering a collection of new and restored houses. The Venetians called this bay Porto Quaglio, after the quails that passed here on migration and were caught in outstretched nets.

Modern Porto Kagio is on the southern side of this bay, normally filled with yachts at anchor. It is a pretty enough setting, with a shingle beach to swim from, and the yacht crowd seem to enjoy it. However, a piratical air seems to hang over the small collection of concrete buildings. There are a couple of fish tavernas here and both of them offer some slightly overpriced rooms; one above the taverna itself and the other in a modern stone building just off the beach.

If you want to stay down here there is a better option at **Marmari** (Μαρμάρι), just to the south and on the opposite coast of the peninsula. This small village clings to the hills over two sandy coves. Above the first of these sprawls the attractive ✳ **Marmari Paradise** (*24 rooms*; ☏ *27330 52101*; e *info@marmariparadise.com*; w *marmariparadise.com*; **€€€**), which has a variety of rooms and also a good taverna.

Cape Tenaro (Ταίναρο)

The main point of coming down this far south is to get to Cape Tenaro (also known as Matapan), which is the southernmost point of mainland Greece, and as atmospheric a place as one could hope to find. Nowadays

One of the first things you notice about the Mani is that it is not particularly fertile. The local story goes that after the creation God was left with a pile of rocks, and with nothing better to do he tipped them on the Mani. Dry stone walls are a feature of the area, making it seem oddly like Yorkshire at times, but here they are rarely used to mark out whose field is whose. Rather they are born of necessity, and are somewhere to pile the infernal rocks so that you can actually find some bare earth to plant crops on. Nowadays the main crop is olives, which actually do rather well in the arid environment, at least farther north, but in the past these fields would have been used for cereal crops and vegetables, so that people could (try) to feed themselves. That land was at a premium can be seen from some of the extraordinary terracing on the mountainsides.

Given that the population of this area was once much higher than it is now, this led to a fierce competition for resources, and it was for this reason, above all others, that the famous Maniat feuds began. If a family, or clan, managed to secure some fertile land, they needed to protect it, and thus were born the tower houses – mini castles used as defensive keeps for the family inside. Often built five storeys high or more, they lacked stairways – ladders were used and could be pulled up behind you to block attack. Holes in the turrets allowed the defenders to shoot downwards on attackers, or douse them in boiling water or hot oil. It all seems pretty medieval, and it is a shock to realise that towers like these were being built and used well into the 19th century.

In the Exo Mani each village was usually ruled by a single 'captain' of a family, and therefore tend to only have one main tower house, or a walled complex of them, as at Kardamyli. It is in the Deep Mani, to the south, that they really come into their own. Here a village such as Vathia could have several feuding clans and came to resemble small Manhattans. The battles took place over the width of an alley, with both rifle and cannon, and sons were called 'guns', as wielding one was their main virtue. Fortunately times have moved on.

the road takes you almost all the way there, finally stopping at a car park and taverna by the ruins of ancient **Tainaron**. There was a temple of Poseidon here, possibly on the same site now occupied by the ruined chapel, and an oracle of the dead. It was also reputedly an entrance to the kingdom of Hades, through which Heracles dragged Cerberus, the three-headed, canine guardian of the underworld. The actual entrance is disputed: some say it is the small cave by the cove below the chapel; others that it's a sea cave to the west only accessible by boat. Neither extends very far back so presumably Hades is not receiving visitors.

A path leads from the car park through bits of ruin (including a well-preserved fragment of mosaic with a wave pattern) towards the cape and its automatic lighthouse. The walk is only half an hour or so each way, but be cautious if there's a wind blowing, unless you want to see why ships still fear this headland. The rocks beyond the lighthouse are not, as some locals would have you believe, the last point of mainland Europe (that honour goes to Tarifa in Spain), but they still feel like the end of the world.

UP THE EAST COAST The east coast of the Mesa Mani is often known as the 'sunward' coast, as opposed to the 'shady' west coast, although there doesn't seem to be much of an actual difference in light quality. It does have a very different character to the west, however, with the mountains coming right down to the sea, and the roads snaking dramatically around them between tower-studded villages that cling to the crags. Until quite recently most travellers would scoot up this coast on the one, bad, road, usually without stopping. Although more of the area has now opened up, with more asphalted roads, travel up this coast still has the air of being well off the beaten track and has the potential to be hugely enjoyable. Apart from the villages and scenery the main attraction is several 'undiscovered' coves that offer lovely, secluded swimming opportunities.

Lagia to Kokkala Travelling from south to north, the first major village of the east coast is **Lagia** (Λαγια), which announces itself with a skyline of tower houses. This profusion is due to the four different clans who lived in the village, each with their own group of towers and a church. Some of the older towers taper inwards as they rise up, perhaps because of the lack of wood in the region for scaffolding. Local legend says that one of the towers was built overnight by a group of 400 men to surprise their adversaries. There is now a smart, modern café/taverna in the main square of the village.

About 3km after Lagia a road leads into the mountains passing the **ancient marble quarries** of *rosso antico*, or Tainaron marble, which was highly sought after in ancient times and has been used in buildings from the Treasury of Atreus at Mycenae (page 74) to Westminster Cathedral. To see this red marble in use nearby follow the road to its end at the church of Profitis Ilias (the last couple of hundred metres are unpaved but driveable).

The marble would reach the harbour of Agios Kyprianos (Αγ Κυπριανός) by a steep road that can still be travelled today. As you enter the village a right-hand turn leads, via a short dirt road, to **Abela Beach** (Άμπελα), a beautiful stretch of pebbles and clear water, but with no facilities at present. This can also be reached by a much gentler road from near Kokkala, but while this is driveable it is not yet asphalted the entire way.

The main road passes the dramatic towers of Dhimaristika (Διμαριστίκα) and the walled village of Spira (Σπίρα) before descending to **Kokkala** (Κοκκάλα). This village, although not the prettiest, does have two pleasant pebble coves (the village derives its name from a dialect word for pebbles) and offers the most choice for accommodation and eating if you want to stay over on this coast. The nicest-looking rooms are above the taverna on Marathos Beach, the more southerly of the two coves. The taverna is also noted for its food, but outside of summer is rarely open.

The only petrol station currently on this coast is 4km north of Kokkala. Just before it is a sharp turn down to the coast, where a large, modern hotel sits beside another pretty cove. Just after the garage and before the village of Nyfi is a sign to the 'Ancient Site of Kournos', although this is actually the name of the ravine. The site is located up in the mountains beyond the monastery of the Panagia. There is some speculation that this may be Aigila, a town mentioned by Pausanias. Aristomenos, a Messinian general, was almost spit-roasted here by some Spartan priestesses. There's little to see at the site or the monastery, but the hard (and thorny) 1½-hour hike up is rewarded by the tremendous views east to Cape Maleas and Kythira.

Nyfi to Ageranos The village of **Nyfi** (Νύφι) is divided into two, with the older half's tower houses located up the slope. The modern half, down by the coast, hides a beautiful, cliff-lined pebble cove with a taverna. Heading north, the landscape gets steadily less barren. There is another outcrop of tower houses at **Flomochori** (Φλομοχώρι) and below this another pebble beach with a taverna that has a few simple rooms.

6

There are more places to stay in **Kotronas** (Κότρωνας), which has the air of a sophisticated resort compared with the rest of the Mesa Mani. It does offer a small choice in eating and sleeping establishments, and a small strip of sand. Enjoy an interesting little wander by following the path down from the children's playground to the west of the village. This takes you down to the 'island' of **Skopa** (Σκοπά), connected to the mainland by a short strip of pebbles. It is a lovely spot and even a quick look round will uncover the remains of medieval fortifications in the undergrowth.

From here you used to have to drive west through the mountains back to Areopoli, but now you can continue around the dramatic headland of **Cape Stavri** (Σταυρί). There are more opportunities to swim here, especially if you have been dying for some sand after all those pebbles. The first is at **Skoutari** (Σκουτάρι), where there are two shingle and sand beaches by a small church and a taverna with basic rooms.

North of here several small roads cross each other in the reedy marshland beside the grey beaches of Kamares (Καμάρες). This area is noted for its migratory birds in the spring. At **Ageranos** (Αγερανός) there are a last few impressive tower houses. The bay below hides the shockingly incongruous Belle Helene Hotel, a 1980s disaster that is signposted for miles around. The surrounding 'resort', while small, is similarly awful. However, another turning slightly farther to the north leads to two campsites on a very pleasant section of sandy beach: **Cronos Camping** (✆ *27330 93093*; **€**) and **Camping Dias** (✆*27330 93293*; m *69391 21613*; e *info@campingdias. gr*; w *campingdias.gr*; **€**).

NORTH FROM AREOPOLI (ΑΡΕΌΠΟΛΗ) TO STOUPA (ΣΤΟΎΠΑ)

The stunning bay of **Itylo** (Οίτυλο), down into which the road descends before leaping back into the mountains on the other side, marks the transition between Exo and Mesa Mani (Outer and Inner or Deep Mani). The bay is lined with various places to stay, but unfortunately the beach, which looks so enticing from above, fails to live up to its promise as it gets hit by the prevailing wind, which also lines the beach with detritus.

The best place to swim is from the rocks in the village of **Limeni** (Λιμένι), in the southern corner of the bay. This is the port for Areopoli and was the ancestral stronghold of the Mavromichalis family, and their (beautifully restored) tower house is still in the family and dominates the small harbour. It is now a rather special hotel: **Pirgos Mavromichali** (✆*27330 51042*; m *69737 57499*; e *info@pirgosmavromichali. gr*; w *pirgosmavromichali.gr*; **€€€€€**). For fresh seafood, the legendary but rather pricey **Taverna Takis To Limeni** (✆ *27330 51327*) has a fantastic setting right on the shore, but it sometimes rests on its culinary laurels. A better option these days is the **Kourmas Restaurant** (✆*27330 51458*; w *kourmas.gr*), which also has a great seafront location and is famed for its spaghetti with lobster.

On the ridge above Limeni can be seen the walls of **Kelefa Castle** (Κελεφά), built by the Ottomans in 1670 in a somewhat vain attempt to stamp their authority on the Maniats. Nothing remains inside the castle, but the imposing fortifications can be reached by a steep road from near Limeni, or by a more gentle drive from the Areopoli–Gythio road.

On the northern side of the bay is **Itylo** itself, once a centre of piracy and the slave trade. Nowadays there is little to detain you, but it is a transport hub with bus travellers from the north or south having to change here. The buses stop at the main square and there are two kafenia nearby. If you are delayed here for an hour or more it is worth walking past these and out of the village to find the sharp left turn to the monastery.

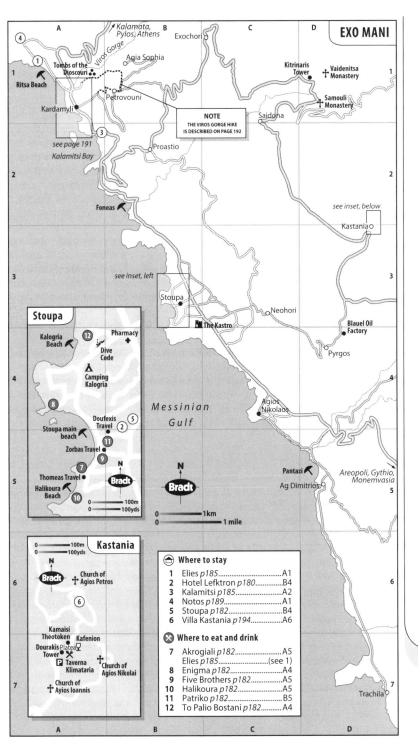

EXO MANI

Kalamata,
Pylos, Athens

Exochori

Viros Gorge

Agia Sophia

Tombs of the
Dioscouri

Ritsa Beach

Kardamyli

Petrovouni

Kitrinaris
Tower

Vaidenitsa
Monastery

Samouli
Monastery

Saidona

NOTE
THE VIROS GORGE HIKE
IS DESCRIBED ON PAGE 192

see page 191
Kalamitsi Bay

Proastio

Foneas

see inset, below

Kastaniao

see inset, left

Stoupa

Neohori

Blauel Oil
Factory

The Kastro

Pyrgos

Stoupa

Kalogria
Beach

Pharmacy

Dive
Code

Camping
Kalogria

Messinian
Gulf

Doufexis
Travel

Stoupa main
beach

Zorbas Travel

Thomeas Travel

Halikoura
Beach

Agios
Nikolaos

Pantazi

Ag Dimitrios

Areopoli, Gythio,
Monemvasia

0 ____ 100m
0 ____ 100yds

0 ____ 1km
0 ____ 1 mile

Kastania

0 ____ 100m
0 ____ 100yds

Church of
Agios Petros

Kamaisi
Theotoken

Kafenion

Dourakis
Tower

Plateia

Taverna
Klimataria

Church of
Agios Nikolai

Church of
Ayios Ioannis

Trachila

🛏 **Where to stay**

1 Elies *p185*.................................A1
2 Hotel Lefktron *p180*..............B4
3 Kalamitsi *p185*.......................A2
4 Notos *p189*..............................A1
5 Stoupa *p182*............................B4
6 Villa Kastania *p194*...............A6

✕ **Where to eat and drink**

7 Akrogiali *p182*.......................A5
Elies *p185*..........................(see 1)
8 Enigma *p182*...........................A4
9 Five Brothers *p182*................A5
10 Halikoura *p182*......................A5
11 Patriko *p182*...........................B5
12 To Palio Bostani *p182*..........A4

179

The **Dekoulou Monastery**, which is best reached by car from the turning down in the bay, has a wonderful setting on the slopes above the bay. The key holders, and their two loud dogs, live next door, so with a bit of luck you should be able to get inside to see the frescoes, which date from 1765. While not that old for the region, they are well preserved, and show the impact of a fully painted church. The *Last Judgement* on the west wall is particularly striking.

The road north is worth it for the route alone. It leaves the coast and climbs into the mountains before passing several interesting Exo Mani villages. Before the first of these there is a chance for a swim stop – take the road down to the right, beside a good bakery, signed to Hotasia. After 2.5km this reaches the sea and, although it is little more than a concrete swimming platform, the water and the spot are lovely. There is a seasonal café here. The first two villages you come to are **Agios Nikon** (Αγ Νικών), named after the 9th-century converter of the Mani to Christianity and **Langada** (Λαγκαδά), with a couple of tower houses and a beautiful church of the Metamorphoses.

Next up is **Thalames** (Θαλάμες), where a kafenion nestles in the shade of a large plane tree. If this tempts you into stopping there are a few other points of interest around the village platea. On the far side is the self-proclaimed **Mani Museum** (⊕ *fairly randomly; €3*), which in fact is the private collection of a rather eccentric local. It's a bit of a mishmash of prints, agricultural equipment and guns, and some of it is of slightly dubious provenance. If he's around the owner will provide commentary in German and the whole experience is just about bizarre enough to warrant the entry fee of a few euros.

More sensible is the **Morea Olive Oil Press** (⭑ *27210 74557;* w *morea-olivenoel. de*) on the other side of the platea. Running on fair-trade principles, this is one of several local oil producers now owned by a foreigner. The shop is often open in the summer and, if they're not busy, you might be able to get a tour of the press itself.

Back in the platea is a reminder of Thalames' ancient history, when it was part of the Free Laconian League. Pausanias writes that there was an oracle and sacred

THE EVIL EYE

You will undoubtedly be exposed to the evil eye while in the Peloponnese. Don't worry too much, though, as it will rarely be directed towards you. The most obvious sign of the lingering belief in its power is the universal gesture of Greek contempt and insult, most often seen flung from one driver to another in traffic jams. This consists of an outstretched arm ending in an open palm with fingers spread (imagine the eye in the centre of the palm with the fingers acting as eyelashes). To double up the insult the other palm is slapped against the back of the first (a complicated manoeuvre, but not unheard of, while driving).

'Giving' someone the evil eye is supposed to result in a string of bad fortune for the receiver. Many people, even today, guard against it with deflecting talismans, generally glass blue eyes of various sizes. Often these will not be displayed openly, but worn or placed somewhere discreetly. Interestingly the evil eye is not always given on purpose. Envy of someone else's good fortune, even if it is unconscious, can bring down the power of the eye. Often when something is admired, particularly a young baby, you will see the person spit over their shoulder, thus deflecting the compliment and guarding against the evil eye. It can be a little disconcerting if it's your baby.

water spring here, and the spring is thought to be where steps go down to two stone arches just to the north of the kafenion.

The last two villages before Stoupa are **Nomitsi** (Νομιτσι), where the 13th-century church of Agios Anargyoi almost straddles the road, and **Platsa** (Πλάτσα), whose centre is just off the main road to the left and boasts a remarkably grand platea. From here the road winds dramatically back down towards the coast.

STOUPA (ΣΤΟΎΠΑ)

The road south from Kardamyli hugs the cliffs above the sea. After 2.5km a sharp hairpin bend takes you round the cove of **Foneas** (Φόνεας) [179 B2], which holds a perfect little pebble beach. It is served by a little beach bar in the summer, but if you come in early spring or late autumn you will probably have the beach all to yourself. Another 2.5km brings you to the outskirts of Stoupa, indisputably the main resort of the Mani. In July and, especially, August the once small village is now overwhelmed by crowds of English, Dutch and visiting Greeks. Outside of this period, however, it remains relatively quiet for a Greek resort and is marketed as a package holiday for Greece lovers, rather than those simply in search of sun and sand. That said, it does have the two best sandy beaches on this coast. With excellent places to eat, all the facilities you might need and plenty of accommodation, Stoupa makes another great base to unwind and do a bit of exploring.

GETTING THERE AND AWAY Stoupa is 10 minutes' drive from Kardamyli and is served by the same buses and taxis (page 185). The best place to catch the buses is on the main road by the bakery. Unlike most villages in the Exo Mani the main road does not go through the middle of Stoupa, but skirts its eastern edge.

TOURIST AGENCIES There are several tourist agencies in Stoupa. They all offer pretty much the same services, including car hire, accommodation, money changing and excursions. They also keep much the same hours in season, opening until 13.00 and then again from 17.00 to 20.00.

Doufexis [179 B5] 27210 77677; e info@doufexis.gr; w doufexis.com. Located up the street that goes off the middle of Stoupa Beach, this is the biggest of the bunch.
Thomeas Travel [179 A5] 27210 77689; e info@thomeastravel.gr; w thomeastravel.gr.

Situated just past the steep bit of road at the south end of the main beach.
Zorbas [179 A5] m 69781 44435; e info@zorbas.de; w zorbas.de. The website hosts a webcam & a discussion forum.

WHERE TO STAY Stoupa is largely geared up to the package-holiday industry, but it should always be possible to find a bed. Try the two hotels listed, or approach the agencies, who will know where there are rooms available. There is also a great online portal for Stoupa and the surrounding area at w insidemani.gr, where you can find accommodation and eating tips as well as a wealth of other local detail. In the summer there is one basic **campsite: Camping Kalogria** (27210 77319; m 69746 07159; e info@campingkalogria.com; w campingkalogria.com; €), as its name suggests, is just above Kalogria Beach. Out of season Stoupa pretty much closes up shop and you are probably better off staying in Kardamyli.

Hotel Lefktron [179 B4] (32 rooms) 27210 77444; e info@lefktron-hotel.gr;
w lefktron-hotel.gr. Next door to the Stoupa, it has slightly better rooms & a pool. €€€

🏠 **Stoupa Hotel** [179 B4] (18 rooms) ✆27210 77308; e hotelstoupa@web-greece.gr; w hotel-stoupa.gr. Bang in the centre of the village on the road leading down to the beach from the bakery. It offers adequate rooms & often stays open off-season. €€

✕ **WHERE TO EAT AND DRINK** For a 'resort', Stoupa's eating options are of a surprisingly high standard, with none of the fish-and-chip rip-off merchants that plague the islands. If you come between October and March, however, it can sometimes be hard to find even a cup of coffee. There are lots of options for after-dinner drinks: among the best are **Patriko**, in a nicely restored old house on the main beach, and **Enigma**, in a prime location on the headland between Kalogria and the main beach.

✕ **Akrogiali** [179 A5] ✆27210 77335; m 69444 20729. This establishment has been in the Rapteas family for years, ever since the Kalamata boat stopped here before the road was built. It has a great location right at the southern end of the main beach & does a surprisingly large b/fast menu.

✕ **Five Brothers** [179 A5] ✆27210 77398. Probably the most old-fashioned of Stoupa's tavernas. It still has a glass counter where the day's hot dishes are displayed, & its chips are renowned. In the winter it stays open as a kafenion for the old men of the village.

✕ **Halikoura** [179 A5] ✆27210 77122. Above Stoupa's smallest & quietest beach, this is often a good place to get away from it all, despite having excellent views along the coast. Their 'village cheese pie' is more of a soufflé, & delicious.

✴ ✕ **To Palio Bostani** [179 A4] ✆27210 78282. Right on Kalogria Beach, the 'old vegetable patch' is a proper family taverna. Dimitri's mother still oversees the vegetable patch itself, while Afi, his daughter, often sets the nets to catch fresh fish (at least when she can spare time from her degree in Marine Biology). A truly delightful spot.

OTHER PRACTICALITIES There are two big supermarkets in Stoupa out on the main road, as well as smaller stores by the main beach. There are a few ATMs in the village, but the only bank caters mainly for the local farmers (even selling their olive oil) and has intermittent opening times. Health problems are best dealt with by the health clinic in Agios Nikolaos (✆27210 77210), but there is a doctor, a dentist and a good pharmacy [179 B4] (out on the main road) in the village.

WHAT TO SEE AND DO

Beaches Stoupa's claim to fame is its beaches, of which there are three. Coming from the north, the first one you reach is **Kalogria** (Καλόγρια) [179 A4], a wedge of golden sand rimmed with cafés and tavernas. It is a great family beach as the water remains shallow for quite a distance, but be warned – it is also very cold, even in the height of summer. This is due to several undersea springs that bring fresh water straight down from the mountains above. One of these springs emerges in the rocks to the right of the beach – the pool is ice cold and, although connected to the sea, just about drinkable. Above the little road down to Kalogria is a bust of the writer Nikos Kazantzakis. He lived here in 1917, running a lignite mine while dodging the draft. His mine manager was one Giorgios Zorbas, who, renamed Alexis and transferred to Crete, became the inspiration for his novel *Zorba the Greek*. Kalogria is the most popular of Stoupa's beaches and can get rather overcrowded in high season, when you might want to head to one of the remoter coves, but for the rest of the year it is a gem. It is also possible to **scuba dive** here at the excellent Dive Code centre (✆27210 64908; m 69763 32919; e dive_code@outlook.com; w divecodegreece.com; closed Nov–Apr).

A short walk over the headland brings you to Stoupa's main beach [179 A5], also blessed with golden sands and skirted by a road lined with gift shops and tavernas. There are undersea springs here too, but they are farther out. Owing to the fresh water mixing in with the sea the beach also supports some ducks – rather an odd sight among the sand and surf. On both these beaches you can hire sun loungers, pedalos, small motor boats and canoes. The last will allow you to explore the small sea cave on the headland between the main beach and Kalogria.

If you want to escape from the crowds in the summer it is worth trying Stoupa's third beach, **Halikoura** (Χαλικούρα) [179 A5]. It is reached by heading south from the main beach and taking the first right. It's only a strip of pebbles and rocks but is rarely busy.

The Kastro [179 B3] Present-day Stoupa is a creation of the holiday trade, but it does have one bit of history, which is represented by the low acropolis at the southern edge of the village. It is now named the Kastro and was the site of Beaufort Castle, built by William de Villehardouin in 1252. It is also thought to be the site of a sanctuary of Athena mentioned by Pausanias (a small marble bust of the goddess was found here and is now in the museum at Kalamata; page 201).

Nothing but a few odd rocks remains of all this, but the short scramble up the hill is worth it for the views up and down the coast. The path up can be found on the most southerly of the roads out of Stoupa, not far from where it joins the main road.

Agios Nikolaos and beyond The holidaymakers in Stoupa seem to be far less keen on hiking than their companions in Kardamyli, but there is a popular short walk along the seashore to **Agios Nikolaos** (Αγ Νικόλαος) [179 C4], the next village to the south. The walk starts by the school in the south of the village and has now been paved so can easily be cycled as well – bike rental is available in both villages. The walk takes a leisurely 45 minutes, and cycling less than half that.

The village itself is a sweet little fishing port (in the mornings you can often buy fish straight off the boats by the marble weighing counter) and there are a few tavernas and rooms here. For eating, try **Elli's Tavern** (✆ *27210 64815;* m *69832 94889;* w *ellhs.weebly.com*), which serves good traditional Greek fare.

You might hear the locals call the village 'Selenitsa', its old Slavic name. The village beach, **Pantazi** (Πανταζή) [179 D5], is a further kilometre south along the seafront road, where there is another taverna. The beach is a mixture of grey sand and pebbles and has plenty of shade provided by tamarisk trees.

For more energetic walkers who don't fancy the mountains, or for those with transport, the road continues along the coast beside cave-riddled cliffs. After 1km it passes **Agios Dimitrios** (Αγ Δημήτριος) [179 D5], another small village with a tower protecting its port. The road comes to an end 5km further on in **Trachila** (Τραχήλα) [179 D7]. There is often a taverna or two open here, but it feels a million miles away from the nearby resorts.

KARDAMYLI (ΚΑΡΔΑΜ'ΥΛΗ)

The road north from Stoupa swings downhill, past the village of **Proastio** (Προάστιο) [179 B2] with its church with a striking bell tower, and then straight into Kardamyli [179 A1], the first of two Exo Mani villages that have devoted themselves to tourism (nearby Stoupa being the other). Despite this, and the main road running straight through the middle of it, Kardamyli is delightful, and has one of the most perfect settings of any Greek village, with the towering Taygetos behind – including a rare glimpse of the pyramid-shaped peak of Profitis Ilias, the range's highest.

OLIVE PICKING

It is sometimes said, somewhat unfairly, that olive farming is the perfect profession for the Greek temperament. For much of the year the trees look after themselves, allowing the 'farmer' to get on with the important business of sitting in the kafenion sorting out the world's problems over sips of coffee. This image is not only a bit of an exaggeration – for a start, olive farming is a second job to most – but it also ignores the fact that at one time of year, when the olives are picked, it is backbreaking work.

People from colder, northern climes, often have rather romantic views of olive picking, usually including a midday picnic under the tress with copious amounts of wine. All of this is entirely accurate, but ignores the difficulty of the work itself, which in the majority of the Peloponnese is done almost entirely by hand.

Olives for eating and for oil actually come from different varieties of trees, the former having larger leaves. The picking season for olives used to make oil starts in November and can continue into early February, each farmer deciding exactly when his olives are ready. Eating olives, which are hand picked and sorted with great care, come off the trees a little earlier.

For oil olives, gangs of three to five people work on each tree. First a large net or tarpaulin is carefully laid on the ground beneath the tree, then one or two people climb into the tree and begin to prune. This is an art, and only the most experienced are allowed this job. It is said that you cut enough branches to allow birds to fly in and out of the tree. These cut branches are allowed to fall to the rest of the team. In a small operation they would then be thrashed repeatedly, either with sticks or large plastic forks, until all the olives have fallen on to the nets below. Larger farms have portable machines that have spiked, rotating cylinders that the branches are held over. The olives still in the tree are removed by plastic combs, or a device a bit like an electric egg whisk on a long pole. Once gathered together in the nets, the olives are sorted by hand to remove any leaves, and sacked up.

In olive areas almost every village has an oil press, sometimes two. The presses either pay the farmer directly for his olives, or give him back a percentage of the oil made. Often lots of farmers work as a co-operative to produce a commercial oil. The most traditional presses work with huge, upright stone discs that rotate. These turn the olives into a kind of pulp, or paste, which is layered on to the press interspersed with 'olive mats' – they look like greasy bits of carpet. This whole lot is then squeezed, and the result is finally put through a centrifuge to get rid of any remaining water. It is at the tap beside this that the anxious farmer waits, glass in hand, to taste this year's crop. A very rough estimate is that a good-sized tree will convert into a five-litre can of oil each year.

Much is made in Western supermarkets about the various 'types' of olive oil. The two main terms used are 'virgin', meaning the oil comes from the first pressing of the olives, and 'cold-pressed', meaning that no heat has been used in the pressing (which produces more oil, but of a lower quality). Many Greeks will get a little confused if you start to talk about this. The vast majority of the village presses in the Peloponnese produce only extra virgin cold-pressed oil, and most locals wouldn't consider anything else olive oil. As to how to use it: 'In the first year on salads, in the second for cooking, in the third in your car.'

HISTORY Kardamyli has a history going back to Classical times. Kardamyle, as it then was, appears in the *Iliad* as one of the seven cities that Agamemnon offered to Achilles to try to persuade him to stop sulking in his tent. The Roman emperor Augustus gave it to the Spartans as an alternative harbour to Gythio, which had rebelled against them. Pausanias briefly mentions the town, saying that the Nereids, sea nymphs, made an appearance off the coast here. A final link to Classical Greece is provided by local legend that claims it as the burial place for Castor and Pollux, the heavenly twins and brothers to Helen of Troy.

In more recent times Kardamyli was the stronghold of the Troupakis-Mourtzinos clan, who dominated the region from the early 18th century. The family claimed descent, probably rather fancifully, from the Byzantine emperors. It was in the Troupakis-Mourtzinos family compound that the armies of Theodoros Kolokotronis and Petrobey Mavromichalis gathered in 1821 before attacking the Ottomans at Kalamata. Legend has it that the two commanders passed the time playing chess, using their soldiers as pieces on a giant board. No-one knows who won. Be careful relating this story to the local villagers, however. They insist that their implacable rival Mavromichalis would never have set foot in the village, and that it was local boy Mourtzinos who played chess with the great Kolokotronis. What's more it was on a perfectly normal-sized chessboard, which they'd be happy to show to you if someone could just remember where they keep the keys… so goes the way of legends.

In the 1950s, the writer Paddy Leigh Fermor arrived in the village, having walked over the Taygetos from Mystra. In his *Mani* he describes a very different, and poorer, Kardamyli from that of the present day. Despite this he clearly fell in love with the area, and later built a house nearby.

GETTING THERE AND AWAY Starting in the early morning there are four buses (three at weekends) daily to and from Kalamata (*1hr*). Coming from the south you will need to change bus at Itylo, from where there are three buses a day (*2 at weekends; 50mins*). The bus stop is on the main road by the square. Local buses also go up to some of the mountain villages, often leaving first thing in the morning.

▶ **WHERE TO STAY** There is a good range of accommodation in Kardamyli, although it does tend to lean towards the expensive end of the market. You should always be able to find somewhere, but in the high season it could be quite a hunt and it might be worth enlisting the tourist agency's help. The nearest camping option is in Stoupa; page 181.

🏠 **Anniska/Liakoto** [191 B4] (22/23 rooms respectively) ☎27210 73600/1; e anniska@ otenet.gr; w anniska-liakoto.com; see ad, 2nd colour section. These 2 hotels, both by the sea, are where to stay if you want luxury in the centre of the village. Run by Gerry, originally from south London, & her Greek husband, both hotels are well appointed. The Liakoto is newer, pricier & has a nice pool, & its top-floor apartment is ideal for families. €€€€ (Anniska) or €€€€€ (Liakato)

🏠 **Elies Hotel** [179 A1] (10 rooms) ☎27219 73021; m 69846 27518; e info@elieshotel.gr; w elieshotel.gr. A lot of new hotels have popped up around Kardamyli in the last few years, not all of them sympathetic to their surroundings, but this effort from the same family that runs the Notos & Lela's continues to set the standard. Beautifully landscaped into its surroundings, it has a great location halfway down Ritsa Beach, nestled behind the taverna of the same name. It has various studios & apartments, all lovingly done up in modern style. €€€€€

🏠 **Kalamitsi** [179 A2] (20 rooms, 15 bungalows) ☎27210 73131; e info@kalamitsi-hotel.gr; w kalamitsi-hotel.gr. Located just to the south of town in Kalamitsi Bay, this beautiful

(At least 5hrs; difficult; cafés at Kambos & Stavropigi)

This is a wonderful, but long hike, that should take the best part of a day if you are going to enjoy it properly. You could shorten it a bit by starting at Kambos (about a third of the way), but you would be missing some of the best bits. On the way you pass through three, very untouristy, Maniat villages, walk on some fantastic *kalderimi* (stone mule paths), see a couple of Byzantine churches and a castle, and end up on a lovely pebble beach to soak off all the sweat.

This is a one-way walk, and you probably won't be up to walking back the other way. The best idea is to start in Kardamyli (the hike's end point) and either get a taxi (which will probably have to be booked in advance), or catch the early morning bus north, getting off at the turn to Sotirianika (inform the conductor of your intention).

Of all the walks included in this book, this is perhaps the easiest to go wrong on, partly on account of the amount of new building work, and thus dirt roads, which are springing up in the area. The directions should be sufficient, but a compass, map, and local advice wouldn't go amiss. Also be aware that some of these paths can be very overgrown and long trousers are a good idea. See the walking guide on page 42.

0mins If you caught the bus, it will probably drop you on the main road at the turning for Sotirianika. Head up the road toward the village. If you are lucky the bus will head into the village. Walk back about 50m after it drops you off to start the walk.

15mins As you come into the village you will see the large olive press on the right. Turn right on to a track by a double telegraph pole. Carry on straight on to a kalderimi that leads into the back section of the village and then down to a riverbed.

20mins When you reach an asphalt road just over a small bridge turn right and carry on straight ahead, ignoring the signed path to the left and any other turns.

37mins Look out for a ruined house just to the right of the road. It has been turned into a small shrine. Turn left, following the string of floodlights, towards the church of Agios Nikolaos, 200m away. This late Byzantine church has good frescoes inside that date to the 17th century but is not always open. There is also a spring here. Carry on past the spring – a fence has been put across the path to deter goats and it is a bit tricky to climb over. The path quickly becomes a well-constructed kalderimi, one of the old, stone mule tracks that were the main form of communication here right up into the second half of the 20th century. It snakes down impressively into the gorge.

50mins You reach the bottom of the gorge, cross over the old stone bridge and start up the other side, turning right when you reach a dirt road, heading up the wide track (which is sometimes concrete) and ignoring a fork to the right. After 500m you pass some derelict houses; the one on the left contains an old olive press. Ignore a right turn here and continue on the main track. Shortly after, ignore a right turn uphill and head down to the left. Carry on along the main track, ignoring roads joining from the left. You will see Zarnata Castle ahead and, shortly, a large building that houses a monastery. Head towards it until you reach a wide tarmac road where you turn left towards Kambos. Ignore side roads and after 1km you hit the main road by a petrol station and turn left.

1hr 35mins After some relaxation at the cafés by the sharp right turn around the church of Agii Theodoroi, head down the alley that runs behind it, quickly turning left around the back of the school. Turn left again around an animal enclosure just past a small chapel on the right. The narrow path continues between stone walls.

1hr 45mins After a small, stone bridge, and just before some stone steps up to the road, a quick detour to the right takes you to the Koumoundouros Tower and a small tholos tomb. Head up the steps back to the main road; cross straight over and head up the faint track directly opposite. When you hit a large track go straight over. There are several new dirt roads here. You are heading up towards the houses on the hillside above, to the right of the castle walls.

1hr 56mins After passing a large oak tree on the right and a pretty church to the left you come into Stavropigi. There are several ways through the village and although confusing, you can't really get lost. Here is one route: cross over another crossroads and then turn right at the next three T-junctions that you pass. Back at the main road turn left and then follow two brown signs, one to Zarnata Castle, up to the left past the triangular platea and then bearing to the left up through the village until you reach the large church of the Koimisis. Follow the main road past it.

2hrs 14mins You reach another brown sign for the church of Zoodochos Pigi. Follow this for a 10-minute detour up to the castle and church (usually locked). The views are worthwhile. Continue on past the sign for another 1km, heading towards a large church. When you reach it follow the road around it and continue until you reach the main road again. Turn right and cross over, shortly taking the next turn up to the left.

2hrs 30mins After 200m turn left up the concrete path where you see both blue-and-yellow stripe and red-dot waymarks (these are the waymarks to follow all the way to Kardamyli, but are sometimes difficult to spot). Keep left at any junctions and carry on relatively straight for about 1.4km. When the road starts to switchback look out for the waymarks that show where stretches of kalderimi cut off the corners of the road. The kalderimi comes to an end and you follow the now dirt road gently downhill and straight for another 1km.

3hrs 10mins After this straight section, just before a bend to the right, look out for the waymarked turn up a bank to the left. Don't miss this and continue down the road. A steep, narrow and rocky path turns into a kalderimi that leads from here up towards a ruined church, a good place for a rest. The kalderimi goes on to a dirt road that leads down to Ritsa Beach by Kardamyli. Again, you are better off following the waymarked kalderimi that cuts across it. The first section is to be found by turning left for a few metres on the dirt road, and the other sections follow on fairly obviously.

4hrs Near to the sea the kalderimi gives out and you follow the road. Where it bends to the left, cross over the olive grove to the lovely pebble beach of Ritsa. You are right by the Elies taverna (page 189), and if you're lucky lunch and a cold beer await. Kardamyli is another 1km walk along the beach to the left.

Born in 1915, Paddy, as friends and fans alike know him, fitted more into his lifetime than should be reasonably possible. The legend begins with him being 'sacked' from Kings Canterbury School, apparently for holding hands with the local grocer's daughter. Rather than be forced into a normal career, in 1933, aged 18, he decided to walk across Europe, from the Hook of Holland to Constantinople. Alternately staying in stables or fields, and then castles and mansions with the aristocracy of central Europe, he travelled through a Germany that had just ushered Hitler into power, and then down through eastern Europe to arrive in Constantinople at the dawn of 1935. Not yet finished, Paddy travelled onward into Greece, where he took part in a cavalry charge during a republican coup. In Athens he met and fell in love with a Romanian princess and, at the outbreak of World War II, he found himself in her family mansion in what is now the region of Moldavia.

Paddy left his princess to join the Irish Guards (the fall of the Iron Curtain meant the parting was permanent). Because of his experiences and linguistic skills he was soon drafted into the Special Operations Executive (SOE), and served as a liaison officer to the Greek army in Albania. After the fall of Greece his talents were put into action in occupied Crete. In 1944, he hatched a plan to kidnap the commanding German general of the island, a piece of comic-book derring-do that involved real danger, both for himself and the Cretans who helped him. After the abduction Paddy and his team spent three weeks crossing the mountains of Crete before being spirited off the wild southern shore.

While on leave in Cairo, he met his wife-to-be (they married in 1968) and lifelong companion Joan, who would later provide the photographs for his two Greek masterpieces: *Mani* (1958) and *Roumeli* (1966). After the war Paddy briefly held his only 'proper' job as a deputy director of the British Institute in Athens. He was soon off travelling again, though, this time in the Caribbean, and it was this that was to provide the material for his first book, *The Traveller's Tree*, published in 1950. This was followed by his only novel, *The Violins of Saint-Jacques* (1953), also based in the Caribbean, and then *A Time to Keep Silence* (1957), a short, but exquisite, meditation on living in monasteries.

His main love remained Greece, and his explorations of this country in the 1950s and 60s led to his twin books on the northern and southern mainland. Indeed *Mani* was originally intended to be about the entire Peloponnese, but Paddy found himself obsessed by the one area. In the 1960s, he and Joan settled in the region, building a beautiful house in what was then a remote bay.

Paddy was never a prolific writer, but the publication of *A Time of Gifts* (1977), and its sequel *Between the Woods and the Water* (1986), confirmed his reputation as one of the best descriptive prose writers of the 20th century. They were a return to the travels of his youth, describing his long trek through pre-war Europe. For a long while the tale of this journey lay unfinished, with the second book ending at the Iron Gates by the Bulgarian border. The last of the trilogy was long awaited while Paddy wrote and revised it, using a typewriter for the first time instead of longhand. The endless tinkering only came to an end when Paddy died in 2011. A biography, by Artemis Cooper, was published in 2012, and was aptly titled *An Adventure*. The final volume of Paddy's journey, called *The Broken Road*, came out in late 2013 (page 273).

complex is worth every penny. Perched above a quiet beach among the olive groves, this is one to lose yourself in for a few days. There is a bar & in season, an excellent restaurant. €€€€€

Notos [179 A1] (13 rooms) \27210 73730; m 69777 16017; e info@notoshotel. gr; w notoshotel.gr. This is another lovely hotel complex, 2km north of town (follow the signposted road that leads off the last bend down from the mountains). The furniture was all designed by Maria, the owner's wife, & built by a local carpenter. €€€€

✳ **Amoni** [191 D6] (2 houses) \27210 73935; m 69343 28148; e amoni.kardamyli@ gmail.com; 🔲 kardamyli. These 2 villas are on the headland above Kardamyli harbour in a secluded olive grove. They are immaculately presented & would make a great base for a longer stay in the area. Jo & Aleko, the hospitable owners, are a mine of information. €€€€

Vardia Hotel [191 D2] (18 rooms) \27210 73777/8; e info@vardia-hotel.gr; w vardia-hotel.gr. This handsome stone-built family-run hotel 10mins' walk from the centre has a splendid location among sloping olive groves that offer great views over the town & ocean.

Accommodation is in light, AC & well-equipped self-catering apartments with kitchen & balcony. Good value. €€€€

Kastro Aggeliki [191 B2] (15 rooms) \27210 73226; m 69734 70561; e info@kastro-aggeliki.gr; w kastro-aggeliki.gr. Just below the old town, this is a good cheaper option with comfortable rooms, small balconies & nice views. €€€

Katerina's Studios [191 A1] (5 rooms) \27210 73445; w kardamyli-katerina.com. Comfortable studios with balcony & a warm welcome in a 2-storey building on a quiet alley 100m from the beach & 200m from the town centre. Good value. €€€

Les Sirenes [191 B4] (10 rooms) m 69803 42020; e e.sirenes@gmail.com; w lessireneskardamili.com. Formerly called Gorgones, this recently renovated block of studio flats is located above the Harilaos Restaurant overlooking the jetty. Comfortable & good value. €€€

Hotel Patriarcheas [191 B2] (15 rooms) \27210 73366. Simple but pleasant rooms with AC & balcony in a 2-storey stone building overlooking the main road at the junction for the old town. €€

WHERE TO EAT AND DRINK In the winter you won't find many places open, although there's always somewhere. In summer, several places open their doors. Kardamyli's visitors are generally a discerning bunch, and there are no bad choices, although a couple stand out as being more reliably excellent than the rest. The café scene in the village is becoming increasingly trendy, especially in season.

✳ ✗ **Café Androuvista** [191 B3] \27210 73788; 🔲 Cafe Androuvista; ⊕ closed in winter. Known to regulars as 'Anna's', this café is a Kardamyli institution (much of the 1st edition of this book was written here). It serves homemade cakes & delicious sandwiches & salads based round local ingredients.

✗ **Elies** [179 A1] \27210 73140. Attached to the hotel of the same name, the kitchen is run by Lela's daughter-in-law, who has obviously been taught the family secrets. At its best during the day when it serves Greek taverna dishes, but with a touch of modern European class. In summer evenings it opens up with a different menu.

✗ **Gialos Restaurant** [191 A2] \27210 73278. This outdoor restaurant on the rocky seafront immediately north of the town centre has pretty tree-shaded garden seating, beer on tap, & a diverse menu of seafood, pizza & traditional Greek fare.

✗ **Harilaos Café & Restaurant** [191 B4] \27210 73373; m 69874 44414. This has a breezy waterfront terrace & a varied menu of seafood, pasta, salads & grilled meat.

✗ **Kalamaki** [191 B3] \27210 73930. Located on the main road, near the butcher's, this is old-style Kardamyli with few tourist pretensions. It is also reliably open all year – grilled meat & chips is the name of the game.

✗ **Kritamos** [191 B4] \27210 64102; m 69723 30217; 🔲 KritamosKardamili; ⊕ year round. This recent addition to the Kardamyli culinary scene is also one of the best, serving a varied selection of tasty & well-priced Greek & international dishes.

✗ **Lela's Taverna** [191 B4] \27210 73541; m 69777 16017; w lelastaverna.com; ⊕ closed Dec–mid-Apr. The eponymous Lela was once the housekeeper to Paddy Leigh Fermor, & she produced taverna classics with a touch of magic for over 25 years. Lela passed away in 2015, but the family-run taverna retains its wonderful seaside location & reputation for excellent Greek food. There are 3 simple rooms upstairs as well.

✕ Psaras Restaurant [191 B3] ✆ 27210 73365. Fresh seafood & pasta are the specialities at this popular terrace restaurant, which also boasts a fine central location overlooking a small pebbly beach & small jetty.

✕ Restaurant Dioskouri [191 C5] ✆ 27210 73236. This place serves more-than-adequate seafood & traditional Greek fare, but the selling point is its unbeatable location on a wide cypress-shaded terrace overlooking St John's Bay 100m south of the town centre.

☆ Aquarella [191 B4] ✆ 27210 75010; **f** aquarella.kardamili. With plenty of terrace seating & an idyllic location on the rocky beachfront next to Lela's, this is a good spot for an outdoor b/fast or snack, but it's first & foremost a café & cocktail bar, with a good wine selection & beer on tap.

OTHER PRACTICALITIES To get about the nearby villages **taxis** are an option, but they tend to prefer to take passengers on longer trips – contact Vassilis and Voula (m *69747 23673*).

Car hire is available at **Trigilidas Travel & Holidays** (*Kardamyli Sq;* ✆ *27210 64150;* m *69367 78127;* e *info@mycarrentals.gr;* w *mycarrentals.gr*), but the office is only open during the tourist season. Within that time, the ever-helpful Denia is a good source of local info.

There are now several small supermarkets in town, as well as a couple of ATMs. On the main road [191 B2–B3] Kardamyli has a post office, a butcher's, a pharmacy, a doctor's and several craft/tourist shops that tend to aim for the 'higher' end of the market. A great place for a more unusual souvenir is the **Bead Shop Kardamyli** [191 C4] (m *69394 55365*) at the south end of the village. Diagonally opposite this, the excellent **Grigoris Bookshop** [191 C4] (✆ *27210 73631*) sells local guides, foreign newspapers, English books and maps.

BEFORE MIDNIGHT – KARDAMYLI ON FILM

In the summer of 2012 the residents (and visiting tourists) of Kardamyli were excited to discover that the bright lights of Hollywood had descended on them in the form of the American actor Ethan Hawke and the French actress Julie Delpy. What exactly they were doing was supposed to be kept secret, but the locals soon ferreted out the details. It turned out that, along with the director Richard Linklater, they were collaborating in the third film of the series that started with *Before Sunrise* in 1995, followed by *Before Sunset* in 2004. The films followed the love affair of the two main characters, and are both set over the course of a conversation-fuelled night or day.

The third film, named *Before Midnight*, was filmed in several locations in and around Kardamyli and the surrounding area, as well as over in Messinia. One prominent location was the beautiful house of Sir Patrick Leigh Fermor in Kalamitsi Bay (see box, page 188).

The movie came out in 2013, and is a fitting conclusion(?) to the trilogy, although somewhat bittersweet. It could also serve as a successful advert for the area, with some gorgeous location shots. The first two movies were set in Vienna and Paris, and it is good to see that the romance of little Kardamyli, and the surrounding area, more than holds its own. Highly recommended.

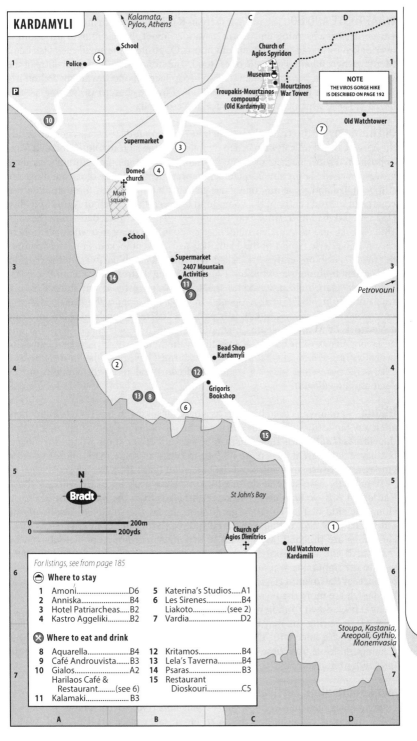

KARDAMYLI

Kalamata,
Pylos, Athens

School

Police

School

Supermarket

Domed
church

Main
square

School

Church of
Agios Spyridon

Museum

Troupakis-Mourtzinos
compound
(Old Kardamyli)

Mourtzinos
War Tower

Old Watchtower

NOTE
THE VIROS GORGE HIKE
IS DESCRIBED ON PAGE 192

Supermarket
2407 Mountain
Activities

Petrovouni

Bead Shop
Kardamyli

Grigoris
Bookshop

St John's Bay

N

Bradt

0   200m
0   200yds

Church of
Agios Dimitrios

Old Watchtower
Kardamili

Stoupa, Kastania,
Areopoli, Gythio,
Monemvasia

For listings, see from page 185

🛏 **Where to stay**

1	Amoni	D6	5	Katerina's Studios.....A1
2	Anniska	B4	6	Les Sirenes	B4
3	Hotel Patriarcheas	B2		Liakoto	(see 2)
4	Kastro Aggeliki	B2	7	Vardia	D2

❌ **Where to eat and drink**

8	Aquarella	B4	12	Kritamos	B4
9	Café Androuvista	B3	13	Lela's Taverna	B4
10	Gialos	A2	14	Psaras	B3
	Harilaos Café &		15	Restaurant
	Restaurant	(see 6)		Dioskouri	C5
11	Kalamaki	B3			

WHAT TO SEE AND DO The main activity in Kardamyli is enjoying the setting. The village itself is charming and worth a wander about. Its harbour to the south is overlooked by an old fortified custom house. Opposite is the small rocky island of Meropi, where a Venetian castle once stood. The stone chimney in the centre of the village belongs to the ruins of an olive-oil soap factory, once owned by Palmolive. Just to the north of town (take the road down by the church) is the long, pebbly beach of Ritsa, which never seems to feel too crowded.

Old Kardamyli The **Troupakis-Mourtzinos compound** [191 C1] is nestled beside the Viros Gorge and can be reached by following the sign to Old Kardamyli from opposite the supermarkets or, more pleasantly, on a stone path through the olive groves, reached via the small square with a war memorial. The outer buildings are still occupied and some new ones have gone up, but if you pass through these you emerge in the old centre of the compound between the church of **Agios Spiridon** [191 C1] and the **Mourtzinos War Tower** [191 C1]. The church dates from the early 18th century, and its Venetian-influenced campanile is decorated with a plethora of carvings in a style typical of the Mani. It is usually kept locked. For safety reasons the tower is also presently kept locked, but you can climb partway up the outside. The present building was rebuilt in 1808 after being destroyed in a feud.

The old clan buildings next to the tower were restored and turned into a small **museum** [191 C1] that opened in 2005 (⊕ *supposedly 08.00–15.00, but only reliable in high season; €2*). It is part of a (currently on hold) plan to create a **Network of Mani Museums**, including one in Areopoli (page 169). The one here contains exhibits on day-to-day life in the Mani. All in all, the site gives an evocative impression of what life in the Mani must have been like in the 18th and 19th centuries, when the clan leaders held court and received tribute from the surrounding villages.

Hiking Kardamyli is used by many as a base for hiking in the Taygetos and there are many fantastic walks around, many using the old stone paths that used to link the villages (*kalderimi*). There are map boards and hiking trails around the village, but if you really want to explore it's best to invest in some maps and/or walking guides, all of which are available at the bookshop (page 190).

If you only have time to do one hike then the walk up to the villages above Kardamyli is the one to go for. A kalderimi leads from the back of the old town along the side of the Viros Gorge. It soon passes the so-called **Tombs of the Dioscouri** [179 A1], the alleged burial spot of Castor and Pollux. The two rock-cut tombs are probably Mycenaean in origin. A half-hour uphill finds you by the church and the outskirts of the village of **Agia Sophia** (Αγ Σοφία), where a path to the right takes you on, crossing a streambed after a while, and then to the outskirts of **Petrovouni** (Πετροβούνι) [179 B1]. The views from here back down to Kardamyli are more than worth the effort so far. Another kalderimi can take you straight back down from here, but it is worth continuing to **Proastio** (Προάστιο) [179 B2]. In spring you may well see orchids, and the village itself is lovely, stuffed to the gills with interesting churches. It also produces a locally famous rosé wine. A kalderimi leads from here down to Kalamitsi Bay (Καλαμίτσι) [179 A2], just to the south of Kardamyli.

Mani Sonnenlink Festival This summer concert programme (❨ *27210 78077; e burgi@mani-sonnenlink.com; w mani-sonnenlink.com*) covers a range of musical styles, including classical, pop, and jazz, etc. It takes place over July and August at a hotel site with a purpose-built amphitheatre in the hills near Pyrgos, but is reached on a 'music bus' that picks people up at several villages along the road from Kardamyli and takes them there. In addition to top-notch musical performances delivered against the backdrop of a stunning sunset over the sea, the price of the day trip includes a superb organic buffet with pudding and wine.

THE MOUNTAINS ABOVE STOUPA (ΣΤΟΎΠΑ) AND KARDAMYLI (ΚΑΡΔΑΜΎΛΗ)

Plenty of visitors to Stoupa or Kardamyli venture no further than a few hundred metres from the sea. They are missing out, because the Taygetos Mountains that loom to the east are spectacularly scenic, as well as being dotted with interesting villages whose lights look like new constellations when seen from the coast at night. Hiking is an excellent way to explore the area, and the excellent **2407 Mountain Activities** ✳ (✆ *27210 73752*; m *69757 85887*; e *info@2407m.com*; w *2407m.com*), on the main street through Kardamyli, sells walking maps and equipment, as well as organising hiking and mountain-biking trips.

There is also a lot that's accessible by paved road. The circular itinerary described below is based on having your own transport, and runs from Stoupa to Kardamyli via Neohori, Kastania, Saidona and Exohori, a total distance of roughly 30km excluding the 8km coastal stretch between Stoupa and Kardamyli. Although the entire route is paved the quality varies from excellent to quite badly pot-holed, sometimes without warning. Still, it could be completed in 3–4 hours with a few stops, though you'd be better off taking a whole day. All of the villages have a kafenion or a basic taverna, and food should be available in at least one of them. Alternatively take a picnic.

It is also possible to get up to some of these villages by bus, generally going up first thing and coming back early afternoon, with the obvious goal being Kastania.

STOUPA TOWARDS KASTANIA At the southern edge of Stoupa, opposite the Kastro Hill, a road heads straight up to the mountains, and then snakes around the village of **Neohori** (Νεοχωρι) [179 C3]. The old centre of the village is handsome, but new houses, mostly built by expats, surround it. Above Neohori these begin to fizzle out, and you pass the village's two oil presses. The next village, **Pyrgos** (Πύργος), is definitely worth a stop. Park just beyond the sharp hairpin and walk back into the village. You will pass a couple of fortified houses and a small 'museum' full of bric-a-brac (🕐 *hardly ever open, but ask for keys at the next-door kafenion*). Carry straight on to the large main church with its imposing tower – this can be seen from the coast and has some nice naïve carvings on it. The main point of coming here, however, is for the truly breathtaking view down to the coast. Don't be fooled by the ancient Greek capitals by the church: the Christian crosses on them point to their 20th-century origin.

Continuing up the road you soon come to the **Blauel Oil Factory** [179 D4] (w *blauel.gr*), a white building on the right. Fritz Blauel moved here from Austria in the 1970s and began bottling olive oil by hand. The company were the first organic producers in Greece and now work with over 500 local farmers. The factory welcomes visitors in the mornings. Past the factory you soon come to a right turn that would take you on another mountain loop via Milia to Platsa. The road straight ahead leads to **Kastania** after another 2km.

KASTANIA Hidden in a fold in the mountains, **Kastania** (Καστανιά) [179 D3], is only 9km from Stoupa by road, but worlds apart in terms of atmosphere. Follow the road into the village past the early Byzantine church of **Agios Ioannis** [179 A7], which is tiny but beautiful. Park in a space just beyond this and continue up on foot to the village platea (square), which is just off to the right. You are now above 550m and will notice the cooler air. The five-storey **Dourakis Tower** [179 A7] dominates the platea, and is a fantastic example of 18th-century defensive architecture. In 1803, Kolokotronis was almost betrayed to the Turks here, but he managed to escape over the mountains. It was restored over 2014/15, when the annex was rebuilt, and the scaffolding that obscured it for the duration has been removed, but it was locked and bolted when we checked it out in 2018, and it's unclear when or indeed whether it is actually open to the public.

Despite its small size, the village contains eight churches dating to between the 12th and 18th centuries, among them the (relatively) large 14th-century **Kamaisi Theotoken** [179 A7] on the platea. To find the others, head out of the platea on the steep path uphill. A path to the right leads to the small **Agios Nikolaos** [179 A7], but the real discovery is made by following the main path all the way to the top of the village. Here is the wonderful church of **Agios Petros** [179 A6], the town's oldest, dating back almost 900 years. Inside the church are some interesting carved decorative marbles and lots of frescoes – the oldest and most beautiful dating from medieval times. Restoration work on the church has been completed and there is now even an information board outside. The key, however, is still to be found in a niche on the left of the door, at least for the moment.

To complete a circuit head down the small steep path just by Agios Petros. Make your way round a long, tiled building, which turns out to be another church to Agios Nikolaos (now often locked, but ask around for a key). Inside, the 18th-century frescoes show all the beasts of the Earth, both real and mythical, praising Jesus, who is surrounded by the zodiac. The paintings are great fun and include werewolves and a two-tailed mermaid. Just around the corner is another tiny church dedicated to the Virgin Mary. This spot catches the breeze and you will often find the village ladies gossiping here. The next right leads back down to the platea. You could think about staying over at the **Villa Kastania** [179 A6] (*6 rooms;* ✆*27210 86324;* **€€€€**), set in a tall, narrow three-storey stone building opposite Agios Petros. For eating, there is a basic, but excellent, taverna and a kafenion on the main square.

KASTANIA TO KARDAMYLI VIA EXOHORI The road from Kastania continues on above a plateau, making it hard to see just how high you are. After 3km it reaches the next village, **Saidona** (Σαϊδόνα) [179 C1]. Just before the village is a war memorial, on the right opposite a parking spot. Saidona was burnt by the Italians in March 1942 in retribution for the locals hiding Allied soldiers who had been left behind in occupied Greece. The memorial commemorates this and other deaths, including those during the civil war of 1945–49. The village was known for its communist sympathies and suffered particularly badly. The road forks just after this, with the left fork going down to the village car park. There's not much to see in Saidona itself but it does have two basic tavernas. The right fork continues on towards Exohori and is paved all the way, whatever maps might tell you.

This is a dramatic bit of roadway and along the route are two fortified monasteries and a tower house that looks like something from a Dracula movie. About 2km beyond Saidona there is a signposted road to the right (with a 4x4 this route can be followed all the way over the mountains). Just beyond this you can park on a track that leads off a hairpin bend. Walk up the track for about 100m until you see a path going steeply up on your right (it's almost at the last point from which you can still see the paved road). This path leads quickly up to the hidden monastery of **Samouli**

[179 D1]. It is fortified and has its own tower and, although largely in ruins, is an evocative site.

Just a bit further along the road the **Kitrinaris Tower** [179 D1] comes into view. It could hardly be in a more imposing position, stuck on a spur of rock high above the valley. The Kitrinaris were feared local bandits and their descendants, somewhat more law-abiding now, still live by the coast below. You can park by the tower and, with care, scramble inside it.

The other monastery, **Vaidenitsa** [179 D1], is visible from the tower. To reach it walk back along the road to the last hairpin and then follow the path up on the left side of the riverbed. Again it is in a lovely setting, and the meadow below is used for village festivities and makes for a great picnic spot.

Exohori (Εξωχώρι) [179 C1] is a further 5km away. Although you might have had your fill of churches, the village contains several more interesting examples. Bruce Chatwin, the travel writer and novelist, requested his ashes scattered by Agios Nikolaos near here. The handsome old school building now contains a good **Historical & Folklore Museum** (✆ 27210 73351; m 69777 41861). It's worth a visit, but has erratic opening hours (these are most reliable in the summer), so check before making a special trip. The road continues downhill through either Proastio or Petrovouni and then to the coast and Kardamyli.

LEAVING THE EXO MANI

Heading north from Kardamyli, the road climbs into the mountains again. Just before it breaches them, there is a truly magnificent view back south, taking in the village of Kardamyli below and several other villages perched above. The Mani itself thrusts off into the distance. It is well worth stopping if you can, and a thoughtfully provided lay-by for this purpose can be found just after a fire service lookout post, which is usually manned throughout the summer.

The first village you pass is Prosilio, meaning 'facing the sun' – its handsome church with its tall tower are rarely in the shade. Next up is **Stavropigi**. Hidden in its backstreets, at the top of the hill, is **Zarnata Castle**. The castle's history goes back at least as far as Byzantine times, and perhaps beyond (it could be the site of Ancient Gerenia, where Nestor, the wise old man of the *Odyssey* and *Iliad*, spent his childhood). There is Byzantine and Frankish masonry in the walls but most of the castle is Turkish.

From Stavropigi an alternative route north is signposted towards the village of **Doli** (Δολοί), where there are several old churches, and through a barren landscape that looks like it belongs further south. It reaches the coast at **Kitries** (Κιτριές), an attractive little fishing village which has a couple of tavernas, and then passes several pebbly beaches and one sandy one, before joining the main road again.

Staying on the main road through Stavropigi you soon start winding down to a plain and the village of **Kambos** (Κάμπος). Just before the village a little ruin on the left is the ancestral home of the Koumoundouros family. Alexandros Koumoundouros, whose bust is outside the tower, was closely involved in Greek politics after independence, holding the post of prime minister on ten occasions. Signposted just by the tower is a Mycenaean tholos tomb. Its ceiling has fallen in but it is still an evocative sight. Entering the village and just before a sharp left-hand turn is the small church of Agii Theodoroi, filled with 18th-century frescoes. Kambos's little bakery, on the main road, is known for the best bread in the area.

A short while after Kambos the main road descends into the **Koskaraka Gorge** (Κοσκάρακα) where it crosses a modern bridge (two other bridges can be seen:

the old concrete one, and beneath it an old stone bridge). Local legend tells that a Turkish commander was skewered on a spit here – a Turkey souvlaki, if you like.

After the gorge a worthwhile diversion is to take the sharp right-hand turn to the village of **Sotirianika** (Σωτηριάνικα). This is the starting point of a fantastic hike (see box, page 186), but if you bear left out of the village, and then another left shortly afterwards, the road winds up through a small village to the **Kapetanakis Castle**. The castle is a good example of one of the incongruities of the Mani: while it looks like a medieval fort, it in fact only dates back to the early 19th century. It was built to protect the Mani against the Ottomans and has wonderful views in all directions, from Kalamata to the north down to Zarnata Castle to the south.

From here the road once again heads dramatically down towards the sea, with superb views of whitewashed Kalamata below. The Mani ends just south of the city where the road flattens out and is joined by the route from Kitries (page 195).

SEND US YOUR SNAPS!

We'd love to follow your adventures using our *Greece Peloponnese* guide – why not send us your photos and stories via Twitter (🐦 @BradtGuides) and Instagram (📷 @bradtguides)? Alternatively, you can upload your photos directly to the gallery on the Peloponnese destination page via our website (**w** bradtguides.com/pelops).

7

Messinia
(Μεσσηνία)

Messinia is the fertile breadbasket of the Peloponnese. Everyone here is a farmer of some sort, and it seems that almost any time of year is the harvest of one crop or another. For the traveller it offers some of the finest beaches to be found in Greece, but also elegant little towns normally huddled beneath impressive medieval castles.

Lastly, despite Mycenae being far to the north, there is an argument to be made for this being the centre of Mycenaean activity. If you go walking, and it is highly recommended, watch your step, or you will find yourself tumbling down one of the countless tholos tombs.

KALAMATA (ΚΑΛΑΜΆΤΑ)

Kalamata is a city built on two products at opposite ends of the health scale. On the good side are olives – as well as the famous table olives it produces a high-quality oil. In the winter months (and often during the rest of the year as well) a string of tankers can be seen coming and going in the Messinian Gulf, exporting the product. Apparently much of it is taken to Italy, where it is mixed in with their own oil to improve its taste. On the other hand the city is home to Karelia, Greece's most famous brand of cigarettes.

If the city itself is not immediately attractive then it has an excuse: on 13 September 1986, a large earthquake destroyed many of the old buildings. There were remarkably few casualties (20 people dead and 330 injured out of a total population of 42,000), as almost the entire city was out watching the inauguration of a new ferry route to Crete. Many were left homeless, and when their houses were rebuilt it was in drab, but safe, concrete. There are appealing parts of the city, however, and plenty to do if you stop over here before heading further south, either into the rest of Messinia or down into the Mani (see *Chapter 6*).

HISTORY In ancient times the city was known as Pharai and, because of its strategic location, was constantly changing hands in the shifting power struggles of the Classical period. It was owned at various times by Messene, Sparta and Athens.

In medieval times the Frankish leader Geoffrey de Villehardouin recognised the importance of the low acropolis and built a castle here in 1208 (his son William, founder of Mystra, was born in it). The castle passed through many hands until it fell to the Turks in 1470.

Kalamata played an important part in the War of Independence and holds the honour of being the first Greek city to gain independence from the Ottomans. On 23 March 1821, an army under the control of Petrobey Mavromichalis, from the Mani, and the great general Theodoros Kolokotronis, liberated the population. This date is still celebrated as Independence Day in the city, two days before the rest of the country.

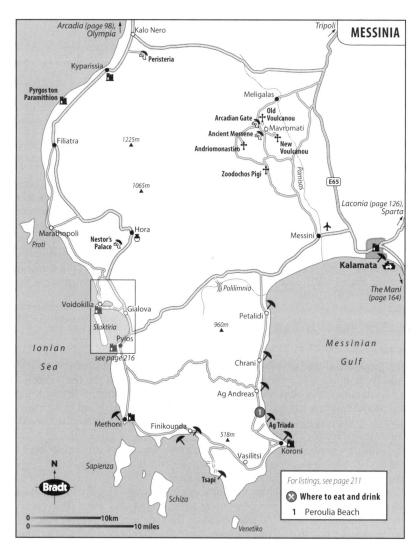

In April 1941, the city was again the scene of warfare as British and Colonial troops tried to evacuate in front of the advancing German army. Despite the Royal Navy's best efforts 7,000 didn't make it and were captured. Some retreated to the countryside, where they were hidden by villagers and often joined the resistance. Veterans of the evacuation still come to commemorate the event each year, but in increasingly dwindling numbers.

GETTING THERE AND AWAY

By air Kalamata International Airport (✆ *27210 63805*) lies aproximately 10km to the west of Kalamata, 2km before the town of Messini. The only scheduled domestic service that operates throughout the year comprises two or three weekly flights in either direction to and from Thessaloniki with Olympic Air (w *olympicair.com*).

During the season there are also charter flights from elsewhere in Europe. The options seem to change yearly, but include easyJet from Gatwick, British Airways from Heathrow, and Thomas Cook Airlines from Gatwick, Birmingham and Manchester. There are also usually seasonal charter flights to/from the Netherlands, Austria, Germany, Russia, Italy, Poland, Israel, France and Norway, among others. There are car-hire offices at the airport and a taxi to Kalamata shouldn't cost more than €20 (unless it is pre-booked).

By car Coming from the north, a 235km multi-lane national toll road now stretches all the way to Athens via Corinth and Tripoli. Allow at least 3 hours to drive there from Athens, longer if the outskirts of the capital are congested. Whichever way you approach Kalamata you are faced with traversing the city, even if you don't want to stop. Despite the heavy traffic, this is not as bad as it sounds; just keep an eye out for signs to your destination. The real nightmare comes if you want to stop. The main car parks are on a concreted-over section of the River Nedontos, in the centre of the city, but these are jam-packed at all hours. Your best bet is to find a quiet back street in the outskirts, and then walk in – not the most enticing prospect.

By bus There are several buses a day each way to Athens (*3½–4hrs*), as well as plenty to the main towns of Messinia. A couple a day go to Sparta (*1hr 40mins*), or up north to Patra (*3hrs 30mins*). Three or four a day head south into the Mani (*1hr to Kardamyli*). The bus station is in the north of the city, to the west of the castle.

By ferry Ferries used to run at least weekly between Kalamata and Crete, via Kythira, and often still do in the summer months, although the timetable seems to change yearly. Check with the local agents for the current situation (see below).

GETTING AROUND Kalamata is a long, thin city which is not desperately pleasant to walk around, especially on the long hike from the old town to the seafront. **Taxi ranks** can be found at the bus and train stations, and at 23 Martiou Square in the old town. They can also be called on ☏27210 26565/ 21112. The most useful **local bus**, the No 1, also starts at this square before going down to and then along the seafront with plenty of stops.

TOURIST INFORMATION The municipal tourist information office in Kalamata seems to have gone out of its way to make itself difficult to find. If you do locate the upstairs office on the undistinguished back street of Polyviou, you'll probably find the hunt wasn't worth the effort. Stick with the commercial operators, who can book car hire and hotels as well as provide information.

Maniatis Travel 1 Iatropoulou St; ☏27210 25300; e info@maniatistravel.com; w maniatistravel.com

Trigilidas Travel & Holidays Polycharous 4; ☏27210 90900; e info@trigilidas.gr; w trigilidas.gr

WHERE TO STAY *Map, page 200*
Kalamata is not the most obvious place to stay, but is very popular among the Greeks, and is a convenient urban base for exploring both Messinia and the Mani. It is also an excellent introduction to a side of Greece that is not centred on tourists.

🏠 **Elite City Resort** (150 rooms) Navirinou; ☏27210 22434; e info@elite.com.gr; w elite.com. gr. This smart, modern hotel offers a variety of rooms & villas to stay in right by the beach. **€€€€€**

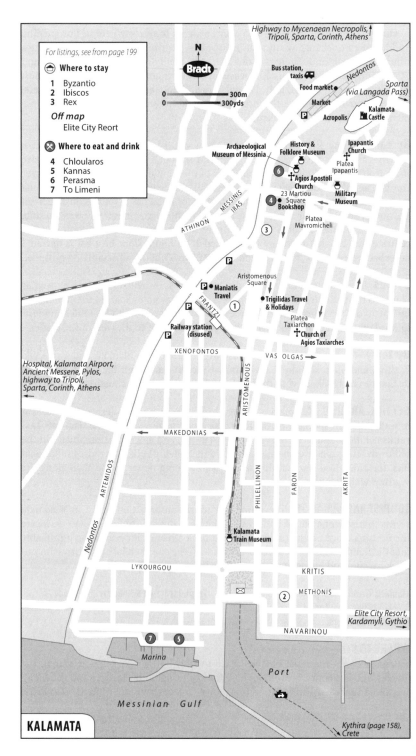

For listings, see from page 199

Where to stay

1 Byzantio
2 Ibiscos
3 Rex

Off map
  Elite City Reort

Where to eat and drink

4 Chloularos
5 Kannas
6 Perasma
7 To Limeni

N

Bradt

0 ⊢——————⊣ 300m
0 ⊢——————⊣ 300yds

Highway to Mycenaean Necropolis,
Tripoli, Sparta, Corinth, Athens

Bus station,
taxis 🚌

Nedontos

Food market ●

Sparta
(via Langada Pass)

Market

P

Acropolis

Kalamata
Castle

Archaeological
Museum of Messinia

History &
Folklore Museum

Ipapantis
Church

6 ✝Agios Apostoli
Church

Platea
Ipapantis

Military
Museum

23 Martiou
4 ● Square
Bookshop

MESSINIS IRAS

Platea
Mavromicheli

ATHINON

3

Aristomenous
Square

P ● Maniatis
Travel

P

● Trigilidas Travel
& Holidays

1

FRANTZI

Platea
Taxiarchon

✝Church of
Agios Taxiarches

P

Railway station
(disused)

P

XENOFONTOS

VAS OLGAS →

Hospital, Kalamata Airport,
Ancient Messene, Pylos,
highway to Tripoli,
Sparta, Corinth, Athens
←

ARISTOMENOUS

MAKEDONIAS ←

ARTEMIDOS

Nedontos

PHILELLINON

FARON

AKRITA

Kalamata
Train Museum

LYKOURGOU

KRITIS

2 METHONIS

Elite City Resort,
Kardamyli, Gythio

NAVARINOU

7 5

Marina

Port

Messinian Gulf

Kythira (page 158),
Crete

KALAMATA

Rex Hotel (45 rooms) 26 Aristomenous; 27210 22334; e rex@rexhotel.gr; w rexhotel. gr. Just up from the central square, next to the City Hall, this hotel was founded in 1899 & still has an air of Neoclassical class. €€€€

Ibiscos Hotel (7 rooms) 196 Faron; 27210 92314; w hotelibiscos-restaurantbar.gr. This lovely boutique hotel occupies a Neoclassical house between the beach & the centre of town. Its name is sometimes anglicised to Hibiscus. Very friendly welcome. €€€€

Byzantio (45 rooms) 13 Sid Stahmou; 27210 86824; e info@byzantiokalamata.gr; w byzantiokalamata.gr. On the right-hand side of the street that runs from opposite the old train station towards the central square of Kalamata. This is a perfectly acceptable budget option, if a little noisy at times. €€

WHERE TO EAT AND DRINK *Map, opposite*

There is lots of choice in Kalamata, and you can eat at plenty of places that cook to an international standard. Old-style tavernas are congregated round the old town and near to the market – try **Perasma** (*57 Nedontos;* 27210 81999) or nearby **Chloularos** (*61 Nedontos;* 27210 27390).

Down by the marina, a string of tavernas specialise in fish; try **To Limeni** (*Cnr Xiou & Poseidonos;* 27210 95670; w tolimeni.gr) or **Kannas** (*12 Poseidonos;* 27210 91596; w kannas.gr), which also does good pasta. On the beach road to the east, there is a wide variety of tavernas, fast-food joints, pizza places and even a Chinese restaurant. The fish tavernas further along the road tend to be good bets, and slightly quieter.

SHOPPING

Kalamata is a cosmopolitan Mecca in the midst of the rural south of the Peloponnese, and as such has a rash of shops selling designer goods of all varieties. Most of these are based around the central Aristomenous Square. It hasn't forgotten its roots, however – the little shops in the old town carry a range of local goods, including the silk scarves that the region was once famous for. The **food market** takes place on Wednesdays and Saturdays and is one of the best in the Peloponnese. It is held in and around the large, hangar-like buildings between the bus station and the castle. Look out for dried figs, another regional speciality (along with olives!), and dried herbs and honey down from the mountains. You don't even have to turn up at the crack of dawn; it's such a big affair that it's still going strong at midday. A **bookshop** near 23 Martiou Square, to the right at the north end of Aristomenous, has English newspapers and a good selection of local guides and maps.

OTHER PRACTICALITIES

Banks and ATMs are plentiful, mostly based in and around Aristomenous Square. The main post office is down by the harbour (⏲ 07.30–14.00 Mon–Fri). The hospital is 5km outside of the city on the Athens road (27210 46000). The tourist police can be contacted on 27210 24680.

WHAT TO SEE AND DO

Unfortunately **Kalamata Castle**, a 13th-century Frankish edifice perched on a hilltop 2km north of the harbour, remains mostly closed off, owing to serious structural damage suffered in the 1986 earthquake. The lower part, where there is a modern amphitheatre, is open sometimes in the mornings and has good views over the city.

The excellent **Archaeological Museum of Messinia** (*Benaki & Agiou Ioannou;* 210 83485; ⏲ *see box, page 52;* €3) is located beside 23 Martiou Square in the old market hall. It opened in 2010 after relocating from smaller premises just down the road. Although there are no stand-out finds here, the museum is well laid out, with English signage, and is definitely worth a visit. Another worthwhile museum in the old town, which nestles around the castle, is the **History and Folklore Museum** (*12 Ag Ioannou;* 27210 28449; ⏲ 09.00–13.00 Tue–Sun; €2), which occupies a triangular two-storey 19th-century building known as Mansion Kyriakou. It has an interesting array of exhibits on traditional life in the region, but the labelling is in Greek only. Fortunately the staff are friendly and enthusiastic, and an English speaker can often be found to show you round.

Although it is rather urban, the **beach** that stretches east from Kalamata is surprisingly good, with clear water and good views down the Messinian Gulf.

One other site worth mentioning is the **Mycenaean Necropolis** on the old Athens road to the north of Kalamata. Look for the brown sign to the right in the rather unlovely community of Ethea. Follow the signs up a narrow road (which is dirt for the last few hundred metres) on to a ridge above the Messinian plain on one side and facing a river gorge on the other. Do be warned that the site is rather isolated, involves some scrambling, and seems to be in a cellphone deadzone – bring a friend along. The setting is fabulous, especially considering the urban sprawl below, but the fenced-in site seems to have little to offer at first. Follow the fencing down the right-hand side, however, and it is easy to enter the Necropolis, or 'City of the Dead'. It consists of 15–20 shaft graves, all set in a row overlooking the gorge, one of which still has carvings over the entrance way. For such a large site, which must date back well over 3,000 years, it is surprisingly little known, and exploring it invokes visions of the intrepid archaeologists of the past – or at least Indiana Jones!

PERIPTEROS AND PANTOPOLEIONS

The *periptero* is as much a part of Greek life as tavernas, ouzo and dancing. These roadside kiosks, looking like overgrown wooden boxes, were originally founded to give employment to war veterans after World War II. Nowadays they are usually family-owned businesses and a periptero in a reasonable location can provide a good income. For a long while they were the only places licensed to sell cigarettes, which guaranteed them good trade. This is no longer the case, and most stock a pretty diverse range of things: soft drinks, beer, condoms, newspapers, phone cards, worry beads, postcards, ice creams and sweets, to name but a few. They also used to act as the local phone booth, but mobiles have made this function obsolete. Yet the periptero, with its long opening hours and wide range of goods, remains a hub of any street. Unfortunately, as part of the imposed austerity regime, it was decided in October 2015 that periptero licences would no longer be renewed. They should be around for a while longer, and who knows what the future may bring, but many will mourn their passing.

While some may try, a mere periptero cannot rival the stock of a good *pantopoleion*. Rarer than they once were, these shops still form the heart of many a small Greek village. The name means 'sells everything' and pantopoleions try to keep true to this. Whether you are after basic food stuffs, DIY tools, pots and pans, electric heaters, books and newspapers, children's toys or alcohol, you merely have to ask; the pantopoleion owner will have what you desire hidden away somewhere on his cluttered shelves. To top all this, the pantopoleion often also serves as the village kafenion and post office (both taking and receiving mail for the village). The only thing that most pantopoleions lack is fresh groceries, but wait around long enough and these will be provided from the back of the loudspeaker-bedecked vans that travel from village to village in rural areas. It is sometimes difficult to see how people survive in these small Greek villages, but dig beneath the surface and you soon find that there is little reason ever to leave one.

Ancient Messene is simply astounding, especially as it comes as such a surprise. Most people have heard of Olympia, and many know of the theatre at Epidavros and the ruins of Old Corinth. Messene rarely gets mentioned in the same breath as these great Classical sites, but its remains are more extensive than any of them. What makes the site so incredible is that this is no mere religious sanctuary, but an *entire* city; from its towering walls, theatre, fountains, marketplace, religious centre, and stadium to the tombs of its prominent citizens.

So why is it so little known? There are a couple of reasons. Firstly it is a little off the beaten track – too far south for the Athens coach tours and not near enough to any prominent road. Secondly, this is a site that has only recently come into its own. Modern archaeological and restoration work has meant that the site has revealed more of itself with every passing year. More visitors are steadily being attracted to this out-of-the-way spot, but on most days of the year you might well find yourself alone with the ruins – a magical experience.

HISTORY The story of the Messinians is dominated by their powerful and aggressive neighbours, the Spartans. They were attracted by the rich agricultural land possessed by the Messinians, as well as by the potential slave labour they represented. In the struggles between the two city states the stronghold of Mount Ithome often played a role.

In the first of these conflicts, known as the First Messinian War (c720BC), the resistance to the Spartans was led by King Aristodemus. He is said to have invented a device that helped his infantry in close combat without compromising their mobility; a distinct advantage on the steep slopes of Ithome. Whatever this device was went to the grave with its inventor. It was not enough, however, and Aristodemus resorted to the custom of human sacrifice to gain the gods' favour, offering his own virgin daughter as the first victim. In a gallant effort to prevent her death her boyfriend promptly removed her from the ranks of the 'pure', making the offering unacceptable. She still died, unfortunately, by the hand of her furious father.

Aristodemus next turned to the oracle at Delphi for help. The advice was of the usual, enigmatic sort: whichever side could first dedicate 100 tripods at the shrine of Ithome would be the victors. The Messinians quickly started constructing large metal tripods. In a moment of brilliance the Spartans read between the lines (always good advice with Delphic prophecies), and quickly knocked up 100 wooden tripods. They were small enough that they fitted in the bag of a spy, who swiftly took them up to Ithome and placed them on the shrine. The Messinians, upon seeing them, simply gave up the fight and submitted to Spartan domination. Aristodemus committed suicide on the same spot that he had killed his daughter.

In the Second Messinian War (685–668BC) the rebellious Messinians based themselves at Eira, to the north. Under the leadership of the legendary Aristomenes, after whom the main street of Kalamata is named, they held out here for 11 years before they were finally defeated. Some Messinians, unwilling to remain *helots* (Spartan slaves), exiled themselves and were given refuge by Athens (they were later to prove their worth, and get some revenge, on the island of Sfaktiria during the Peloponnesian War – see pages 14 and 225).

Another revolt, the Third Messinian War, took place when Sparta suffered a devastating earthquake in 465BC. They recovered quickly, and soon the Messinians had again retreated to the fastness of Mount Ithome, where they were again defeated.

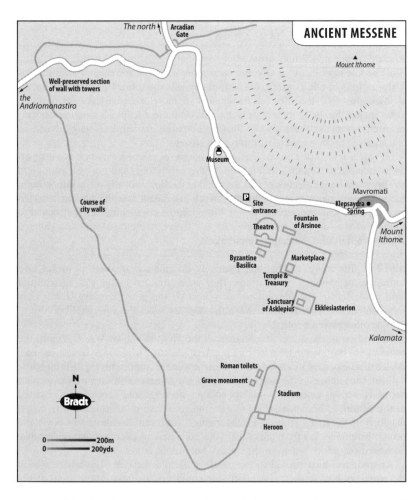

It would take the intervention of the Thebans, and their great general Epaminondas, to finally free Messinia. In the Battle of Leuctra (371BC) his armies, which included many Messinians, crushed the Spartans. In order to keep them on their knees Epaminondas founded a series of fortress cities, including that of Messene, nestled beneath the bulk of Mount Ithome.

The city survived into Roman times, and there was still a settlement here in the 7th century AD. It declined in Byzantine times and by the modern era only the small village of Mavromati remained.

GETTING THERE AND AWAY

By car The common approach is from the modern town of Messini (Μεσσήνη). The way is signposted from the roundabout on the Kalamata side of the town all the way to Mavromati (Μαυρομάτι).

A more interesting way to come is to take the old Athens road north out of Kalamata and turn off towards the charmingly named Meligalas (Μελιγαλάς), 'Honey milk', after about 25km. Head west out of town towards Neochori (Νεοχώρι). You will pass a huge, concrete cross: a **memorial to a massacre** that took place here during the civil war. Just before Neochori, the road passes straight over an **ancient bridge** at the confluence of two rivers. The piers (with their large stones) date back to the time of Ancient Messene, 2,500 years ago, while the seven arches are mainly Turkish. The tarmac top surface is, of course, rather more modern. The small village of Neochori was the home of the family of **Maria Callas** (who were then named Kalogeropoulos). The famous opera star was conceived here, but was actually born and raised in the States. From here signed roads lead to Ancient Messene, passing through its walls at the Arcadian Gate (see below).

By bus Two buses run from Kalamata to the site daily, the first leaving at 09.00 and the second at 15.00. Both drop passengers at the museum then turn around and head straight back to Kalamata. This means that unless you want to spend the night in Mavromati, you need to take the first bus and be at the museum in time to catch the second one back to Kalamata.

WHERE TO STAY AND EAT *Map, opposite*
The little village of Mavromati (which means 'black eyes', after the black staining on a rock that issues sacred spring-water) is yet to be overrun by tourists, or even mildly bothered by them, unlike so many villages near the ancient sites. The **Ithomi Taverna** (✆*27240 51298;* w *ithomi.gr*), owned and managed by the same family since 1987, serves above-average Greek fare and the terrace offers a great view down to the ruins. For overnight stays, **rooms** are available at **Guesthouse Lykourgos** (✆ *27240 51297;* m *69726 07391;* e *roomslykourgos@yahoo.gr;* w *guesthouselykourgos.gr;* **€€€**). Apart from a little **souvenir shop** that is sometimes open in the summer, and a **kafenion**, that's it for facilities for the foreseeable future.

WHAT TO SEE AND DO
The walls and the Arcadian Gate The best way to approach Messene is the old-
fashioned way, through the gates in its magnificent walls. The best preserved of the four gates that once existed is the **Arcadian Gate**. Coming from Mavromati head past the museum and the entrance to the main site on the left, and after another kilometre you will come to the impressive remains of this ancient portal. The first surprise is that the road north still runs through the gate, which does indeed then lead on towards the region of Arcadia. It is, in fact, a double gateway with a circular courtyard in the middle. The inner entrance has a monumental doorpost that has half tumbled to the ground. Inside the courtyard are two niches in the wall which would have held statues of the gods; Pausanias mentions that one was of Hermes.

Another imposing section of the city walls, and several watchtowers, can be seen by carrying on a bit further on the road that runs to the south. Messene originally had fully 9km of walls, running around the lower city and then up to the acropolis atop Mount Ithome. They are not particularly high, but were built to take advantage of the local topography and would have been difficult to assault. They are faced with large, locally quarried stones that are fitted together without mortar, and then filled with a rubble core. Pausanias thought them the most impressive city walls he had seen, and they have lost little of their power.

Ancient Messene (✆ *27240 51201;* w *ancientmessene.gr;* ⊕ & *entrance fees, see box, page 52*) The entrance to the site is down a road just past the museum building on the western edge of Mavromati. After many years the little ticket booth at the site finally opened for business in 2015. Keep in mind that there is a lot to explore here, and that to get back to the entrance can be a long haul and is uphill all the way: take

water and sun protection if needed, and wear reasonable shoes. Note also that there are no toilets on site (the museum has some), though there is now a fresh drinking water pipe just to the left of the steps down to the stadium. You will need at least a couple of hours to do the site justice.

You emerge into Messene above its large **theatre**, where the stage area and first few rows of seats are currently being restored. At 100m wide it is one of the largest of the ancient world. From this vantage point you can see down to some, but certainly not all, of what awaits in the city.

Follow the path past the theatre and down into the site and you will pass a long building on the left. This is the **Fountain of Arsinoe**, the city's water supply. The ground around it is still damp and, just as in antiquity, it still receives its water from the Klepsaydra spring, now in the village of Mavromati, which takes its name ('Black Eyes') from the holes that the spring emerges from. The fountain stood at the edge of the city marketplace, which filled the space right down to the Sanctuary of Asklepius. At the moment the area is mainly grassland, but who knows what may be discovered soon?

It is worth heading back towards the theatre to examine it close up. You will also notice another small ruin just below it. This building shows the longevity of Messene; it is a **Byzantine basilica**, built in the 7th century AD. Much of it was constructed of what is known as *spolia* – basically bits nicked from older buildings, a practice common in Greece right up to modern times.

Heading back into the main part of the city you pass the remains of a **temple**, currently thought to be dedicated to an ancient deification of the land as a mother goddess. Next door to this is a room buried in the ground with a removable stone roof. This is known as the **treasury**. In 183BC, Philopoemen, a general in the Achaean League and known to the Romans as 'the last of the Greeks', was captured by the Messinians and imprisoned in this hole. They did not want to leave such a powerful man alive, so rather shamefully they sent him poison in the night. Uncowed, Philopoemen asked after his men, and learning they were mostly safe calmly drank the proffered cup knowing it would be his death. Standing in this spot his act of bravery seems like it could have happened yesterday.

Beyond this you come to the spiritual centre of the city of Messene – the **Sanctuary of Asklepius**. A monumental staircase leads down into a large open-air courtyard, almost square in shape (72m × 67m). It was surrounded by an internal colonnade of Corinthian columns. This would have been full of statues, of political figures as well as heroes and gods. The bases for at least 140 of these have been found. In the centre stood the Temple of Asklepius.

The right side of the sanctuary, as you enter it, is taken up with cult rooms, where various deities would have been worshipped. On the other side is the **Ekklesiasterion**, or Assembly Room. This looks like a small theatre, but unlike its larger counterpart it would have had a roof. The multi-coloured tiled floor looks bizarre, but is a faithful reproduction of the original – sometimes you can get too used to all the white marble and forget that the ancient Greeks were just as much into colourful decoration as we are. This room was used for musical and theatrical tributes to the gods, as well as political gatherings. Near the Ekklesiasterion are the remains of a **Roman villa** covered by a large steel roof. Beneath this are some impressive **mosaics**.

Carrying on further downhill you come to the **stadium**. Its remains, helped by some judicious restoration, are amazingly complete, down to the lion paws carved on the VIP seats to the left. Looking at the far end you can trace how the stadium, used by the Greeks for athletics, was closed off in Roman times to make an amphitheatre for gladiator and animal fights – each to their own.

Heading down the right side of the stadium there are a couple of things of note. The first is another Roman innovation, a row of **toilets**. Ingeniously these were flushed by diverted water from the spring back up the hill. A bit further on is a very odd building. From the outside it looks like a small stone cube, with sides 5m long. Inside the floor is divided up like a crossword puzzle. It is in fact a **grave monument** of an aristocratic Messinian family. Its roof was an inverted funnel shape, topped by a Corinthian capital, a bizarre construction that currently lies in pieces on the floor nearby. With any luck it will be restored to its rightful place in the near future.

There is one more building to be seen, and it is worth a last stroll to the bottom end of the stadium. The **Heroon** was a mausoleum for the Saithidae family, prominent in the city from the 1st to the 3rd century AD. It is also an oddity, being a Doric temple sat on top of an absurdly large podium.

The museum (✆27240 51201; ⏲ 08.30–15.00 Tue–Sun) The small museum, back by the turning down to the site, is worth a quick glance. It consists of just three rooms. In the first is a wonderful statue of a naked Hermes which was found near the stadium. This is appropriate as it presents an athletic ideal of the male form – exactly the kind of image you expect in Greek sculpture. It dates from the 1st century AD, but is a Roman copy of a 4th-century BC original. Also found nearby was the torso of Theseus, with similarly athletic features.

The second room is mainly devoted to various works by the famous sculptor Damophon. Pausanias rates his work extremely highly (he even says that he was given the job of repairing damage to Phidias's famous gold and ivory statue of Zeus at Olympia – one of the Seven Wonders of the ancient world).

The last room is dominated by another fantastic statue, this time depicting the female form. It is Artemis, goddess of the hunt, with one arm reaching delicately over her shoulder probably searching for an arrow from her quiver. It is also a Roman copy of a 4th-century BC original. Nearby a crude statue of a Roman emperor proves that the evolution of art is not always one of upward progress.

While in the museum, it is also worth looking out for a reconstructed model of the city, which brings across its scale and ties together the ruins you have seen.

Mount Ithome and the Voulcanou monasteries (Ιθώμη & Βουλκάνου)

Despite the imposing bulk of Ithome that looms over Messene and the modern village of Mavromati, it's actually not that difficult to get to its summit, especially with your own transport. The reward is an incredible view, both down to the ruins, but also across vast swathes of Messinia and over to the mountains of Laconia.

There are two wonderful, and contrasting, monasteries: one abandoned and one still working. If you are walking, taking in all of these would take about 3½ hours with no stops. Realistically set aside half a day to explore. Even with a car you may not want to attempt the dirt track up the mountain (this is currently driveable with care, but do not attempt it in the wet). If so, park by the Laconian Gate and walk (an hour each way).

Coming back through Mavromati from Messene you pass the spring on the left and the taverna on the right. Just after these a small road turns up to the left. This skirts the mountain for a few hundred metres before coming to the remains of the **Laconian Gate**, opposite a modern shrine. It is not as well preserved as its Arcadian cousin, but it is impressive how the walls of the city must have marched up the mountainside.

Just before you reach the Laconian Gate a dirt road leads off to the left, heading up Ithome. It soon passes the remains of a **temple of Artemis**. As it nears the summit the road widens out and you can see a section of fortified wall above you. If you have brought a vehicle up this far, then park here and continue on foot. A few more minutes brings you to the top of the mountain, more of a saddle or plateau than a peak, and the **Old Monastery of Voulcanou**. This attractive, and isolated, collection of stone buildings within a walled compound was only finally abandoned in the 1950s. Various legends are attached to its foundation. One story sets its origin during the reign of the Byzantine emperor Leo III the Isaurian, who ruled from AD717 to 741, claiming it was a refuge for monks fleeing the iconoclasts (a sect then powerful in the Church who opposed the use of images in worship). Another tradition ascribes the foundation of the monastery to the wife of the emperor Andronikos Palaiologos, which would make it late 13th century. Most of the buildings you see now date back to the 16th century. It is reasonably easy to hop over the wall to explore, but the chapel is kept locked. It is possible to glimpse some of the frescoes within, which were painted in 1638, from the doorway. This was probably the site of the sanctuary to Zeus Ithomatas, where Aristodemus killed his daughter and then himself.

Back down at the Laconian Gate head onwards through it on the tarmac road. You will soon see the large **New Voulcanou Monastery** below you. You can see why the monks might prefer the location to the windy summit of Ithome, and the views are still breathtaking. It is only comparatively new, and was founded in 1625 in buildings originally occupied by the Knights of St John. Most of it now is 19th century, as the monastery was burnt down by Ibrahim Pasha in the War of Independence. In one corner, however, you can see the original gateway that dates back to the 15th century. If you want to look inside dress respectfully and try not to turn up at lunch or siesta times. The most important relic in the monastery is an icon of the Virgin Mary, said, like countless others, to be painted by Luke the Evangelist. It originally lived in the old monastery, and still visits there on the feast of the Assumption (15 August).

If you haven't had your fill of monasteries and churches, and have your own transport, there are a couple more in the area that are worth hunting out. The first is the **Andromonastiro** (Ανδρομονάστηρο), which is signposted off the road south from the Arcadian Gate. Turn left just before the village of Petralona (Πετράλωνα); the road to the monastery is now tarmac all the way. The walled compound is set in an attractive spot and is interesting to explore (but care is needed). If the front doors are locked, try round the back. The oldest parts of the church are early 14th century.

The second is the exquisite 12th-century church of **Zoodochos Pigi** (Ζωοδόχος Πηγή), 'Fountain of Life' – an aspect of the Virgin Mary. Just past the village of Ellinoeklisia (Ελληνοεκλησιά), on the road to Androusa (Ανδρούσα), look out for a brown sign to the right, beside a large shrine. What makes this church special is that it has been largely untouched since it was built. It still has an outside porch, which in other churches is often walled in, and its original belfry, also often replaced by a taller, Venetian-style affair elsewhere. The church is kept pretty firmly locked, but is beautiful enough on the outside to warrant a stop.

SOUTH TO KORONI

The westernmost of the three fingers that stick down into the Mediterranean from the Peloponnese is Pylia, named after the town of Pylos. Its coast is dotted with pretty towns and villages, along with some excellent stretches of sand. You could whip round the peninsula in a day in a car and get a reasonable taste of the area, but it is worth lingering and there are plenty of nice places to stay.

The eastern coast, along with Finikounda in the south, has been developed for resort holidays for tourists, primarily from northern Europe, mainly because of the proximity of the airport at Kalamata. Do not be put off; it's all pretty low key with the few big hotels being relatively unobtrusive. Only in the midst of the high season does it really begin to get going, and even then a short drive inland will return you to rural, and unspoilt, Messinia.

The first little harbour you come to is **Petalidi** (Πεταλίδι), still very much a working market town with a handsome main square. Just to the north there is a good, sandy beach with views across to Kalamata. There is nothing here apart from **Petalidi Beach Camping** (✆ *27200 31154*; e *info@campingpetalidi.gr*; w *campingpetalidi.gr*; €), which offers a pleasantly shady and quiet site right by the sand. They can also sell drinks to those who just want to enjoy the beach.

Further south is **Chrani** (Χράνοι), the proper resort along this coast, although it is barely more than a little village really, surrounded by a few large hotels. It is a delightful little place, uncrowded even at the height of the season, and serviced by a few tavernas of higher standard than might be expected but not expensive. Parking for the beach is down the road opposite the now-closed Blue Waves Tavern on the main road. If you want to overnight, try the beachfront **Ilaira Apartments** (m *69835 11833*; e *info@ilaira.gr*; w *ilaira.gr*; €€€), a family-run set-up with fun hosts, a lovely swimming pool, spacious and well-equipped apartments, and a good restaurant. A number of marked walks run up to the villages on the hills behind Chrani – the 2½-hour route to the abandoned village of Vigla and then on to Kakkorevma via the Vigla Gorge is marked from the bus stop outside Billy's Supermarket.

Agios Andreas (Αγ Ανδρέας) is very easy to scoot straight past on the main road without realising it's there. It is a much more authentic kind of place than Chrani, with its pretty little harbour filled with fishing boats and the occasional yacht. A sandy beach lined with eucalyptus trees lies just to the south of the harbour and has another campsite, **Agios Andreas Beach** (✆ *27250 31881*; €). If you want to do a minor bit of exploring there are a few remains of a **temple of Apollo** in the olive groves behind the village. To get there, head up the inland road towards Longa (Λογγά). After 100m there is a 12th-century Byzantine church on the left, although it has been extensively restored. The temple is another 30m up the road and then about 100m into the olives to the right of the road. You can make out the base of the building, and two sections of column lie on the ground.

More good beaches lie on the coast between here and Koroni. The best of them is at **Agios Triada** (Αγ Τριάδα). Look out for the sign to the left about 2km after you have passed through the inland market town of Harokopio (Χαροκοπιό). This is a wonderful strip of golden sand, fringed with lush vegetation and steep cliffs. There are no facilities.

KORONI (ΚΟΡΏΝΙ)

Koroni is one of the prettiest towns of the Peloponnese. It is reminiscent of some of the islands, with its whitewashed houses set round a small port rising up to a low hill behind, on which perches the castle. It has that sleepy air of everyone waiting for the daily ferry to arrive, when they will all suddenly burst into frenetic action. Except, in Koroni, the ferry never comes.

HISTORY This was apparently the site of Ancient Asini, but no significant Classical remains have been found in the town. Koroni really came into its own in medieval times. In 1205, it was captured by the Frankish knights of the elder Geoffrey de Villehardouin, but he only managed to hold on to it for one year before ceding it to the Venetian Republic, who held on to it until 1500. These years were its crowning glory, and the Venetian influence has a lot to do with the special feeling the town still exudes. It became one of the chief ports of call on Venice's trade routes to the crusader kingdoms of the Middle East. Together with Methoni, its sister town on the coast to the west, it was known as the 'eyes of the republic'.

This era ended with the coming of the Ottomans, under the command of Bayezit II. They first took Methoni, and treated its inhabitants so brutally that Koroni gave up without a fight. The Venetians got their revenge in 1685 when the soon-to-be doge, Francesco Morosini, put the town to siege. After an attempted truce was ended by a Turkish cannon misfiring, Morosini put the 1,500 defenders of the castle to death. Venice's decline in power led to the Ottomans retaking the town in the early 18th century, and it remained under their control until the end of the War of Independence.

GETTING THERE AND AWAY

By car There is a fast road connecting Koroni to Finikounda via Vasilitsi (Βασιλιτσι) that is only shown on recent maps. Driving into Koroni, head down to the harbour where there is plenty of parking at the far end. The town is small and mainly pedestrianised anyway.

By bus There are at least six buses a day to and from Kalamata (*1hr 20mins*). There's one bus a day on to Finikounda (*30mins*) and Methoni (*40mins*) from here. The main bus stop is in the square just before the harbour, by the large church.

WHERE TO STAY

Xenios Zeus Rooms (6 rooms) 27250 22509; m 69740 47580; e malliosdim@yahoo.gr; w xenioszeuskoroni.com. A handsome building right on a small pebble beach at the far end of the harbour is the home of the Mallios family. They have converted their lower floor into a series of comfortable rooms. They also have larger apartments a street away & 2 villas out of town. €€€

Hotel Diana (8 rooms) 27250 22312; w dianahotel-koroni.gr. A pretty Neoclassical building on the small street down from the square to the start of the harbour. All rooms have a side view of the sea. Noise may be a problem in the evenings. €€

Koroni Camping 27250 22119; m 69471 98228; e info@koronicamping.com; w koronicamping.com. Set above the small Artaki Beach on the way into town from the north, it's close enough to walk in easily. There's a nice pool & all the facilities you'd expect. €

WHERE TO EAT AND DRINK
The harbourfront is lined with countless eateries, ranging from unpretentious seafood restaurants and tavernas to stylish crêperies and modern cafés. Unlike many other seaside resorts, most places seem to stay open out of season, so there is plenty of choice at all times of year. In the summer there are a couple of **clubs** that operate by Memi Beach to the south of town. Ask around to find out what they are currently called and which is in favour.

Barbarossa Restaurant 27250 29039; barbarossakorwnh. Formerly known as Flisvos, this is probably the pick of the terrace eateries that line Koroni's waterfront. Seafood is the speciality, & it is excellent & very well priced, but it also does good steak & meatballs, & the house wine is above par.

Café & Restaurant Resalto 27250 23064. At the east end of town on the corner of a square with the playground, this has candlelit tables with a view of the floodlit castle walls & offers Greek cooking with a classy twist from a smallish but creative menu. Try the beetroot in mustard sauce or cod with spinach. Costlier than the other tavernas but worth it for a treat.

✕ La Famiglia   m 69723 63202; **f** lafamigliakoronimessinia. Offering a welcome change from taverna fare, this genuine Italian eatery specialises in pasta & pizza, & has a nice waterfront location.

✕ Peroulia Beach Restaurant   [map, page 198] 📞27250 41777; m 69463 33728; e info@peroulia. gr; w peroulia.gr. Situated on sandy Peroulia Beach 8km north of Koroni by road, this long-serving restaurant (established 1984) is worth the diversion assuming you have a car, both for the fabulous seaside setting & for the great seafood & salads.

✕ Taverna Bogris   📞27250 22947. Situated in a plant-filled cobbled courtyard at the west end of the harbour, this is an old-style taverna where you are invited into the kitchen to choose from a wide selection of well-cooked oven dishes, as well as all the usual grilled meats, salads, etc. Staff are friendly, service good, portions large, & prices reasonable.

OTHER PRACTICALITIES   Koroni has a couple of supermarkets, two banks with ATMs, and a post office. It is a town to walk about, but if you need a taxi they hang out in the main square, just off the start of the harbour. There is also a useful map board here showing all the important features of the town.

WHAT TO SEE AND DO   Koroni is a town for wandering around and its backstreets are largely pedestrianised, and often actual staircases. The inhabitants of the town clearly realise what a little gem they have and take evident pride in it. The whitewash is immaculate and enlivened with splashes of colour (and not just the ubiquitous blue), while potted flowers spill over the balconies. The occasional gift shop is of good quality, rather than tacky, and there are enough little surprises to make wandering a delight: small churches, Venetian fountains, and a disused windmill that looks out over the rooftops.

The castle   (⊕ *daylight hours*) Any wandering will take you up to the castle at some point. Outside of high season, you can drive up here and park inside near to the convent, but it is worth checking first as if this option is closed there is nowhere else to park and it is hard to turn around. You enter the castle, which is surrounded by water on three sides, through a tall, arched gateway, and are confronted by its decidedly unmilitary interior. For a start, people still live within the castle walls and there are plenty of houses surrounded by well-tended vegetable patches. Carrying straight on you are next confronted by a convent, the **Timiou Prodromou** dedicated to John the Baptist. The friendly nuns welcome visitors (dressed appropriately) and some of the best views of the town and surrounds are from the castle walls within. The convent itself only dates back to the early 20th century.

Near to the convent's entrance are the ruins of an 8th-century Byzantine church, **Agia Sophia**. Beside it you can see the remains of a **temple of Apollo**, on top of which it was built. A stairway near to here can take you down towards Zaga Beach (page 212).

Following the walls round away from the houses and the convent, things get a bit more castle-like. The most impressive feature is a large bastion that overlooks the last half-kilometre of land before the cliffs drop to the sea. A dark passage spirals downward from on top of it into its interior. You can also reach this through a nearby breach in the wall. This breach used to be another bastion, but during the war the Germans used it as an ammunition store, and they blew it up in 1944 when they left. Inside the still-standing bastion the ceiling is supported by a huge octagonal pillar, some 15m high. These fortifications are Turkish, dating from the 16th century.

Nearby beaches The north end of town has the small, sandy beach of **Artaki** (Αρτάκι). Just to the south is a 2km-long beach with two names: close to the town it is called **Zaga** (Ζάγκα), and further on it turns into **Memi** (Μεμί). This stretch of sand and shale is remarkably underdeveloped, with only the two ends having the odd café or taverna on them.

A little further away are **two isolated coves**. On the road towards Finikounda, after about 12km, look out for a road to the left signposted to the sandy beach of **Tsapi** (Τσαπί). In the summer two tavernas set up shop here, as well as a **campsite** (\ *27250 51503;* e *campingtsapi@gmail.com;* w *campingtsapi.gr;* €). I have heard that this beach, and the facilities, can get a bit overrun in midsummer, but it has always been pristine when I have visited. On the way to Tsapi there is a right turn down a steep, rough track to **Marathi** (Μαράθι), an even more isolated and picture-perfect cove, which you can also reach on a boat trip from Finikounda.

FINIKOUNDA (ΦΟΙΝΙΚΟΎΝΤΑ)

Finikounda is no longer the secret gem it used to be. Once a quiet fishing village blessed with a string of sandy beaches, it now announces itself with two large roundabouts, separated by a wide section of road with a central reservation. This is a bit of an overkill, however, and despite the arrival of package tours this is still a fairly sleepy kind of resort, and the beaches remain excellent. A lot of the accommodation is booked up by travel companies, but outside of August there is usually something to spare. The younger crowd, often attracted by the good **windsurfing** (boards are easily available to hire), tend to stay in the **campsites**. The best of these, and nearest to the village, is **Anemomilos** (\ *27230 71360;* f *campinganemomilos.finikounda;* €) on the beach of the same name. It is set on many levels with plenty of shade and has a bar, but no restaurant. The old favourite for eating, and with a prime spot overlooking the harbour from the west, is the **Taverna Elena** (\ *27230 71235*) which does all the normal taverna fare and has live music in the summer.

The main **beach**, called simply Finikounda, is the most sheltered and best for swimming, as well as backing on to the village with its bars and tavernas. **Anemomilos** (Ανεμόμυλος), to the west, is where to head for windsurfing – the name means 'windmill'. **Loutsa** (Λούτσα), to the east, is often the least crowded of the three main beaches. The best of all, however, takes a bit of work to get to. This is **Turtle Cove**, a sliver of sand visible on the headland past Loutsa. To get there you either have to walk (*40mins, ask directions in the village*), or take a **boat**: Kostas Apostolidis can take you here, and elsewhere, on the *Bebis* (m *69445 65421*).

METHONI (ΜΕΘΏΝΗ)

Sister town to Koroni, Methoni is not as immediately pretty as its sibling. It more than makes up for it by having one of the best castles going, as well as being the jumping-off point for a visit to the island of Sapienza, an uninhabited natural paradise, just to the south. It is also more of a working town, with a distinct air of hustle and bustle, which can come as a bit of a relief after sleepy Koroni. The town beach is sandy and narrow, and good for kids as it remains shallow for a long distance.

HISTORY Like Koroni, the important part of Methoni's story belongs to the medieval period and later. Once known as the haunt of pirates, it was here that Geoffrey de Villehardouin landed in 1204 and began the Frankish conquest of the Peloponnese. He did not hold the town for very long, however, and the Venetians came in 1206. They were formally ceded the town in the 1209 Treaty of Sapienza. The story of Methoni now mirrors that of Koroni, the other 'eye' of Venice. It was known as Modon and was famous for its wine and bacon.

It was the first of the two towns to fall to the Ottomans in 1500. The Turkish forces were 100,000 strong with 500 cannons, while 7,000 Venetians defended the castle. Despite being heavily outnumbered the Venetians held out for a month. Then, on 9 August, four Venetian ships managed to break through the Turkish blockade, bringing much-needed supplies and reinforcements. In a bizarre incident the defenders, overcome with joy at this turn of events, left the walls unmanned and the Turks were able to storm the castle. The Venetians made a last stand in the Bourtzi tower, at the castle's end, but were massacred to a man.

One of the more famous visitors to Methoni during the Ottoman occupation was Cervantes, the Spanish author of *Don Quixote*. We can presume that he didn't enjoy it much, as he was a galley slave at the time.

During the War of Independence, Ibrahim Pasha, on his way to lay waste to the Peloponnese, disembarked his Egyptian army here. Three years later, after Greek victory, a French force came under General Maison. They were the equivalent of a modern UN peacekeeping expedition, and handed out much-needed supplies as well as rebuilding houses. They tore down the old town, which was then mostly within the fortress walls and dreadfully unsanitary, and relocated it to its present site.

GETTING THERE AND AWAY

By car Arriving by car from any direction, make your way towards the seafront, where parking is plentiful.

By bus The bus stop is in the centre of town, where the road coming in from Pylos forks into Methoni's two main, parallel streets. There are seven buses a day to and from Pylos (*30mins*) and Kalamata (*1hr 30mins*) and a couple to Finikounda (*15mins*).

WHERE TO STAY

Although the accommodation in Methoni is not going to win any prizes at present, it is perfectly acceptable.

Castello (13 rooms) 27230 31300; e info@ castello.gr; w castello.gr. Close to the entrance to the castle, the Castello is a bit bland from the outside, but is pleasant enough inside & has a pretty little garden where b/fast is served. €€€

Methoni Beach Hotel (13 rooms) 27230 31555; m 69784 18710; e info@ methonibeachhotel.gr; w methonibeachhotel. gr. This is the one to pick for the views, which encompass the castle, the sea & the islands. It's just beside the castle walls, by the beach, & was designed, partly successfully, to blend in with the fortifications. €€€

Ulysses Hotel (9 rooms) 27230 31600; e ulysseshotel@yahoo.com; w ulysseshotel. com. Although it lacks a waterfront location, this small owner-managed hotel scores highly when it comes to character, friendly service, comfort & a top-notch home-cooked Greek b/fast – & it's still only 2mins' walk from the beachfront & castle. Recommended. €€€

Methoni Campsite 27230 31228; e info@ campingmethoni.gr; w campingmethoni.gr. This used to be the municipal campsite & was somewhat basic, but it looks like it has had a bit of a renovation recently. It's just by the beach, at the opposite end to the castle & with good views back to it. €

WHERE TO EAT AND DRINK

Taverna Nikos 27230 31282. Situated practically opposite Methoni Castle, this family-run

stalwart – established back in 1976 – serves a varied selection of well-priced typical taverna fare including delicious kleftiko & plenty of vegetarian choices.

✕ To Meltemi ☎ 27230 31042. The most homely & wallet-friendly of the half-dozen tavernas that enclose the main beachfront square serves a predictable selection of seafood, meat & vegetarian, but portions are generous & prices low.

OTHER PRACTICALITIES The two parallel roads through the centre of town have all you could need, including supermarkets, two banks with ATMs, a pharmacy and a post office.

WHAT TO SEE AND DO

Methoni Castle (⊕ *see box, page 52; €2*) While the warlike nature of the castle at Koroni seems to have been mitigated by its vegetable gardens and nunnery, there is no escaping the intent of this castle. There has been a fortification here since ancient times. A German dynamite explosion in 1944 revealed Mycenaean foundations. You enter the castle over an elegant, 14-arched, stone **bridge**, built by the French in 1828 to replace an earlier wooden one. The inland-facing walls, unsurprisingly, are the most impregnable part of the fortifications. The bridge crosses a large **moat** started by the Venetians with the original intention of flooding it with sea water, thus entirely surrounding the castle. Their work was interrupted by the Turkish attack of 1500.

On either side of the bridge are **artillery bastions**; the one on the right built under the command of the Venetian governor Giovanni Bembo in 1460, and the one to the left constructed by Antonio Loredan in 1714. On the walls of this bastion can be seen the Venetian emblem of the Lion of St Mark. It is easy to see how cannon from these bastions would have dominated the castle entrance.

Once over the bridge and through the **gate**, with its carved pillars, a sharp left turn acts as a further defensive measure, and then leads through a further two gates, one of which is pierced by a cannon hole. The second gate leads you into the interior of the castle itself. This is where the **old town** of Methoni was, with a far larger population than in modern times. There are only a handful of buildings remaining now, including a few ruined Turkish baths and a more recent Orthodox church. A **granite column** right by the gate is of disputed origin, but was probably put up in commemoration of Giovanni Bembo in 1494. The odd pyramid-roofed building opposite the gate was an **armoury**.

It is worth heading for the southernmost wall of the castle, where a large **sea gate** is in the process of being restored. From this a causeway leads you to the **Bourtzi tower**, perched on a rocky islet. This is where the last survivors of the Turkish assault of 1500 were put to the sword. Despite its dark past it is a beautiful and romantic spot.

Back near the granite column the landward wall, with its single gate, separates the 'habitable' side of the castle from the defensive part above the twin bastions. This section of the fortress makes for great exploring. Follow the path past the **old barracks**, and then down a dark tunnel of stairs. You emerge into a series of fortifications and passageways lined with cannon holes. Follow them round until you end up by the entrance gate once again.

Sapienza Island (Σαπιέντζα) To the south of Messinia are the **Inouses**, an uninhabited group of islands that dominate the sea views. The most interesting of them, and the most easily visited, is **Sapienza**. Many ships have come to grief around the island: a Roman sarcophagus can still be seen in the waters just to the north, and the islet of Bomba on the east coast is one of the many places St Paul is said to have been shipwrecked. It was also on Sapienza, in 1209, that the treaty ceding Methoni and Koroni from the Franks to the Venetians was signed.

Today Sapienza is known for nature, which flourishes away from human influence. The overgrown forests are extremely atmospheric, with large spider webs stretching from tree to tree. Many of these are large *Arbutus*, or the **strawberry tree**, named for its bright-red fruit that appears in winter (they taste bitter, but make a nice jam, apparently). The pollen of these trees has stained the earth a bright orange colour, most obviously seen in a central clearing known as the **Spartolaka**.

The island is also home to two non-native endangered species: the **kri kri**, or Cretan wild goat, and the **mouflon sheep**. The latter are easier to spot and resemble small deer. The best place to see these is on the lovely little beach of **Ammos**, on the north coast of the island. In 1986, 20 kri kri and 26 mouflon sheep were released. Now there are estimated to be about 300 kri kri and 400 sheep. In fact, at a price, you can even hunt the animals now.

Sapienza is best reached on a boat excursion, which is easy to organise from the harbour.

PYLOS AND GIALOVA (ΠΎΛΟΣ & ΓΙΆΛΟΒΑ)

The area around the great natural harbour of Navarino Bay shows off Greece doing what it does best. It is an intoxicating mix of environment and history, with 3,500-year-old ruins competing for your attention with perfect crescents of soft sand. The modern town of Pylos adds an air of sophistication, with its café culture and smart, 'new' castle, while Gialova is for nature- and beach-lovers; set beside a lagoon that sees the first resting place for flocks of thirsty birds on the way north from Africa. All the while the still waters of the bay and its low-lying islands hide the violent past of the area, where two of the most important battles in European history took place.

The charms of this corner of Greece have not gone unnoticed, and in 2010 the hugely ambitious Costa Navarino complex opened, combining luxury hotels, and golf courses (page 217).

HISTORY Homer called it 'sandy Pylos', an epithet that certainly rings true, and made it the kingdom of the wise old Nestor. For a long time this was consigned to the realms of mythology, but in the mid 20th century it was proved that there was indeed a Mycenaean kingdom here, although its palace was to the north of the modern town (page 221).

In Classical times it was called Koryphasia, and was located on the hills beside Gialova Lagoon. It was part of Spartan-occupied Messinia, and it was here that the famous warriors of Sparta suffered one of their few defeats, at the hands of the Athenians during the Peloponnesian War (page 14).

From the 6th to the 9th century AD the area was dominated by the Avars, a Turkic group of nomads who controlled much of eastern Europe at the time. They gave the region its medieval name, Navarino, which is still kept by the bay itself. In 1278, the Frankish Nicholas II of St-Omer built a castle here (the Paleokastro, page 221). In 1501, it was occupied by the Turks, who in 1572 decided to relocate and built a new castle above the site of modern Pylos.

In 1825, during the War of Independence, Ibrahim Pasha made it his base while he operated a scorched earth policy on the ravaged Peloponnese. This led, in 1827, to the Battle of Navarino and the end of the war, the second decisive battle of the area (see box, page 218). The French peacekeeping force under General Maison arrived in 1828 and rebuilt Pylos in its present location, where it reverted to the old, Homeric name.

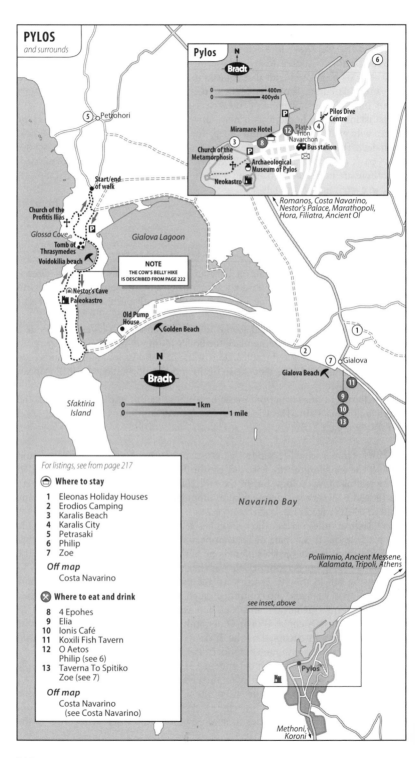

PYLOS
and surrounds

Pylos

Bradt

0 ———————— 400m
0 ———————— 400yds

⑥

Petrohori ⑤

Pilos Dive Centre

Miramare Hotel

Platéa Trión Navarchon ④
⑫
⑧

Bus station

Church of the Metamorphosis ③

Archaeological Museum of Pylos

Neokastro

Romanos, Costa Navarino, Nestor's Palace, Marathopoli, Hora, Filiatra, Ancient Ol

Start/end of walk

Church of the Profitis Ilías

Glossa Cove

Gialova Lagoon

Tomb of Thrasymedes

Voidokilia beach

NOTE
THE COW'S BELLY HIKE IS DESCRIBED FROM PAGE 222

Nestor's Cave
Paleokastro

Old Pump House

Golden Beach

Gialova ⑦

Gialova Beach
⑪
⑨
⑩
⑬

①

②

N

Bradt

Sfaktiria Island

0 ———————— 1km
0 ———————— 1 mile

Navarino Bay

Polilimnio, Ancient Messene, Kalamata, Tripoli, Athens

see inset, above

Pylos

Methoni, Koroni

For listings, see from page 217

🛏 Where to stay

1 Eleonas Holiday Houses
2 Erodios Camping
3 Karalis Beach
4 Karalis City
5 Petrasaki
6 Philip
7 Zoe

Off map
Costa Navarino

🍴 Where to eat and drink

8 4 Epohes
9 Elia
10 Ionis Café
11 Koxili Fish Tavern
12 O Aetos
Philip (see 6)
13 Taverna To Spitiko
Zoe (see 7)

Off map
Costa Navarino
(see Costa Navarino)

GETTING THERE AND AWAY

By car The most scenic approach to Pylos is from the north, which is the direction you come if you have driven from Gialova or Kalamata. There are fantastic views over the town and bay as you descend into it. Whichever way you come, as is almost always the case with coastal towns, you want to head straight for the harbour where there is plenty of parking space by the water. The entrance into the small, beachfront hamlet of Gialova is to the left on a sharp right-hand bend in the road 6km north round the bay from Pylos. If you are driving to or from Kalamata, you should work in a stop at the pools and waterfalls of Polilimnio (page 226).

By bus There are seven buses a day to and from Kalamata (*1hr 20mins*), five south to Methoni (*30mins*), three to Finikounda (*35mins*), and four that head north up the coast passing Gialova and Nestor's Palace (*40mins*). One bus runs directly to and from Athens daily. The bus station (✆ 27230 22230) is at the back of the main square.

WHERE TO STAY *Map, opposite*

Around Navarino Bay you have the choice of either staying in the provincial style of modern Pylos or relaxing into the rural charms of Gialova and its surroundings. Both have their attractions, and neither precludes enjoying the other.

Pylos

🏠 **Karalis City & Karalis Beach** (35 & 14 rooms) ✆ 27230 22960 & 27230 23021; e info@hotelkaralis.gr & info@karalisbeach.gr; w hotelkaralis.gr/en & karalisbeach.gr/en. These are 2 sister hotels, the larger of which (Karalis City) is right by the central square of Pylos, overlooking the harbour. The quieter sister establishment (Karalis Beach) is almost opposite it, a short walk out of town underneath the walls of the castle. Both are attractive locations, & the rooms have all the mod cons. €€€

🏠 **Philip** (17 rooms) ✆ 27230 22741; e info@hotelphilip-pylos.com; w hotelphilip-pylos.com. On the road into Pylos from the north, & overlooking the harbour, the Philip has some of the best views in town & a b/fast (€8) based on local produce that goes on until midday. €€€

Gialova

🏠 **Costa Navarino** (750 rooms) ✆ 27230 95000/96000; w costanavarino.com. Despite its vast size, this modern resort is impressive in terms of architecture, attention to detail, eco-credentials & deference to local culture & history. It comprises 2 side-by-side complexes, with the Westin being slightly smarter & the Romanos being more child-friendly. Activities include 2 golf courses, watersports, philosophy walks, a spa, 10-pin bowling lanes, an ecological museum, squash courts & tennis. Food, including

an impressive b/fast, is sourced locally, in keeping with the resort's mission to help the surrounding community. The complex's cosmopolitan selection of restaurants is of a high standard but extremely pricy for the area. One final fact: the beach here is a nesting place for the loggerhead turtle (page 9). Because of this, the whole of this huge hotel complex, although right by the beach, is entirely invisible from it. €€€€€

🏠 **Eleonas Holiday Houses** (8 villas) ✆ 27230 22696; e info@eleonas.com; w eleonas.villas. Set on a citrus- & olive-strewn slope offering stunning views to Pylos & the Paleokastro, this attractively sprawling complex comprises a collection of handsome standalone 1- to 3-bedroom villas, all with well-equipped kitchenettes & some with shared or private swimming pool. €€€€€

🏠 **Zoe** (24 rooms & 16 apts) ✆ 27230 22025; e hotelzoe@otenet.gr; w hotelzoe.com. The Zoe is a bit of an institution in Gialova. The main hotel is right on the beach, while the newer apartments are set back behind the large pool in a converted wine warehouse. Stavros & Voula are passionate about the area & are a good source of information on everything from walks to wildlife. It is located right next to Gialova's beachfront mall, which means you have more than a dozen eateries within easy walking distance. Apts €€€€, rooms €€€

🏠 **Petrasaki** (8 bungalows) ✆ 27230 41814; m 69484 84148; e info@petrasaki.de;

In 1825, Ibrahim Pasha took an army of 16,000 Egyptian troops into the Peloponnese with the intention of laying it to waste. At the same time the European powers – England, France and Russia – were realising that some sort of resolution to the problems in Greece was becoming necessary.

In 1827, the Treaty of London called for autonomy for Greece as a tribute-paying dependency of the Ottomans, although many wanted to take things further. Meanwhile an Ottoman fleet of some 100 ships had sailed out to join Ibrahim Pasha at Pylos.

In reaction a joint navy set out under the command of Count Heiden for Russia, Count de Rigny for France, and Sir Edward Codrington for the British, whom the others deferred to. The Ottoman fleet joined up with Ibrahim in Navarino Bay, and were shortly followed by the allied navy, who took up position outside the bay.

They failed to intimidate the Ottomans, however, and Ibrahim's forces continued to harass the Greek population. In the end the allies lost patience and, on 20 October, their fleet, fewer than 30 ships, entered the bay to face down the larger Turkish force.

Exactly what happened next remains unclear, but it seems that a lack of discipline among the Ottoman forces led to shots being fired, which escalated into a general engagement. It was one of the most extraordinary naval battles ever fought. It was the last major confrontation between ships with sails, but one of the first where the ships remained stationary, slogging it out with cannon and sword. In the end the bay was filled with smoke and blood, and the allies emerged triumphant.

Ibrahim was now cut off from any support, and the eventual defeat of his troops was inevitable. This accidental battle, while not entirely unwelcome, was something of an embarrassment back in Britain. The king's speech of 1828 referred to the conflagration in Navarino Bay as 'an untoward event'. In Greece it is commemorated in countless streets and squares named after the Trion Navarchon, the 'Three Admirals'.

w petrasaki.de/wo.htm. Run by a Greek/English couple, this is a group of small & simple self-contained cottages arranged like a mini village in lushly wooded hilltop grounds in Petrohori, close to Voidokilia Beach, among others. Peaceful with good views. €€€

À **Erodios Camping** \27230 23269; m 69733 80550; e info@erodioss.gr; w erodioss.gr. This is the nicer of the 2 campsites at Gialova. Right on the beach, on the way to the lagoon, it has excellent facilities, including bungalows to rent. €, bungalows €€€

✘ **WHERE TO EAT AND DRINK** *Map, page 216*
Even if you are in the Costa Navarino resort, with its plethora of eating options, it is worth going further afield to try other options. Messinia is farming country, and the food is always fresh and delicious.

Pylos

✘ **4 Epohes** \27230 22739; m 69774 37729. On the Pylos seafront just past the Hotel Miramare, the 'Four Seasons' has been popular for many years & is where to come for

fish (which can be expensive) as well as normal taverna dishes.

✘ **O Aetos** \27230 22783. Probably the current pick of a dozen or more eateries on the main waterfront square, this has plenty of terrace seating, but a small interior, so book if you want to sit indoors. The emphasis is on seafood but it also serves salads & meat stews. Well priced.

✕ Philip ✎27230 22741. At the hotel of the same name, this terrace restaurant has lovely views over the bay.

Gialova

The beach at Gialova is now fringed by a low-rise open-air arcade that incorporates a supermarket, a beauty salon & a few craft shops, as well as a dozen or more restaurants, cafés & cocktail bars. Follow your nose or try one of the recommendations below.

✳ ✕ Elia Restaurant ✎27230 23503; w elia-gialova.gr. This 'creative local soul kitchen' has a very friendly vibe & serves a great selection of traditional Peloponnese dishes, often with a modern twist. Seafood is well represented. Ingredients are mostly sourced from local suppliers & the imaginative menu is complemented by a wide selection of local & regional wines.

✕ Ionis Café ✎27230 23181. Situated next to Elia, this funky café has plenty of terrace seating & is a great spot for coffee accompanied by a light snack – sweet or savoury filled crêpes being the speciality.

✕ Koxili Fish Tavern ✎27230 23259. It may not look much from the outside, but this unpretentious eatery on the beach 100m past the mall serves the best seafood in town at very reasonable prices.

✕ Taverna To Spitiko ✎27230 22138; w spitikogialova.gr. At the far end of the short beachfront mall. The name is a reference to home cooking, with dishes such as lountza (smoked pork fillet) & seftalies (grilled meatballs) giving it a Cypriot slant.

✕ Zoe ✎27230 22025. Stavros is the chef at the restaurant beneath the Zoe Hotel in Gialova. The veg comes from their own organic garden, just around the corner. The tables are practically on the sand.

OTHER PRACTICALITIES Most things you might need can all be found round the main square of Pylos, the **Platea Trion Navarchon** or 'Square of the Three Admirals', by the harbour, including banks and ATMs. This is also where to find taxis. The post office is just up a street to the right, at the back of the square. The health centre (✎27320 23779) is on the way out of town towards Methoni. Perhaps because of the lagoon, mosquitoes and other insects can be bothersome around this area – be sure to wear repellent.

WHAT TO SEE AND DO
Pylos and the Neokastro (Νιόκαστρο) Pylos retains a Gallic flavour, left over from its reconstruction by the French troops of General Maison. The hub of the town is the harbour and the adjacent **Platea Trion Navarchon**, where a monument celebrates the three admirals from England, Russia and France who defeated the Ottomans. This victory is celebrated every **20 October** with parades in the morning and music and dancing in the evening. The Greek and Russian navies send warships, while the British and French tend to make do with representatives.

Looking inland, the road that leads from halfway up the right-hand side of the square climbs uphill then bends to the left where a track to the right leads to the **Neokastro** (✎27230 22010; ⊕ 08.00–15.00 Tue–Sun; €3), or 'New Castle'. Started in the 16th century, it was called this to distinguish it from the old castle above Voidokilia. You would barely notice the castle was here from the modern town – which makes sense, as it was built to dominate the sea, not the land. It is surprisingly large, and consists of an outer curtain wall built upon recessed arches, and an inner, hexagonal citadel with a moat around it. It is possible to walk around almost all of the walls, which provide good views of Navarino Bay and its islands. The inner **citadel** is a particularly fine bit of military architecture. It was used as a prison for feuding Maniats in the 19th century, and the courtyard had to be divided by walls to keep them apart from each other. These walls are now gone and there is an exhibition on **maritime archaeology** (the Ephorate of Maritime Antiquities have their offices here). The only other buildings that survive in the interior of the castle are the church of the **Metamorphosis**, originally a mosque, and the Turkish barracks that now contains a collection of engravings, mostly to do with the War of Independence.

Recently relocated to within the walls of the Neokastro, the small **Archaeological Museum of Pylos** (✆ *27120 63100;* w *pylos-museum.gr;* ⊕ *08.00–15.00 Tue–Sun*) displays a variety of locally excavated Neolithic and Roman-era items, including votive gifts from the vaulted tombs Voidokilia and Koukounara, and the remains of a Mycenaean boar's tusk helmet.

If you go further along the road past the castle you will see an **Ottoman aqueduct** that used to bring water to the castle. Other sections of this can be glimpsed up in the hills as you come along the road from Kalamata.

Navarino Bay (Όρμος Ναβαρίνου)

If you imagine Navarino Bay as forming the arch of some great bow, then the island of **Sfaktiria** (Σφακτηρια) forms the taut bowstring across its entrance. It only allows access to the bay at its two extremities: to the north is a thin, shallow channel, only accessible to the smallest of fishing boats; to the south a kilometre-wide gap is studded with rocky islets and watched over by the Neokastro above Pylos. Inside, the bay is 5.5km long and up to 3km wide, and reaches a depth of 55m. It sometimes feels that the bay is a natural theatre, and was just waiting for great events of history to take place on its stage.

If you want to explore further then **boat trips** run around the bay from the harbourfront in Pylos. These tend to wait until they have four to seven people before they go, so you may be out of luck if you turn up on your own out of season (€10–20pp). These trips tend to focus on the various **memorials** to the Battle of Navarino that dot the islands in the bay. The British one is on the small islet of Chelonaki ('Turtle') in the centre of the bay. The French one is up a long staircase on one of the rocky crags to the south of Sfaktiria. The Russian one is on the main island and includes a wooden chapel, built entirely without nails. On a calm day you will also be able to see the **Turkish wrecks**, still littering the bottom of the bay.

Gialova Lagoon

Just to the north of Gialova, on the main road, is the left turn towards this fabulous lagoon, now a part of the European NATURA 2000 network (page 9). The road runs along the edge of **Golden Beach**, whose sandy shores have lovely views back towards Pylos. If you want to know more about the lagoon you are best to head for the **Old Pump House**, which is manned during spring and summer days by knowledgeable volunteers, and is next to a **nature walk** with informative boards in English and Greek.

Gialova is a natural paradise, home to over 265 varieties of bird (79 of which are protected), 26 species of reptile, 16 of fish, and 28 different types of mammal. It is also heart-stoppingly beautiful. It is extraordinary to think that it was almost all destroyed. In the 1950s, as part of a national plan to increase agricultural land and reduce malaria (both much-needed ends to be sure), the government attempted to drain the lagoon. Thankfully they failed, but its size was reduced by a third.

It is not out of danger yet. In recent years it was discovered that the lagoon was the only European habitat of the endangered African chameleon (*Chamaeleo africanus*). Almost as soon as the discovery was made, the small population started disappearing to the exotic pet stores of Athens. Now it barely exists here.

As you explore this unique environment take care to disturb as little of it as possible. Prominent signs give advice on how to do this.

Voidokilia Beach and the Paleokastro (Βοιδοκοιλία & Παλιόκαστρο) The best way to explore the area around this superlative beach and dramatic castle is to enjoy the walk described on page 222, which should be done over a leisurely half to a whole day, including swimming and a picnic.

If you don't have the time for this, then the **Paleokastro** ('Old Castle') is most easily approached from Gialova. Follow the main road into the lagoon area with Golden Beach on your left; a path leads up to the castle from just beyond the car park at the end of the road. It takes about 15 minutes to get up to the castle. Signs warn that the castle is closed as it is dangerous – it is possible to explore it, but do take care.

You will probably have already seen a picture of **Voidokilia Beach**; it is a common postcard subject. It does look like it has been magically transported here from the Caribbean or the South Seas: a golden crescent of sand lapped by azure waters and backed by the lagoon. Unfortunately it can get quite crowded in the high summer and at weekends. Come here in the spring or autumn, however, and you will likely have this paradise to yourself. The easiest way to get here is to take the left turn (on a sharp right-hand bend) 6km north of Gialova, and then follow the signs past the villages of Romanos and Petrohori.

Above the beach and below the castle can be seen the gaping hole of **Nestor's cave**. An obvious path leads up to it through the dunes at the end of Voidokilia (*10mins*). It was supposedly used as a cattle pen by the wise old king.

Diving There is plenty of opportunity for diving in the area, both snorkelling and full scuba. The **Pilos Dive Center** (*10 Kalamatas, Pylos;* ☏ *27230 22408;* 📱 *69764 37515;* e *pilosmarine@yahoo.com;* w *pilosmarine.com*), next to the Karalis City Hotel, rents out equipment and organise trips. They also offer boat hire.

NORTH OF GIALOVA
Nestor's Palace (☏ *27630 31437;* ⊕ *08.00–15.00 Tue–Sun;* €6) Even if you are just passing through this area you will notice the plethora of brown signs pointing to tholos tombs, the conical, beehive-like grave chambers favoured by Mycenaean nobles. Many of these are nowadays little more than holes in the ground, but their abundance is an indication that 3,500 years ago a great kingdom was centred here, perhaps the 'sandy Pylos' of wise King Nestor that Homer wrote of. The epicentre of this kingdom was probably this palace complex, which stands on the left side on the road north from Gialova towards Hora (Χώρα), and is now widely associated with King Nestor. A fascinating site, it recently reopened after several years' closure for restoration, and is now covered by an impressive curved steel roof and raised walkway (with disabled access) offering a bird's-eye view of the excavations (as well as fabulous views back to Voidokilia, the Paleokastro and Pylos).

The excavations of Troy and Mycenae by Schliemann in the late 19th century, and of Knossos in Crete by Sir Arthur Evans in the early 20th century, had shown that there was a lot more truth to Homer's poetry than had been hitherto supposed. Nestor's kingdom, therefore, was surely worth hunting for as well. The *Iliad* has Nestor sending 90 ships to the siege of Troy, second only to the great king Agamemnon of Mycenae himself.

In 1938 and 1939, the area was surveyed by a joint Greek and American team led by Konstantine Kourouniotis and Carl Blegen. This 'survey' mainly took the form of asking local villagers if they knew of any 'old walls' – a surprisingly effective technique.

One of the sites identified as being promising was the low hill of Epano Englianos, which had sweeping views down to the sea. Blegen decided to dig here first, noting

2½hrs min; mostly easy with 1 hard scramble; no facilities

This walk explores the area around the stunning beach at Voidokilia (which literally means 'Cow's Belly') and the Gialova Lagoon behind it, taking in castles and caves on the way. It's a lovely way to explore this area and not very taxing, especially if, as intended, you take a whole day to complete it: stopping to swim, picnic, or just to enjoy the magnificent scenery.

There is no drinking water anywhere on the walk. Don't forget to take swimming things, and remember not to disturb the wildlife in the lagoon area. If you come out of season the paths around the lagoon can often be in poor condition, sometimes disappearing into the water itself. Also note that mosquitoes can be very active around the lagoon. See the walking guide on page 42.

0mins The walk begins about 800m south of the village of Petrohori, where a small blue-and-white Greek-only sign points to the church of Profitis Ilias (Προφιτις Ηλιας) up a dirt road to the right. If you have driven you might be able to park here; if not carry on to the car park by the beach (200m) and come back.

15mins At the top of the hill is the small, modern church of Profitis Ilias (the prophet Elijah), which has great views both up and down the coast. Head back down the road for a couple of minutes to the second clearing, where an initially indistinct footpath leads into the undergrowth to the right, passing a small cave used as an animal shelter.

27mins You emerge into an open meadow opposite a brown sign that simply reads 'Archaeological Site'. Ignore this for the moment and head right on a path through the trees.

32mins This takes you down to a secret cove, called Glossa, which only has a narrow outlet to the sea. If you swim here watch out for urchins on the rocks. Afterwards make your way back to the brown sign and follow it towards the Tomb of Thrasymedes.

that, 'If I were building a palace, this is where I'd build it.' Digging started on 4 April 1939 and immediately hit pay dirt, discovering the stone walls of a palace and, more importantly, the first five of more than 600 fire-baked tablets with Linear B script on them (see box, page 226).

The remains of the palace are not as immediately impressive as those at Mycenae or Tiryns. There are no great defensive walls, although these may yet be discovered, and the main ruins are just those of the central palace complex. However, these are much better preserved than elsewhere, with walls almost 1m high giving an excellent idea of the ancient floor plan. The building would have been two storeys, with a wooden roof and wooden columns. The profusion of timber aided the fire that destroyed the palace in the 12th century BC (and incidentally hard-baked the Linear B tablets). The modern shelter is meant to reflect where the original roof stood.

You enter the palace past a **sentry tower** to the right. There is also a sentry stand to the left, which may have guarded the two **archive rooms** here. It was in these that the hoard of Linear B tablets was discovered. The entrance leads through a pair of porches to an open-roofed **courtyard**. To the left is a **waiting room**,

39mins Thrasymedes was the son of Nestor, and this tomb, traditionally ascribed to him, is one of the oldest in Greece. It's pretty ruined, but make your way round the fence for lovely views down to the beach. Again make your way back to the brown sign and follow the path down to the beach, where you walk round the sand to the other side, with Nestor's cave and the Paleokastro above you.

51mins Ignore the obvious path up to the cave and instead cut into the dunes about 40m before the end of the beach. There is no set way through; just make for the cliffs below the castle. After about 5 minutes you will find yourself on a delightful flat path that runs by the water of the lagoon immediately below the cliffs.

1hr 6mins Golden Beach begins near the end of this path, but instead of going on it, head round to the right beneath a watchtower, opposite the strait that separates the mainland from Sfaktiria, to start up the path towards the castle. Go to the right whenever the path forks.

1hr 21mins Once in the castle take the path to the right that leads through its centre towards the far wall. Watch your footing among the undergrowth and ruins.

1hr 26mins In the back wall of the castle you will come across a V-shaped notch in the stone, with views over the beach. It is fairly easy to climb down through here to a path that leads downhill. This is slightly precipitous, but is fine in dry weather.

1hr 36mins The path leads down to the entrance to Nestor's cave. From here an easy route leads back to the beach.

1hr 56mins When you reach the far end of Voidokilia, turn right just before the beach ends to the car park, then continue on a dirt road with a river to your left for about 200m before crossing a bridge over the river back to the walk's starting point at the junction for Profitis Ilias.

where supplicants to the king were sequestered before being admitted to the royal presence. It has the air of a doctor's waiting room.

From the courtyard you carry on to the centre of the palace complex, the **megaron** (or throne room) itself. The main feature of this is the great circular **hearth** in its centre. It was surrounded by four columns that supported a balcony above, from where observers could look down on the actions of the court. The throne would have stood on the right-hand wall; next to it is a curious pair of hollows connected by a thin channel into which the king may have poured offerings to the gods. These rooms were originally full of colour, with decorative floor tiles and frescoes on the walls. Behind the megaron can be seen the **magazines** used for storage. The *pithoi*, or large storage jars, which held oil or wine, are still in place. Messinia is still famous for the production of jars such as these.

To the right of the courtyard are a set of apartments that belonged to the king's wife, including the **Queen's Megaron**, a smaller version of the king's, with its own hearth. Next to this is a bathroom, with an evocative terracotta tub still on display. For those who know their Homer it is impossible not to recall his description of Telemachus' visit to the palace:

Just when you think Greek archaeology has lost the ability to surprise, something new always turns up. In late 2015, the discovery of a new grave at the site of Nestor's Palace near Pylos was announced. This, in such a well-explored area, would be news on its own, but what was astonishing was the extent of the findings, with archaeologists saying that not since the 1950s had such a rich tomb been excavated.

The grave is that of a warrior, aged 30–35, and buried around 1500BC along with his bronze sword and a collection of gold rings, precious jewels, gold and silver cups, and beautifully carved seals. Between his legs was an ivory plaque carved with a griffin, from which archaeologists have given him his title.

Not only are the artefacts stunning, but they also provide an important insight into the interplay between Minoan culture from Crete, from where most of the carving seems to emanate, and the Mycenaean civilisation of the mainland. More information is sure to come and DNA extracted from the warrior's teeth could tell us where exactly he was born. For those wishing to explore Nestor's Palace, the site has recently reopened (page 221).

The fair Polycaste, the youngest daughter of Nestor, son of Neleus, bathed Telemachus. And when she had bathed him and anointed him richly with oil, and had cast about him a fair cloak and a tunic, forth from the bath he came in form like unto the immortals; and he went and sat down by Nestor, the shepherd of the people. Now when they had roasted the outer flesh and had drawn it off the spits, they sat down and feasted, and worthy men waited on them, pouring wine into golden cups.

Don't leave the palace without going down to the lower of the two car parks, from where a path leads to a large, restored **tholos tomb**. When it was found the roof had collapsed and it was full of earth, but was cleared out and restored in 1957, and the acoustics underneath the 'beehive' are magnificent.

If you want to get a clearer picture of the palace then a visit to the **museum** (⊕ *08.30–15.00 daily; €2*) in Hora, 4km to the north, is highly recommended. To find it follow the signs toward Kalamata through the town. It is in the outskirts on the left of the road. Its three rooms contain a variety of finds from here and elsewhere. Of particular note are the gold artefacts from the tombs at Peristeria (page 228), fragments of wall fresco from the palace itself that have been reconstructed, and casts of the famous Linear B tablets. There is also an extremely useful model of the palace in its heyday, including its colourful interior.

Up the coast: more beaches and a fairytale castle If you do arrive on an August weekend and find that Voidokilia and the beaches near Gialova are awash with bodies, do not despair. Starting by the villages of **Petrohori** (Πετροχώρι) and **Romanos** (Ρωμανός), and then continuing up the attractive coastal road north, there are a series of long sandy beaches and little coves, often backed by tavernas. The Costa Navarino complex (page 217) is also hidden behind the dunes.

Marathopoli (Μαραθόπολη), 15km north of Gialova on the coast opposite the little island of Proti (Πρώτη), is renowned for its fish tavernas, which line the seafront. These are at their best, and busiest, on a holiday weekend. Look for the one the Greeks are favouring and try and squeeze yourself in.

In the spring of 425BC, the Spartan army was carrying out its annual destruction of the countryside around Athens (for a fuller context of the Peloponnesian War, see page 14), while Athens had sent a fleet of 40 ships around the Peloponnese. On board was Demosthenes (not to be confused with the famed later orator), who built a fortification near modern Pylos in an attempt to incite the Messinian *helots* to rebellion, and to take the land war to the Spartans for the first time.

The Spartans quickly saw the new threat and returned their forces to Sparta after only 15 days campaigning against Athens, the shortest invasion of the war so far. Their fleet, which could get there quicker, was also dispatched.

The Spartans occupied all of the land around the bay, including the island of Sfaktiria, where they sent 420 soldiers. With the Spartans gathering around him Demosthenes recalled the Athenian fleet. Seeing that he would be forced to defend his position while waiting for the fleet to relieve him, Demosthenes sought to encourage his hugely outnumbered troops, reminding them of the difficulties of attacking a well-defended land position from the sea, something the Athenian sailors were well aware of. In the end the Athenians held out for two days. On the third day the Athenian navy arrived and quickly gained control of the bay, isolating the 420 Spartans on the island of Sfaktiria. This put the Spartans in a terrible position. Although it seems a small number now, it represented a tenth of their army, and a good number of them were from the elite class. Sparta called a truce.

With the benefit of hindsight, Athens should have accepted a final peace treaty at this point, but many opposed this, including Cleon, who was sent with more troops to help Demosthenes.

Initially they tried to starve the Spartans off Sfaktiria, but Spartan *helots*, promised their freedom, managed to get food to them, some even swimming underwater across the small strait from the mainland, dragging wrapped parcels behind them. The Athenian forces now greatly outnumbered the soldiers stuck on the island, but faced the same difficulties of attacking fortified land positions from the sea. They attacked quickly, from both sides of the island. Demosthenes realised that mobility was the key to an attack of this nature. His lightly armed soldiers moved fast to seize the island's high points, from where they harried the encumbered Spartans from all sides, retreating if they came too close. The Spartans made their last stand behind fortifications at the highest point of the island, from where they were dislodged by a Messinian contingent. What happened next was extraordinary. The remaining Spartans laid down their arms.

The reaction to this around the Greek world was spectacular. Spartan soldiers *never* surrendered; they died rather as they had done at Thermopylae. Although they eventually won the war, it was the beginning of the end for the carefully fostered image of the Spartan warrior.

Filiatra (Φιλιατρά), another 11km to the north, is a prosperous market town, with a grand central square and fountain. Driving out of it you might be slightly surprised to see the **Eiffel Tower**, or at least a 12m-high version of it. This is the work of local philanthropist and clear eccentric, Charlambos Fournarakis. To see his crowning achievement look out for the turn to the coastal village of

Agrilis (Αγρίλης). Keep an eye to the left and you will soon spot the **Pyrgos ton Paramithion**, or 'Fairytale Castle', looking like something Walt Disney might have created if he had fallen in love with concrete. It is surrounded by a collection of statues culled from various Greek myths, including a full-size Trojan Horse. Lord knows what wonders await inside the castle, but it remains closed at present.

EAST OF PYLOS

Polilimnio (Πολυλίμνιο) The Polilimnio, or 'Many Lakes', used to be a bit of a local secret, but they are being increasingly recognised as an attraction. Out of season you may well find yourself alone here, but it can be very busy over June to August, when you might be greeted by a stream of people climbing up and down the rocks (most in very unsuitable flip-flops or sandals), and jostling to get changed or take selfies. They're far away from being spoilt, however, and with careful management, and the consideration of visitors, they'll long remain so.

To get to Polilimnio, head roughly halfway along the road from Kalamata to Pylos, then follow the large blue metal road signs that point you through the village of **Haravgi** (Χαραυγή), to the car park (a 10-minute drive from the main road). To properly explore you'll need reasonable shoes and at least a couple of hours. Take water, swim things if it is hot, and a picnic if you fancy it. Do take care if you are going to swim, especially after heavy rains. A cantina, operational in the high season only, stands next to the car park.

DECIPHERING LINEAR B

It is not often that an entire new script is discovered, and the first job, when it is, is to try to find out what the symbols mean. The best-known example is the decipherment of Egyptian hieroglyphics with the help of the Rosetta stone. Less familiar, although perhaps more interesting, is the story of Linear B. The Rosetta stone made things relatively easy, with consecutive copies of the same text in three different languages, two of them known. There was no such 'key' in the case of Linear B.

The tale begins in the late 19th century when Arthur Evans, curator of the Ashmolean Museum in Oxford and an amateur archaeologist, began to come across a certain kind of engraved gemstone on which his sharp eyes discerned various symbols which he believed came from a hitherto unrecorded form of writing. His enquiries into their origin all led in one direction: the island of Crete, at that time still occupied by the Ottomans. Evans travelled to the island in the 1890s and found many more of the stones; the local women called them 'milk stones' and believed they aided fertility.

Evans became convinced that they were the remnants of an important ancient culture, and he knew just where to look for the evidence. A low hill, not far from the Cretan capital of Iraklion, had long been identified as the site of Ancient Knossos, the capital of the legendary King Minos (he of the labyrinth and the bull-headed minotaur) mentioned by Homer. Taking his lead from Heinrich Schliemann (see box, page 69), Evans suspected that the myths had more truth to them than had been assumed. He got his chance to prove it when the Turks began to withdraw from Crete and he was able to purchase the site of Knossos and begin digging in 1900.

Initially just chasing down what he thought was a lost script, Arthur Evans managed to discover a whole new ancient civilisation, called the Minoans,

The lakes, varying in size from bathtub-sized pools upwards, are formed by the River Kalorema ('Beautiful Stream') as it tumbles down a hidden gorge in a series of small waterfalls. From the main car park head down the steep track past the cantina. You also have the option of a rough path through the trees, which is preferable on a hot day. At the bottom you can turn left to explore two reed-choked lakes before the gorge walls close around the river. This section of the Polilimnio is overgrown and mysterious.

More open and full of light is the section to the right. You pass two main pools, and the path gets rougher and rougher, before you get to **Kadi Lake**, into which falls the highest of the waterfalls (roughly 20m high). The path does continue up past this, but it is not for the fainthearted and is almost vertical in places (although iron rungs provide some support). If you don't fancy it there's an alternative route.

Make your way back to the car park and head back towards Haravgi, but take the first left you see, signposted towards Mavrolimna, and follow the main dirt road to another small car park. This is right beside the most accessible of all the lakes, used as the village swimming pool for many years. A path starts from here back towards the other lakes; at first easily, but becoming increasingly difficult. You will find yourself descending a small waterfall, helped by iron rungs, then crossing a plank suspended above the water, before ending up on the shore of **Mavrolimna**, perhaps the most beautiful of all the lakes. You can continue past it to see the climb up from Kadi.

who were clearly at least an influence on the later Mycenaean culture that had recently been uncovered in the Peloponnese. During the excavation of the palace complex he found many baked clay tablets with examples of the script on them, now named Linear B, but he remained unable to decipher them right up to his death in 1941.

Part of the problem had been that Evans was very proprietorial about his discoveries, and was somewhat slow to publish examples of the script, which would have allowed other scholars to help him. This situation was altered in 1939 by the discovery of over 600 more Linear B tablets by Carl Blegen at the Palace of Nestor in the southern Peloponnese. This opened the door to a new, young scholar named Michael Ventris, an architect by trade, but also an amateur cryptologist.

Ventris initially agreed with Evans that Linear B could not possibly bear any relationship to the Greek language. As his work continued, however, during the early 1950s, he came to the surprising conclusion that Linear B was, in fact, Greek, thus pushing the written evidence of the language back by 600 years in one fell swoop. How he reached this impressive revelation is far too complicated to go into here; suffice to say that he was a very clever chap, and was aided by some inspired guesswork.

Unfortunately what was written in Linear B, although hugely valuable to archaeology, proved to be rather mundane. The tablets generally concerned administrative matters, such as how many sheep were owned by such-and-such a person, and it is believed that the use of the script was confined to a limited number of 'civil servants'. Perhaps a new epic poem, or another series of mythological tales, written in Linear B, awaits our discovery, but in all probability it will just be more lists.

Most people travel through the northern part of Messinia without stopping, either on the way up the coast towards Olympia and Patra, or up into the mountains of Arcadia. There are at least a couple of diverting stops, however, and the rural hinterland, as the foothills rise up to the mountains to the north, rewards exploration.

KYPARISSIA (ΚΥΠΑΡΙΣΣΊΑ) The modern part of Kyparissia, laid out in a grid pattern around its harbour, isn't much to look at, although it does have several hotels – one of the better ones is the **Kanellakis** (*20 rooms;* ╲ *27610 24464;* w *kanellakishotel.gr;* **€€€**).

The **old town**, up the hill towards the castle, has more to offer. An effort has been made to celebrate the cultural heritage of the town, and an informative leaflet is available. The various cobblestone paths, fountains and old buildings are well signposted. Most date back to the 18th and 19th centuries, when the town was under Turkish occupation. Near to the castle is the old square, named **Arkadia** (Αρκαδία) after the town's medieval name. A **taverna** of the same name does good food (╲ *27610 24522*).

The **castle** (⊕ *daylight hours*) is a mishmash of Byzantine, Frankish and Turkish remains and is a little scruffy, but the views are exquisite, especially at sunset. On a clear day you can see over to the Ionian Islands. Just past the castle is the town **museum**, which contains folk artefacts, but you'll be lucky to find it open. The building was once the home of Greek poet Kostis Palamas (1859–1943). He composed the *Olympic Hymn*, the official anthem of the Olympic Games.

AROUND KYPARISSIA To the north of Kyparissia, near to the village of **Kalo Nero** (Καλό Νερό), 'Good Water', starts what is perhaps the longest stretch of beach in Greece, and certainly in the Peloponnese. The gravelly sands go on from here, with only a few breaks, almost all the way to Patra, over 150km away. This southern part, which can be accessed at a few points from the road north, is a favoured breeding ground of the endangered loggerhead turtle (*Caretta caretta*), so do not dig or disturb the sand in any way.

In the hills above Kyparissia **Peristeria** (⊕ *08.30–15.00 daily*) is one of Greece's best-preserved tholos tombs, and also where the golden cups now in the Hora museum were found. To get here look for the sign to the right 4.5km north of Kyparissia that goes through the village of Raches (Ράχες).

The site consists of **three tholos tombs** dating back to the 16th century BC. Two of them have collapsed roofs, but the third, and largest, has been expertly restored. You will see its dome poking out of the top of the hill as you approach. The lintel stone above its entrance weighs an estimated 25 tons and inside the conical dome sweeps up to over 10m – a truly impressive piece of construction. Have a careful look at the outside of the entranceway: on the left-hand side two of the highest stones have faint scratched markings on them. The highest represents the branch of a tree, most probably an olive, and the other is a double-headed axe. They are thought to be masons' marks. If so the axe symbol might point to the builders being from Crete (it is commonly associated with Minoan sites), perhaps refugees from the destruction wrought by the eruption of the volcano on Santorini. These marks were initially thought to be birds, giving the tombs their name (*peristeri* means pigeon or dove in Greek).

8

The North

The northern and western coasts have plenty of good beaches, but so does the rest of Greece. In fact there would be no particular reason to come to this area, bar transport links, were it not for the secret that lies inland. For the northern Peloponnese is not only the site of Olympia – the ancient city that housed the original Olympic Games – but it also has mountain landscapes to rival anything in Europe. The hiking is fabulous and just driving around takes your breath away. You can even ski in the winter. Add to that one of the most fun train rides anywhere, and it's worth stopping off for a while.

OLYMPIA (ΟΛΥΜΠΊΑ)

Olympia is by far the most famous site in the Peloponnese. Situated in the northwesterly province of Ilia (Ancient Elis), this is where the most important festival of the ancient world took place, in both Greek and Roman times. And it still has a place in modern world culture. It is here, every four years, that the Olympic flame is first lit (by the power of the sun) before being taken to whichever city is hosting the modern games.

Most ancient ruins in Greece seem to be located in fantastically dramatic locations; think of the Temple of Apollo at Vasses to the south, or Mycenae rising up on its crag of rock, or, indeed, the Parthenon itself. Olympia, in contrast, is set in a lush and bucolic valley, watered by the famous Alphios to the south and its tributary, the Kladeos, to the west. The mighty-sounding Mount Kronos (he was Zeus's father) which lies just to the north of the site is, in reality, a small hill, barely 100m tall. The white columns of the ruins lay below it, shaded not only by the ubiquitous olive, but also by plane trees, oaks and poplars.

The forest fires of 2007 came close to destroying this idyll, turning the hill of Kronos into a charcoal mound and coming within metres of the ruins themselves. They were saved by the concerted efforts of the locals, whether they worked on the site or not, and now the slopes of Kronos have been replanted. Olympia remains a remarkable place, peaceful and romantic, especially in the spring, when wild flowers surround the ruins.

That said, it can also come as something of a disappointment to many visitors. This is partly due to false expectations. Perhaps people anticipate something on the scale of the modern stadiums that are built to host the Games, or at least something comparable to the Parthenon, or the theatre at Epidavros, rather than the somewhat jumbled, and often confusing, ruins that do remain. There is also no denying that the modern village next to the site, while functional, lacks charm or character. On top of this the site itself is often crowded, even first thing in the morning.

Please don't be discouraged. Olympia is a place that repays the effort you put into it. Away from the coach parks and the tourist facilities, the atmosphere of the place still prevails, giving some idea of why the ancients chose the site in the first place. Even on a busy day you will be able to find a quiet corner to sit and

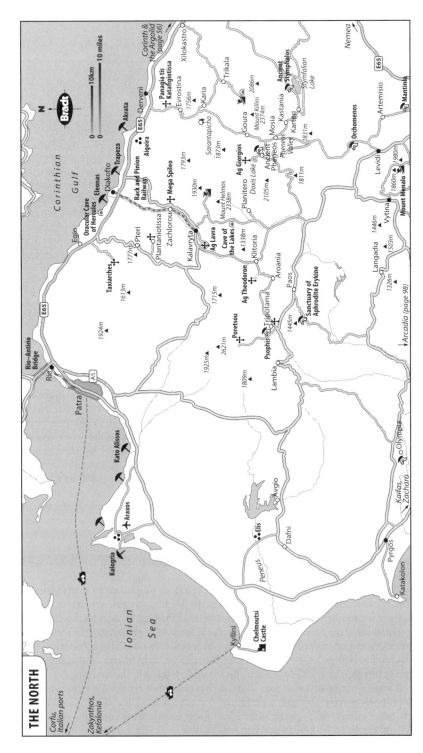

THE NORTH

contemplate the place, and on a cloudy, wet day in autumn you might have the ruins to yourself. The Olympic ideal, peace between states fostered by friendly competition, was difficult to achieve even in Classical times, but here, in this Arcadian glade, you can still feel its power.

GETTING THERE AND AWAY

By car Olympia is 20km from the main coastal road that runs north from Pylos to Patra; the turning is near to the unattractive town of Pyrgos. Coming from the east, a scenic route to Olympia winds through the mountains of northern Arcadia, starting at a junction on the national road 10km above Tripoli. Another attractive route approaches from the north via the back roads through Lalas (Λάλας).

By bus There are numerous buses to and from Pyrgos (*30mins*), three or four of which also serve Patra (*2hrs*) and Athens (*3hrs 30mins*). Two or three buses a day go back and forth to Tripoli (*2hrs 30mins*). The bus station is on the main road.

By train A modern train service covers the 32km between Olympia and the cruise-ship port of Katakolon three times a day (*45mins; €10 round trip*). It makes several stops on the way, including Pyrgos.

WHERE TO STAY *Map, page 232*

The modern village is not very inspiring, but it has plenty of decent hotels. The main reason to stay here is to arrive at the archaeological site as soon as it opens, and get a jump on the tour buses, but even this is hard in high season. You could also consider staying a bit farther afield, especially if you have your own transport. If you want to stay on the coast, avoid Pyrgos, which vies with Megalopoli and Tripoli as the Peloponnese's most boring town; rather head further south to Zacharo, which has a few beachside options.

Olympia town

🏠 **Europa** (80 rooms) ✆26240 22650; e hoteleuropa@hoteleuropa.gr; w hoteleuropa.gr. Set on a hill above the village & site, this sets out to be the best hotel in town. Has a pool & a rooftop restaurant. Book online for the best rates. €€€€€

✳ 🏠 **Leonidaion Guesthouse** (8 rooms) 3 Spiliopoulou; ✆26240 23507; e info@leonidaion. gr; w leonidaion.gr. This contemporary-feeling guesthouse is distinguished by its energetic & friendly owner-manager, a funky yet minimalist ground-floor wine bar selling traditional local produce, & the bright, colourful & spacious rooms with balcony & good amenities. A real winner. €€€

🏠 **Hotel Hercules** (11 rooms) 2 Tsoureka; ✆26240 22696; e info@hotelhercules.gr; w hotelhercules.gr. This central budget hotel has small but very clean rooms with TV & a decent ground-floor restaurant. Good value. €€

🏠 **Pelops** (18 rooms) 2 Varela; ✆26240 22543; e hotelpelops@gmail.com; w hotelpelops.gr. Almost 50 years old & still in the same family, this comfortable Neoclassical hotel offers excellent value for money at the quieter end of the village but still within walking distance of the ruins. The large rooms all have a combined tub-shower & wide balcony. The hands-on Greek-Australian owner-managers also offer traditional Greek cooking lessons & can provide good local recommendations. €€

🏕 **Camping Diana** ✆26240 22314; w campingdiana.gr. This is the closest campsite to the ruins & it has a pool. It's a small space, but the owners provide a friendly welcome. €

Further afield

🏠 **Hotel Lambia Ori** (22 rooms) ✆26240 81323; m 69720 92563; e info@lampeia-ori.gr; w lampeia-ori.gr. In the attractive mountain village of Lambia, 40km to the north, this is a modern hotel, but built in stone in the traditional style. €€€€

🏠 **Hotel Rex** (21 rooms) 10 Dimokratias, Zacharo; ✆26250 31221; m 69373 56856; e reservations@rexhotel-zacharo.gr; w rexhotel-zacharo.gr. Although it stands on the main road

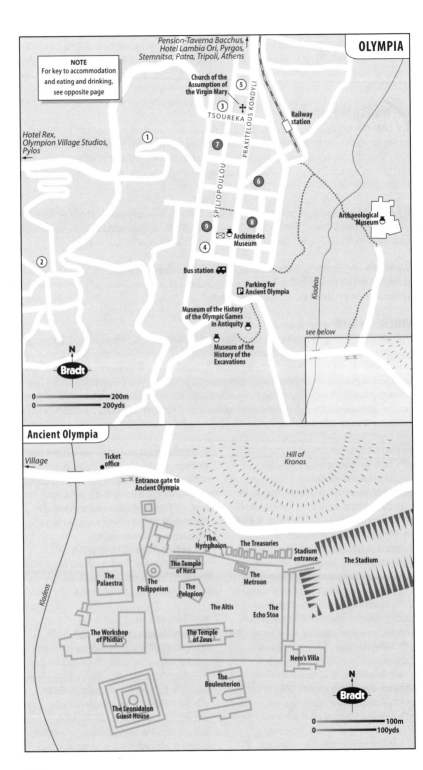

OLYMPIA

NOTE
For key to accommodation
and eating and drinking,
see opposite page

Pension-Taverna Bacchus,
Hotel Lambia Ori, Pyrgos,
Stemnitsa, Patra, Tripoli, Athens

Church of the
Assumption of
the Virgin Mary ⑤

③ ✝

TSOUREKA

PRAXITELOUS KONDYLI

Railway
station

Hotel Rex,
Olympion Village Studios,
Pylos

① ⑦

SPILIOPOULOU

⑥

Archaeological
Museum

⑨ ⑧

✉ Archimedes
Museum

④

Bus station 🚌

Parking for
P Ancient Olympia

Museum of the History
of the Olympic Games
in Antiquity

Kladeos

see below

Museum of the
History of the
Excavations

N

Bradt

0 ————— 200m
0 ————— 200yds

Ancient Olympia

Village ←

Ticket
office ●

✕—✕ Entrance gate to
Ancient Olympia

Hill of
Kronos

The
Nymphaion

The Treasuries

Stadium
entrance

The Stadium

The Temple
of Hera

The Metroon

Kladeos

The
Palaestra

The
Philippeion

The
Pelopion

The Altis

The
Echo Stoa

The Workshop
of Phidias

The Temple
of Zeus

Nero's Villa

N

Bradt

The
Bouleuterion

The
Leonidaion
Guest House

0 ————— 100m
0 ————— 100yds

232

2km from the beach, this modern 5-storey hotel compensates with its warm family-run feel, tastefully decorated & well-equipped rooms & great ground-floor restaurant. **€€€**

🏠 **Pension-Taverna Bacchus** (11 rooms) 📞 26240 22298; **m** 69371 44800; **e** info@ bacchustavern.gr; **w** bacchustavern.gr. Situated in the amusingly named Ancient Pissa, next to the turn-off to Lalas, only 3km out of Olympia, this pension is renowned for the home-cooking & terrace view at its long-serving taverna, but the rooms, built with traditional stone, are also very comfortable & well priced. **€€€**

🏠 **Olympion Village Studios** (15 rooms) Zacharo; 📞 26250 31659. Good budget hotel only 100m from Zacharo's beach. **€€**

WHERE TO EAT AND DRINK *Map, opposite*

The many tavernas interspersed between the gift shops and other cruise passenger bait that lines the main road through Olympia cater almost exclusively to tour groups and tend to be overpriced and low on quality. Fortunately, however, a few excellent little tavernas and restaurants are dotted around the flanking back roads, and it is these that are listed below. Alternatively, you could picnic. There are a few supermarkets about, and the surrounding countryside is surprisingly lovely; try the banks of the river or the slopes of Mount Kronos. Lastly, several of the nearby villages have tavernas desperate for some of the business that the tourist village gets, and prepared to go out of their way to impress.

✖ **Aegean Restaurant** 35 Praxitelous Kondyli; 📞 26240 22540. Set under a shady plane tree, this vegetarian-friendly restaurant just south of the central square dishes up excellent traditional home-style cooking by a skilled Canadian-Greek chef. Summer only.

✖ **Grillhouse Anesis** 13 Spiliopoulou; 📞 26240 22644. The most reasonably priced eatery in Olympia, this unpretentious grillhouse is popular with locals for its generous servings of souvlakia & other meat dishes. Pavement seating available.

✖ **Mythos Family Grill & Taverna Odos** Aimiliou Kountse; **m** 69706 05395. Small family-run taverna serving good-quality souvlakia, seafood & oven-baked dishes.

✖ **Taverna Orestis** 5 Spiliopoulou; 📞 26240 26046; **e** tavernaorestis@gmail.com. Owned by a fisherman who is also a superb chef, this is the place to head to for seafood, but it also does great oven-baked lamb & has a decent vegetarian selection.

OTHER PRACTICALITIES As you would expect from a village that owes its entire existence to tourism, the facilities are good. Pretty much everything you might need is on, or by, the main street, Praxitelous Kondyli, including banks with ATMs, a post office, and supermarkets. Most of the shops are squarely aimed at tourists and several sell English newspapers and books.

There is also a **tourist information office** (📞 *26240 23100;* ⊕ *all day in the summer, more erratically in winter*). It is run by the municipality, rather than the government as is usual, and is a model of what these offices should be, with a good map of the village, accurate transport info, and staff who realise that you are the reason they have their jobs in the first place. There is also a good website at **w** olympia-greece.org.

The original Olympic Games lasted, uninterrupted, for over 1,000 years, making the modern run of just over 100 years, with a couple of suspensions owing to world wars, look pretty flat. They officially started, according to the ancient Greeks, in 776BC, but evidence shows that there was probably some kind of athletic festival taking place here even earlier. The importance of this starting date cannot be overemphasised. The Greeks based their dating system on the four-yearly Olympics, so for them 776BC was literally the beginning of history. Anything before that time was relegated to the field of myth.

The Games started off as a mainly religious festival with an attached running race. This developed over time to have many more events, and an emphasis that increasingly strayed away from its religious origin, while never entirely losing the connection. At its height the Games attracted thousands of spectators, hailing from every corner of the Mediterranean. Most of them camped out in the surrounding countryside. The sport was not the only event they had come to watch. Olympia was also a place where poets and musicians could display their talents to the widest crowd possible. Herodotus, the great historian, was one of the many who orated his work here. Imagine if the modern Games were combined with Glastonbury and the Cannes Film Festival, and then took place in the Vatican!

At its heart, however, remained the athletics. For most of its history the festival was run, and judged, by the population of Elis, the small, nearby, city state (page 240). Every four years they would send out heralds to announce the new Games and the start of the sacred truce that went with them. Surprisingly this was widely kept, and taken very seriously. Small and weak as Elis was, it still had the power to fine mighty Sparta when it infringed the truce.

The centre of the Games were the running races, oldest of all the events. These were run in the stadium by naked athletes (the entire Games were an all-male affair), and were of varying lengths: the most basic was one length of the stadium, about 200m, followed by a race of two lengths, and lastly by an endurance test of 24 lengths, almost 5km. Almost equally prestigious was the pentathlon, which attempted to discover the most all-round athlete with a five-part competition in wrestling, running, long jumping (seemingly done without a run up and while carrying weights), discus throwing, and the javelin.

Other events were also added, including boxing and chariot racing. The latter was the most dangerous of the sports, and often ended in injury or even death. In this it surpassed even the brutal *pancration*, a mixture of boxing and wrestling

WHAT TO SEE AND DO You will rarely find the site and the main museum free of crowds, unless you come on a weekday in winter, and even then a busload of Greek schoolchildren is apt to appear. Fortunately the ruins themselves are large enough to swallow the crowds on all but the busiest days. Not so the museum, however, and it is worth considering visiting this first thing in the morning when there are fewer people around; most tour groups tend to visit the ruins first. Conversely the most peaceful time to contemplate the ruins is often just before the site closes. The other museums at Olympia (page 240) are mostly skipped, and can be visited more easily.

Ancient Olympia (✆26240 22517; ⊕ & entrance fees, see box, page 52) The ancient site is only 200m from the car park at the southeast end of the modern village.

with few, if any, rules. In all of these the victors' only prizes were a palm branch, an olive wreath, and the chance to erect a statue in the Altis, the sacred precinct of Zeus.

One must not imagine, however, that everything was a mix of friendly competition and brotherly love. Politics and money, as in the modern Games, were not far below the surface. Above all, an athlete represented his city, and a win brought high prestige for them both. Accordingly an Olympic champion could expect great fame and also monetary rewards. Cheating and the bribing of judges were not unknown, although never as blatantly as done by the Emperor Nero in the 211th Olympiad. This had already been delayed by two years, to AD69, in order to let Nero take part, and a new contest, in singing, had been introduced just so he could win it. The biggest farce, however, was the chariot race. The emperor competed with a team of ten horses, while the other charioteers had to make do with four. Nero had difficulty controlling this number and fell out of his chariot twice. He was still declared the winner.

Nero would have been horrified to know that it was Christianity that brought an end to the Games. In AD393, Theodosius I declared all pagan festivals to be illegal, and the Games came to an end. Thirty-three years later his successor ordered the sanctuary destroyed, and soon after a church was built over the workshop of Phidias (page 238). A final blow was dealt by the changing course of the nearby rivers, which dumped silt on to the buildings. For much of the last 2,000 years the site was lost under 3m of mud. It was only rediscovered in 1766, by the Englishman Richard Chandler. The bulk of the excavation work was done by German archaeologists.

Partly inspired by the old ruins emerging from the mud, the Olympic Games were revived in 1896, taking place in an unabashedly 'Classical' stadium in Athens. Fittingly a Greek, Spyridon Louis, won the first marathon (see box, page 236). The Greeks thought it was their right to host the centenary of the modern Games, and were furious when it went to Atlanta, Georgia in 1996. When they reapplied to be the hosts in 2004, most people feigned indifference, but there was widespread celebrating when they won. This soon turned to concern when it seemed that nothing would be ready in time and that the Greek nation would be shamed on the world stage. No-one was more surprised than the Greeks themselves when they pulled off a successful and well-regarded set of Games. Unfortunately their legacy has not been quite as impressive, but that is another story.

From the car park, the pedestrianised road there passes below the large Neoclassical Museum of the History of the Olympic Games in Antiquity (page 240), then crosses over the Kladeos River to an area that houses the ticket office and a café. The main site is to the right, while a path to the left leads to the Archaeological Museum (page 238).

Olympia can be a confusing site and, oddly, suffers from too much excavation. Two stones next to each other can come from periods centuries, if not an entire millennium, apart. The trick is not to worry about it too much, unless you are an archaeologist or historian yourself (and sometimes even if you are). Just let the atmosphere of the place soak into you, and concentrate on some of the major features. Obsessing too much on the details, and trying to discern the purpose of every building, will only lead to headaches.

Much of the ruins belong to the **Altis**, or sacred precinct of Zeus, filled with temples to the gods. It was a kind of neutral area, where people from different cities could come together in peace. Entry was only allowed to free-born, Greek (and later Roman) males. As you enter the site from the modern entrance you are at the

SPYRIDON LOUIS

One of the good things about history is that it contains stories that you wouldn't dare make up. One of these is the story of Spyridon Louis; still a hero among the Greeks, this magnificent fellow deserves to be better known elsewhere.

At the revived Olympic Games in 1896 at Athens, one of the premier events was to be the marathon, a re-creation of the feat of a legendary soldier who had run to Athens to announce the Athenian victory in the Battle of Marathon, a distance of 42.2km. No-one in modern times had competed over such a large distance.

As the Games progressed the Greeks, while proud to be hosting the events, became increasingly disgruntled that they were not winning anything. Particularly galling was the loss of the discus throw, one of the favourites of the Classical Greeks, to an American. The final event was the marathon, to be ended with a final lap around the stadium in the centre of Athens watched by the Greek king and the two crown princes.

Spyridon Louis, not long out of the army, was a poor farmer's son, who made his living on the streets of Athens as a water carrier. Piped water had yet to come to the city, and drinking water was pushed around in large tanks on handcarts. Spyridon's talent for running had been spotted in the army, and with the help of a borrowed pair of shoes he entered the marathon.

At first Spyridon didn't seem to be taking it very seriously, and he stopped in a village taverna for a glass of wine. Nonchalantly asking how far ahead the other athletes were he confidently said that there was plenty of time to catch them up. It was not his only stop; his run was also fuelled by milk, orange juice, a red, hard-boiled egg (traditional at Easter), and a beer.

The leader of the race was an Australian named Edwin Flack, who had already won the 800m and 1,500m, and when a cyclist announced this to the crowds waiting in the stadium a wave of anxiety came over them.

Slowly, however, as he had predicted, Louis was catching up. In one last dramatic turn, Flack, not used to running such distances, collapsed only a few kilometres from the finish line. When Spyridon Louis entered the stadium as the leading runner the crowd erupted. The two royal princes ran down on to the track and completed the final lap with him. Even the foreigners present were caught up in the wave of Greek pride and emotion.

Presenting him with his medal, the Greek king is said to have offered Spyridon any gift he might desire. After a short moment's thought the athlete replied that a donkey would be nice, to help him pull his water cart through the Athenian streets.

Spyridon Louis never took part in a competitive race again, preferring to live a quiet life. His last appearance in the public eye was as an old man at the 1936 Olympics in Berlin, where, dressed in full Greek traditional costume, he led the national team in. Presented to Adolf Hitler he gave the dictator a gift of an olive branch from Ancient Olympia, a token of peace. Spyridon died before war broke out, never knowing how forlorn his gift would become.

northwest corner of the Altis, which was originally walled and was roughly a square shape with sides about 150m long. Bearing left will take you into it.

The first building you see of any note is the circular **Philippeion** with some restored columns. If your head is full of the Olympic ideal, then this monument might give you pause. It was started by Philip of Macedon to commemorate his victory over the rest of Greece in the Battle of Chaironeia (338BC), and probably finished by his son, Alexander the Great, a man not noted for his love of peace and democracy. The inside originally held statues, covered in gold and ivory, of Philip, his parents, his wife Olympias, and their son Alexander.

Continuing onward, with the Hill of Kronos rising on your left, you come to the **Temple of Hera**. This is among the best preserved of all the remains at Olympia, which is a little surprising as it is also the oldest. It was started in the 6th century BC, and was originally made of wood. The wooden columns were slowly replaced by stone ones as they rotted over the course of the years. This was a long drawn-out process, and a wooden column survived even when Pausanias visited here (2nd century AD). The remarkable statue of Hermes, now in the museum, was found in the temple. The low mound to the south is the **Pelopion**, or Grove of Pelops, dedicated to the first hero of the Games (see box opposite).

To the right of the temple is the semicircular **Nymphaeum of Herodes Atticus**. Herodes was a wealthy Roman philanthropist who lived during the reign of Hadrian (AD117–138). The source of his wealth was the chance discovery by his father of pots of cash buried beneath their house, something we can all dream of. His son paid off their luck by building public works all over the empire. This particular one was a fountain, providing clean drinking water to the spectators of the Games. It was here that the fires of 2007 approached closest to the ruins, burning down to the base of the hill just over the small road behind the fountain.

Also beneath the hill, and leading along from the fountain, is a row of **treasuries** dating from c600–450BC. Built like small temples, they were set up by various cities and were full of offerings to the gods. Their main, secular, purpose was to act as advertisements to a city's wealth and power. The ruined temple in front of them was the **Metroon**, dedicated to the mother of the gods.

The treasuries lead on to the passageway into the **stadium** itself. Originally a vaulted corridor, only one arch of this remains, but it is still not too hard to imagine the roar of the crowd as you pass under it. The stadium was actually a fairly simple affair. It had no seats and the spectators merely lined the grassy banks that surrounded it (it is estimated they could number up to 45,000) as well as perching on the hill above. The start and finish lines still remain, and it is hard to resist having a quick sprint. To be authentic, remember that Classical athletes used a standing start (you might want to ignore the running in the nude bit, though). The fact that the 2004 Olympic shot put finals were held here was somewhat marred by a drugs scandal. Nero would have probably approved.

Running south from the entrance to the stadium is the scant remains of the **Echo Stoa**, a once impressive colonnade built in about 350BC. It got its name because of the echoes that would repeat themselves seven times within the building. Beyond it are the remains of **Nero's Villa**, built in the 1st century AD for the cheating emperor.

Turning back west, and into the site, the dominant building in the centre of the Altis is the **Temple of Zeus** (c470BC), set on a massive platform. It is one of the largest temples in mainland Greece. The outside was covered with sculptured pediments, many of which can still be seen in the museum (page 238). Inside was one of the Seven Wonders of the ancient world, the **Statue of Zeus** carved by Phidias, the most famous sculptor of the ancient world. The main structure of the statue, which stood 12m high, was in fact plain old wood, but this was covered in ivory to represent skin, and then highlighted with sheets of gold. The seated god held a figure of Nike, the goddess of victory, in his right hand, and an eagle-topped sceptre in his right.

The statue has long been lost, but various odd stories are connected to it. In 167BC, the King of Syria, according to Pausanias, dedicated a 'woollen curtain' to the statue. Many believe this to have been the veil that covered the Holy of Holies in the temple of Jerusalem. During the reign of Julius Caesar the statue was struck by lightning, an odd fate for the thunder god. Caligula, never counted among the saner of the Roman emperors, wanted to replace Zeus's head with his own countenance, but whenever this was tried the statue, disconcertingly, erupted into laughter. Eventually, after the destruction of the sanctuary, it was carted off to the new imperial capital at Constantinople. Here it is said to have been destroyed by a fire in AD475.

South of the temple, and outside the Altis, lie the ruins of the **Bouleuterion**, or council chamber, where, among other things, the athletes swore that they would not commit any foul play during the Games. The large, jumbled ruins to the east are the **Leonidaion**, a luxury hotel and exact ancestor of the many in the modern village.

Heading back north, towards the site entrance, you pass a 5th-century AD **Christian basilica**. The main interest of this is that it was built on top of the studio where the sculptor Phidias worked. This was proved by the mass of artist's materials found here, as well as a cup with the great man's name on it (now in the museum).

The last major ruin you pass, on the left as you come back towards the site entrance, is the **Palaestra**, a large, colonnaded, square structure. This was used for the athletes' training, as well as being a place where they could meet and socialise.

The Archaeological Museum ☏ 26240 22742; ☉ see box, page 52; entrance included in the archaeological site ticket) The museum is reached by the 200m path away from the site, past the Hill of Kronos. It had a facelift in time for the 2004 Olympics and, having survived the 2007 fires, remains spick and span. For a smallish museum it has one of the finest collections in Greece, if not the world.

The entrance hall contains a good model of the site, and the first of many information boards that are all well presented and translated into English. The staff here can also give you a useful leaflet describing the museum. The general plan is to present finds chronologically, starting with the prehistoric period in the room to the left, and proceeding round in a clockwise direction to the final years of the sanctuary, which are in the room to the right. The highlights are the sculptures that surrounded the Temple of Zeus, which fill the large central room, and two superb statues, which each have a room to themselves at the back of the museum.

The first of these, in Room 6, is the **Nike of Paionios**, the Greek goddess of victory (yes, the trainers are named after her). It dates from the 5th century BC, and was probably dedicated by the Messinians who helped Athens defeat Sparta on the island of Sfaktiria in 425BC (see box, page 225). The statue originally had wings and is shown swooping down from the heavens. Her dress billows around her, barely disguising the shape of the goddess's body, and it is a highly sensual piece of sculpture.

The second of the famous statues is in Room 8, and is the **Hermes of Praxiteles** found in the Temple of Hera in 1877, exactly where Pausanias said it was 1,700 years previously. It is most probably a Greek sculpture from the 4th century BC, and represents the acme of their style. Hermes is having a rest while carrying his young brother Dionysus, another product of Zeus's infidelities, away from the jealous Hera. He leans nonchalantly against a tree trunk, entirely nude, and representing the ideal athletic figure. Dionysus is shown reaching for whatever is in Hermes's missing right hand. Knowing the god's later interests, it might well have been a bunch of grapes.

The **monumental sculpture** from the Temple of Zeus is laid out in the central Room 5, in such a way as to suggest how it was laid out on the temple itself. It consists of two scenes from the **pediments**, the triangular spaces formed under the roof at each end of the temple, and the **metopes**, square panels that decorated the area under the pediments. The scenes from the **east pediment** are, perhaps, the least interesting, and are executed in the aptly named Severe style, dating from the 5th century BC. They depict the start of the chariot race between Pelops and Oenomaus (see box, page 12). The large central figure is Zeus, with Oenomaus to his right, and Pelops to the left. The two characters at either edge of the pediments are personifications of the two rivers of Olympia, the Alphios and the Kladeos.

The **west pediment** is a bit more fun, and depicts a common subject in Greek art, the fight between the Lapiths and the Centaurs at the wedding feast of Pirithous. The centaurs, half-man and half-horse, got drunk and began to assault all the women present (and the boys, as well). You can see that one of them has, rather impolitely, grabbed the bride by the breast. The large central figure is the god Apollo, who has come to help the Lapiths, who represent civilisation, against the Centaurs, emblematic of savagery.

The 12 **metopes** represent the **Twelve Labours of Heracles** (page 10). It is fun to try to avoid the labels and guess which Labour is which just from the sculptures, a much harder task than you would think as some are very fragmentary. It is worth remembering that these would have originally been brightly painted, as were the pediments and most other Greek sculpture.

Other museums Olympia houses a couple of other museums, which are mostly overlooked by the visitors who are carted in and out by tour bus. If you are here for a little longer they are worth checking out, especially the first two.

Newest and arguably the most interesting is the private **Archimedes Museum** (*9 Praxitelous Kondyli;* m *69318 31530;* e *kkotsanas@hotmail.com;* w *archimedesmuseum.gr;* ⏰ *10.00–15.00 Mon–Sat all year through & 11.00–15.00 Sun in summer only; free entrance*), which focuses on the many innovative engineering, mathematical, astronomical and other scientific achievements of its Sicilian-born namesake and his near contemporaries. Listed second in FlightNetwork's 2018 list of Europe's Best-Kept Secret Museums, it is an absolutely fascinating installation, incorporating working re-creations of the world's first robot (an 'automatic servant' dedicated to pouring wine designed by Philon of Byzantium), a proto-cinema (the automatic theatre of Heron of Alexandria), and various artefacts designed by the great Archimedes, an innovator cited as an inspiration by such post-renaissance giants as da Vinci, Galileo and Newton. Don't miss it, and despite its small size, allow at least an hour to take it all in.

The **Museum of the History of the Olympic Games in Antiquity** (✆ *26240 29119;* ⏰ *mid-Apr–Oct 08.30–20.00, Nov–mid-Apr 08.30–15.00 daily*) was set up in time for the Athens games in 2004, and was clearly named by someone with a fondness for pithy titles. It is housed in the old museum building, on the way from the village to the ancient site. The collection is surprisingly large and interesting, and attempts to give a rounded picture of how the ancient Games operated, using a thematic approach.

The small **Museum of the History of the Excavations** (✆ *26240 20128;* ⏰ *mid-Apr–Oct 08.30–20.00, Nov–mid-Apr 08.30–15.00 daily*) is just next door. Its chief interest to the non-archaeologist are the photos of the site before it was entirely dug up.

The coast west of Olympia Comprising an almost continuous beach, mostly backed by dunes, the coast west of Olympia is accessible at various points, and there are also a few low-key 'resorts' which would make pleasant places to stay and are within striking distance of the ruins at Olympia. This stretch of coast is a nesting ground for the loggerhead turtle, so try not to disturb the sand too much.

About 25km south of Pyrgos the waters of the sulphurous lagoon at **Kaiafas** (Καϊάφας) are known for their spa-like qualities. Unfortunately the facilities here have seen better days. The dune-backed beach, however, is superb – park near the dusty old train station of Kaifas.

To the south of the lagoon is the resort town of **Zacharo** (Ζαχάρω), which is almost as sweet as its name implies (it means 'sugar'). There are lots of options to stay here, many of which are close to the beach (page 231).

Katakolo (Κατάκολο) is on the coast near Pyrgos and serves as the port of Olympia for the many cruise ships that visit. It is pleasant enough, and has some good beaches nearby, but needn't detain the non-cruising visitor.

ANCIENT ELIS (ΗΛΙΣ)

The ruins of the city that once ran the Olympic Games are near the village of Avgio (Αυγείο), inland of the main road north from Pyrgos towards Patra. Look out for the signs as you head through the village; you probably want to go to the museum first, before heading towards the ruins themselves. The museum (✆ *26220 41415;* ⏰ *08.00–15.00 Tue–Sun; €2*) is in the nearby village of Ilida (Ηλιδα) and comes as a bit of a surprise. If you have made it this far – and you really need your own transport to do so – you will feel like you are in a rural backwater. To then find a large, modern museum in this small village is a shock. Inside, however, reality takes back over and you discover that the finds on display don't really live up to the impressive exterior. Still, it's worth a stop, if only for the English leaflets that the friendly staff provide, which will make your visit to the ruins more illuminating.

Head back towards Avgio and then follow the signs for the **ruins** themselves (⏲ *08.00–15.00 Tue–Sun*). The road passes straight through the middle of these; park next to the old museum. You can follow a roughly circular path from here, past the grassy theatre and other scattered remains. Mapboards provide additional information to that on the leaflets. While the site is not spectacular, it is rural and peaceful, and you are likely to be able to soak up the atmosphere on your own.

Since you are already here, it might be worth heading just a little bit further in order to explore the isolated remains of a **Mycenaean cemetery**. Be warned, however, that this is one for archaeology fanatics only. Head south past Avgio for about another 8km to the village of Dafni (Δάφνη). Just outside the village large brown signs will point you up the concrete road towards the cemetery. This soon turns to dirt, but is driveable. Head straight until a white sign points up a concrete road to the left (you are best to park here and walk the last 100m). If you reach a small chapel on the right you have gone too far, although this would make a great picnic spot, with benches, shade and a great view. The cemetery itself is little more than a few shaft graves (short, horizontal tunnels) dug into the hillside. It is enclosed, but you can scramble in around the back if you want to explore – you'll feel like a proper archaeologist, or possibly a grave robber. The last of these is not too much of a stretch. In 2012, during the financial crisis, it was discovered that someone was trying to dig up the cemetery, presumably in the hope of finding buried treasure. In a heartening sign the local villagers, who gain nothing from this unknown ancient site near their land, spent ten consecutive nights camped out around the cemetery in order to protect the site.

THE COAST FROM PYRGOS (ΠΎΡΓΟΣ) TO PATRA (ΠΆΤΡΑ)

There are plenty of places to stop and stay on the west coast of the Peloponnese when heading to or from Patra, ranging from campsites to huge holiday complexes block-booked by foreign companies. The coastline consists of long swathes of sandy beaches, but there are other reasons to stop off along this route, including one of the most impressive castles in the Peloponnese, an isolated Mycenaean citadel and a transport 'hub' if you are heading on to the Ionian Islands.

CHELMOUTSI CASTLE (⏲ *08.30–15.00 Tue–Sun; €3*) This used to be a rather forlorn, if romantic, place. It's a great Frankish ruin visited only by bats and the occasional eccentric tourist. Without your own transport it's still a bit of a mission to get to, but several years of restoration have perked the place up a bit, the downside being a ticket booth. The ruins, with a hexagonal keep inside the outer walls, and great vaulted chambers where knights and their ladies once feasted, are impressive, and the battlements, famous for their views towards the Ionian Islands, are a highlight. It was originally built in 1220 by Geoffrey I de Villehardouin.

KYLLINI (ΚΥΛΛΉΝΗ) This is where to catch ferries over to **Kefalonia** (Κεφαλωνιά) and **Zakynthos** (Ζάκυνθος) – there are several services a day and e-tickets can be booked on their website (w *21094 99400;* w *ionianferries.gr*). In medieval times this was a major city, named Clarence, but it is a bit drab now. It has a beach and a few places to stay. One of the few remnants of its past is the **13th-century church** at the working monastery of **Vlachernon** (🕐 *10.00–noon & 16.00–18.00 daily*) – look out for the signs (some the normal brown variety, and some larger and wooden) to the west of the port – which has plenty of Frankish elements.

THE NORTHWEST The extreme northwest of the Peloponnese is normally only visited by those using the small **Araxos airport** (Άραξός). Carry on past it, however, and two unexpected treasures await. First off is a little-visited **Mycenaean citadel** (🕐 *08.30–15.00 daily*) set upon an imposing crag. This goes by a couple of different names, but no-one knows what it was called when it was first built. In Classical times it was called the Dymaion wall, and was believed to have been constructed by Heracles. In more modern times it was simply called Kalogria Castle, after the nearby beach. The site is impressive, with some truly monumental architecture, but perhaps the biggest reward are the extensive views. These stretch down, past a series of marshes that teem with birdlife, to **Kalogria Beach**, a firm favourite of the students and other inhabitants of nearby Patra.

PATRA (ΠΑΤΡΑ)

Despite being the Peloponnese's main city, or maybe because of this, Patra seems to have little to offer the visitor. The city itself is a transport hub, particularly for passenger ferries and cargo coming to and from Italy. The coastal roads that run east, or west and then south, have plenty of reasonable stretches of beaches edging the agricultural land, but not much else of interest, at least at first glance. Dig a little bit deeper, both in town and in its surroundings, and unexpected pleasures begin to emerge.

HISTORY Patra seems to have always been an important crossroads, mainly for trade, but never one of the 'big names' of Greek history, despite, in Classical times, having 'long walls' down to its port, similar to those between Athens and Piraeus.

Its major claim to fame is being the site of the martyrdom of St Andrew. He was crucified, but legend has it he was too humble to be killed in the same way as Christ and insisted that his cross be X-shaped instead. The relics of the saint were given to Pope Pius II by Thomas Palaeologus in 1461. In 1964, Pope Paul VI sent them back to Patra. The relics, which consist of a bit of the saint's finger and the top of his head, are kept in the cathedral where his saint's day is celebrated on 30 November.

GETTING THERE AND AWAY
By car Unless you are desperate to see the city, or are using the ferries to Italy, you're probably best to give Patra a miss. There is now a fast, two-lane bypass that whizzes you past with little difficulty. The **Rio-Antirio Bridge**, completed in 2004, connects the Peloponnese with the mainland to the north and is a surprisingly beautiful construction – it even has its own website (**w** *gefyra.gr*). The current toll for a car is €13.30.

If you do drive in be prepared for a one-way system of Byzantine complexity. Keep your eyes peeled for signs, which are not always obvious. Parking is stressful; there are now large, free car parks by the sea, close to the cathedral of Agios Andreas, but these seem to attract a large transient population, and you wouldn't want to leave your vehicle here overnight. If you are getting a ferry, try to time it so that you spend the minimum time here.

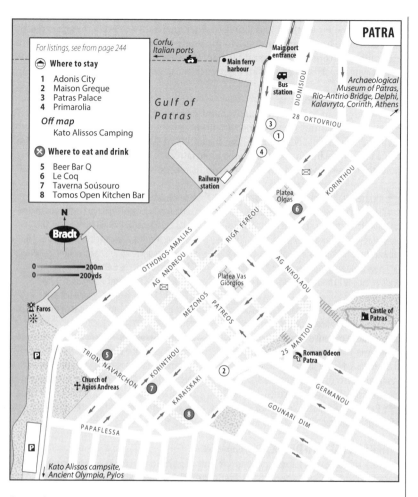

For listings, see from page 244

Where to stay
1 Adonis City
2 Maison Greque
3 Patras Palace
4 Primarolia

Off map
Kato Alissos Camping

Where to eat and drink
5 Beer Bar Q
6 Le Coq
7 Taverna Soúsouro
8 Tomos Open Kitchen Bar

Corfu,
Italian ports

Main ferry
harbour

Main/port
entrance

Bus
station

Archaeological
Museum of Patras,
Rio-Antirio Bridge, Delphi,
Kalavryta, Corinth, Athens

DIONISIOU

28 OKTOVRIOU

3
1
4

KORINTHOU

Gulf of
Patras

Railway
station

Platea
Olgas

6

N

Bradt

0   200m
0   200yds

OTHONOS-AMALIAS

AG ANDREOU

RIGA FEREOU

Platea Vas
Giorgios

MEZONOS

PATREOS

AG NIKOLAOU

Castle of
Patras

Faros

P

TRION NAVARCHON

5

KORINTHOU

Church of
Agios Andreas

7

KARAISKAKI

2

25 MARTIOU

Roman Odeon
Patra

GERMANOU

8

GOUNARI DIM

PAPAFLESSA

P

Kato Alissos campsite,
Ancient Olympia, Pylos

By train The only trains currently departing from Patra only run as far as Rio, just along the coast.

By bus You can get direct buses from here to northern Greece, to several islands including Crete (they go by ferry, in case you were wondering), as well as Romania, Albania and Bulgaria.

For those with more modest ambitions, the most useful services are along the coast towards Corinth (*2hrs*) and Athens (*3hrs*), passing through Diakofto (*frequent; 1hr*), and those heading south towards Pyrgos (*frequent; 1hr 30mins*) and on to Kalamata (*2 a day; 3hrs 30mins*).

There are at least two major bus stations in Patra, as well as some minor ones. Fortunately they are all close by each other, on the harbourside road. The principal one is just to the north of the train station.

By ferry For more on arriving and departing by ferry, see page 33. There are plentiful ticket offices around, including those of the ferry companies themselves, but you are better off organising things in advance over the internet. Your best bet is to head straight for the docks, but be warned there are several of these. Ferries for Italy currently leave from the docks to the south, although the signs try to make you enter the city from the north and then get lost driving straight through the middle of it. Try to check beforehand, and approach these docks from the south if you can.

🏠 WHERE TO STAY *Map, page 243*

Ideally you want to time your arrival and departure from Patra so that you don't have to hang around for too long. If you do get stuck here overnight, options are plentiful, if not hugely inspiring. Noise can be an issue. If you want to get out of town just a little bit, there are close-by alternatives to the hustle and bustle of Patra, both to the east and west, which have rooms places, as well as campsites.

🏠 **Primarolia** (14 rooms) 33 Othonos-Amalias; ☎26106 24900; e primarolia@ arthotel.gr; w arthotel.gr. This central 'art hotel', distinguished by its neat grey façade opposite the railway station, is the place to splash out. Care & skill have gone into its presentation & running, & it seems a bit odd to find it in the bustling streets of Patra. €€€€€

🏠 **Maison Grecque** (8 rooms) 25 Martiou; ☎26102 41212; e info@mghotels.gr; w mghotels.gr. Occupying a converted 19th-century mansion about 5mins' walk inland of the harbour, this characterful & dynamically managed boutique hotel has small but very comfortable double & family rooms individually decorated in period style. €€€€

🏠 **Patras Palace Hotel** (60 rooms) 15 Leoforos Othonos; ☎26106 23131; e patraspalace@gmail.com; w patraspalace.gr. Conveniently located right next to the bus station & close to all the waterfront ferry offices, this 4-star high-rise is a typical city business hotel but very well equipped & reasonably priced (especially if you shop online). €€€

🏠 **Adonis City Hotel** (56 rooms) 9 Zaimi; ☎26102 24213. Adequate budget hotel in a high-rise overlooking the harbour & just by the main bus station. €€

🅰 **Kato Alissos Camping** ☎26930 71249; m 69773 59889; e demiris-cmp@otenet.gr; w camping-kato-alissos.gr; ⏰ closed Nov–Mar. This is currently the nearest campsite to the west (21km) & is well signposted. Reasonable facilities, above a beach. The attached taverna has good views. €

✖ WHERE TO EAT AND DRINK *Map, page 243*

As you might expect for a port town that also holds a large student community, Patra's main culinary speciality is **fast food**. This is no bad thing, and there's some good, informal eating to be had near the port and around the central squares. Good **cafés** can be found round the three main squares, and also up towards the Odeon from Platea Vas Giorgios (which even has a Starbucks on it). For more **traditional tavernas,** try the semi-pedestrianised street of Trion Navarchon that runs up from near Agios Andreas Cathedral towards the Roman Odeon.

✖ **Beer Bar Q** 182 Riga Fereou; ☎26103 46097; m 69075 23528; 🇫 beerbarQ1. Situated just off Trion Navarchon, this lively venue offers an immense choice of draught beer & has a varied international menu. It often hosts live music. The dark interior can get a bit smoky when busy but there's garden seating too.

✖ **Le Coq** Platea Olgas; ☎26105 28777. Inexpensive grilled chicken served in clean & comfortable surroundings.

✖ **Taverna Soúsouro** 45 Trion Navarchon; ☎26106 72522. Established in 1984, this ranks among the very best of the many tavernas on this pedestrian-only street. Very popular with locals at lunchtime, it has a characterful interior hung with old photos & plenty of pavement seating. Strong on grills & seafood, & very well priced.

✖ **Tomos Open Kitchen Bar** 77 Sachtouri; ☎26103 11141; e mixalistomos@gmail.com. Situated opposite a small park at the inland end of Trion Navarchon, this funky fine-dining venue serves beautifully presented Mediterranean fusion cuisine & has a good wine list & pavement seating.

OTHER PRACTICALITIES Car-hire offices cluster around the port and include the usual suspects, but you are likely to get cheaper rates booking online in advance. Tourist police are contactable on ☎26106 95190.

WHAT TO SEE AND DO If you haven't realised by now, Patra is not the best place in the world to hang around. That said, beyond, but not far from, the never-ending chaos that surrounds the port are some reasonably elegant squares. One pleasant option, if you have time to kill, is to install yourself in a bar or café and people-watch. Patra has a large student population, so look for them if you want to be in a trendy spot.

If you have the energy, and it is not a hot day, the climb up the steps to the **castle** (⊕ 08.30–15.00 Tue–Sun) provides good views. A **Roman odeon** (⊕ 08.30–14.30 Tue–Sun), nearby, is often used for modern performances.

The modern cathedral of **Agios Andreas** is not often described as beautiful. 'Striking', 'colourful' or 'gaudy' are frequently deployed, but perhaps just 'big' is the best summation. The saint's head is in a silver reliquary at the end of the right-hand aisle, behind which parts of his cross are displayed.

During Lent, Patra is the venue for one of the biggest **carnivals** in Europe; check w carnivalpatras.gr for details. Be aware that it can be a hard place to travel through, or stay in, at this time.

Archaeological Museum (*36–40 Patras–Athens New National Rd;* ☎ *21636 16100;* ⊕ *08.00–20.00 Tue–Sun; €4*) This modern museum, which opened in 2009, is housed in rather swish buildings on the right-hand side of the main route out towards Athens. The air-conditioned calm that prevails provides a welcome relief from the bustle of the city. The exhibitions are organised under three headings (Private Life, Public Life and Cemeteries). Of particular note are the collection of large Roman mosaics and some fascinating examples of funeral wreaths still in place on the owners' skulls.

THE NORTH COAST

It is possible to whizz along the north coast of the Peloponnese on the national toll road that runs from Patra to Corinth (or at least it will be when they finally make all of the road two-lane, a project that seems endless). If you have time, however, it is well worth getting on to the old road, which tends to hug the coast more closely, and is much more attractive. It also offers several worthwhile stops.

EGIO AND AROUND The town of **Egio** (Αίγιο) is an attractive place, built on three levels above the sea, with some handsome churches and good cafés. The hinterland in the mountains south of Egio is ripe for exploring, and the best way to do this is to head towards the **Taxiarches Monastery** (Μόνη Ταξιαρχών). On the way east out of Egio look out for the signs for the monastery. There are several ways you can head; the most obvious is to the right opposite the Carrefour supermarket. The road will take you past the hospital and then up through the village of Mavriki (Μαυρίκι). Keep following the brown signs, which will take you down one side of a spectacular gorge, across the river, and then up the other side where there is soon a right turn. It is another 6km, through great scenery, to the monastery (⊕ *closed 13.00–17.00, you are best to visit mid morning*) which is set round a pleasant courtyard. Even more rewarding is the old monastery of Leonidas, which can be found by taking the little road onwards. This soon turns to dirt, but is driveable with care, and continues for another 2km. The old monastery clings below to some dramatic cliffs with astounding views down to the 'modern' monastery. To get as high as you can, you climb an impressive freestanding stone staircase, which ends in a wooden ladder – for the brave only.

ORACULAR CAVE OF HERACLES   As you approach Diakofto (Διακοφτό), the coastal terminus for the rack-and-pinion railway to Kalavryta (page 251), look out for where the old road passes beneath the new national road and, unusually, runs south of it for a short period. To the right here (south) is a brown sign to the Oracular Cave of Heracles. Parking is a little tricky, but possible in lay-bys on either side of the site. It is a 5-minute scramble up to the cave itself, which is fairly small, but the views towards the coast are well worth it.

AIGEIRA   There are plenty of places to stay along this coast, not many of which are hugely inspiring (head into the mountains for that), but there are a few camping opportunities. One of them is **Akrata Beach Camping** (\ *26960 31988;* e *info@ akrata-beach-camping.gr;* w *akrata-beach-camping.gr;* **€**). It's a small site, but friendly, and is signposted off the old road. Nearby are the ruins of **Aigeira**, which are well worth hunting out. Look out for the brown sign that initially takes you left (north) of the old road, before turning back and passing under the national road. It then winds upwards for about 5.5km (past an antenna mast) before the site is signposted to the left. Although not huge, the ruins are impressive, not least because of their lovely setting. Not a huge amount is known about the settlement here. The most noticeable remains, including the theatre, date from Hellenistic times (post Alexander the Great), but archaeologists can often still be seen digging here, so we may know more soon. The site is fenced, but often open during the day, and also still viewable if the gate is locked.

KALAVRYTA (ΚΑΛΆΒΡΥΤΑ)

Considering its size – you can easily walk from one end to the other – the little town of Kalavryta ('Good Springs') definitely punches above its weight. It would be well known just for its history, which mixes heroism and tragedy (see below), but it has much more to offer. First and foremost it is the final destination of the wonderful rack-and-pinion railway that snakes up the mountains from the coastal port of Diakofto, a ride not to be missed. In recent years it has also developed into rather a trendy little ski resort (yes, you read that correctly). While most of us don't connect Greece with skiing it is well worth considering if you are here at the right time of year. In the spring the area is a walker's paradise and in the summer its height, 900m, provides a welcome relief from the heat of the lowlands.

There is plenty more. Kalavryta makes a fantastic base for exploring the northern mountains of the Peloponnese, which have only just started to be easily accessible to the traveller. This is changing fast as the Greeks rediscover the delights of their highlands, but this area is still full of little-known gems.

HISTORY   Two events stand out in the history of Kalavryta, and still reverberate in the collective Greek psyche. The first was the official start of the War of Independence against the Turks. The story has it that in the nearby monastery of Agia Lavra, on 25 March 1821, Germanos, Archbishop of Patra, raised the standard of revolt here, surrounded by various local leaders. In fact the precise details of this event are difficult to ascertain, and fighting had in fact broken

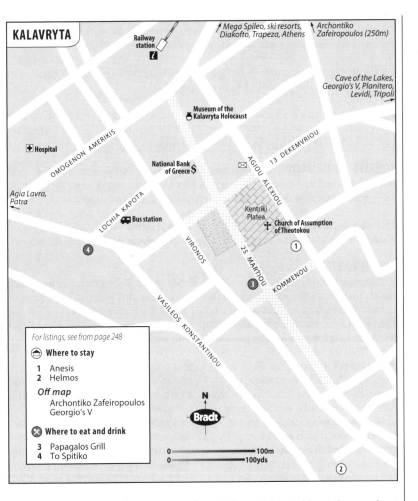

KALAVRYTA

Mega Spileo, ski resorts,   *Archontiko*
Diakofto, Trapeza, Athens   *Zafeiropoulos (250m)*

Railway
station

Cave of the Lakes,
Georgio's V, Planitero,
Levidi, Tripoli

Museum of the
Kalavryta Holocaust

Hospital

Agia Lavra,
Patra

National Bank
of Greece

Kentriki
Platea

Church of Assumption
of Theotokou

Bus station

OMOGENON AMERIKIS

LOCHIA KAPOTA

VIRONOS

25 MARTIOU

AGIOU ALEXIOU

13 DEKEMVRIOU

KOMMENOU

VASILEOS KONSTANTINOU

4

1

3

2

N

Bradt

For listings, see from page 248

Where to stay

1   Anesis
2   Helmos

Off map
   Archontiko Zafeiropoulos
   Georgio's V

Where to eat and drink

3   Papagalos Grill
4   To Spitiko

0   100m
0   100yds

out before this date (Kalamata fell to the Greeks on 23 March). At the very least the raising of the standard was a well-planned propaganda event, rather than a spontaneous act. Nevertheless there is no denying its importance in the collective Greek imagination.

Another, darker, image is also associated with this mountain town. On 13 December 1943, the German occupying troops, in reprisal for the shooting of 78 of their men captured by ELAS guerrillas, rounded up every male member of the town over the age of 15 and massacred them. Exact figures are disputed, but a figure of 696 Greeks killed, along with 25 surrounding villages burnt, is what one reliable source states. What is certain is that it was the worst, but not the only, atrocity committed by the Germans during the occupation. Although the town has now recovered, if not forgotten, it was for a long time a village full of mourning widows.

GETTING THERE AND AWAY

By car The main approach to Kalavryta comes up from the north coast near to the village of Trapeza (Τράπεζα). While it can't compete with the railway, it is a dramatic route in its own right. There are also extremely attractive routes through the mountains on back roads west to Patra and south into Arcadia.

By train The train up from Diakofto (Διακοφτό) is one of the few still running in the Peloponnese and shouldn't be missed (page 251).

By bus There are a couple of buses a day to and from Corinth (*2hrs*), three or four from Patra (*2hrs*) and one from Tripoli (*2hrs*). The bus station is in a small square just to the west of Kentriki Platea (the central square).

TOURIST INFORMATION During the skiing season the best source for local information and advice on all sorts of activities are the various ski-hire shops. There are several of these in town, as well as a couple at the slopes themselves.

Antonopoulos Ski Centre ✆26920 22667
Klaoudatos ✆26920 24464; w klaoudatos.gr

Kokkotis Ski Bill ✆26920 23027
Kosmopoulos Snow Shop ✆26920 22465

WHERE TO STAY *Map, page 247*

Accommodation in Kalavryta is mainly aimed at the skiing community, which means that the normal Greek seasons are reversed and that prices in winter can be almost double those of summer. The hotels in the town are good, particularly the friendly Anesis, but there are also tempting places to stay on the 14km road that winds up to the ski resort. The price indications are for August, as usual.

Georgio's V (15 rooms) ✆26920 24600; m 69447 58595; e info@georgiosv.gr; w georgiosv.gr. Lying about 3km above town, this collection of stone houses is set in a large estate where the owners keep horses. The rooms have fireplaces for winter visitors. €€€€€

Archontiko Zafeiropoulos (15 rooms) 19 Efseviou Kipourgou; ✆26920 24500; m 69720 80291; e info@archontiko.gr; w archontiko. gr. Located within the town centre, this friendly owner-managed 'manor house' has comfortable & well-equipped rooms & suites that lead out on to a pretty garden. €€€€

Helmos (22 rooms & 6 suites) Platea Eleftherias 1; ✆26920 29222; e info@hotelhelmos.

gr; w hotelhelmos.gr. This smart, Neoclassical building has been the main hotel of Kalavryta since it was built in 1922. Unfortunately the restored interior, while comfortable, is a bit anonymous. The suites, if you can afford them, have more character. It is at the opposite end of town to the railway station. €€€€

Anesis (14 rooms) Kentriki Platea; ✆26920 23070; m 69444 60665; e anesis@anesishotel. gr; w anesishotel.gr. Run for the last 20 years by a friendly Greek-Australian family. Each of the rooms has its own character & is decorated with unique artwork. 3 rooms have fireplaces. Set right on the central square. €€€

WHERE TO EAT AND DRINK *Map, page 247*

During the winter there are several tavernas and restaurants that open on the road up to the ski resort, all with roaring fires and superb views. These sometimes open up at the weekends in the rest of the year, but there are also a couple of good options in town. Another place to head for, if you have transport, is the village of **Planitero** (Πλανητέρο), where a grove of large plane trees surround the springs of the Ladonas River. Various tavernas have grown up here, specialising in trout from the river. They are most likely to be open on weekend and holiday lunchtimes.

Papagalos Grill ✆26920 29400. A cheap-&-cheerful grillhouse on the central, pedestrian

street of town. The 'Parrot' of its name entertains from a corner cage.

✕ To Spitiko ✎ 26920 24260. Opposite the bus station, this is the locals' choice, either spilling out on to the pavement on summer nights, or in the cosy interior. The soups are particularly recommended, but it is worth watching out for the lamb offal soup (a sovereign hangover cure, but not for the fainthearted).

OTHER PRACTICALITIES Taxis (✎ 26920 22127) tend to hang out on the roads near the central square, and the post office and National Bank with an ATM are also just by here. There is a **health centre** (✎ 26920 22222) on the main road in and out of town, not far past the train station if you are coming up from the coast. Most other useful shops can be found on the main pedestrian street that runs through the central square. It also has several gift shops that sell 'mountain' products (look out for the local sweets made from rosehip) and a bookshop that has maps and sometimes English newspapers.

WHAT TO SEE AND DO The recently introduced Kalavryta CityPASS costs €24.80 and includes a return trip on the rack-and-pinion railway between Kalavryta and Diakopto (valued at €19), as well as entrance to the Holocaust Museum and Cave of Lakes, and a free ride on the ski lift to the Mount Helmos resort. The pass can be bought at the railway stations in Kalavryta, Diakopto or Patra.

Museum of the Kalavryta Holocaust (✎ 26920 23646; w dmko.gr; ⊕ 09.00–16.00 Tue–Sun; €3) The museum that commemorates the massacre is housed in the old school building on the pedestrian road between the railway station and the central square. It was in this very building that the town's population was gathered on 13 December 1943. The men over 15 years old were separated from the women and infants and led out through the main door of the school. It closed behind them and their wives and children never saw them alive again; the door has not been reopened since that day. The last room of the museum contains a wall of photos of those who were killed.

Two other memorials to the massacre can be seen in the town. The first is the large white cross on the hillside above, and the second is the clock of the main church, stuck forever at 14.34, the time of the deaths.

Agia Lavra (Αγ Λαύρα) (⊕ variable opening hours, the morning is best) The monastery where Greeks proclaimed their freedom from the Turks is about 5km southwest of Kalavryta, close to an imposing monument to the same event. It has been rebuilt several times over the years and, to be honest, there is little of interest for the visitor. If the small museum is open you can see the flag that Archbishop Germanos raised. It depicts the Assumption of the Virgin Mary and was made in Smyrna (now Izmir in Turkey) in the 16th century.

The **old monastery** can be reached by walking up a path to the left, shortly past the modern one. You can see the ruins of its 10th-century church and some badly damaged frescoes.

Mega Spileo (Μέγα Σπήλαιο) (⊕ closed in the afternoons) A more worthwhile monastery to visit is the so-called 'Great Cave', 8km north down the road towards the coast. It is also fairly modern (it burnt down in 1934 when a powder magazine left over from the War of Independence exploded), but the situation more than makes up for it, with the buildings clinging to the side of a tall, overhanging cliffside. It looks rather like the hideout of a Bond villain.

The story goes that it was founded in AD362, when the monks Symeon and Theodorus were led to the cave by a shepherdess and found within it an icon of the Virgin Mary, painted by St Luke himself. The icon performed many miracles, including blasting an evil serpent with fire.

The monastery is an extremely rich one and some of its treasures can be seen in the small museum within. Just past this is the monastery church, carved into the rock. The icon is hung here, a dark relief image of wax and wood. Despite the story it probably 'only' dates back to the 10th century. Past the church is the cave itself, where the icon's discovery and miracles are represented with cardboard cut-outs. The dripping water here is called the 'tears of the Virgin'.

Often packed with hordes of pilgrims who come here in tour buses, the monastery is an odd mix of the sacred and the profane, the old and the new, and is all the more interesting because of it. Be warned that monks take the dress code for visitors seriously.

🚶 DOWN THE TRACKS

(At least 5–6hrs; medium–hard; water & a taverna at Zachlorou)
This is a long walk, but spectacular and well worth the effort. Beginning at the railway station in Kalavryta, you simply follow the tracks all the way down to the coast at Diakofto (just over 22km away). If you time it right you can have a quick dip and then catch the train back up, with the smug knowledge that you have had a much closer view of the wonders of the gorge than any of the other passengers.

It seems odd to be walking on a railway track, but this is, in fact, part of the cross-Europe E4 hiking trail (another part of which is covered in the walk on page 141) and the train drivers are used to seeing hikers on the rails. In the narrow sections they hoot their horns to give walkers plenty of warning, and there are always spaces by the side of the track to shelter in, even in the short tunnels. Nonetheless it is a good idea to study the timetable so that you know roughly when to expect trains, and have a good listen before heading through the tunnels. Torches might be a good idea for these tunnel sections, but are not vital. Water is available at Zachlorou, which is a bit over a third of the way down, as well as other drinks and food. See the walking guide on page 42.

0mins The walk begins at Kalavryta railway station, where you simply begin to follow the tracks – you can't get lost on this walk! You start off on the flat, fertile plain that surrounds the town.

40mins A road crosses the railway track on its way up to the village of Rogi. The main road is still above you on the right, but out of sight, and the Vouraikos River is below on the left.

55mins Not far past Kerpini station you come to the first bridge, an arched metal structure surrounded by forest. You cross it on a central walkway.

1hr 13mins Another road crosses the railway track and then runs parallel to, but above, it, towards Zachlorou. Cliffs begin to close in on the left while the river flows through the forest to the right.

1hr 31mins You pass the ruins of an old stone bridge to the right, and can trace the old, pre-railway path on the other side of the river. Cliffs begin to close in from the right as well, and the river descends in a series of small waterfalls.

The rack-and-pinion railway (☎ 26920 22245 *(Kalavryta), 26910 43206 (Diakofto)*; **e** *odon totos@yahoo.gr*; **w** *odon totos.com*; *€9.50 one way*) This short section of railway, just over 22km between Diakofto on the coast and Kalavryta, runs up the gorge of the Vouraikos River and, with its tunnels and bridges, ranks as one of the most entertaining and spectacular train rides in Europe. It was built by Italian engineers, who were used to planning routes through the Alps, between 1885 and 1895, and was officially opened by the Greek king George I on 10 March 1896. The carriages were pulled by narrow-gauge steam trains until the 1960s when they were replaced by diesel engines (you can see one of the originals at Diakofto). At the steepest sections of the line the trains are pulled up the slope by a rack-and-pinion system – the 'teeth' as the Greeks put it. The track underwent extensive repair

1hr 36mins You arrive in Zachlorou and cross a bridge to where there is a taverna and the station. An outside tap provides drinking water.

1hr 51mins The first section of rack, or 'teeth', starts, dropping steeply down as the valley opens up. The river is down to the left, audible, but generally out of view.

1hr 56mins You cross a bridge and the rack ends. Shortly after this another bridge spans a tributary to the main river.

2hrs 1min The first tunnel goes through the rock next to the 'Portes', the narrowest part of the gorge. An abandoned bridge crosses the gorge to a tunnel that partially collapsed and was replaced after World War II. The new bridge crosses after another section of tunnel. Shortly after, another rack begins.

2hrs 16mins You reach Triklion station, where there is a place where trains can pass each other. Shortly after you cross the river again.

2hrs 34mins The last, and longest, section of rack begins just before a short tunnel.

2hrs 44mins A long, slightly vertiginous, bridge crosses the river.

2hrs 57mins Cross back to the left-hand side of the river past some dramatic waterfalls. From here the railway passes through a series of tunnels and overhangs.

3hrs 2mins Look out for a cave in the cliffs to the right. It is called the 'courtroom' by the locals and the stalagmites are supposed to represent the judge, jury and other characters.

3hrs 7mins You cross the last of the bridges. The gorge starts to widen and the rack ends. The last tunnel has the Greek royal crest over it, and the date 1890.

3hrs 27mins The gorge narrows for the last time. When it opens up again look back up it for a dramatic view. The railway levels out as it approaches Diakofto.

4hrs 7mins You reach the final station. If you want a swim, there is a beach if you go straight ahead and then to the right.

a few years back, in order to introduce new rolling stock, and only started to reopen in late 2008. There are now five trains a day at weekends and in the high season, starting from Diakofto at 09.05, and with the last one returning from Kalavryta at 17.23. Out of season there are still three trains daily, with the last one down at 15.28.

Perhaps the best way to explore the railway and the gorge is to hike down it and then catch a train back up (this is described in the walk on page 250). At the very least you should plan a stop in the village of **Zachlorou** (Ζαχλωρού) at roughly the halfway point. This sleepy and isolated hamlet only really comes alive when the train passes through. The monastery of Mega Spileo is in the hills above (a 45-minute walk up a path, although occasionally taxis meet the train). The charming, and quirky, taverna of **Romantzo** (↖26920 22758; m 69442 58506) is almost on the train track, and you could even rent simple rooms here.

Mount Helmos ski resort (Χελμός) (↖26920 24451; e mail@kalavrita-ski.com; w kalavrita-ski.gr; €25 for a lift pass, €20 per day for equipment hire) On the slopes of Mount Helmos (2,338m), just 14km from Kalavryta, is this small but popular ski resort. It is known for its spectacular views with slopes starting at 1,650m. It offers 12 runs with a total length of 20km and catering to all levels of skier, served by seven ski lifts that can accommodate up to 5,000 people in an hour.

There are two ski lodges, and the higher lodge provides a magnificent view of the Gulf of Corinth. The two main runs are the 1,400m-long Stiga trail 1, and the even longer 2,200m-long Stiga trail 2. The resort is also noted for its off-piste and cross-country skiing.

You are best to rent equipment in the town (page 248), not the resort, as prices are lower. Also, the resort is very popular and can get crowded at weekends.

Cave of the Lakes (Σπήλαιο των Λιμνών) (↖26920 31001; e kastcave@otenet. gr; w kastriacave.gr; ⊕ 09.00–16.30 daily; €9) This cave system, 17km south of

---

ROADSIDE SHRINES

You won't go far on the Greek road system, whether on large national roads, or country back roads of churned earth, without seeing a shrine by the roadside. These vary from a small metal box with a glass door set on a pole, with enough room inside for an oil candle and a small icon, to shed-sized replicas of whole churches done in stone, from which you expect a mini priest to emerge.

There seems to be a lot of misinformation and misconception around the purpose of these structures. Most often you will hear, even from Greek tour guides, that they mark the spot where someone has died in a traffic accident. Their profusion then leads visitors to the country to hardly dare set foot, or tyre, on the roads.

Now, while it is true that this *could* be what a shrine has been placed there for, most likely it is not, and there are countless other reasons why they are set up. A common one, in fact, is to mark a lucky escape from serious injury or death. They are also put up to fulfil obligations made when a prayer is answered. They might also mark the route to a more inaccessible church or monastery that is off the road. This allows a traveller to pay due respect in passing without going out of their way.

In short don't see every roadside shrine as a marker of hideous death and destruction, but do continue to drive safely!

Kalavryta, is an ancient subterranean riverbed. Almost 2km of cave system have been explored, of which about 500m is open to visitors, who are led through on 20-minute tours (the guides don't always speak English, but an information leaflet is provided). They are best seen in the winter and early spring when the 'lakes' fill with crystal-clear water. Human and animal fossils have been found in the caves including, rather startlingly, that of a hippo.

North of Kalavryta
With a vehicle you can undertake a pleasant half day to a day circuit to the west and north of Kalavryta. Head down to the coast via the monastery of Mega Spileo. If you fancy a swim, the beaches at Trapez (Τραπέζα) and Eleonas (Ελαιώνας) are pleasant. Drive west and then near Egio head back into the mountains towards **Pteri** (Πτέρη), marked Fteri (Φτέρη) on some maps and signs. The views from the road are excellent. Pteri itself is surprisingly smart for a mountain village. In the past it was used by the well-to-do people of Patra as a fresh-air getaway, and it still has a few tavernas and places offering rooms.

A bit farther on take a road to the left towards **Plantaniotissa** (Πλατανιώτισσα). Follow the (Greek) signs through the village to the **Church of the Panagia**. This bizarre little structure is built inside a plane tree, and has a glass roof. Inside is preserved a knot of wood that is said to represent an icon of the Virgin and Child. Interestingly this is not too far away from the spot that Pausanias found 'a sacred wood of plane trees, mostly hollow from old age and so huge that parties are given inside the trunks and as many feel like it sleep there afterwards'.

The main road continues south through some lovely mountain scenery, before looping round back to Kalavryta.

South to Arcadia
If you are making your way to or from Arcadia, and you have your own transport, then the mountain roads south of Kalavryta make for some fantastic exploring, and there are a few minor 'sights' to make for – all of them not only well off the main tourist track, but across several fields and over a hill.

The road from **Klitoria** (Κλειτορία) towards **Aroania** (Αροανία) is spectacular, clinging to the mountainsides. Look out for the signed road to the right to the monastery of **Agios Theodoron** which is a large, walled complex that looks potentially very interesting.

As you approach Aroania you can see its large, modern, grey church and surrounding pilgrims' complex. It is more attractive from afar than close to, but the village does boast a smart café.

The scant ruins of Ancient **Psophis** (Ψωφίς) are near to the village of **Tripotama** (Τριπόταμα), next to a walled church. The city was destroyed by Philip V of Macedon, but is most famous as the site of Heracles' Fourth Labour, the capturing of the Erymanthian Boar (page 11). If you want to explore the slopes of the modern **Mount Erimanthos** (Ερύμανθος) (2,223m), take the scenic road up to the **Poretsou Monastery** (Πορετσού), which contains good frescoes that, because of an inscription, can be accurately dated to 12 March 1614.

Heading back east on the main road, look for a small turning south near to the village of Paos (Πάος) that heads over **Mount Aphrodisio** (Αφροδισίο) (1,446m) towards Kontovazena (Κοντοβάζαινα). Despite what many maps say this road is entirely tarmac, if narrow and sometimes precipitous. It is a dramatic route, switchbacking up to almost 1,000m. At the very top stop near to a small church (Agios Petros) to admire the views. You will also be surprised to see the ruins of the **Sanctuary of Aphrodite Erykine** which gave the mountain its name. It's a windswept and evocative spot.

The area around this mountain, often called Ziria (Ζήρεια), its medieval name before the Greeks restored the Classical one, has only recently begun to open up to visitors, and most of those are Greek. It's a difficult area to travel in, most especially without your own transport, and the roads are small and sometimes precipitous. Don't be put off, as there is a lot to see here, with hidden valleys, cliff-hugging churches, and a string of attractive stone villages. It is a special place with its own unique feeling – somehow more akin to the Balkans and eastern Europe than the Mediterranean coast.

MYTHOLOGY Hermes, the messenger and trickster god of Greek mythology, was born on Mount Killini. His father was Zeus himself, and his mother Maia, one of the thunder god's many conquests, was a nymph. She was one of the Pleiades, daughters of Atlas the Titan, and later immortalised in the stars.

Hermes was a precocious child. At only a day old he invented the lyre, making it out of one of the numerous tortoise shells to be found on the mountainside. By nightfall of the same day, he had rustled the immortal cattle of Apollo. When Apollo came to accuse the young Hermes, he pretended to be asleep like a normal baby, and his mother defended him. In the end Apollo was placated by a gift of the newly invented lyre.

GETTING THERE AND AWAY This area can only really be explored properly with your own transport. Even some of the bigger villages only see one bus a week. There

OUT WITH THE OLD, IN WITH THE NEW

As Christianity began to spread through the Roman, and then the Byzantine, empire, one must not imagine the population immediately dropping all their pagan ways. Shifting belief systems were one of the features of paganism, where gods came and went, gradually absorbing each other's spheres of influence and sometimes even names. All a new set of gods needed to do was to take over the existing temples, change the names a bit, and everything carried on as normal. Christianity, however, was something different: a religion that allowed for only one god.

Or at least so it would at first seem. For starters you have the endlessly confusing Trinity, with the added bonus of the Virgin Mary, regarded as semi-divine herself. On top of this you have a legion of saints, all of whom can be objects of veneration, if not actual worship. Thus the early Christians, rather than just abandoning their old customs, could just subtly adjust them; a temple of Dionysus, the god of wine, would be rebuilt as the church of Agios Dionysus, the patron saint of wine-growers, and so on.

There are countless examples of this, but one of the most striking is the case of Profitis Ilias, or the prophet Elijah. It is not unusual, when you reach the top of a Greek hill or mountain, to find a little chapel built there, often in the midst of the wilderness, and it is almost certain that it will be dedicated to Ilias. Back in the pagan days these high places were sacred to the sun god, Helios. It can already be seen that there is a similarity in names, but the bond goes deeper than that. In Greek mythology the sun god crossed the sky in a chariot and, in the Bible, Elijah is taken up to heaven in a fiery chariot of his own. So, while Helios does not become Ilias, the leap from one to the other is made easier.

are a number of ways in and out of the region. From the north coast, roads lead up from near Derveni (Δερβένι), Xilokastro (Ξυλόκαστρο) and Kiato (Κιάτο). From the east, various back roads lead up into the mountains from the wine routes of Nemea (page 66). A road now leads from Pheneos west through a high mountain pass towards Arcadia, or north to Kalavryta. Note that most maps are not up to date on which roads are tarmac.

WHERE TO STAY AND EAT The villages that surround Killini are home to an increasing number of boutique hotels, mainly catering to Greeks wishing to escape the smog and heat of Athens. The best of them are either new stone houses that blend in with the mountain 'style', or old village buildings that have been converted. Most of the villages have good 'mountain' tavernas that specialise in grilled and oven-baked meat. Some local recommendations include **Staikou** in the village of Pheneos, **Zacholi** in Evrostina, and **Ta Efta Adelfia** and **Ta Tria Platania** in Mesea Trikala.

🏠 **Astra Hotel** (10 rooms) Kastania; 🗔 27470 61202; **m** 69450 46208; **e** info@astrahotel. gr; **w** astrahotel.gr. Situated in the highland village of Kastania a short distance west of the Stymfalian Lake, this tranquil boutique hotel is set in a restored traditional stone house close to extensive pine forests – a great location for hiking & birdwatching. **€€€**

🏠 **Evrostini Guesthouse** (5 rooms) Evrostina; 🗔 27430 32122; **m** 69733 79465; **e** evrostini@ evrostini.gr; **w** evrostini.com. Constantina is the hostess, & heart, of this comfortable guesthouse. She knows the area well & can recommend places to see & explore. **€€€**

🏠 **Kallisto** (4 rooms) Goura; 🗔 21099 39999; **m** 69772 26514; **e** contact@xenonascallisto.gr; **w** xenonascallisto.gr. This is a renovated mansion from 1885. The rooms are simple, but beautifully done, & the breakfast is full of local products. **€€€**

🏠 **Karteri tou Leonida** (16 rooms) Karteri; 🗔 27470 31203. In a village close to the Stymfalian Lake, this is a slightly simpler option, housed in a concrete extension to the excellent roadside taverna. All the rooms have a fire & the owner, Giorgios, is another one with good local knowledge. **€€€**

🏠 **Pigi Tarlamba** (20 rooms) Ano Trikala; 🗔 27430 91267; **m** 69441 68571; **e** info@ pigitarlamba.gr; **w** pigitarlamba.gr. A large, stone-built structure with its own restaurant & excellent views from most rooms, which are decorated with 1930s furniture. **€€€**

🏠 **Predari** (8 rooms) Goura; **m** 69389 00200; **e** info@arhontiko-predari.gr; **w** arhontiko-predari.gr. In a restored building from 1870, right by the attractive village square. It is next door to its own trendy café. **€€€**

OTHER PRACTICALITIES You are best to stock up on cash and other essentials before heading up to the mountains. There is a small health centre in Goura.

WHAT TO SEE AND DO
Mount Killini The mountain dominates the region. It has two peaks: a lesser one to the east (2,086m) and a higher one to the west (2,374m). The easiest way to approach the summit is to drive up past the various villages of Trikala (Τρίκαλα). This road is tarmac all the way up to a mountain refuge and a small **ski centre** (🗔 27430 22229; **m** 69453 75693; **e** info@orosziria.gr; **w** orosziria.gr). Paths lead from here to the summit (*2hrs, difficult*) and the **Hermes' Cave** (*30mins, signposted*). There is also a 24km dirt road that circles the mountain. In fact, there are plenty of walking opportunities on the mountain and in the local area. Take local advice and purchase the *Upland Corinth* map produced by Anavasi.

Panagiatis Katafigiotissa The name of this wonderful chapel and its surrounding refuges roughly translates as 'Our Lady of the Shelter'. It was built

8

c1782 and the shelter was from the Turkish occupiers. It allowed the local people, and the *klephts* (bandit-like freedom fighters), to worship and live in safety.

The effectiveness of the hiding place is evident from the road, where the only sign of its presence is a modern shrine and information board. It is on the left-hand side on the way up into the mountains from Derveni, a few kilometres before Evrostina (Εβροστίνα). At the top of the cliff are some impressive battlements that look out over breathtaking views south to Mount Killini. From here follow the steps down the 40m of cliff. The first detour takes you right along the cliff face to one of the refuges, where the villagers lived in times of trouble. Be warned that these paths are not for the nervous. They have been restored and are quite safe, but are rather vertiginous. They are also extremely narrow.

Another refuge, reached up a steep metal staircase, has a bucket and pulley system for lifting supplies. Below this you reach the church complex, clinging to the cliffside. The main chapel has a painted wooden ceiling and iconostasis. A metal, spiral staircase leads to another refuge, while steps from the chapel lead up to a room that has been set up as a hermitage for pilgrims. It has a rather interesting 'toilet with a view'.

Pheneos Valley (Φενεός)

The Pheneos Valley, or Basin, is an extraordinary piece of landscape. Flat as a pancake, and extremely fertile, it is ringed on all sides by towering mountains: Killini to the east, and the start of Helmos to the west. It can be driven into from the village of Mosia (Μοσιά), where a tarmac road begins to skirt its edge. It is interesting to see all the settlements clinging to the edge of the mountains, leaving the fertile ground entirely to planting. It is a somewhat otherworldly place to explore, with only the odd tractor driver to keep you company. Unfortunately the road turns to dirt before it makes a complete circuit.

Monastery of Agios Giorgios

Above the village of **Ancient Pheneos** (there are very sparse remains of a Classical temple here) is the beautiful **Doxis Lake** (Δόξια). Despite being a manmade body of water it still manages to be incredibly picturesque, surrounded by fir trees and with a postcard-perfect chapel jutting out into the lake on a spit of land. This chapel is all that's left of the old monastery, which moved up the hill after the lake was filled. A road runs all the way round the shore, and from the far side a turn leads up through the fir trees to the 'new' monastery.

This **monastery** dates back to the 18th century, although it has an air of being older, and is a rather wonderful building of old stone supplemented with wooden balconies and overhanging rooms. The two monks who live here are very friendly and enjoy visitors (try to avoid siesta time), and may well offer you a coffee with the traditional glass of water and spoon of homemade sweet jam. The monastery courtyard is delightful, with well-tended plants climbing up the walls. The door into the church is well worth examining. Made of carved wood it is faced with a bronze representation of St George slaying the dragon. Inside, the church is decorated with 18th-century frescoes and an elaborately carved iconostasis. From the top floor of the monastery there are good views back down to the lake, and the monks have a small shop of religious knick-knacks here.

Sarantapicho Forest (Σαραντάπηχο)

On the road from Evrostina to Karia a right turn leads down towards the **pine forest** of Sarantapicho. The road soon turns into a dirt track. The forest is criss-crossed with countless paths and would be a great place to explore on foot or bike.

Stymfalian Lake (Στυμφαλία) Perhaps the most famous of the things to see in this region is this lake, site of the Sixth Labour of Heracles, killing the man-eating birds that lurked here. Nowadays, the lake is a sanctuary to more peaceful varieties of **birdlife**, including great crested grebe, water rail, migratory herons and the rare golden eagle. The surrounding mountains are still home to small and secretive populations of lynx, golden jackal and otter.

Stymfalian is the only highland lake in the Peloponnese, set in a basin fed by the water that drains off the mountains that surround it on all sides, and then in turn is drained by sinkholes. On account of this, it is subject to wide fluctuations in area, sometimes extending over as much as 30km², but often disappearing almost entirely in summer, leaving an endless plain of reeds waving in the dramatic mountain light. In Roman times, the lake was an important source of water for Corinth, to which it was connected by an 84km aqueduct that was constructed under Emperor Hadrian around AD130 and carried up to 80,000m³ to the city daily.

The obvious starting point for exploration is the small village of Stymfalia, a few hundred metres from the lake's northern shore. This village lies about 50km/1 hour by road from Levidi via Kandila, 60km/1 hour from Corinth via Kiato, and 75km/1½ hours from Kalavryta via Likouria. Overlooking the lake about 1km west of Stymfalia village, the **Environment Museum of Stymfalia** (℘27470 22296; e *piop@piraeusbank.gr;* w *piop.gr;* ⊕ *16 Oct–Feb 10.00–18.00 Wed–Mon, Mar–15 Oct 10.00–17.00 Wed–Mon; adult/concession €3/1.50*) is a well-thought-through modern installation that forms part of the excellent Piraeus Bank Group Cultural Foundation network. Worth 45–60 minutes of your time, the museum contains informative displays about the area's history, geology, flora and fauna.

Two interesting ruins lie close to Stymfalia village. Set alongside the main road immediately to its west, as if to emphasise that this area is different from the rest of Greece, lies a Gothic ruin, looking like something out of a horror movie. This is the remains of the **Cistercian Abbey of Zaraka**, built around AD1225 when the area was in the control of the Franks, and abandoned 50 years later. Some 600m south of the ruined abbey, the more low-key ruins of **Ancient Stymphalos** – one-time starting point of Hadrian's aqueduct – stand on a narrow acropolis by the lake shore.

If you fancy a leg stretch, you can take in the two above-mentioned ruins on a short walk that starts in the museum car park, shouldn't take longer than an hour, and also allows you to get a bit closer to the surrounding nature. From the car park, an obvious path leads 800m east along the lake shore to the low acropolis upon which stands Ancient Stymphalos. Here, you first come upon the base of a tower, with polygonal stone work, before heading on through the undergrowth to the remains of another building, apparently a temple to Athena. From here make your way down to the lake side, where you will find a spring house and a small theatre. This is a lovely spot, out of sight of the road or any other reminder of the modern world. Walk along to the end of the acropolis; round the corner from here a farm track leads back towards the Cistercian Abbey. This walk is part of a network of others in the area, marked with green boards.

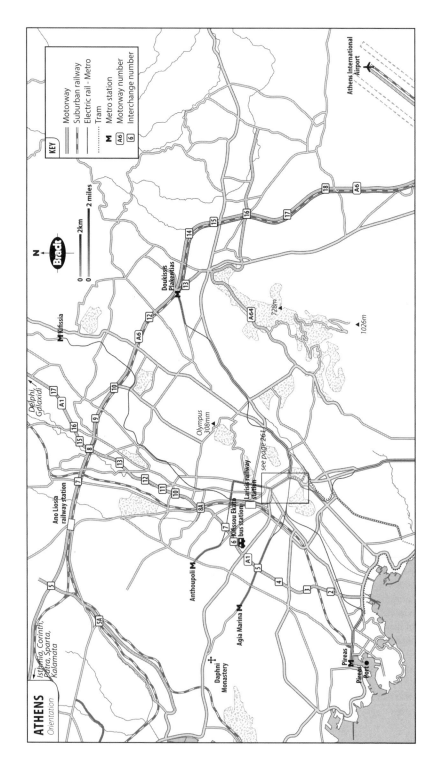

ATHENS
Orientation

KEY

Motorway
Suburban railway
Electric rail - Metro
Tram
M Metro station
A6 Motorway number
6 Interchange number

N

Bradt

0 ————— 2km
0 ————— 2 miles

*Isthmia, Corinth,
Patra, Sparta,
Kalamata*

Ano Liosia
railway station

*Delphi,
Galaxidi*

M Kifissia

Doukissis
Plakentias

Athens International
Airport

*Olympus
308mm*

▲728m

▲1026m

Larisi railway
station

see page 261

Kifissou Ekita
bus station

Anthoupoli **M**

Agia Marina **M**

✝
Daphni
Monastery

Pireas

Pireas
Port

9

Beyond the Peloponnese: Athens and Delphi

There is plenty in the Peloponnese to keep you going for a lifetime (believe me), let alone for a holiday, but you are also close to many other of the delights of Greece. This section will provide a brief introduction to a couple of them. Athens is an obvious attraction, and is only an hour away from Corinth, as well as being a convenient entry point to the country itself. It manages to blend its extraordinary history with the buzz of a modern city rather well. Delphi, on the other hand, is embedded in the Classical past, and makes an obvious addition to a tour of the Peloponnese, lying just to the north, with a setting that is simply breathtaking.

ATHENS (AΘHNA)

I resisted including Athens in the first two editions of this guidebook, not because I dislike the city – it's wonderful – but because to do it justice would involve a whole new guidebook. However, if you are flying in or out of Athens it would be foolish not to stop in on the city itself. To help with this, especially for the traveller who is only spending a day or two here, I have included a few personal highlights in this fourth edition, but I must point out that Athens has far more to offer than this. My best advice is to make friends in the city, a much easier task than you might imagine. No-one can show you round Athens better than an Athenian.

MYTHOLOGY The myth behind the naming of Athens involves its first king Cecrops, an odd character who had the torso and head of a man, but the tail of a snake. Early versions of the myth have Cecrops judging a race between Poseidon and Athena as to who should be patron deity of his new city. The most popular story nowadays has Cecrops asking each god to present the city with a gift. Poseidon struck the ground with his trident and produced a flowing spring out of a rock. Unfortunately, and unsurprisingly for the sea god, the spring was salty and not much good for anyone. For her turn, Athena struck the ground with her spear, and planted the hole she made with an olive branch, which then grew into the ever useful tree. Athena duly won and the city was dedicated to her. However, Poseidon took his revenge by making sure that the city would forever be short of water.

HISTORY The Classical history of the city is well known, and widely covered elsewhere. It is worth remembering that after these glory days (post the rise of Alexander the Great in the 4th century BC), through medieval times, and right up to recent history (it became the capital of the modern country in 1834), Athens was somewhat of a historical backwater and visitors (such as Lord Byron and Mark Twain) initially found it rather a disappointment. Having said that, it is also worth remembering that there is more to the city than the famous ruins walked by Plato and Pericles. Athens is layered with history, and its delights often come from surprising eras, with Byzantine churches poking out between concrete office blocks, and tavernas, shops and markets that don't seem to have changed décor since the 1920s.

GETTING THERE AND AWAY

By air For information on getting between Athens International and the southeast of the city, see page 31.

By bus Buses from the Peloponnese will set you down at the large bus station known as Kifissou 100 (Kifissou Ekato in Greek). From here, it is a short(ish) ride to near Omonia Square on Bus 051, which will put you on the Metro. For more details on connections to the Peloponnese, see page 31.

By car Driving into any city can be complicated, but the ring road means that you can get to central Athens quicker than you might think, at least if you are lucky with traffic. It can also be done with no more help than a map app on your smartphone, but can be stressful if you're not used to driving abroad. Once in Athens, you are better to leave your car and use public transport or walk to explore. Parking is possible in central Athens, sometimes on the street, but more often in private car parks – these are fairly inexpensive (around €12–15 a day) and are a safer option. If staying in Athens, you are best advised to book accommodation in advance and ask them for parking advice.

By train You can get to Corinth by train by joining the Proastiakos service from the airport. Take the train from Larisis (Λάρισιζ) station (also on the metro) towards the airport and change at Ano Liosa (Ανω Λιοσια) for trains towards Corinth. See page 61 for more details on this line.

By ferry Piraeus, the port of Athens, can be reached on the metro. From here the Greek islands are your oysters, but the hydrofoils that once ran to Monemvasia and elsewhere on the east coast of the Peloponnese no longer seem operational.

GETTING AROUND **Taxis** are cheap in Athens, and most trips in the centre will only cost a few euros. Your best bet is to get your accommodation to call you one. If you try to hail one, make sure they run the meter and don't be surprised if you have to share it with other passengers – this is perfectly normal. The **Metro** is excellent and also cheap, with day and family tickets available.

Walking around Athens can be great fun, and the centre is small enough to make this a good option for many visitors. Just be aware that pavements sometimes disappear on smaller streets, or will be full of parked cars. Traffic can be hairy when crossing roads, and even pedestrian streets often have mopeds going up them – keep your wits about you.

All the listed places to stay can provide you with good advice and a map, as will most other good hotels – Athenians are friendly and proud of their city.

WHERE TO STAY *Map, opposite*
There are plenty of options in Athens, with places to suit all budgets in many different areas. If you're not staying for long, you will want to be in the centre of things. The

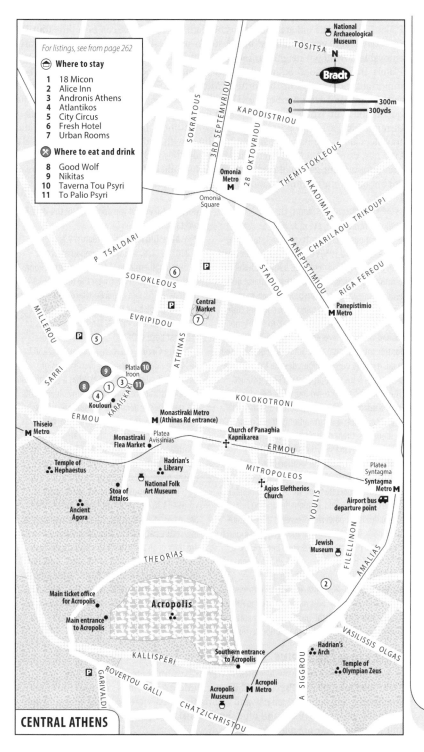

For listings, see from page 262

🛏 **Where to stay**
1 18 Micon
2 Alice Inn
3 Andronis Athens
4 Atlantikos
5 City Circus
6 Fresh Hotel
7 Urban Rooms

🍴 **Where to eat and drink**
8 Good Wolf
9 Nikitas
10 Taverna Tou Psyri
11 To Palio Psyri

National Archaeological Museum

TOSITSA

Bradt

0 ————— 300m
0 ————— 300yds

SOKRATOUS

3RD SEPTEMVRIOU

KAPODISTRIOU

28 OKTOVRIOU

THEMISTOKLEOUS

AKADIMIAS

CHARILAOU TRIKOUPI

Omonia Metro Ⓜ

Omonia Square

PANEPISTIMIOU

STADIOU

RIGA FEREOU

P TSALDARI

SOFOKLEOUS ⑥

🅿

Central Market ⑦

EVRIPIDOU

MILLEROU

🅿

ATHINAS

Panepistimio Ⓜ Metro

SARRI ⑤ 🅿

⑨ Platia Iroon ⑩

⑧ ①③ ⑪
④
Koulouri

ERMOU

KARAISKAKI

KOLOKOTRONI

Monastiraki Metro Ⓜ (Athinas Rd entrance)

Thiseio Ⓜ Metro

Monastiraki Flea Market ●

Platea Avissinias

Church of Panaghia Kapnikarea ✝

ERMOU

Temple of Hephaestus

Hadrian's Library

MITROPOLEOS

Platea Syntagma

Syntagma Ⓜ Metro

Stoa of Attalos

National Folk Art Museum

Agios Eleftherios Church ✝

VOULIS

Airport bus 🚌 departure point

Ancient Agora

THEORIAS

Jewish Museum

FILELLINON

AMALIAS

②

Main ticket office for Acropolis ●

Acropolis

Main entrance to Acropolis ●

KALLISPERI

🅿

ROVERTOU GALLI

GARIVALDI

Southern entrance to Acropolis

A SIGGROU

VASILISSIS OLGAS

Hadrian's Arch

Temple of Olympian Zeus

Acropoli Ⓜ Metro

Acropolis Museum

CHATZICHRISTOU

CENTRAL ATHENS

Beyond the Peloponnese: Athens and Delphi   ATHENS

9

Plaka (Πλάκα), the old area of Athens beneath the Acropolis, can be a little touristy nowadays, and you would be better to go a little further afield. A particularly enjoyable downtown neighbourhood to settle into is Psyri (Ψυρρή), whose central Plateia Iroon (Heroes' Square; Πλατεία Ηρώων) is located halfway between two important metro stops in the form of Monastiraki (Μοναστηράκι; direct trains to the airport) and Omonia Square (Πλατεία Ομονοίας; direct buses to Kifissou, the bus station from where all buses to/from the Peloponnese leave/arrive). Once rather disreputable, Psyri now possesses a grungy trendiness that appeals to Athenians and travellers alike, and its roads are liberally lined with budget hostels, boutique hotels, tavernas, cafés and other restaurants. Psyri also lies within easy walking distance of the Acropolis, the National Archaeological Museum, and many other sites of interest. All but one of the accommodation options listed below is in Psyri.

✵ 🏠 **18 Micon** (15 rooms) Cnr Esopou & Mykonos; 📞 21032 35307; e reservations@18miconstr.com; w 18miconstr. com. A converted 1950s warehouse set in the heart of Psyri, this lovingly decorated boutique hotel has unusually spacious rooms whose minimalist décor reflects the building's industrial roots. In-room amenities include everything from a proper coffee machine & a well-stocked minibar, to smartphones loaded with local recommendations & software for free international calls. Set on a pedestrianised road, it is very quiet at night, despite the plethora of eateries & bars within easy walking distance. The buffet b/fast is stellar too. €€€€€

🏠 **Andronis Athens** (6 rooms) 33 Karaiskaki; 📞 21032 32244; e info@andronisathens.com; w andronisathens.com. Another superlative boutique hotel in Psyri, the Andronis has a couldn't-be-more-central location just 10m from Plateia Iroon & massive trendily decorated rooms with treated concrete floor, well-stocked minibar & the choice of an old-fashioned standing tub in the bedroom or powerful shower in the en-suite bathroom. B/fast is taken in the delightful ground-floor I Feel pavement café & wine bar. €€€€€

🏠 **Fresh Hotel** (133 rooms) 26 Sofokleous; 📞 21052 48511; e info@frehhotel.gr; w freshhotel.gr. Not quite as fresh as it once was, this is still one of the best modern hotels in Athens, & is located just near the bustling market area. Rooms are stylish & bold, & the rooftop terrace is worth a visit even if you don't stay for the view & cocktails. €€€€€

🏠 **Alice Inn Athens** (5 rooms) 9 Tsatsou; 📞 21032 37139; e stay@aliceinnathens.com; w aliceinnathens.com. A home away from home on the edge of the Plaka, near the National Gardens. Each room is individually & very tastefully done up, & you have the use of a communal kitchen. Small & stylish, & John, the owner, is an excellent host. €€€€

🏠 **City Circus** (15 rooms) 16 Sarri; 📞 21302 37244; e info@citycircus.gr; w citycircus.gr. Although it calls itself a hostel & has a youthful air, it is sophisticated enough that many older guests will be perfectly happy here. Double & private family rooms with bunk beds available, as well as dormitories. The communal areas are relaxed & informal, & the included b/fast is a sociable event. Staff are friendly & knowledgeable. Dorms €€, private rooms €€€

🏠 **Urban Rooms** (8 rooms) 30 Evripidou; m 69463 36795; w urban-rooms.hotelsathens. org. As good value as you'll find in central Athens, this secure backpacker-oriented hotel is set on the 3rd floor of an apartment block & has spacious clean double rooms with writing desk & spotless shared bathroom & toilets. Rooms at the front are larger, those at the back quieter. The hands-on owner is very communicative & a good source of local travel advice. €€

✕ **WHERE TO EAT AND DRINK** *Map, page 261*
A bustling warren of alleyways hiding trendy bars and cafés cheek-by-jowl with old-fashioned food places, Psyri has a buzzing student vibe, but is not at all intimidating for families or older travellers, and seems to give a view of a more 'real' Athens. Even the graffiti is artistic and often humorous. New places are always popping up, but for eating here are a few favourites.

✳ ✖ **Atlantikos** 7 Avliton; ☎ 21303 30850. This is quite possibly one of the best seafood joints in Athens, but you wouldn't believe it at first glance. Odd tables & chairs sit in a graffiti-clad alley in front of what looks like a cheap cafe. Don't be put off – the prices are indeed reasonable, but the food is a treat.

✖ **Good Wolf** 10 Navarchou Apostoli; ☎ 21303 67395; m 69743 20286; ⓕ okalosolykos1. A refreshing break from the stereotypical traditional eateries that dominate Psyri, this restaurant/bar with pavement seating has an alternative feel, playfully eclectic décor, & very reasonable-priced mains that cater better to vegetarians than most.

✖ **Nikitas** 19 Ag Anargiron; ☎ 21032 52591. This is an old-fashioned place that made its name catering for traders at the nearby market, as it still does. Because of this, it is only open for lunch on weekdays (although being Greece, lunch can stretch into the early evening). The grilled meats are well renowned.

✖ **Taverna Tou Psyri** 12 Eschilou; ☎ 21032 14923. Plateia Iroon is a bit of a foodie Mecca, with its famous pastry shop, cheese market, and rash of restaurants. This taverna, just off it, has been here forever, & is still serving delicious home-cooked dishes alongside a more regulation set of grills.

✖ **To Palio Psyri** Plateia Iroon; m 21032 13131. Walls decorated with photos of old Athens, this refreshingly inexpensive & down-to-earth option in the heart of the city's best-known foodie district serves excellent giro- or souvlakia-filled pitas at €2.50 (but do specify if you prefer tzatziki to mayonnaise). More expensive plates are available too.

OTHER PRACTICALITIES ATMs and banks are plentiful in Athens. For other practicalities you are best off to rely on your accommodation – all the places listed give good information and advice, as well as dealing with post and other things.

WHAT TO SEE AND DO I am not going to belabour the many obvious attractions of Athens, but first: a word of warning. Athens is a modern city that often seems to be collapsing under its own weight. The Classical glory, Byzantine churches, backstreet tavernas, and traditional shops are all here, but they sometimes seem obscured behind the frenetic traffic and pollution. Give it a little bit of effort, however, and Athens quickly grows on you. Listed below are a few suggestions on how best to spend a short stay.

The Acropolis (Ακρόπολη) (☎ 21032 14172 – call for wheelchair access; ⊕ 08.00–20.00 daily; €20) The rock that looms over central Athens, and the extraordinary ruins on top and around it, are unavoidable, and you shouldn't attempt to try. Some iconic world sights disappoint at first view, but this is not one of them. The Parthenon, which is the main event, just somehow works. You can read about its perfect proportions and lack of straight lines, and you can argue that when complete and covered with paint it was a very different building, but even as a ruin, even covered with scaffolding, this is still a building that takes the breath away. Try to visit the museum first (see below). The entrance ticket covers several of the surrounding sites and is valid for four days.

The Acropolis Museum (☎ 21090 00900; w theacropolismuseum.gr; ⊕ summer: 08.00–16.00 Mon, 08.00–20.00 Tue–Thu, Sat & Sun, 08.00–22.00 Fri, winter: 09.00–17.00 Mon–Thu, 09.00–22.00 Fri, 09.00–20.00 Sat & Sun; €5) This is a fabulous and well-thought-out museum which would be a fitting repository of all the sculptures that once adorned the Parthenon. Try to ignore all the incomparable displays as you first walk in and go straight up to the top floor and turn left for the best view of the Acropolis in the city. Pause for a moment – the sight has reduced some to tears. On a more prosaic note, the videos and displays here are a great introduction before going around the site itself.

Walking around As mentioned above, the best way to explore Athens is to wander, perhaps using the Metro to scoot back home again at the end (some of its stations are worth visiting on their own). As well as the immediate area around the Acropolis and the touristy Plaka below it, the most rewarding places to explore on a short visit are Monastiraki (Μοναστηράκι), Psyri (Ψυρρή), and the area around the markets and shops of Athinas Street (Οδος Αθηνάς). These areas are interconnected and could be toured in half a day, although longer exploration is worthwhile.

Monastiraki is best known for its 'flea market', although this is no longer quite the collection of chaos it once was. Nowadays, it is still well worth an explore, and the shops get more interesting as you delve further, particularly around Platea Avissinias (Αβησσυνίας), where antiques and bric-a-brac compete and the café is a great place to people-watch, particularly on a Sunday morning.

Psyri has already been mentioned as a good place to seek out food and drink. For a snack, look out for the small *koulouri* shop on Karaiskaki (Καραϊσκάκη). *Koulouri* (sesame-seed bread rings) are the mid-morning snack of choice for Greek workers, and this shop seems to keep half of Athens going on them (watch out for the queue of mopeds waiting to whizz off the next load).

Athinas Street bounds the west side of Psyri, and is flanked by the main Athens fruit and veg market and the fish and meat market. These are both still thriving, and make no compromises for tourists. The meat market is housed in a wonderful old 19th-century building, with ironwork reminiscent of a Victorian train station, but don't enter if you're squeamish about dead animals. The shops on and around Athinas still cluster in the old-fashioned manner, with lines of tool yards, salami stores, or herb and spice shops. This is perhaps the best place to look for an authentic souvenir.

To see these things and more through local eyes, it is a great idea to book a **walking tour**, which have become increasingly popular in recent years. Don't think of the herds following around a bored guide with a raised umbrella – these are personalised, small group tours. Some of the best are organised by **Alternative Athens** ＊ (m *69484 05242*; e *info@alternativeathens.com*; w *alternativeathens. com*), who provide a great range of tours, including several family-friendly ones.

National Archaeological Museum (ℂ *21321 44800*; w *namuseum.gr*; ⊕ *summer: 08.00–20.00 daily, winter: 13.00–20.00 Mon, 09.00–16.00 Tue–Sun; €7*) Unless museums leave you completely cold, this should be another unmissable visit, especially for travellers to the Peloponnese where so many of the artefacts were found. Almost every room contains pieces of work that the educated traveller will find familiar. Particularly worth looking for are the gold mask of Agamemnon (page 73), the frescoes from Knossos on Crete, the gold cups dug up at Vapheio (page 144), the statue of Poseidon rescued from the sea near Evia, and the amazing complexity of the Antikythira Mechanism (see box, page 161). You can see the highlights in a few hours, or spend several days here; your choice. Other extremely worthwhile museums include the Benaki (w *benaki.gr*), which has an extraordinarily eclectic collection that includes something for everyone, and the Museum of Cycladic Art (w *cycladic.gr*), which is the best place to see the mesmerising figurines that inspired modern artists from Brancusi to Picasso.

Monastery of Daphni (ℂ*21058 11558*; ⊕ *09.00–14.00 Tue & Fri; free entrance*) This is a very personal recommendation. I visited this 11th-century Byzantine monastery – now a UNESCO World Heritage Site – many years ago, and was bowled over by its superb, almost overwhelming, mosaics. In 1999, it was damaged by an earthquake and it has been under restoration ever since, but the work is now almost complete and the mosaics are once again accessible to visitors. It lies about 10km west of Monastiraki in central Athens and can be reached by catching the Metro to Agia Marina, which lies about 2km to its east, then hopping on the A16, 811 or 866 bus. Alternatively, take a taxi, but make sure your driver knows where he is going.

DELPHI (ΔΕΛΦΟΊ)

Delphi lies just to the north of the Peloponnese, across the Gulf of Corinth, and is another worthy addition to any itinerary of the area. The ancient Greeks thought that this was the centre of the world, and coming here it is quite easy to agree with them.

MYTHOLOGY AND HISTORY The name Delphi has a couple of origins: one meaning 'womb', which is connected to the old mother goddess of the Earth, Gaia; the other from the word 'dolphin', this being the disguise Apollo adopted when he came here. Apollo battled with Gaia's child: the Python, a snake-like dragon. After its defeat, Apollo founded the Pythian Games, which took place here every four years. Another myth tells how Zeus released eagles from the edges of the Earth, and they met above Delphi, proving that this was the 'navel' of the Earth.

Delphi is most known for its oracle, a priestess called the Pythia. She would go into a sacred trance induced by noxious gases (thought by some to be ethylene) that emerged from the chasm where Apollo threw the Python's body, as well as chewing on herbs (possibly oleander), and then prophesise in rather peculiar terms. Her ravings were 'translated' by the temple's priests, and given how long the oracle lasted, their advice must have been pretty good.

The oracle was also known for its ambiguous advice. Most famously, Croesus, when he asked whether he should attack the Persians, was told his actions would destroy a great empire (and they did – his). The Athenians were told to rely on wooden walls to defeat the Persians – but these turned out to be the walls of their ships, not their city. The oracle survived from the 9th or 8th century BC until the 400s AD when it was closed by the Christian emperors of Rome, and it received tributes from all around the Mediterranean world, making it one of the most important Classical shrines.

GETTING THERE AND AWAY

By bus Buses to Delphi run from Athens's other bus station (Liossion 260) to Delphi (*at least 6 a day; 3hrs*), and from Patra in the Peloponnese (page 243). There are also plenty of coach trips that can be booked from Athens, but these are not recommended – you will spend most of the day on the bus, and arrive at the site at its busiest time.

By car Delphi can be reached either from Athens or the Rio-Antirio Bridge near Patra (page 242). Either drive is very pleasant. Coming from Athens takes about 2½ hours and you should consider a stop at Osios Loukas (page 267). The drive from Patra is a little shorter. Parking on the road outside the site entrance is normally fairly easy.

WHERE TO STAY AND EAT The modern town of Delphi is not really worth bothering with, although, like the site itself, the views are good. Like Olympia, most visitors only stay a night here and never return so the establishments don't need to impress. There is some cheap accommodation available, but it's nothing special. The exception is the nearby **campsite** (*Apollon Camping;* ✆ *22650 82750;* e *apollon4@ otenet.gr;* w *apolloncamping.gr;* €), which has the views and everything else you'd expect, as well as a free transfer to the site on one of those mini tourist road trains.

It is worth staying, however, as the site takes at least a full day to explore. Your best bet is to head a little further afield. To the west, and down on the coast, is Galaxidi (Γαλαξίδι), a charming port town with good options to stay and eat (*30–40mins' drive*). To the east is Arachova (Αράχωβα), a far more appealing village than Delphi that is almost as spectacularly situated (*10–15mins' drive*) and is surprisingly trendy as it supports the nearby ski resort. Arachova has several reasonable hotels, but the best options are in the surrounding mountains.

🏠 **Amfikaia Farm** (16 houses) ✆ 22340 48860; m 69775 96196; w amfikaia.gr. These traditional stone houses are set on a mountain farm on the other side of Parnassos to Delphi (about 1hr drive). You are encouraged to explore the farm & the surrounding countryside. A top-notch place to while away a few days. €€€€

✳ 🏠 **Ganimede & Miramare hotels** (7 rooms each) Galaxidi; ✆ 22650 41328; m 69371 54567; e info@ganimede.gr; w ganimede. gr. Looked after by Chrisoula, an active & knowledgeable host, these 2 family-run hotels both offer great value for money, good amenities & superb home-cooked b/fasts. The Ganimede, 5mins' walk from the harbourfront, has quaint

rooms based round a green courtyard. The Miramare is less characterful but it has larger rooms with kitchenette & stands only 10m from the harbourfront. Thoroughly recommended. €€€

✗ **To Steki ins Nilas** Galaxidi; ✆ 22650 42079. The best budget eatery in Galaxidi, this grillhouse stands on the harbourfront opposite the main square & has plenty of terrace seating. The mixed grill at €7 is fabulous value & a real treat for meat lovers.

✗ **Zygos** Galaxidi; ✆ 22653 01071. There are a string of cafés & restaurants set beside Galaxidi's small harbour. This vies for title of the best one (Tasos down the road is the other bet) & specialises in seafood, as you would expect.

WHAT TO SEE AND DO Once past the modern village, the large ruins of the site of Ancient Delphi sprawl across the hillside with grandstand views down towards the valley below. There's lots to see and you should aim to spend most of the day exploring.

The Sanctuary of Apollo (✆ *22650 82313;* ⊕ *timings & entrance fees, see box, page 52*) The main site of Delphi is set above the road on the west side of the old town, and is impressively arrayed up the mountain slopes that stare down on the valley below. It has one of the most impressive situations of any ancient Greek site, and the competition is pretty stiff. Make sure you get hold of the free map that comes with your ticket, which will allow you to identify the various ruins that dot the Sacred Way that winds up to the Temple of Apollo. Look out for the *omphalos* as you go. This stone is the 'navel of the world' and is a copy of the one that marked where Zeus's eagles met (page 265). The original is in the museum and it is interesting to note that the world has an 'outie'. The temple itself is an impressively big structure, but has only a few columns left standing. Above it lies a theatre with a view and finally the path winds up to the stadium where the Pythian Games took place.

Castalian Spring (⊕ *closed at present*) To the east of the sanctuary in a cleft of the mountains, this spring was where pilgrims to Delphi cleansed themselves. It brings water down from Mount Parnassos above it, the mythical home of the Muses. The old story was that anyone who drank from its waters would receive artistic inspiration. Unfortunately, it is closed due to the danger of rock falls.

The Marmaria (*same details as the Sanctuary*) This adjunct to the site, a sanctuary dedicated to Athena, is a bit further along from the spring. The walk along the road is still a bit awkward as the pavement gives out, so take care, but because of this few tour groups bother with it. The chief thing to see is the round marble tholos, with its three re-erected columns – the picture postcard of Delphi.

The Museum (⊕ *09.00–16.00 daily; entrance inc in ticket for main site*) The modern museum, to the west of the main site, not only provides welcome air conditioning on a hot day, but has a superb collection. The most famous of its statues is that of the Charioteer, whose piercing eyes seem to stare at you from across the ages.

Osios Loukas (⊕ *09.00–17.00 daily; €3*) This is an ancient walled monastery with impressive buildings that lies between Athens and Delphi. More of a museum than a monastery these days, and it gets plenty of coach tour visits, but if you have a car it is still worth visiting for its lavish mosaics.

Appendix 1

LANGUAGE

The first battle when dealing with Greek is the alphabet. While never an easy one, this is somewhat helped by the fact that letters, with a few exceptions, are always pronounced the same. This means that once you learn the alphabet, with due notice to proper word stress, you are fully able to read Greek. You won't understand any of it, of course, but it can come in useful when transliterating signs and menus.

Greek grammar can also be a bit of a nightmare, with all nouns being masculine, feminine or neuter. Adjectives and articles then have to agree with them. For instance 'a beer' is 'mia birra', while 'a coffee' is 'ena kafe' (Greek does not distinguish between 'a' and 'one'). Verbs are even more complicated, but be of good cheer, the Greeks themselves cheerfully admit that they make mistakes all the time. They will love you for making an attempt at the language, and will excuse even major mangling.

Greek letter	Sound	Name
Αα	a normal 'a' sound	alpha
Ββ	'v'	vita
Γγ	a mixture between 'g' and 'y'	gamma
Δδ	somewhere between 'd' and 'th'	delta
Εε	'e'	epsilon
Ζζ	'z'	zita
Ηη	'i'	ita
Θθ	'th'	thita
Ιι	'i'	yiota
Κκ	'k'	kappa
Λλ	'l'	lamda
Μμ	'm'	mi
Νν	'n'	ni
Ξξ	'x'	xi
Οο	'o'	omicron
Ππ	'p'	pi
Ρρ	'r'	ro
Σσ (ς at the end of a word)	's'	sigma
Ττ	't'	taph
Υυ	'i'	ipsilon
Φφ	'f'	fi
Χχ	'h' or 'ch' as in loch	chi
Ψψ	'ps'	psi
Ωω	'o'	omega

SOME ODD COMBINATIONS

αυ	'av' or 'af'
ευ	'ev' or 'ef'
αι, ει, οι	'e'
ου	'oo'
μπ	between 'b' and 'mb'
ντ	between 'd' and 'nd'

WORDS AND PHRASES
Essentials

Do you speak English?	*Miláte angliká?*
Good morning	*Kalí mèra*
Good evening	*Kalí spèra*
Good night	*Kalí níkta*
Hello	*Yássas* (formal or plural)
	Yássou (informal singular)
Goodbye	*Yássas* or *yassou* as above
My name is …	*Me lène …*
What is your name?	*Póse lène?*
I am from …	*Apó tin …*
… England/Britain	*…. angliá*
… America	*… amerikí*
How are you?	*Ti kánete?* (formal or plural)
	Ti kánis? (informal singular)
Fine, and you?	*Kalá, ke esis?*
Please	*Parakaló*
Thank you	*Efharistó*
Excuse me/pardon me/sorry	*Signómi*
OK	*Endáxi*
Yes	*Ne*
No	*Óhi*
Certainly	*Málista*
I understand	*Katalavèno*
I don't understand	*Den katalavèno*
Do you understand?	*Katalavènis?*
Have a good trip!	*Kaló taxídi!*

Questions

How?	*Pos?*	When?	*P te?*
What?	*Ti?*	Who?	*Pios?*
Where?	*Poo?*	How much?	*Póso?*
Which?	*Píos?*	Why?	*Yiatí?*

Numbers

1	*èna* or *miá*		8	*októ*
2	*dío*		9	*enèa*
3	*tría*		10	*dèkka*
4	*tèssera*		11	*èndekka*
5	*pènde*		12	*dódekka*
6	*èxi*		13	*dekkatría*
7	*eftá*		14	*dekkatèssera*

20	èkosi	200	diakósa
21	èkosi èna	300	trakósa
30	triánda	400	tetrakósa
40	saránda	500	pendakósa
50	penínda	600	eksakósa
60	exínda	700	eftakósa
70	evdomínda	800	oktakósa
80	ogdónda	900	eneakósa
90	enenínda	1,000	hília
100	ekató		

Time

What time is it?	Ti óra ine?	tomorrow	ávrio
It's . . . o'clock	Íne . . .	yesterday	kthès
today	símera		

Days

Monday	Deftèra	Friday	Paraskeví
Tuesday	Triti	Saturday	Sávatto
Wednesday	Tetárti	Sunday	Kiriakí
Thursday	Pèmpti		

Months

January	Yenáris	July	Ioólios
February	Fevrooários	August	Ávgoostos
March	Mártios	September	Septèmvrios
April	Aprílios	October	Októvrios
May	Máios	November	Noèmvrios
June	Ioónios	December	Dekèmvrios

Getting around

I'm going to …	Páo sto …	train	trèno
How far is it?	Póso makriá ine?	plane	aeropláno
How long will it take?	Póses ores? (how many hours?)	ship	plío
		taxi	taxí
ticket	Isitírio	car	aftokínito
bus station	Staphmos leoforíon	scooter	papáki
train station	Staphmos too trèno	petrol	venzíni
airport	Aerodrómo	bicycle	podílato
port	Limáni	on foot	me ta pódia
bus	Leoforío		

Directions

Where is … ?	Poo íne … ?	south	nótia
left	aristerá	east	anatoliká
right	dexiá	west	ditiká
north	vória		

Signs

| Entrance | ΕΙΣΟΔΟΣ | Open | ΑΝΟΙΚΤΟ |
| Exit | ΕΞΟΔΟΣ | Closed | ΚΛΕΙΣΤΟΣ |

270

Accommodation

hotel	*xenodohío*	shower	*dous*
campsite	*cámping*	air conditioning	*klimatismós*
I'd like a room …	*Thèlo èna domátio …*	toilet	*tooalèta*
… for one night	*… yia mía vradís*	breakfast	*proinó*
bed	*kreváti*		

Food and drink

I'm vegetarian	*Ime hortofágos*	water	*neró*
bread	*psomí*	milk	*gála*
eggs	*avgá*	coffee	*kafè*
fish	*psári*	tea	*tsái*
cheese	*tyrí*	beer	*bírra*
yoghurt	*yiaoúrti*	wine (white,	*krasí (aspro* or *lefká,*
honey	*mèli*	rose, red)	*rosè, kókkino)*
the bill	*to logariasmó*	cheers!	*yámas!*

Shops

bank	*trápeza*	pharmacy	*farmakío*
post office	*taxidromió*	bakery	*fóurno*

Emergencies and health

Help!	*Voíthya!*	Go away!	*fiye!*
police	*astinomía*	hospital	*nosokomío*
doctor	*yatró*		

Other

boy/girl	*agóri/korítsi*	hot/cold	*zestí/krío*
big/small	*megálo/mikró*	good/bad	*kaló/kakós*

Greek gestures

No	*Anything from a slight raising of the eyebrows to a huge shrug and upward nod of the head*
Yes	*A tip of the head to the side*
Rude	*A flat palm with fingers outstretched*

PELOPONNESE ONLINE

For additional online content, articles, photos and more on The Peloponnese, why not visit **w** bradtguides.com/pelops?

Appendix 2

FURTHER INFORMATION

BOOKS There are thousands of books written about the Peloponnese and Greece in general, as well as fiction and poetry from the earliest times right up to today. What follows is a fairly idiosyncratic list of some favourite books, plus one website. Hopefully they will lead you on to other things, as they did me. The latest UK publisher is listed, but even the out-of-print (op) books are fairly easy to get hold of on the internet, often via companies such as Amazon, from where you can buy print-on-demand editions.

Andrews, Kevin *The Flight of Ikaros* (op). In 1947 a young American archaeologist received a fellowship to study the Frankish castles of the Peloponnese. Unfortunately the civil war was raging, but Andrews still managed to come into intimate contact with the Greek people and landscape. The Peloponnese seems to have inspired some of the best travel writing of the 20th century, and this is a great start.

Barrow, Bob *Inside the Mani* Matthew Dean, 2006. Bob Barrow retired to the Mani after a varied career as a policeman and pub landlord. He discovered a new passion in the mountains of the Mani and became an expert on the local culture, and especially the Byzantine churches. This is an excellent guide to the nooks and crannies of this incredible region. The publisher also produces a yearly magazine, back issues of which are obtainable locally.

Bostock, Andrew *Inside Messinia* Matthew Dean, 2009. The most comprehensive guide available to the region. The author, who knows his stuff, drove down almost every back road of Messinia in order to produce this comprehensive guide to the region. His car suffered in the process.

Brewer, David *The Flame of Freedom* John Murray, 2003. By far the best, and most modern, account of the War of Independence against the Ottomans in English. Much of this took place in the Peloponnese, and saw heroism and brutality on both sides.

Brewer, David *Greece, the Hidden Centuries* I B Tauris, 2012. After his magisterial work on the Greek struggle for freedom Brewer turned his hand to the centuries of occupation that preceded it. This is a much neglected period, at least for popular history books, and some of the conclusions will come as a surprise to those who thought they knew Greek history.

Coats, Lucy *Atticus the Storyteller's 100 Greek Myths* Orion, 2003. To really understand the Greek myths you should first encounter them while young. Some of these tales, while confusing to adults, make perfect sense to kids. This is the best modern version of them aimed at children, and is not a bad read for adults either.

Cottrell, Leonard *The Bull of Minos* Tauris Parke, 2009. This is a bit dated, but is still an exciting and easy introduction to the world of the Minoans and Mycenaeans, although much of it focuses on Crete.

Facaros, Dana *Northern Greece* Bradt Travel Guides, 2019 A new Bradt guide to the regions of Épirus, Thessaly, Macedonia and Thrace, including cities, mountains, lakes, beaches and the world's deepest gorge.

Holst-Warhaft, Gail *Road to Rembetika* (op). Rembetika are the 'Greek Blues', and grew up in the backstreets of Athens after the 1920s exchange of populations with Turkey. Once slightly shocking, the music has now become somewhat mainstream. This introduction to the music reveals its poetry and power.

Hughes, Bettany *Helen of Troy* Pimlico, 2006. This book serves as a welcome reminder that although the works of Homer concentrate on Troy, their heart is surely in the Peloponnese. In particular this is worth reading while exploring the Spartan plain.

Leigh Fermor, Patrick *Mani* John Murray, 2004. Paddy Leigh Fermor travelled into the Mani in the 1950s and wrote sublime prose about it. His other Greek book, *Roumeli*, is also well worth it, as is everything he wrote. His final book came out after his death in 2011. Titled *The Broken Road*, it included diary entries from his time in Mount Athos, northern Greece. Artemis Cooper's biography of Paddy, titled *An Adventure*, includes some nice details on his life in Kardamyli.

Levi, Peter *Hill of Kronos* Eland, 2007. Another archaeologist falls in love with the Peloponnese, this time during the military dictatorship of the 1960s and 70s. Once again an author is brought to Greece by its antiquities, but finds the modern reality just as compelling. Levi even manages to make the drab town of Pyrgos sound enticing.

Mazower, Mark *Inside Hitler's Greece* Yale University Press, 2001. An excellent insight into the most effective resistance movement in Europe, which took much of its inspiration from the Far Left. It also relates how the country then descended into civil war, and the complicity of Great Britain and the US in this. Difficult reading.

Miller, Henry *The Colossus of Maroussi* Summersdale, 2007. Miller, one of the most admired novelists of the 20th century, gets intoxicated by Greece, and often quite drunk as well. An account of a visit in 1939, it touches on many themes, but the love of the country and its characters shines through. Miller considered it his best work.

Milona, Marianthi *Culinaria Greece* Ullmann, 2008. Not just a recipe book, but a cultural guide as well. Surprisingly cheap considering its size and breadth.

Norwich, John Julius *A Short History of Byzantium* Penguin, 1998. Not perfect, but still the best introduction to the Byzantines available. If you hadn't heard of them before, this is the way in, but we're still waiting for the great popular history of this civilization.

Pausanias *Guide to Greece* Penguin, 2006. Pausanias is a bit dense and difficult at times, but his wit and character shines through, even over the centuries, making him a surprisingly good travel companion. Better to dip into while in the area than to read straight through. Both of the two volumes cover the Peloponnese, and Peter Levi's notes are excellent.

Powell, Dilys *An Affair of the Heart* Souvenir Press, 1999. This time an archaeologist's wife falls in love with the area, while remaining aware of its frustrations and ambiguities. Her book on Cretan archaeology and history, *The Villa Ariadne*, also contains many insights.

Salmon, Tim and Cullen, Michael *Trekking in Greece: The Peloponnese and Pindos Way* Cicerone, 2018. This guidebook presents four specially devised treks in the mountains of Greece.

Sterry, Paul *Complete Mediterranean Wildlife* Collins, 2000. The best overall guide to the flora and fauna of the region. Essential if you have more than a passing interest the stunning diversity of its nature.

WEBSITES

Most information and tourism websites in Greece, including the ones listed in this book, are still frustrating, and are poorly translated, if at all. While surfing look out for a UK flag, or the tab 'En', to turn the website into some sort of English. If this is unavailable sites such as Google Translate will make a decent attempt at deciphering the website. There are some good exceptions, and these are listed in the text. One other website should be mentioned:

www.maniguide.info is the result of one man's slightly unhealthy but impressive obsession with the Mani and its churches and towers. It is a fantastic resource (although it could do with an update).

Index

Page numbers in **bold** indicate main entries; those in *italics* indicate maps.